14th European Workshop on Natural Language Generation

(ENLG 2013)

Sofia, Bulgaria
8 – 9 August 2013

ISBN: 978-1-62748-992-8

Printed from e-media with permission by:

Curran Associates, Inc.
57 Morehouse Lane
Red Hook, NY 12571

Some format issues inherent in the e-media version may also appear in this print version.

Printed by Curran Associates, Inc. (2013)

For permission requests, please contact the Association for Computational Linguistics at the address below.

Association for Computational Linguistics
209 N. Eighth Street
Stroudsburg, Pennsylvania 18360

Phone: 1-570-476-8006
Fax: 1-570-476-0860

acl@aclweb.org

Additional copies of this publication are available from:

Curran Associates, Inc.
57 Morehouse Lane
Red Hook, NY 12571 USA
Phone: 845-758-0400
Fax: 845-758-2634
Email: curran@proceedings.com
Web: www.proceedings.com

ENLG 2013

14th European Workshop on Natural Language Generation

Proceedings of the Workshop

August 8-9, 2013
Sofia, Bulgaria

Preface

We are pleased to present the papers accepted for presentation at the 14th European Workshop on Natural Language Generation (ENLG 2013), held in conjunction with the 51st Annual Meeting of the Association for Computational Linguistics (ACL 2013). The ENLG workshop will be held on August 8th and 9th in Sofia, Bulgaria.

This year's workshop forms part of a biennial series that has been running since 1987 and have been held at Royaumont, Edinburgh, Judenstein, Pisa, Leiden, Duisburg, Toulouse, Budapest, Aberdeen, Dagstuhl, Athens and Nancy. Together with the International Conference on Natural Language Generation (INLG), which is held in alternate years, ENLG is the main forum for research on all aspects of the generation of natural language.

For this year's edition, we invited submissions on all topics related to natural language generation. We received a total of 36 submissions from all over the world, and accepted 13 as long papers for oral presentation, and 10 as short papers for poster presentation. In addition, there were two papers accepted as demos. The first part of this volume contains all the accepted papers, as well as the abstracts by the two invited speakers for the workshop.

ENLG 2013 also hosts this year's edition of the Generation Challenges, where two shared task evaluation competitions will be presented: The KBGen Challenge (Banik, Gardent and Kow) and the Content Selection Challenge (Bouayad-Agha, Casamayor, Wanner and Mellish). Overviews of both challenges, together with short contributions by all participating teams, are found in the second part of the volume.

Another special event at this year's edition of ENLG 2013 is a panel on convergences and divergences between generating natural language from raw data or based on textual input. We have invited four panelists, two from each area, to give brief presentations. These will be followed by an open discussion.

Finally, we would like to thank the authors and the members of our program committee, whose work helped to ensure that the research papers collected herein are of a high standard. We are also delighted that Guy Lapalme and Pablo Gervás accepted our invitation to give invited talks at ENLG 2013.

Albert Gatt and Horacio Saggion
Program co-Chairs for ENLG 2013

Program Co-Chairs:

Albert Gatt, University of Malta, Malta
Horacio Saggion, Universitat Pompeu Fabra, Spain

Program Committee:

Kalina Bontcheva, University of Sheffield, UK
Nadjet Bouayad-Agha, Universitat Pompeu Fabra, Spain
Giuseppe Carenini, The University of British Columbia, Canada
Reva Freedman, Northern Illinois University, US
Claire Gardent, CNRS/LORIA, France
Konstantina Garoufi, University of Potsdam, Germany
Raquel Hervàs, Universidad Complutense de Madrid, Spain
Srinivas Janarthanam, Heriot-Watt University, UK
Alistair Knott, University of Otago, New Zealand
Alexander Koller, University of Potsdam, Germany
Leila Kosseim, Concordia University, Canada
Emiel Krahmer, Tilburg University, Netherlands
Elena Lloret Pastor, University of Alicante, Spain
Chris Mellish, University of Aberdeen, UK
Margaret Mitchell, University of Aberdeen, UK
Paul Piwek, Open University, UK
Ehud Reiter, University of Aberdeen, UK
Verena Rieser, Heriot Watt University, Edinburgh, UK
Advaith Siddharthan, University of Aberdeen, UK
Manfred Stede, Universitaet Potsdam, Germany
Kristina Striegnitz, Union College, US
Irina Temnikova, University of Wolverhampton, UK
Mariet Theune, University of Twente, The Netherlands
Takenobu Tokunaga, Tokyo Instiute of Technology, Japan
Kees van Deemter, University of Aberdeen, UK
Ielka van der sluis, University of Groningen, Netherlands
Keith vanderLinden, Calvin College, US
Sebastian Varges, University of Potsdam, Germany
Jette Viethen, Tilburg University, Netherlands
Leo Wanner, Universitat Pompeu Fabra, Spain
Michael White, The Ohio State University, US
Sandra Williams, Open University, UK
Tie-jun Zhao, Harbin Institute of Technology, China

Additional Reviewers:

Hailong Cao, Harbin Institute of Technology, China
Gerard Casamayor, Universitat Pompeu Fabra, Spain
Allan Third, Open University, UK
Xiaoning Zhu, Harbin Institute of Technology, China

Invited Speakers:

Pablo Gervás, Universidad Complutense de Madrid, Spain
Guy Lapalme, Université de Montréal, Canada

Table of Contents

Long papers

Poster papers

Demo papers

Generation Challenges posters

Workshop Program

Thursday, August 8, 2013

8:45–9:00	Opening Remarks
	Session 1: NLG from Semantic Representations and Knowledge Bases
9:00–9:30	*Aligning Formal Meaning Representations with Surface Strings for Wide-Coverage Text Generation* Valerio Basile and Johan Bos
9:30–10:00	*Exploiting Ontology Lexica for Generating Natural Language Texts from RDF Data* Philipp Cimiano, Janna Lüker, David Nagel and Christina Unger
10:00–10:30	*User-Controlled, Robust Natural Language Generation from an Evolving Knowledge Base* Eva Banik, Eric Kow and Vinay Chaudhri
10:30–11:00	Coffee Break
	Session 2: Realisation, Aggregation and Variation
11:00–11:30	*Enhancing the Expression of Contrast in the SPaRKy Restaurant Corpus* David Howcroft, Crystal Nakatsu and Michael White
11:30–12:00	*Generating Elliptic Coordination* Claire Gardent and Shashi Narayan
12:00–12:30	*Using Integer Linear Programming for Content Selection, Lexicalization, and Aggregation to Produce Compact Texts from OWL Ontologies* Gerasimos Lampouras and Ion Androutsopoulos
12:30–14:00	Lunch

Thursday, August 8, 2013 (continued)

Session 3: Referring Expressions and Multimodality

14:00–14:30 *Generating and Interpreting Referring Expressions as Belief State Planning and Plan Recognition*
Dustin Smith and Henry Lieberman

14:30–15:00 *Graphs and Spatial Relations in the Generation of Referring Expressions*
Jette Viethen, Margaret Mitchell and Emiel Krahmer

15:00–15:30 *What and Where: An Empirical Investigation of Pointing Gestures and Descriptions in Multimodal Referring Actions*
Albert Gatt and Patrizia Paggio

15:30–16:00 Coffee Break

Invited Talk I

16:00–17:00 *Natural Language Generation and Summarization at RALI*
Guy Lapalme

Generation Challenges

17:00–17:30 *The KBGen Challenge*
Eva Banik, Claire Gardent and Eric Kow

17:30–18:00 *Overview of the First Content Selection Challenge from Open Semantic Web Data*
Nadjet Bouayad-Agha, Gerard Casamayor, Leo Wanner and Chris Mellish

Friday, August 9, 2013

	Invited Talk II
09:00–10:00	*Narrative Composition: Achieving the Perceived Linearity of Narrative* Pablo Gervás
	Session 4: NLG for Learner Support
10:00–10:30	*Generating Natural Language Questions to Support Learning On-Line* David Lindberg, Fred Popowich, John Nesbit and Phil Winne
10:30–11:00	Coffee Break
11:00–11:30	*Generating Student Feedback from Time-Series Data Using Reinforcement Learning* Dimitra Gkatzia, Helen Hastie, Srinivasan Janarthanam and Oliver Lemon
	Session 5: NLG from Textual Input
11:30–12:00	*Deconstructing Human Literature Reviews – A Framework for Multi-Document Summarization* Kokil Jaidka, Christopher Khoo and Jin-Cheon Na
12:00–12:30	*Abstractive Meeting Summarization with Entailment and Fusion* Yashar Mehdad, Giuseppe Carenini, Frank Tompa and Raymond T. NG
12:30–14:00	Lunch
14:00–15:30	Poster Session
15:30–16:00	Coffee Break
16:00–17:30	Round table discussion: Generating language from raw data vs. Generating language from textual input
17:30–17:45	Conclusion

Friday, August 9, 2013 (continued)

Demos

MIME- NLG Support for Complex and Unstable Pre-hospital Emergencies
Anne Schneider, Alasdair Mort, Chris Mellish, Ehud Reiter, Phil Wilson and Pierre-Luc Vaudry

Thoughtland: Natural Language Descriptions for Machine Learning n-dimensional Error Functions
Pablo Duboue

Generation Challenges Posters

An Automatic Method for Building a Data-to-Text Generator
Sina Zarriess and Kyle Richardson

LOR-KBGEN, A Hybrid Approach To Generating from the KBGen Knowledge-Base
Bikash Gyawali and Claire Gardent

Team UDEL KBGen 2013 Challenge
Keith Butler, Priscilla Moraes, Ian Tabolt and Kathy McCoy

Content Selection Challenge - University of Aberdeen Entry
Roman Kutlak, Chris Mellish and Kees van Deemter

UIC-CSC: The Content Selection Challenge Entry from the University of Illinois at Chicago
Hareen Venigalla and Barbara Di Eugenio

Aligning Formal Meaning Representations with Surface Strings for Wide-coverage Text Generation

Valerio Basile **Johan Bos**

{v.basile,johan.bos}@rug.nl
Center for Language and Cognition Groningen (CLCG)
University of Groningen, The Netherlands

Abstract

Statistical natural language generation from abstract meaning representations presupposes large corpora consisting of text–meaning pairs. Even though such corpora exist nowadays, or could be constructed using robust semantic parsing, the simple alignment between text and meaning representation is too coarse for developing robust (statistical) NLG systems. By reformatting semantic representations as graphs, fine-grained alignment can be obtained. Given a precise alignment at the word level, the complete surface form of a meaning representations can be deduced using a simple declarative rule.

1 Introduction

Surface Realization is the task of producing fluent text from some kind of formal, abstract representation of meaning (Reiter and Dale, 2000). However, while it is obvious what the output of a natural language generation component should be, namely *text*, there is little to no agreement on what its input formalism should be (Evans et al., 2002). Since open-domain semantic parsers are able to produce formal semantic representations nowadays (Bos, 2008; Butler and Yoshimoto, 2012), it would be natural to see generation as a reversed process, and consider such semantic representations as input of a surface realization component.

The idea of using large text corpora annotated with formal semantic representations for robust generation has been presented recently (Basile and Bos, 2011; Wanner et al., 2012). The need for formal semantic representations as a basis for NLG was expressed already much earlier by Power (1999), who derives semantic networks enriched with scope information from knowledge representations for content planning. In this paper we take a further step towards the goal of generating text from deep semantic representations, and consider the issue of aligning the representations with surface strings that capture their meaning.

First we describe the basic idea of aligning semantic representations (logical forms) with surface strings in a formalism-independent way (Section 2). Then we apply our method to a well-known and widely-used semantic formalism, namely Discourse Representation Theory (DRT), first demonstrating how to represent Discourse Representation Structures (DRSs) as graphs (Section 3) and showing that the resulting Discourse Representation Graphs (DRGs) are equivalent to DRSs but are more convenient to fulfill word-level alignment (Section 4). Finally, in Section 5 we present a method that generates partial surface strings for each discourse referent occurring in the semantic representation of a text, and composes them into a complete surface form. All in all, we think this would be a first and important step in surface realization from formal semantic representations.

2 Aligning Logic with Text

Several different formal semantic representations have been proposed in the literature, and although they might differ in various aspects, they also have a lot in common. Many semantic representations (or logical forms as they are sometimes referred to) are variants of first-order logic and share basic building blocks such as entities, properties, and relations, complemented with quantifiers, negation and further scope operators.

A simple snapshot of a formal meaning representation is the following (with symbols composed out of WordNet (Fellbaum, 1998) synset identifiers to abstract away from natural language):

$$blue\#a\#1(x) \wedge cup\#n\#1(x)$$

How could this logical form be expressed in natural language? Or put differently, how could we realize the variable x in text? As simple as it is, x describes "a blue cup", or if your target language is Italian, "una tazza blu", or variants hereof, e.g. "every blue cup" (if x happens to be bound by universally quantified) or perhaps as "una tazza azzurra", using a different adjective to express blueness. This works for simple examples, but how does it scale up to larger and more complex semantic representations?

In a way, NLG can be viewed as a machine translation (MT) task, but unlike translating from one natural language into another, the task is here to translate a formal (unambiguous) language into a natural language like English or Italian. Current statistical MT techniques are based on large parallel corpora of aligned source and target text. In this paper we introduce a method for precise alignment of formal semantic representations and text, with the purpose of creating a large corpus that could be used in NLG research, and one that opens the way for statistical approaches, perhaps similar to those used in MT.

Broadly speaking, alignments between semantic representations and surface strings can be made in three different ways. The simplest strategy, but also the least informative, is to align a semantic representation with a sentence or complete text without further information on which part of the representation produces what part of the surface form. This might be enough to develop statistical NLG systems for small sentences, but probably does not scale up to handle larger texts. Alternatively, one could devise more complex schemes that allow for a more fine-grained alignment between parts of the semantic representation and surface strings (words and phrases). Here there are two routes to follow, which we call the *minimal* and *maximal alignment*.

In maximal alignment, each single piece of the semantic representation corresponds to the words that express that part of the meaning. Possible problems with this approach are that perhaps not every bit of the semantic representation corresponds to a surface form, and a single word could also correspond to various pieces in the semantic representation. This is an interesting option to explore, but in this paper we present the alternative approach, minimal alignment, which is a method where every word in the surface string points to exactly one part of the semantic representation. We think this alignment method forms a better starting point for the development of a statistical NLG component. With sufficient data in the form of aligned texts with semantic representations, these alignments can be automatically learned, thus creating a model to generate surface forms from abstract, logical representations.

However, aligning semantic representations with words is a difficult enterprise, primarily because formal semantic representations are not flat like a string of words and often form complex structures. To overcome this issue we represent formal semantic representations as a set of tuples. For instance, returning to our earlier example representation for "blue cup", we could represent part of it by the tuples ⟨blue#a#1,arg,x⟩ and ⟨cup#n#1,arg,x⟩. For convenience we can display this as a graph (Figure 1).

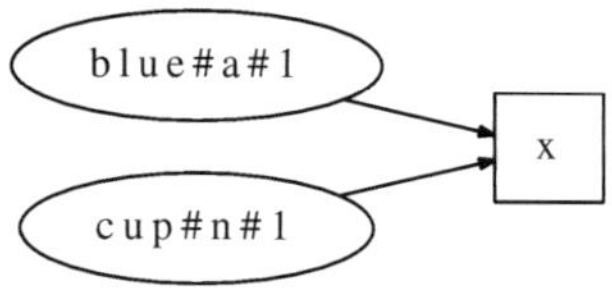

Figure 1: Logical form graph.

Note that in this example several tuples are not shown for clarity (such as conjunction and the quantifier). We show below that we can indeed represent every bit of semantic information in this format without sacrificing the capability of alignment with the text. The important thing now is to show how alignments between tuples and words can be realized, which is done by adding an element to each tuple denoting the surface string, for instance ⟨cup#n#1,arg,x,"tazza"⟩, as in Figure 2.

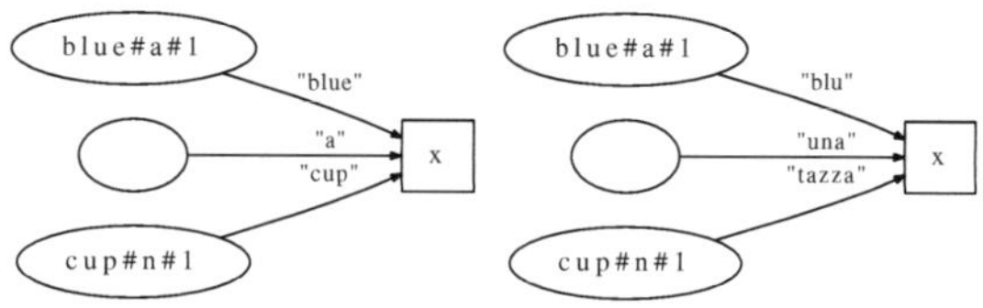

Figure 2: Logical form graphs aligned with surface forms in two languages.

We can further refine the alignment by saying something about the local order of surface expressions. Again, this is done by adding an element to the tuple, in this case one that denotes the local order of a logical term. We will make this clear by continuing with our example, where we add word order encoded as numerical indices in the tuple, e.g. ⟨cup#n#1,arg,x,"tazza",2⟩, as Figure 3 shows.

From these graphs we can associate the term

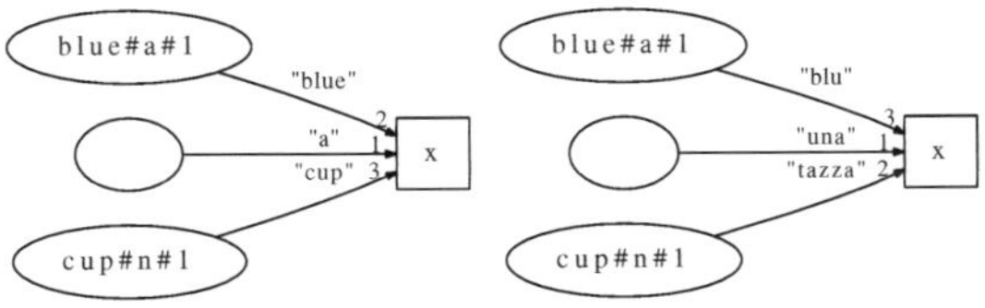

Figure 3: Encoding local word order.

x with the surface strings "a blue cup" and "una tazza blu". But the way we express local order is not limited to words and can be employed for partial phrases as well, if one adopts a neo-Davidsonian event semantics with explicit thematic roles. This can be achieved by using the same kind of numerical indices already used for the alignment of words. The example in Figure 4 shows how to represent an event "hit" with its thematic roles, preserving their relative order. We call surface forms "partial" or "incomplete" when they contain variables, and "complete" when they only contain tokens. The corresponding partial surface form is then "y hit z", where y and z are placeholders for surface strings.

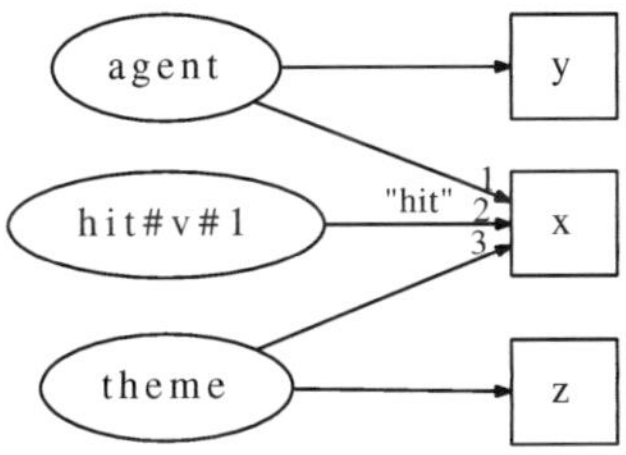

Figure 4: Graph for a neo-Davidsonian structure.

This is the basic idea of aligning surface strings with parts of a deep semantic representation. Note that precise alignment is only possible for words with a lexical semantics that include first-order variables. For words that introduce scope operators (negation particles, coordinating conjuncts) we can't have the cake and eat it: specifying the local order with respect to an entity or event variable directly and at the same time associating it with an operator isn't always possible. To solve this we introduce *surface tuples* that complement a semantic representation to facilitate perfect alignment. We will explain this in more detail in the following sections.

3 Discourse Representation Graphs

The choice of semantic formalism should ideally be independent from the application of natural language generation itself, to avoid bias and specific tailoring the semantic representation to one's (technical) needs. Further, the formalism should have a model-theoretic backbone, to ensure that the semantic representations one works with actually have an interpretation, and can consequently be used in inference tasks using, for instance, automated deduction for first-order logic. Given these criteria, a good candidate is Discourse Representation Theory, DRT (Kamp and Reyle, 1993), that captures the meaning of texts in the form of Discourse Representation Structures (DRSs).

DRSs are capable of effectively representing the meaning of natural language, covering many linguistic phenomena including pronouns, quantifier scope, negation, modals, and presuppositions. DRSs are recursive structures put together by logical and non-logical symbols, as in predicate logic, and in fact can be translated into first-order logic formulas (Muskens, 1996). The way DRSs are nested inside each other give DRT the ability to explain the behaviour of pronouns and presuppositions (Van der Sandt, 1992).

Aligning DRSs with texts with fine granularity is hard because words and phrases introduce different kinds of semantic objects in a DRS: discourse referents, predicates, relations, but also logical operators such as negation, disjunction and implication that introduce embedded DRSs. A precise alignment of a DRS with its text on the level of words is therefore a non-trivial task.

To overcome this issue, we apply the idea presented in the previous section to DRSs, making all recursion implicit by representing them as directed graphs. We call a graph representing a DRS a Discourse Representation Graph (DRG, in short). DRGs encode the same information as DRSs, but are expressed as a set of tuples. Essentially, this is done by reification over DRSs — every DRSs gets a unique label, and the arity of DRS conditions increases by one for accommodating a DRS label. This allows us to reformulate a DRS as a set of tuples.

A DRS is an ordered pair of discourse referents (variables over entities) and DRS-conditions. DRS-conditions are basic (representing properties or relations) or complex (to handle negation and disjunction). To reflect these different constructs, we distinguish three types of tuples in DRGs:

- ⟨K,referent,X⟩ means that X is a discourse referent in K (**referent tuples**);
- ⟨K,condition,C⟩ means that C is a condition

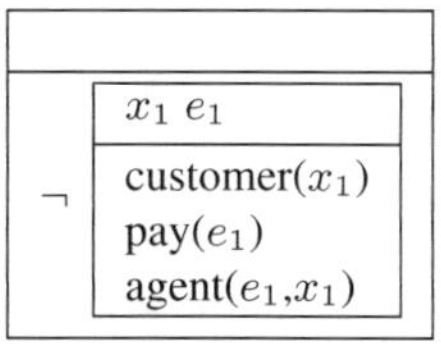

k_1	unary	¬
¬	scope	k_2
k_2	referent	e_1
k_2	referent	x_1
k_2	event	*pay*
k_2	concept	*customer*
k_2	role	*agent*
customer	instance	x_1
pay	instance	e_1
agent	internal	e_1
agent	external	x_1

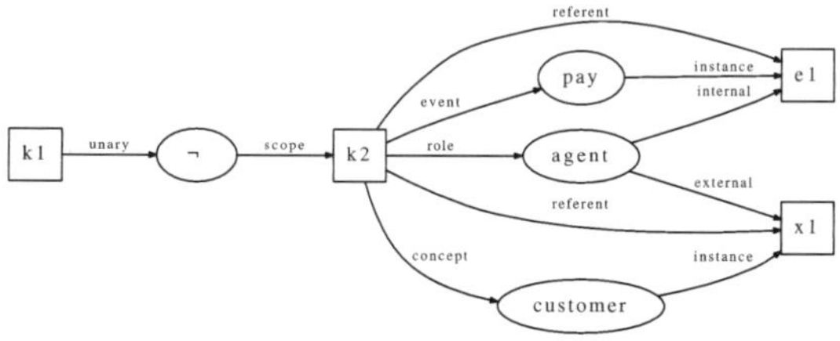

Figure 5: DRS and corresponding DRG (in tuples and in graph format) for "A customer did not pay."

in K (**condition tuples**), with various sub-types: concept, event, relation, role, named, cardinality, attribute, unary, and binary;

- ⟨C,argument,A⟩ means that C is a condition with argument A (**argument tuples**), with the sub-types internal, external, instance, scope, antecedent, and consequence.

With the help of a concrete example, it is easy to see that DRGs have the same expressive power as DRSs. Consider for instance a DRS with negation, before and after labelling it (Figure 6):

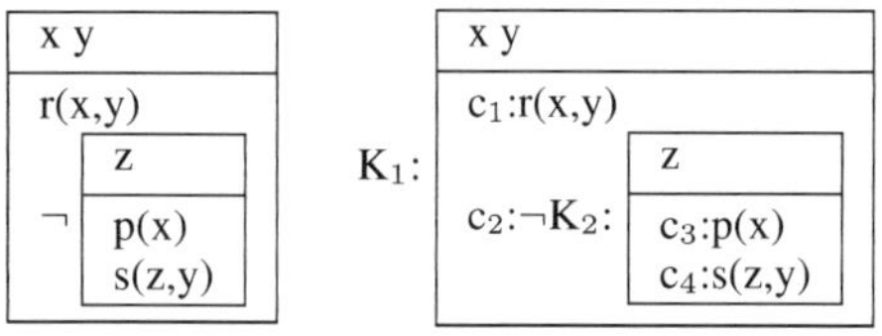

Figure 6: From DRS to DRG: labelling.

Now, from the labelled DRS we can derive the following three referent tuples: ⟨K_1,referent,x⟩, ⟨K_1,referent,y⟩, and ⟨K_2,referent,z⟩; the following four condition tuples: ⟨K_1,relation,c_1:r⟩, ⟨K_1,unary,c_2:¬⟩, ⟨K_2,concept,c_3:p⟩, and ⟨K_2,relation,c_4:s⟩; and the following argument tuples: ⟨c_1:r,internal,x⟩, ⟨c_1:r,external,y⟩, ⟨c_2:¬,scope,K_2⟩, ⟨c_3:p,instance,x⟩, ⟨c_4:s,internal,z⟩, and ⟨c_4:s,external,y⟩. From these tuples, it is straightforward to recreate a labelled DRS, and by dropping the labels subsequently, the original DRS resurfaces again.

For the sake of readability we sometimes leave out labels in examples throughout this paper. In addition, we also show DRGs in graph-like pictures, where the tuples that form a DRG are the edges, and word-alignment information attached at the tuple level is shown as labels on the graph edges, as in Figure 9. In such graphs, nodes representing discourse referents are square shaped, and nodes representing conditions are oval shaped.

Note that labelling conditions is crucial to distinguish between syntactically equivalent conditions occurring in different (embedded) DRSs. Unlike Power's scoped semantic network for DRSs, we don't make the assumption that conditions appear in the DRS in which their discourse referents are introduced (Power, 1999). The example in Figure 6 illustrates that this assumption is not sound: the condition p(x) is in a different DRS than where its discourse referent x is introduced. Further note that our reification procedure yields "flatter" representations than similar formalisms (Copestake et al., 1995; Reyle, 1993), and this makes it more convenient to align surface strings with DRSs with a high granularity, as we will show below.

4 Word-Aligned DRGs

In this section we show how the alignment between surface text and its logical representation is realized by adding information of the tuples that make up a DRG. This sounds more straightforward than it is. For some word classes this is indeed easy to do. For others we need additional machinery in the formalism. Let's start with the straightforward cases. Determiners are usually associated with referent tuples. Content words, such as nouns, verbs, adverbs and adjectives, are typically directly associated with one-place relation symbols, and can be naturally aligned with argument tuples. Verbs are assigned to *instance* tuples linking its *event* condition; likewise, nouns are typically aligned to *instance* tuples which link discourse referents to the *concepts* they express; adjectives are aligned to tuples of *attribute* conditions. Finally, words expressing relations (such as prepositions), are attached to the *external* argument tuple linking the relation to the discourse referent playing the role of external argument.

Although the strategy presented for DRG–text

alignment is intuitive and straightforward to implement, there are surface strings that don't correspond to something explicit in the DRS. To this class belong punctuation symbols, and semantically empty words such as (in English) the infinitival particle, pleonastic pronouns, auxiliaries, *there* insertion, and so on. Furthermore, function words such as "not", "if", and "or", introduce semantic material, but for the sake of surface string generation could be better aligned with the event that they take the scope of. To deal with all these cases, we extend DRGs with *surface tuples* of the form ⟨K,surface,X⟩, whose edges are decorated with the required surface strings. Figure 7 shows an example of a DRG extended with such surface tuples.

k_1	unary	$\neg$		
$\neg$	scope	k_2		
k_2	referent	e_1		
k_2	referent	x_1	**1**	**A**
k_2	event	*pay*		
k_2	concept	*customer*		
k_2	role	*agent*		
customer	instance	x_1	**2**	**customer**
pay	instance	e_1	**4**	**pay**
agent	internal	e_1	**1**	
agent	external	x_1		
k_2	**surface**	e_1	**2**	**did**
k_2	**surface**	e_1	**3**	**not**
k_2	**surface**	e_1	**5**	**.**

Figure 7: Word-aligned DRG for "A customer did not pay." All alignment information (including surface tuples) is highlighted.

Note that surface tuples don't have any influence on the meaning of the original DRS – they just serve for the purpose of alignment of the required surface strings. Also note in Figure 7 the indices that were added to some tuples. They serve to express the local order of surface information.

Following the idea sketched in Section 2, the total order of words is transformed into a local ranking of edges relative to discourse referents. This is possible because the tuples that have word tokens aligned to them always have a discourse referent as third element (the *head* of the directed edge, in terms of graphs). We group tuples that share the same discourse referent and then assign indices reflecting the relative order of how these tuples are realized in the original text.

Illustrating this with our example in Figure 7, we got two discourse referents: x_1 and e_1. The discourse referent x_1 is associated with three tuples, of which two are indexed (with indices 1 and 2). Generating the surface string for x_1 succeeds by traversing the edges in the order specified, resulting in [A,customer] for x_1. The referent e_1 associates with six tuples, of which four are indexed (with indices 1–4). The order of these tuples would yield the partial surface string [x_1,did,not,pay,.] for e_1.

Note that the manner in which DRSs are constructed during analysis ensures that all discourse referents are linked to each other by taking the transitive closure of all binary relations appearing in a DRS, and therefore we can reconstruct the total order from composing the local orders. In the next section we explain how this is done.

5 Surface Composition

In this section we show in detail how surface strings can be generated from word-aligned DRGs. It consists of two subsequent steps. First, a surface form is associated with each discourse referent. Secondly, surface forms are put together in a bottom-up fashion, to generate the complete output. During the composition, all of the discourse referents are associated with their own surface representation. The surface form associated with the discourse unit that contains all other discourse units is then the text aligned with the original DRG.

Surface forms of discourse referents are lists of tokens and other discourse referents. Recall that the order of the elements of a discourse referent's surface form is reflected by the local ordering of tuples, as explained in the previous section, and tuples with no index are simply ignored when reconstructing surface strings.

The surface form is composed by taking each tuple belonging to a specific discourse referent, in the correct order, and adding the tokens aligned with the tuple to a list representing the surface string for that discourse referent. An important part of this process is that binary DRS relations, represented in the DRG by a pair of internal and external argument tuple, are followed unidirectionally: if the tuple is of the *internal* type, then the discourse referent on the other end of the relation (i.e. following its *external* tuple edge) is added to the list. Surface forms for embedded DRSs include the discourse referents of the events

$$\frac{k_1 : e_4 \qquad \dfrac{\dfrac{x_1 : \text{Michelle} \qquad e_1 : x_1 \text{ thinks } p_1}{e_1 : \text{Michelle thinks } p_1} \qquad \dfrac{p_1 : \text{that } e_2 \qquad \dfrac{x_2 : \text{Obama} \qquad e_2 : x_2 \text{ smokes .}}{e_2 : \text{Obama smokes .}}}{p_1 : \text{that Obama smokes .}}}{e_1 : \text{Michelle thinks that Obama smokes .}}}{k_1 : \text{Michelle thinks that Obama smokes .}}$$

Figure 8: Surface composition of embedded structures.

they contain.

Typically, discourse units contain exactly one event (the main event of the clause). Phenomena such as gerunds (e.g. "the laughing girl") and relative clauses (e.g. "the man who smokes") may introduce more than one event in a discourse unit. To ensure correct order and grouping, we borrow a technique from description logic (Horrocks and Sattler, 1999) and invert roles in DRGs. Rather than representing "the laughing girl" as [girl(x) $\wedge$ agent(e,x) $\wedge$ laugh(e)], we represent it as [girl(x) $\wedge$ agent^{-1}(x,e) $\wedge$ laugh(e)], making use of R(x,y) $\equiv$ R^{-1}(y,x) to preserve meaning. This "trick" ensures that we can describe the local order of noun phrases with relative clauses and alike.

To wrap things up, the *composition* operation is used to derive complete surface forms for DRGs. Composition puts together two surface forms, where one of them is complete, and one of them is incomplete. It is formally defined as follows:

$$\frac{\rho_1 : \tau \qquad \rho_2 : \Lambda_1 \rho_1 \Lambda_2}{\rho_2 : \Lambda_1 \tau \Lambda_2} \tag{1}$$

where ρ_1 and ρ_2 are discourse referents, τ is a list of tokens, and Λ_1 and Λ_2 are lists of word tokens and discourse referents. In the example from Figure 7, the complete surface form for the discourse unit k_1 is derived by means of composition as formulated in (1) as follows:

$$\frac{k_2 : e_1 \qquad \dfrac{x_1 : \text{A customer} \qquad e_1 : x_1 \text{ did not pay}}{e_1 : \text{A customer did not pay .}}}{k_2 : \text{A customer did not pay .}}$$

The procedure for generation described here is reminiscent of the work of (Shieber, 1988) who also employs a deductive approach. In particular our composition operation can be seen as a simplified *completion*.

Going back to the example in Section 4, substituting the value of x_1 in the incomplete surface form of e_1 produces the surface string [A,customer,did,not,pay,.] for e_1.

6 Selected Phenomena

We implemented a first prototype using our alignment and realization method and tested it on examples taken from the Groningen Meaning Bank, a large annotated corpus of texts paired with DRSs (Basile et al., 2012). Naturally, we came across phenomena that are notoriously hard to analyze. Most of these we can handle adequately, but some we can't currently account for and require further work.

6.1 Embedded Clauses

In the variant of DRT that we are using, propositional arguments of verbs introduce embedded DRSs associated with a discourse referent. This is a good test for our surface realization formalism, because it would show that it is capable of recursively generating embedded clauses. Figure 9 shows the DRG for the sentence "Michelle thinks that Obama smokes."

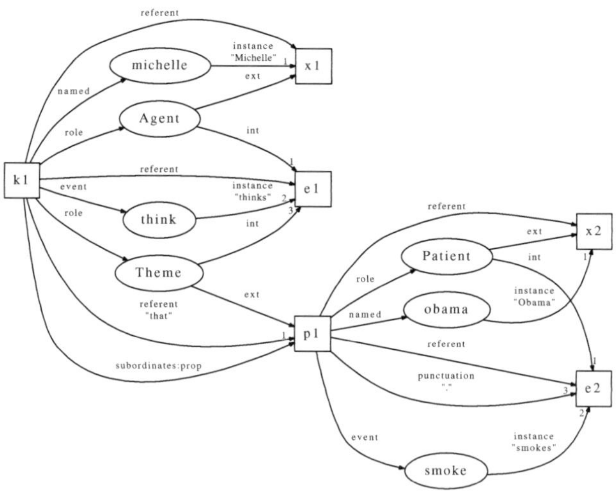

Figure 9: Word-aligned DRG for the sentence "Michelle thinks that Obama smokes."

Here the surface forms of two discourse units (main and embedded) are generated. In order to generate the complete surface form, first the embedded clause is generated, and then composed with the incomplete surface form of the main clause. As noted earlier, during the composition process, the *complete* surface form for each discourse referent is generated (Figure 8), showing a clear alignment between the entities of the semantic representation and the surface forms they represent.

6.2 Coordination

Coordination is another good test case for a linguistic formalism. Consider for instance "Subsistence fishing and commercial trawling occur within refuge waters", where two noun phrases are coordinated, giving rise to either a distributive (introducing two events in the DRS) or a collective interpretation (introducing a set formation of discourse referents in the DRS). We can account for both interpretations (Figure 10).

Note that, interestingly, using the distributive interpretation DRG as input to the surface realization component could result, depending on how words are aligned, in a surface form "fishing occurs and trawling occurs", or as "fishing and trawling occur".

6.3 Long-Distance Dependencies

Cases of extraction, for instance with WH-movement, could be problematic to capture with our formalism. This is in particular an issue when extraction crosses more than one clause boundary, as in "Which car does Bill believe John bought". Even though these cases are rare in the real world, a complete formalism for surface realization must be able to deal with such cases. The question is whether this is a separate generation task in the domain of syntax (White et al., 2007), or whether the current formalism needs to be adapted to cover such long-distance dependencies. Another range of complications are caused by discontinuous constituents, as in the Dutch sentence "Ik heb kaartjes gekocht voor Berlijn" (literally: "I have tickets bought for Berlin"), where the prepositional phrase "voor Berlijn" is an argument of the noun phrase "kaartjes". In our formalism the only alignment possible would result in the sentence "Ik heb kaartjes voor Berlijn gekocht", which is arguably a more fluent realization of the sentence, but doesn't correspond to the original text. If one uses the original text as gold standard, this could cause problems in evaluation. (One could also benefit from this deficiency, and use it to generate more than one gold standard surface string. This is something to explore in future work.)

6.4 Control Verbs

In constructions like "John wants to swim", the control verb "wants" associates its own subject with the subject of the infinitival clause that it has as argument. Semantically, this is realized by variable binding. Generating an appropriate surface form for semantic representation with controlled variables is a challenge: a naive approach would generate "John wants John to swim". One possible solution is to add another derivation rule for surface composition dedicated to deal with cases where a placeholder variable occurs in more than one partial surface form, substituting a null string for a variable following some heuristic rules. A second, perhaps more elegant solution is to integrate a language model into the surface composition process.

7 Related work

Over the years, several systems have emerged that aim at generate surface forms from different kind of abstract input representations. An overview of the state-of-the-art is showcased by the submissions to the Surface Realization Shared Task (Belz et al., 2012). Bohnet *et al.* (2010), for instance, employ deep structures derived from the CoNLL 2009 shared task, essentially sentences annotated with shallow semantics, lemmata and dependency trees; as the authors state, these annotations are not made with generation in mind, and they necessitate complex preprocessing steps in order to derive syntactic trees, and ultimately surface forms. The format presented in this work has been especially developed with statistical approaches in mind.

Nonetheless, there is very little work on robust, wide-scale generation from DRSs, surprisingly perhaps given the large body of theoretical research carried out in the framework of Discourse Representation Theory, and practical implementations and annotated corpora of DRSs that are nowadays available (Basile et al., 2012). This is in contrast to the NLG work in the framework of Lexical Functional Grammar (Guo et al., 2011).

Flat representation of semantic representations, like the DRGs that we present, have also been put forward to facilitate machine translation (Schiehlen et al., 2000) and for evaluation purposes (Allen et al., 2008), and semantic parsing

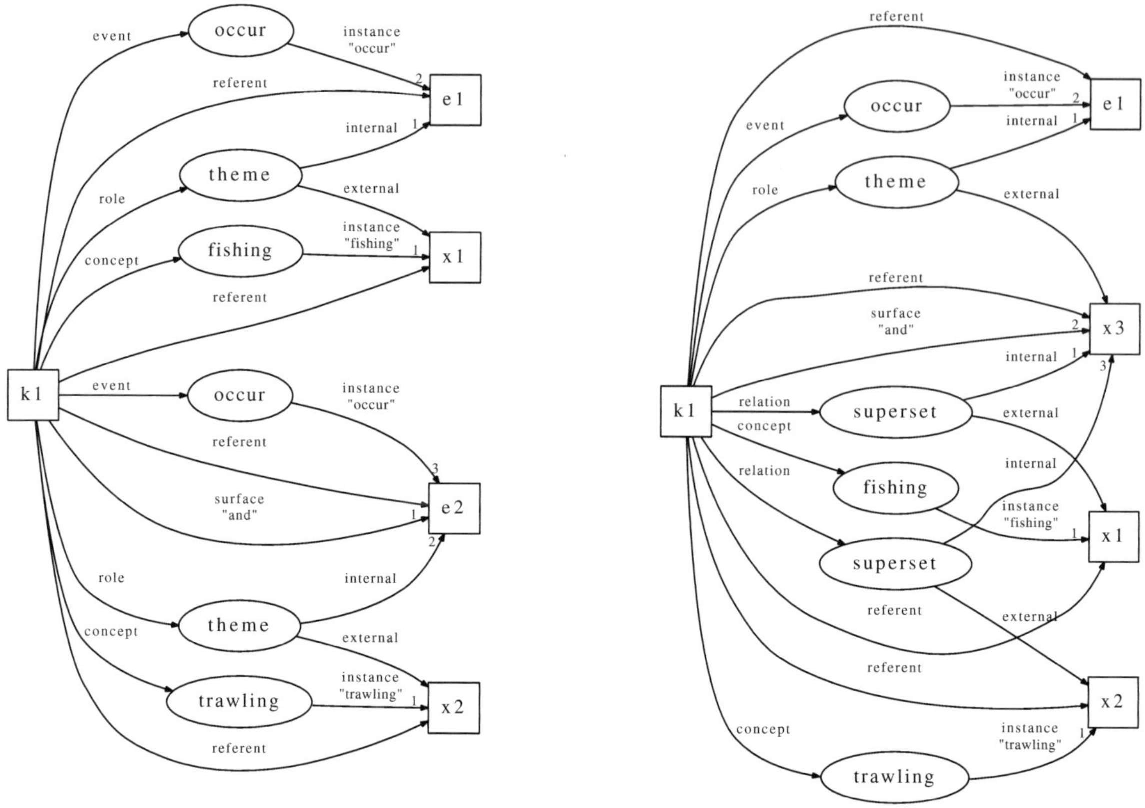

Figure 10: Analysis of NP coordination, in a distributive (left) and a collective interpretation (right).

(Le and Zuidema, 2012) just because they're easier and more efficient to process. Packed semantic representations (leaving scope underspecified) also resemble flat representations (Copestake et al., 1995; Reyle, 1993) and can be viewed as graphs, however they show less elaborated reification than the DRGs presented in this paper, and are therefore less suitable for precise alignment with surface strings.

8 Conclusion

We presented a formalism to align logical forms, in particular Discourse Representation Structures, with surface text strings. The resulting graph representations (DRGs), make recursion implicit by reification over nested DRSs. Because of their "flat" structure, DRGs can be precisely aligned with the text they represent at the word level. This is key to open-domain statistical Surface Realization, where words are learned from abstract, syntactic or semantic, representations, but also useful for other applications such as learning semantic representations directly from text (Le and Zuidema, 2012). The actual alignment between the tuples that form a DRG and the surface forms they represent is not trivial, and requires to make several choices.

Given the alignment with text, we show that it is possible to directly generate surface forms from automatically generated word-aligned DRGs. To do so, a declarative procedure is presented, that generates complete surface forms from aligned DRGs in a compositional fashion. The method works in a bottom-up way, using discourse referents as starting points, then generating a surface form for each of them, and finally composing all of the surface form together into a complete text. We are currently building a large corpus of word-aligned DRSs, and are investigating machine learning methods that could automatically learn the alignments.

Surprisingly, given that DRT is one of the best studied formalisms in formal semantics, there isn't much work on generation from DRSs so far. The contribution of this paper presents a method to align DRSs with surface strings, that paves the way for robust, statistical methods for surface generation from deep semantic representations.

References

James F. Allen, Mary Swift, and Will de Beaumont. 2008. Deep Semantic Analysis of Text. In Johan Bos and Rodolfo Delmonte, editors, *Semantics in Text Processing. STEP 2008 Conference Proceedings*, volume 1 of *Research in Computational Semantics*, pages 343–354. College Publications.

Valerio Basile and Johan Bos. 2011. Towards generating text from discourse representation structures. In *Proceedings of the 13th European Workshop on Natural Language Generation (ENLG)*, pages 145–150, Nancy, France.

Valerio Basile, Johan Bos, Kilian Evang, and Noortje Venhuizen. 2012. Developing a large semantically annotated corpus. In *Proceedings of the Eight International Conference on Language Resources and Evaluation (LREC 2012)*, pages 3196–3200, Istanbul, Turkey.

Anja Belz, Bernd Bohnet, Simon Mille, Leo Wanner, and Michael White. 2012. The surface realisation task: Recent developments and future plans. In Barbara Di Eugenio, Susan McRoy, Albert Gatt, Anja Belz, Alexander Koller, and Kristina Striegnitz, editors, *INLG*, pages 136–140. The Association for Computer Linguistics.

Bernd Bohnet, Leo Wanner, Simon Mille, and Alicia Burga. 2010. Broad coverage multilingual deep sentence generation with a stochastic multi-level realizer. In *Proceedings of the 23rd International Conference on Computational Linguistics*, pages 98–106.

Johan Bos. 2008. Wide-Coverage Semantic Analysis with Boxer. In J. Bos and R. Delmonte, editors, *Semantics in Text Processing. STEP 2008 Conference Proceedings*, volume 1 of *Research in Computational Semantics*, pages 277–286. College Publications.

Alastair Butler and Kei Yoshimoto. 2012. Banking meaning representations from treebanks. *Linguistic Issues in Language Technology - LiLT*, 7(1):1–âĂŞ22.

Ann Copestake, Dan Flickinger, Rob Malouf, Susanne Riehemann, and Ivan Sag. 1995. Translation using Minimal Recursion Semantics. In *Proceedings of the Sixth International Conference on Theoretical and Methodological Issues in Machine Translation*, pages 15–32, University of Leuven, Belgium.

Roger Evans, Paul Piwek, and Lynne Cahill. 2002. What is NLG? In *Proceedings of the Second International Conference on Natural Language Generation*, pages 144–151.

Christiane Fellbaum, editor. 1998. *WordNet. An Electronic Lexical Database*. The MIT Press.

Yuqing Guo, Haifeng Wang, and Josef van Genabith. 2011. Dependency-based n-gram models for general purpose sentence realisation. *Natural Language Engineering*, 17:455–483.

Ian Horrocks and Ulrike Sattler. 1999. A description logic with transitive and inverse roles and role hierarchies. *Journal of logic and computation*, 9(3):385–410.

Hans Kamp and Uwe Reyle. 1993. *From Discourse to Logic; An Introduction to Modeltheoretic Semantics of Natural Language, Formal Logic and DRT*. Kluwer, Dordrecht.

Phong Le and Willem Zuidema. 2012. Learning compositional semantics for open domain semantic parsing. Forthcoming.

Reinhard Muskens. 1996. Combining Montague Semantics and Discourse Representation. *Linguistics and Philosophy*, 19:143–186.

R. Power. 1999. Controlling logical scope in text generation. In *Proceedings of the 7th European Workshop on Natural Language Generation*, Toulouse, France.

E. Reiter and R. Dale. 2000. *Building Natural Language Generation Systems*. Cambridge University Press.

Uwe Reyle. 1993. Dealing with Ambiguities by Underspecification: Construction, Representation and Deduction. *Journal of Semantics*, 10:123–179.

Michael Schiehlen, Johan Bos, and Michael Dorna. 2000. Verbmobil interface terms (vits). In Wolfgang Wahlster, editor, *Verbmobil: Foundations of Speech-to-Speech Translation*. Springer.

Stuart M. Shieber. 1988. A uniform architecture for parsing and generation. In *Proceedings of the 12th conference on Computational linguistics - Volume 2*, COLING '88, pages 614–619, Stroudsburg, PA, USA. Association for Computational Linguistics.

Rob A. Van der Sandt. 1992. Presupposition Projection as Anaphora Resolution. *Journal of Semantics*, 9:333–377.

Leo Wanner, Simon Mille, and Bernd Bohnet. 2012. Towards a surface realization-oriented corpus annotation. In *Proceedings of the Seventh International Natural Language Generation Conference*, INLG '12, pages 22–30, Stroudsburg, PA, USA. Association for Computational Linguistics.

Michael White, Rajakrishnan Rajkumar, and Scott Martin. 2007. Towards broad coverage surface realization with CCG. In *Proceedings of the Workshop on Using Corpora for NLG: Language Generation and Machine Translation (UCNLG+MT)*.

Exploiting ontology lexica for generating natural language texts from RDF data

Philipp Cimiano, Janna Lüker, David Nagel, Christina Unger
Semantic Computing Group
Cognitive Interaction Technology – Center of Excellence (CITEC),
Bielefeld University, Germany

Abstract

The increasing amount of machine-readable data available in the context of the Semantic Web creates a need for methods that transform such data into human-comprehensible text. In this paper we develop and evaluate a Natural Language Generation (NLG) system that converts RDF data into natural language text based on an ontology and an associated ontology lexicon. While it follows a classical NLG pipeline, it diverges from most current NLG systems in that it exploits an ontology lexicon in order to capture context-specific lexicalisations of ontology concepts, and combines the use of such a lexicon with the choice of lexical items and syntactic structures based on statistical information extracted from a domain-specific corpus. We apply the developed approach to the cooking domain, providing both an ontology and an ontology lexicon in *lemon* format. Finally, we evaluate fluency and adequacy of the generated recipes with respect to two target audiences: cooking novices and advanced cooks.

1 Introduction

The goal of the Semantic Web is to enrich the current web by a layer of machine-readable and machine-understandable content (Berners-Lee et al., 2001). In recent years, the growth of data published on the web according to Semantic Web formalisms and data models (e.g. RDF(S) and OWL) has been exponential, leading to more than 30 billion RDF triples[1] available as part of the *Linked Open Data* cloud, which contains a wide range of factual knowledge that is very interesting to many applications and for many purposes. However, due to the fact that it is available as RDF, it is not directly accessible to humans. Thus, natural language generation from RDF data has recently become an important topic for research, leading to the development of various systems generating natural language text from knowledge bases (Bouayad-Agha et al., 2012a; Mellish and Sun, 2006; Sun and Mellish, 2007; Wilcock and Jokinen, 2003) as well as corresponding shared tasks (Banik et al., 2012; Bouayad-Agha et al., 2012b).

Natural language generation (NLG) from knowledge bases requires knowledge about how the concepts in the underlying ontology—individuals, classes and relations—are realised linguistically. For this purpose, *lemon*, a lexicon model for ontologies, has been developed (McCrae et al., 2011). One of the use cases of *lemon* is to support natural language generation systems that take as input a knowledge base structured with respect to a given ontology. In this paper, we present a system that relies on *lemon* lexica for selecting suitable lexicalisations of a given concept, showing how ontology lexica can be exploited in a standard generation architecture.

We apply our system to the domain of cooking, generating natural language texts for recipes modeled as RDF data based on a cooking ontology. Our system relies on a large text corpus of cooking recipes that is used to extract frequency information for single terms and n-grams as well as syntactic trees, which are then used in the selection process for lexicalisation and surface realisation. Additionally, we provide a manually created *lemon* lexicon for the underlying ontology that was enriched with inflectional variants derived from

[1] `http://www4.wiwiss.fu-berlin.de/lodcloud/state/`

Wiktionary. The lexicon also includes contextual information regarding which lexicalisations to prefer depending on the target group, and thereby allows our system to personalize the output to different groups of users. We demonstrate the flexibility of our system by showing that it can be easily tuned to generate recipe descriptions both for novices and for advanced cooks and that this adaptation is clearly recognized by users.

The remainder of this paper is structured as follows. In Section 2 we describe the resources we created and employed, in particular a domain ontology, a corresponding ontology lexicon enriching ontology concepts with lexical information, and a parsed domain corpus. In Section 3 we describe the architecture of the system, in particular the use of a corpus for selecting appropriate syntactic structures and surface realisations of concepts. Then we present the results of an extensive user study in Section 4, compare our approach to related work in Section 5 and finally give an outlook on future work in Section 6.

2 Resources

2.1 Domain ontology and lexicon

In order to be able to model cooking recipes as RDF data, we created a domain ontology in which recipes are modeled comprising the following information (for a similar modeling see (Ribeiro et al., 2006)):

- An indication of the number of people that it serves.
- A set of ingredients used in the recipe.
- An ordered list of steps involving a certain action (e.g. cutting) on a set of ingredients. Each action in turn allows one or many modifiers (e.g. to indicate cutting granularity).
- Interim ingredients that are produced as the result of some step and can be reused later in another step.

An excerpt from the RDF recipe for marble cake is given in Figure 1. It shows two steps, one for mixing the ingredients butter, flour and egg, using a bowl, thereby creating

```
:Marmorkuchen a :Nachspeise;

  :hasStep [ a :Step ;
  :hasStepNumber 7^^xsd:integer ;
  :hasAction     action:mischen ;
  :hasMixType    prop:vermengen ;
  :hasIngredient
       [ a ingredient:Butter ;
         :hasAmount amount:Gramm ;
         :hasValue  "300" ],
       [ a ingredient:Mehl ;
         :hasAmount amount:Gramm ;
         :hasValue  "375" ],
       [ a ingredient:Ei ;
         :hasAmount amount:Stueck
         :hasValue  "5" ] ;
  :hasIndirectIngredient
                  tool:Schuessel ;
  :creates tool:Marmorkuchen_Interim_1
  ] ;

  :hasStep [ a :Step ;
  :hasStepNumber 8^^xsd:integer ;
  :hasAction     action:backen ;
  :isPassive     "true"^^xsd:boolean ;
  :hasTimeUnit   prop:Minute ;
  :hasTimeValue  45.0^^xsd:double ;
  :hasIngredient
      tool:Marmorkuchen_Interim_1 ;
  :hasIndirectIngredient
      tool:Backofen
  ] .
```

Figure 1: An excerpt from the RDF recipe for marble cake.

the dough as an interim object, and a subsequent one in which this interim object is being baked in the oven for 45 minutes.

In general, each step comprises:

- A *step number* indicating the order in a list of steps.
- An associated *action* indicating the type of action performed in the step, e.g. *to fold in.*
- One or more *ingredients* used in the action. This is either an ingredient from the ingredient list of the recipe, or an object that was created as a result of some other step.
- A *passivity* flag indicating whether a step does not require an active action by the cook, e.g. *Let the cake cool for 1 hour.*
- Further modifiers such as *mixType* indicating the way in which the ingredients

are mixed (e.g. *beating* or *folding*), temporal modifiers specifying a *time unit* and *time value* (e.g. 45 minutes). These modifiers later affect the grouping of steps and their lexicalisation.

- A flag indicating whether this is a *key step* within the recipe, for example a step that requires particular care and thus should get emphasis in the verbalization, like *Quickly fry the meat!*

Overall, the ontology comprises 54 different action types that we used to manually model 37 recipes. Further, we created a *lemon* lexicon specifying how the different actions and ingredients specified in the ontology are verbalized in German. In total the lexicon contains 1,530 lexical entries, on average 1.13 lexical variants for each ingredient and 1.96 variants for each action.

Figure 2 gives an example entry for the verb *schneiden* (*to cut*), specifying its part of speech, two form variants, the infinitive and the past participle, and a semantic reference to the ontology action of cutting. Figure 3 gives an excerpt from the lexical entry for *tranchieren* (*to carve*), which refers to the same cutting action but is restricted to cases where the ingredient is of type *meat*, modelled using a logical condition that can be issued as a query to the knowledge base. This verb would therefore only be used in the context of technical registers, i.e. with advanced cooks as target group.

After having manually created lexical entries with their base forms, we automatically enrich them with inflectional forms extracted from Wiktionary, as already indicated in Figure 2.

The ontology, the RDF recipes as well as the ontology lexicon can be accessed at `http://www.sc.cit-ec.uni-bielefeld.de/natural-language-generation`.

Although the manual creation of *lemon* lexica is feasible for small domains (and supported by tools such as *lemon source* (McCrae et al., 2012)), it does not scale to larger domains without a significant amount of effort. Therefore corpus-based methods for the semi-automatic creation of ontology lexica are currently developed, see (Walter et al., 2013).

```
:schneiden a lemon:LexicalEntry ;
 lexinfo:partOfSpeech lexinfo:verb ;

 lemon:canonicalForm [
 lemon:writtenRep "schneiden"@de ;
  lexinfo:tense lexinfo:present ;
  lexinfo:mood  lexinfo:infinitive
 ];
 lemon:otherForm [
  lemon:writtenRep "geschnitten"@de ;
  lexinfo:verbFormMood
                 lexinfo:participle ;
  lexinfo:aspect lexinfo:perfective
 ];

 lemon:sense
 [ lemon:reference action:schneiden ].
```

Figure 2: Lexical entry for the verb *schneiden*, denoting a cutting action.

```
:tranchieren a lemon:LexicalEntry ;
 lexinfo:partOfSpeech lexinfo:verb ;

 lemon:canonicalForm [
  lemon:writtenRep "tranchieren"@de ];

 lemon:sense
 [ lemon:reference action:schneiden;
   lemon:condition [ lemon:value
    "exists ?x :
     :hasIngredient(?x,?y),
     :Step(?x),
     ingredient:Fleisch(?y)" ];
   lemon:context
     isocat:technicalRegister ] .
```

Figure 3: Lexical entry for the verb *tranchieren*, denoting a cutting action restricted to meat and marked as a technical term.

2.2 Domain corpus

In order to build a domain corpus, we crawled the recipe collection website `http://www.chefkoch.de`, which at that point contained more than 215 000 recipes with a total amount of 1.9 million sentences. We extracted the recipe text as well as the list of ingredients and the specified level of difficulty – *easy*, *normal* and *complicated*.

The extracted text was tokenized using the unsupervised method described by Schmid (Schmid, 2000), and for each recipe an *n*-gram index (considering 2, 3 and 4-grams) for both the recipe text and the ingredient list was constructed. Furthermore, 65 000 sentences were parsed using the Stanford parser, trained on the German TIGER corpus, also enriching the training data of the parser with fragments derived from the ontology lexicon in order to ensure that the lexical entries in the ontology lexicon are actually covered. This resulted in 20 000 different phrase structure trees where the leafs were replaced by lists of all terms occurring at that position in the parse tree. Both trees and leaf terms were stored together with the number of their occurrences. Leaf terms were additionally annotated with lexical senses by comparing them to the already created lexical entries and thus connecting them to ontology concepts.

3 System architecture

Our system implements a classical NLG pipeline comprising the following three steps (Reiter and Dale, 2000):

- Document planning
- Microplanning
- Surface realisation

Document planning in our case is quite straightforward as the recipes already comprise exactly the information that needs to be verbalized. In the following we present the two remaining steps in more detail, followed by a brief description of how the text generation is parametrized with respect to the target group (novices or experts).

3.1 Microplanning

Following Reiter & Dale (Reiter and Dale, 2000), microplanning comprises three steps: aggregation, referring expression generation, and lexicalisation.

Aggregation Aggregation serves to collapse information using grouping rules in order to avoid redundancies and repetitions. In our case, the main goal of aggregation is to group steps of recipes, deciding which steps should be verbalized within the same sentences and which ones should be separated, based on the following hand-crafted rules:

- Steps are grouped if
  - they have the same step number, or
  - the actions associated with the steps are the same, or
  - the same ingredient is processed in subsequent actions, e.g. peeling and chopping onions.
- Steps that are marked as *important* in the ontology can only be grouped with other important steps.
- If the grouping of steps would result in too many ingredients to still form a readable sentence, the steps are not grouped. Currently we consider more than six ingredients to be too many, as there are hardly any trees in the corpus that could generate corresponding sentences.
- If there is a big enough time difference between two steps, as e.g. between baking a cake for 60 minutes and then decorating it, the steps are not grouped.

Each of these rules contributes to a numerical value indicating the probability with which steps will be grouped. The use of the rules is also controlled by a system parameter λ_{length} that can be set to a value between 0 and 1, where 0 gives a strong preference to short sentences, while 1 always favors longer sentences.

Referring expression generation The generation of referring expressions is also rule-based and mainly concerns ingredients, as actions are commonly verbalized as verbs and tools (such as bowls and the oven) usually do not re-occur often enough. In deciding whether to generate a pronoun, the following rule is used: A re-occurring ingredient is replaced by a pronoun if there is no other ingredient mentioned in the previous sentence that has the same number and gender. A system parameter $\lambda_{pronoun}$ can be set to determine the relative frequency of pronouns to be generated.

If an ingredient is not replaced by a pronoun, then one of the following expressions is generated:

- A full noun phrase based on the verbalization given in the ontology lexicon, e.g. *two eggs*.
- A definite expression describing a super-category of the given ingredient. The super-category is extracted from the ontology and its verbalization from the on-

tology lexicon. For instance, if the ingredient in question is *pork*, the expression *meat* would be generated.

- A zero anaphora, i.e. an empty referring expression, as in *Bake for 60 minutes* or *Simmer until done.*

The use of those variants is regulated by a system parameter $\lambda_{pronoun}$, where a high value forces the use of abstract expressions and zero anaphora, while a low value prefers the use of exact ingredient names. In future work the decision of which referring expression to use should be decided on the basis of general principles, such as uniqueness of the referent, avoidance of unnecessary and inappropriate modifiers, brevity, and preference for simple lexical items, see, e.g., (Reiter and Dale, 1992).

An exception to the above rules are interim ingredients, whose realisation is determined as follows. If there is a lexical entry for the interim, it is used for verbalization. If there is no lexical entry, then the name of the main ingredient used in the creation of the interim is used. Furthermore, we define and exploit manually specified meaning postulates to create names for specific, common interims. For example *dough* is used if the interim is generated from *flour* and at least one of the ingredients *butter*, *sugar*, *egg* or *backing powder.*

Lexicalisation In order to lexicalise actions and ingredients, the ontology lexicon is consulted. Especially for actions, the lexicon contains several lexical variants, usually accompanied by a restriction that specifies the context in which the lexicalisation is appropriate. For example the action *to cut* can be lexicalised in German as *hacken* (*to chop*) if the specified granularity is *rough*, as *blättrig schneiden* (*to thinly slice*) if the specified granularity is *fine*, or *tranchieren* (*to carve*) in case the ingredient is of type *meat.*

The conditions under which a lexicalisation can be used felicitously are given in the lexicon as logical expressions, as exemplified in Figure 3 above, which are translated into SPARQL queries that can be used to check whether the condition is satisfied with respect to the recipe database.

In addition, we rely on statistics derived from our domain corpus in order to choose a lexicalisation in case the conditions of more than one lexical variant are fulfilled, by preferring terms and term combinations with a higher frequency in the domain corpus. Again, the system implements a parameter, $\lambda_{variance}$, that regulates how much overall lexical variability is desired. This, however, should be used with care, as choosing variants that are less frequent in the corpus could easily lead to strange or inappropriate verbalizations.

3.2 Surface realisation

The input to the surface realisation component is a list of concepts (spanning one or more recipe steps) together with appropriate lexicalisations as selected by the lexicalisation component. The task of the surface realiser then is to find an appropriate syntactic tree from the parsed corpus that can be used to realise the involved concepts. An example of such a parse tree with annotated leaf probabilities is shown in Figure 4.

All trees retrieved from the index are weighted to identify the best fitting tree combining the following measures: i) the normalized probability of the syntax tree in the domain corpus, ii) a comparison of the part-of-speech tag, synonyms and the lexical sense of a given lexicalisation with those of the terms in the retrieved tree, iii) the node distances of related words inside each tree, and iv) an n-gram score for each resulting sentence. These scores are added up and weighted w.r.t. the size of n, such that, for example, 4-grams have more influence on the score than 3-grams. Also, sentences with unbalanced measure, i.e. that score very well w.r.t. one measure but very poorly w.r.t. another one, are penalized.

3.3 Personalization

On the basis of conditions on the context of use provided in the ontology lexicon, it is possible to distinguish lexicalisations that are suitable for experts from lexical variants that are suitable for novices. Thus, texts can be generated either containing a high amount of technical terms, in case the user has a high proficiency level, or avoiding technical terms at all, in case the user is a novice. Furthermore, the complexity of texts can be varied by adjusting the

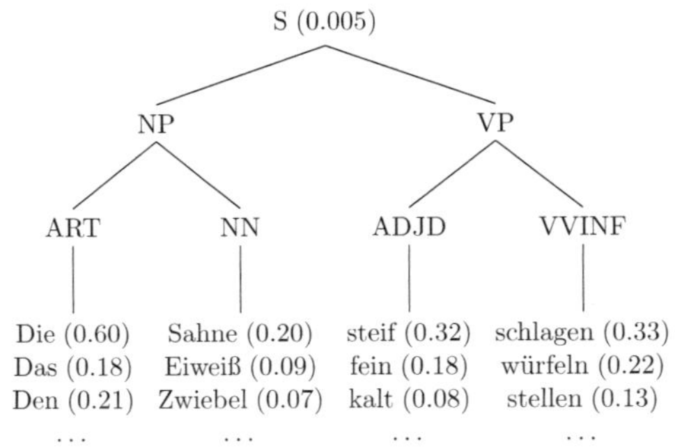

Figure 4: Example of a parse tree extracted from the corpus, annotated with leaf probabilities

sentence length and the number of adjectives used. We used this as an additional parameter $\lambda_{context}$ for tailoring texts to their target group, preferring complex structures in expert texts and simple structures in texts for novices. The influence of this parameter is tested as part of the user study described in the next section.

Personalization thus has been implemented at the level of microplanning. In addition, personalization is possible on the level of text planning. For example, experts often require less detailed descriptions of actions, such that they can be summarized in one step, while they need to be broken down into several steps for beginners. This will be subject of future work.

4 Evaluation

The system was evaluated in an online study with 93 participants—mainly students recruited via email or Facebook. The majority of the participants (70%) were between 18 and 34 years old; the native tongue of almost all participants (95%) was German. About half of the participants regarded themselves as novices, while the other half regarded themselves as advanced cooks.

For each participant, 20 recipes were randomly selected and split into two groups. For ten recipes, test subjects were asked to rate the fluency and adequacy of the automatically generated text along the categories *very good*, *good*, *sufficient* and *insufficient*. The other ten recipes were used to compare the effect of parameters of the generation system and thus were presented in two different versions, varying the sentence length and complexity as well as the level of proficiency. Participants were asked to rate texts as being appropriate *for novices* or *for advanced cooks*.

The parameters that were varied in our experimental setting are the following:

- $\lambda_{context}$: The context of the used terms, in particular *novice* or *advanced*.
- $\lambda_{pronoun}$: Amount of proper nouns, where a high value prefers pronouns over proper nouns, while a low value generates only proper nouns.
- $\lambda_{variance}$: Amount of repetitions, where low values lead to always using the same term, whereas high values lead to fewer repetitions.
- λ_{length}: Length of the created sentences, where a low value creates short sentences, and high values merge short sentences into longer ones.

The values of these parameters that were used in the different configurations are summarized in Table 1. The parameter $\lambda_{pronoun}$ is not varied but set to a fixed value that yields a satisfactory generation of referring expressions, as texts with smaller or higher values tend to sound artificial or incomprehensible.

	$\lambda_{context}$	$\lambda_{pronoun}$	$\lambda_{variance}$	λ_{length}
Standard	*novice*	0.5	0.5	0.5
Novice vs	*novice*	0.5	0.5	0.3
Advanced	*advanced*	0.5	0.5	0.7
Simple vs	*novice*	0.5	0.0	0.3
Complex	*novice*	0.5	1.0	0.7

Table 1: The used parameter sets

Fluency and adequacy of the generated texts Each participant was asked to rate fluency and adequacy of ten automatically generated texts. The results are given in Figures 5 and 6. The fluency of the majority of generated texts (85.8%) were perceived as *very good* or *good*, whereas only 1% of the generated texts were rated as *insufficient*. Similarly, the adequacy of 92.5% of the generated texts were rated as *very good* or *good*, and again only 1% of the generated texts were rated as *insufficient*. There was no significant difference between judgments of novices and experts; neither did the category of the recipe (main or side dish, dessert, etc.) have any influence. Overall, these results clearly show that the quality of the texts generated by our system is high.

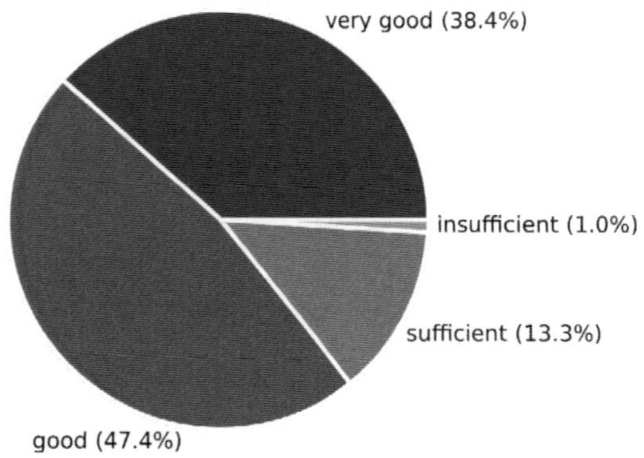

Figure 5: Results for text fluency

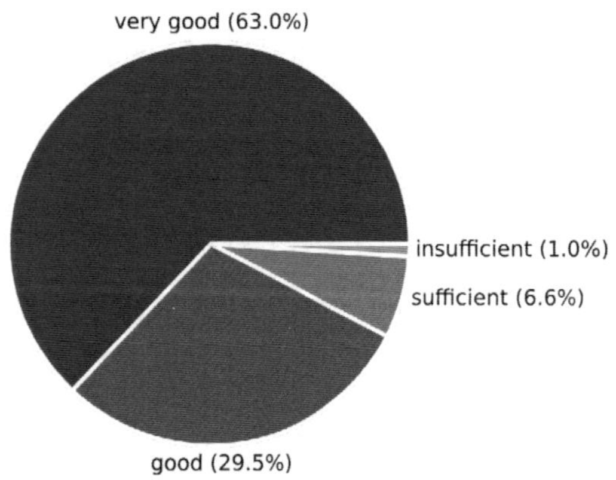

Figure 6: Results for text adequacy

Error analysis The most frequent errors found in the generated texts can be grouped into the following categories:

- **Content (39.4%):** Errors in document planning (e.g. due to the ontology missing details about tools, such as for cutting cookies, or the recipe missing information about the amount of ingredients) or aggregation (e.g. sentences with highly related content were not aggregated), as well as sentence repetitions.
- **Language (29.4%):** Errors in the referring expression generation or lexicalisation steps (e.g. wrong use of function words like *as well*) and grammar errors (e.g. wrong use of definite or indefinite determiners).
- **Other (31.3%):** Some users specified that they would prefer another ordering of the involved steps, or that they lack knowledge of particular terms. Also short sentences with exclamation marks are often perceived as impolite.

Influence of parameter settings We set up the following hypotheses, validating them by means of a χ^2-test by comparing answers across two conditions corresponding to different parameter settings. We regarded a p-value of 0.05 as sufficient to reject the corresponding null hypothesis.

H1 Users prefer longer sentences: Rejecting the null hypothesis that users rate texts with longer sentences and texts with shorter sentences in the same way (p-value: $3 * 10^{-5}$).

H2 Texts for professionals are regarded as not suitable for novices: Rejecting the null hypothesis that texts generated for professionals are regarded as many times as suitable for novices as for professionals (p-value: $2 * 10^{-7}$).

H3 Beginners prefer texts generated for novices: The null hypothesis that novices equally prefer texts targeted to novices and texts targeted to experts could not be rejected.

H4 Advanced cooks prefer texts generated for advanced cooks: Rejecting the null hypothesis that advanced cooks equally prefer texts targeted to novices and texts targeted to experts (p-value: 0.0005).

The confirmation of H1 shows that users perceive a difference in sentence length and prefer texts with longer sentences, probably due to perceived higher fluency. The confirmation of H2 and H4, on the other hand, corroborates the successful adaptation of the generated texts to specific target groups, showing that texts generated for professionals are indeed perceived as being generated for professionals, and that such texts are preferred by advanced cooks. The rejection of H3 might be caused by the fact that recipes for advanced cooks include some but actually not many technical terms and are therefore also comprehensible for novices.

5 Related work

There have been different approaches to natural language generation, ranging from template-based to statistical architectures. While early NLG systems were mainly based on manually created rules (Bourbeau et al., 1990; Reiter et al., 1992), later approaches started applying statistical methods to the subtasks involved in generation (Belz, 2005), focusing on scalability and easy portability and often relying on overgeneration and subsequent ranking of generation possibilities. Personalization has been a concern in both strands of research. PEBA-II (Milosavljevic et al., 1996), for example, generates target-group-specific texts for novice and experts users from taxonomical information, relying on a phrasal lexicon that is similar in spirit to our ontology lexicon. Statistical approaches such as (Isard et al., 2006), on the other hand, use text corpora to generate personalized texts.

Our approach is hybrid in the sense that it enriches a classical rule-based approach with statistical data in the microplanning and realisation steps, thus being comparable to systems like HALogen (Langkilde and Knight, 1998) and *p*CRU (Belz, 2008). The main difference is that it uses Semantic Web data as base.

Since the emergence of the Semantic Web there has been a strong interest in NLG from Semantic Web data, especially for providing users with natural language access to structured data. Work in this area comprises verbalization of ontologies as well as RDF knowledge bases; for an overview see (Bouayad-Agha et al., to appear). Of particular interest in the context of our work is NaturalOWL (Galanis and Androutsopoulos, 2007), a system that produces descriptions of entities and classes relying on linguistic annotations of domain data in RDF format, similar to our exploitation of ontology lexica. We thus share with NaturalOWL the use of linguistic resources encoded using standard Semantic Web formats. The main difference is that the annotations used by NaturalOWL comprise not only lexical information but also microplans for sentence planning, which in our case are derived statistically and represented outside the lexicon. Separating lexical information and sentence plans makes it easier to use the same lexicon for generating different forms of texts, either with respect to specific target groups or stylistic variants.

6 Conclusion and future work

We have presented a principled natural language generation architecture that follows a classical NLG architecture but exploits an ontology lexicon as well as statistical information derived from a domain corpus in the lexicalisation and surface realisation steps. The system has been implemented and adapted to the task of generating cooking recipe texts on the basis of RDF representations of recipes. In an evaluation with 93 participants we have shown that the system is indeed effective and generates natural language texts that are perceived as fluent and adequate. A particular feature of the system is that it can personalize the generation to particular target groups, in our case cooking novices and advanced cooks. The information about which lexicalisation to prefer depending on the target group is included in the ontology lexicon. In fact, the ontology lexicon is the main driver of the generation process, as it also guides the search for appropriate parse trees. It thus is a central and crucial component of the architecture.

While the system has been adapted to the particulars of the cooking domain, especially concerning the generation of referring expressions, the architecture of the system is fairly general and in principle the system could be adapted to any domain by replacing the ontology, the corresponding ontology lexicon and by providing a suitable domain corpus. This flexibility is in our view a clear strength of our system architecture.

A further characteristic of our system is the consistent use of standards, i.e. OWL for the ontology, RDF for the actual data to be verbalized, SPARQL for modelling contextual conditions under which a certain lexicalisation is to be used, and the *lemon* format for the representation of the lexicon-ontology interface. One important goal for future work will be to clearly understand which knowledge an ontology lexicon has to include in order to optimally support NLG. To this end, we intend to test the system on other domains, and at the same time invite other researchers to test their systems on our data, available at `http://www.sc.cit-ec.uni-bielefeld.de/natural-language-generation`.

Acknowledgment

This work was partially funded within the EU project PortDial (FP7-296170).

References

E. Banik, C. Gardent, D. Scott, N. Dinesh, and F. Liang. 2012. KBGen: text generation from knowledge bases as a new shared task. In *Proc. Seventh International Natural Language Generation Conference (INLG 2012)*, pages 141–145.

A. Belz. 2005. Statistical generation: Three methods compared and evaluated. In *Proc. 10th European Workshop on Natural Language Generation (ENLG '05)*, pages 15–23.

A. Belz. 2008. Automatic generation of weather forecast texts using comprehensive probabilistic generation-space models. *Natural Language Engineering*, 14(4):431–455.

T. Berners-Lee, J. Hendler, and O. Lassila. 2001. The Semantic Web. *Scientific American Magazine.*

N. Bouayad-Agha, G. Casamayor, S. Mille, M. Rospocher, H. Saggion, L. Serafini, and L. Wanner. 2012a. From ontology to NL: Generation of multilingual user-oriented environmental reports. In *Proc. 17th International Conference on Applications of Natural Language Processing to Information Systems (NLDB 2012)*, pages 216–221.

N. Bouayad-Agha, G. Casamayor, L. Wanner, and C. Mellish. 2012b. Content selection from Semantic Web data. In *Proc. Seventh International Natural Language Generation Conference (INLG 2012)*, pages 146–149.

N. Bouayad-Agha, G. Casamayor, and L. Wanner. to appear. Natural Language Generation in the context of the Semantic Web. *Semantic Web Journal.*

L. Bourbeau, D. Carcagno, E. Goldberg, R. Kittredge, and A. Polguère. 1990. Bilingual generation of weather forecasts in an operations environment. In *Proc. 13th International Conference on Computational Linguistics (COLING 1990)*, pages 318–320.

D. Galanis and I. Androutsopoulos. 2007. Generating multilingual descriptions from linguistically annotated OWL ontologies: the NaturalOWL system. In *Proc. 11th European Workshop on Natural Language Generation (ENLG '07)*, pages 143–146.

A. Isard, C. Brockmann, and J. Oberlander. 2006. Individuality and alignment in generated dialogues. In *Proc. Fourth International Natural Language Generation Conference (INLG 2006)*, pages 25–32.

I. Langkilde and K. Knight. 1998. Generation that exploits corpus-based statistical knowledge. In *Proc. 17th International Conference on Computational Linguistics (COLING '98)*, pages 704–710.

J. McCrae, D. Spohr, and P. Cimiano. 2011. Linking lexical resources and ontologies on the semantic web with lemon. In *Proc. 8th Extended Semantic Web Conference on The Semantic Web: Research and Applications (ESWC 2011)*, pages 245–259.

J. McCrae, E. Montiel-Ponsoda, and P. Cimiano. 2012. Collaborative semantic editing of linked data lexica. In *Proceedings of the 2012 International Conference on Language Resource and Evaluation.*

C. Mellish and X. Sun. 2006. The Semantic Web as a linguistic resource: Opportunities for natural language generation. *Knowl.-Based Syst.*, 19(5):298–303.

M. Milosavljevic, A. Tulloch, and R. Dale. 1996. Text generation in a dynamic hypertext environment. In *Proc. 19th Australian Computer Science Conference*, pages 417–426.

E. Reiter and R. Dale. 1992. A fast algorithm for the generation of referring expressions.

E. Reiter and R. Dale. 2000. *Building natural language generation systems.* Cambridge University Press.

E. Reiter, C. Mellish, and J. Levine. 1992. Automatic generation of on-line documentation in the IDAS project. In *Proc. Third Conference on Applied Natural Language Processing (ANLP)*, pages 64–71.

R. Ribeiro, F. Batista, J.P. Pardal, N.J. Mamede, and H.S. Pinto. 2006. Cooking an ontology. In *Proceedings of the 12th international conference on Artificial Intelligence: methodology, Systems, and Applications*, AIMSA'06, pages 213–221. Springer.

Helmut Schmid. 2000. Unsupervised learning of period disambiguation for tokenisation. Technical report, IMS-CL, University of Stuttgart.

X. Sun and C. Mellish. 2007. An experiment on "free generation" from single RDF triples. In *Proc. 11th European Workshop on Natural Language Generation (ENLG '07)*, pages 105–108.

S. Walter, C. Unger, and P. Cimiano. 2013. A corpus-based approach for the induction of ontology lexica. In *Proceedings of the 18th International Conference on the Application of Natural Language to Information Systems (NLDB 2013)*.

G. Wilcock and K. Jokinen. 2003. Generating responses and explanations from RDF/XML and DAML+OIL. In *Knowledge and Reasoning in Practical Dialogue Systems, IJCAI 2003 Workshop*, pages 58–63.

User-Controlled, Robust Natural Language Generation from an Evolving Knowledge Base

Eva Banik
Computational Linguistics Ltd
London, UK
ebanik@comp-ling.com

Eric Kow
Computational Linguistics Ltd
London, UK
kowey@comp-ling.com

Vinay Chaudhri*
SRI International
Menlo Park, CA
chaudhri@ai.sri.com

Abstract

In this paper we describe a natural language generation system which produces complex sentences from a biology knowledge base. The NLG system allows domain experts to discover errors in the knowledge base and generates certain parts of answers in response to users' questions in an e-textbook application. The system allows domain experts to customise its lexical resources and to set parameters which influence syntactic constructions in generated sentences. The system is capable of dealing with certain types of incomplete inputs arising from a knowledge base which is constantly edited and includes a referring expression generation module which keeps track of discourse history. Our referring expression module is available for download as the open source Antfarm tool[1].

1 Introduction

In this paper we describe a natural language generation system we have developed to interface with a biology knowledge base. The knowledge base (KB) encodes sentences from a biology textbook, and the ultimate goal of our project is to develop an intelligent textbook application which can eventually answer students' questions about biology[2] (Spaulding et al., 2011).

*The work reported in this paper was supported by funding from Vulcan, Inc. We would also like to thank the members of the Inquire Biology development team: Roger Corman, Nikhil Dinesh, Debbie Frazier, Stijn Heymans, Sue Hinojoza, David Margolies, Adam Overholtzer, Aaron Spaulding, Ethan Stone, William Webb, Michael Wessel and Neil Yorke-Smith.

[1] https://github.com/kowey/antfarm

[2] http://www.aaaivideos.org/2012/inquire_intelligent_textbook/

The natural language generation module is part of a larger system, which includes a question understanding module, question answering and reasoning algorithms, as well as an answer presentation module which produces pages with information from the KB. We measure the progress and consistency of encoding by asking "what is an X?" type questions of the application and evaluate the quality of answers. In response to these questions, the system generates "glossary pages" of concepts, which display all information about concept X in the KB that are deemed relevant. The NLG module is used for two purposes in our system: to check the completeness and consistency of the KB (instead of looking at complex graphs of the encoded knowledge, it is easier to detect errors in natural language sentences), and to present parts of answers in response to questions.

One goal of our project was to develop a tool which empowers biology teachers to encode domain knowledge with little training in formal knowledge representation. In the same spirit, we aimed to develop an NLG system which allowed domain experts to easily and intuitively customize the generated sentences as much as possible, without any training on the grammar or internal workings of the system. This was necessary because many domain-specific concepts in the KB are best expressed by biology terminology and linguistic constructions specific to the domain. We developed a utility which allows encoders to not only associate lexical items with concepts in the KB but also customise certain lexical parameters which influence the structure of sentences generated to describe events.

Another requirement was robustness: since the knowledge base is constantly edited, the NLG system had to be able to deal with missing lexical information, incomplete inputs, changing encoding guidelines, and bugs in the KB as much as possible. The system also had to be flexible in the sense

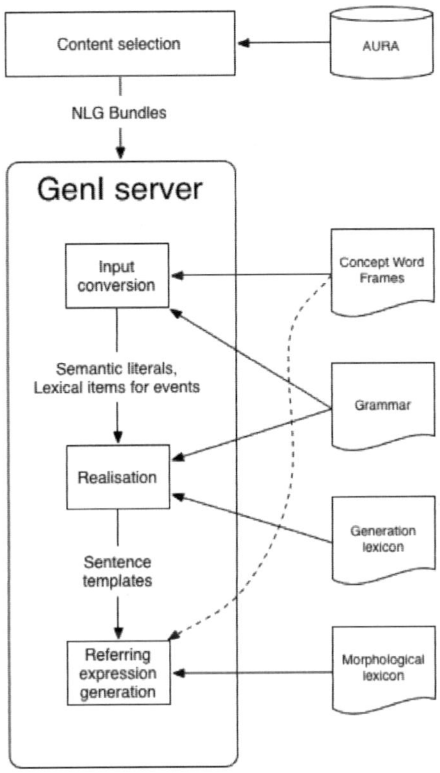

Figure 1: Architecture of the AURA NLG system

that it had to be able to generate different versions of the same output to suit specific contexts or types of concepts in its input. Our system therefore generates all possible realizations for a given input, and allows the answer presentation module to send parameters to determine which output is returned in a specific context.

After describing the architecture of the NLG module in detail we explain how the system is able to deal with unseen combination of event-to-entity relations when describing events. We illustrate the utility we developed to allow domain experts to customize the system's output by adding parameters to lexical entries associated with concepts.

2 Related Work

Work on natural language generation from ontologies and knowledge bases tends to fall into two groups. On the one hand, there are tools for ontology verbalization which tend to handle a limited number of relations, and where the goal of the system is to help the work of knowledge engineers. These systems produce template based outputs, and the texts closely follow the structure of the ontology (Wilcock, 2003; Galanis and Androutsopoulos, 2007). Some of these systems attempt to minimize reliance on domain-specific linguistic resources and attempt to detect words in the labels of the ontology to use as lexical items (Mellish and Sun, 2005). On the other hand there are NLG systems which take their input from complex knowledge bases (Reiter et al., 2003; Paris, 1988) and produce fluent texts geared towards users other than knowledge engineers. These systems produce outputs tailored to the user or the context and they are difficult for non-NLG-experts to customize or port to a different domain. Our system falls halfway between these two groups: like ontology verbalizers, we wanted to produce output for all inputs, using ontology labels if necessary in the absence of lexical entries. However, like sophisticated NLG systems, we also wanted to generate good quality output for inputs for which the system had lexical resources, and we also wanted to be able to tailor the generated output to the context in which it is displayed. Our input was also more expressive than the input of ontology verbalizers, because of the presence of cardinality constraints and co-references in our KB. Our work is perhaps most closely related to the MIAKT system which also allows domain experts to edit lexical knowledge and schemas (Bontcheva, 2004; Bontcheva and Wilks, 2004). Like MIAKT, we also aimed to develop an NLG system which can be easily maintained as the KB changes.

3 Architecture of the AURA NLG system

Our NLG system generates complex sentences from the AURA knowledge base (Gunning et al., 2010), which contains information from a college-level biology textbook. AURA is a frame-based KB which encodes events, the entities that participate in events, properties, and roles that the entities play in an event (e.g., catalyst, reactant, messenger, parent). The KB specifies relations between these types, including event-to-entity, event-to-event, event-to-property, entity-to-property. The AURA KB is built on top of the CLIB ontology of general concepts (Barker et al., 2001), which was extended with biology-specific information. The KB consists of a set of concept maps, which describe all the statements that are true about a concept in our KB. The input to our NLG system is a set of relations extracted from the KB either in response to users' questions or when generating glossary pages that describe specific concepts in detail. The generation pipeline consists of four main stages: content selection, input conversion, realisation and referring expression generation, as illustrated in Fig1.

3.1 Content Selection

Question answering and reasoning algorithms that return answers or other content in AURA are not engineered to satisfy the purposes of natural language generation. The output of these algorithms can be best thought of as pointers to concepts in the KB, which need to be described to provide an answer to the user. In order for the answer to be complete in a given context, the output of reasoning algorithms have to be extended with additional relations, depending on the specific question that was asked, and the context in which the answer was found in the KB. The relations selected from the KB also vary depending on the type of concept that is being described (event, entity, role, property). For example, a user might ask "What is a catalyst?". To answer this question, AURA will retrieve entities from the KB ("role players") which play the role of catalyst in various events. For example, it will find "adenylyl cyclase", which is defined in the KB as a universal catalyst, i.e., this information is encoded on the concept map of Adenylyl cyclase and is regarded as a "universal truth". In this case, our content selection algorithm will return a single `plays` triple, and the NLG system will produce *"Adenylyl cyclase is a catalyst'.'*
Another entity that will be returned in response to the question is "ribosomal RNA". However, ribosomal RNA is a catalyst only in specific situations, and therefore we need to give more detail on the contexts in which it can play the role of a catalyst. This includes the event in which ribosomal RNA is a catalyst, and perhaps the larger process during which this event occurs. Accordingly, content selection here will return a number of relations (including `agent`, `object`, `subevent`), and our NLG system will produce:
"In translation elongation, ribosomal RNA is a catalyst in the formation of a peptide bond by the ribosomal RNA and a ribosome."
Similarly, for "triose phosphate dehydrogenase" we will produce
"In energy payoff phase of glycolysis, NAD plus is converted by a triose phosphate dehydrogenase to a hydrogen ion, an NADH and a PGAP. Here, the triose phosphate dehydrogenase is a catalyst."
For "cellulose synthase" the situation is slightly different, because the event in which this entity plays the role of catalyst is not part of a larger process but the function of the entity. So we need slightly different information to produce the correct sentence: *"The function of cellulose synthase is conversion of a chemical in a cell to cellulose. Here, a cellulose synthase is a catalyst."*
The task of the AURA content selection module is to determine what information to include for each entity or event that was returned as the answer to the question. We do this by retrieving sets of relations from the KB that match contextual patterns. We also filter out relations which contain overly generic classes (e.g., Tangible-Entity), and any duplication arising from the presence of inverse relations or inferences in the KB. The output of content selection is a structured bundle (Fig. 2), which contains
(1) the relations that form the input to NLG
(2) information about concepts in the input: what class(es) they belong to, cardinality constraints
(3) parameters influencing the style of output texts.

3.2 Input Conversion

The realisation phase in our system is carried out by the GenI surface realizer (Kow, 2007), using a Tree-Adjoining Grammar (Joshi and Schabes, 1997). The task of the input conversion module is to interpret the structured bundles returned by content selection, and to convert the information to GenI's input format. We parse the structured bundles, perform semantic aggregation, interpret parameters in bundles which influence the style of the generated text, and convert triples to semantic literals as required by GenI.

4 Handling Unseen Combinations of Relations

As Fig 3 shows, a combination of event-to-entity relations are associated with elementary trees in the grammar to produce a full sentence. The domain of the relations associated with the same tree is the event which specifies the main predicate of the sentence and the range of the relations are entities that fill in the individual argument and modifier positions. Depending on the event, different relations can be used to fill in the subject and object positions, and verbs might determine the prepositions needed to realize some of the arguments. Ideally the mapping between sets

```
(TRIPLES-DATA
  :TRIPLES
    ((|_Cell56531|               |has-part|       |_Ribosome56523|)
     (|_Ribosome56523|           |has-part|       |_Active-Site56548|)
     (|Enzyme-Synthesis17634|    |base|           |_Cell56531|)
     (|Enzyme-Synthesis17634|    |raw-material|   |_Free-Energy56632|)
     (|Enzyme-Synthesis17634|    |raw-material|   |_Monomer56578|)
     (|Enzyme-Synthesis17634|    |raw-material|   |_Activation-Energy56580|)
     (|Enzyme-Synthesis17634|    |raw-material|   |_Monomer56581|)
     (|Enzyme-Synthesis17634|    |raw-material|   |_Amino-Acid56516|)
     (|Enzyme-Synthesis17634|    |result|         |_Free-Energy56575|)
     (|Enzyme-Synthesis17634|    |result|         |Protein-Enzyme17635|))
  :CONSTRAINTS
     ((|Enzyme-Synthesis17634|   |raw-material|   (|at-least| 3 |Amino-Acid|)))
  :INSTANCE-TYPES
    ((|_Ribosome56523|           |instance-of|  |Ribosome|)
     (|_Active-Site56548|        |instance-of|  |Active-Site|)
     (|_Cell56531|               |instance-of|  |Cell|)
     (|_Free-Energy56632|        |instance-of|  |Free-Energy|)
     (|_Monomer56578|            |instance-of|  |Monomer|)
     (|_Activation-Energy56580|  |instance-of|  |Activation-Energy|)
     (|_Monomer56581|            |instance-of|  |Monomer|)
     (|_Amino-Acid56516|         |instance-of|  |Amino-Acid|)
     (|_Free-Energy56575|        |instance-of|  |Free-Energy|)
     (|Enzyme-Synthesis17634|    |instance-of|  |Enzyme-Synthesis|)
     (|Protein-Enzyme17635|      |instance-of|  |Protein-Enzyme|)
     (|Free-Energy|              |subclasses|   |Energy|)
     (|Activation-Energy|        |subclasses|   |Energy|)
     (|Free-Energy|              |subclasses|   |Energy|))
  :CONTEXT NIL
  :OUTPUT-PARAMETERS NIL)
```

A protein enzyme is synthesized in an active site of a ribosome of a cell using at least 3 amino acids and 2 monomers. This process transforms activation energy and free-energy to another free-energy.

Enzyme synthesis – a protein enzyme is synthesized in an active site of a ribosome of a cell using at least 3 amino acids and 2 monomers. This process transforms activation energy and free-energy to another free-energy.

Synthesis of a protein enzyme in an active site of a ribosome of a cell using at least 3 amino acids and 2 monomers. This process transforms activation energy and free-energy to another free-energy.

Figure 2: An example input bundle and the three outputs generated by our system for this input

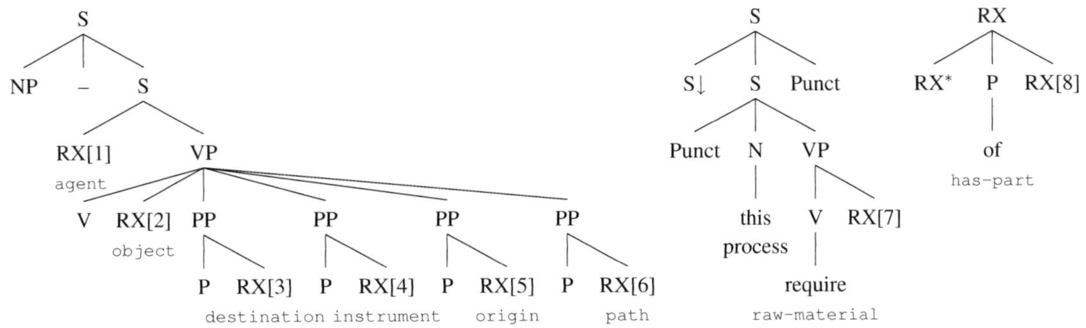

Figure 3: Tree selection

of event-to-entity relations and sentences would be given based on encoding guidelines used to create the knowledge base. However, the goal of our project is to continuously expand the knowledge base with more information, encoding new types of events, and enriching existing events with more detail as we go along (e.g., by specifying energy consumption and regulation mechanisms for processes), therefore our encoding guidelines are continuously revised. In order to produce output, our realizer requires a generation lexicon, which maps sets of relations onto elementary trees in the grammar. Determining this mapping would require knowing the number of entities that can be associated with each event type, and the relations that can be used to express them. However, because our knowledge base is continuously changing, neither the number of entities linked to specific events, nor the types of relations used are stable and therefore it was impossible to build such a generation lexicon from the KB. Instead, we adopted an approach where we detect "event frames" in the input of the system, and automatically create entries for them in the generation lexicon, guessing sentence structure and ordering based on the event participants. An event frame is a set of event-to-entity relations which have the same event in the domain of the relations, and participating entities in the range. We currently distinguish between two types of event frames, depending on the type of the entities in the range of relations: participant frames (ranges are of type Tangible-Entity) and energy frames (ranges are type Energy). An example of a participant frame and an energy frame extracted from the input illustrated in section 4.2 is illustrated below:

Participant frame:

```
(Uptake07 path Plasma-membrane78)
(Uptake07 origin Extracellular-Side52)
(Uptake07 destination Cytoplasm39)
(Uptake07 agent Cell-Surface-Receptor79)
(Uptake07 instrument Coated-Vesicle49)
(Uptake07 object Cholesterol08)
```

Energy frame:

```
(Uptake07 raw-material Chemical-Energy70)
(Uptake07 raw-material Free-Energy89)
```

Our input conversion module detects event frames and automatically creates an entry in GenI's generation lexicon for each frame, anchored on a noun or verb associated with the event in our concept-to-word mapping lexicon. The entries link the sets of relations in the frame to a tree with the same number of arguments, attempting to place entities that play `agent` and `object` participants into subject/object positions in the tree if they exist. Our algorithm also attempts to determine the best syntactic construction for the specific combination of participant relations, and decides between selecting an active sentential tree, a passive sentential tree, a complex noun phrase, or a combination of these. This process also involves deciding based on the event participants whether the tree will be anchored on a transitive verb, an intransitive verb, or a verb with a prepositional object, and assigning default prepositions to event participants (unless we have more detail specified in the lexicon, as described in the next section). The elementary trees in the grammar are named after the number of referring expressions and prepositional phrases in the tree, and we use this naming convention to automatically generate tree names (or tree family names) for lexical entries, thereby linking trees in the grammar to GenI's generation lexicon. The two S-rooted trees in Fig 3 were selected based on automatically generated lexical entries for the two frames above.

4.1 Realisation

The GenI surface realizer selects elementary TAG trees for (sets of) relations in its input and combines them using the standard operations of substitution and adjunction to produce a single derived tree. We have developed a feature-based lexicalized Tree Adjoining Grammar to generate sentences from relations in the KB. Our grammar has two important properties, following the approach in (Banik, 2010):

(1) our grammar includes discourse-level elementary trees for relations that are generated in separate sentences, and

(2) instead of the standard treatment of entities as nouns or NPs substituted into elementary trees, our grammar treats entities as underspecified referring expressions, leaving the generation of noun phrases to the next stage. The underspecified referring expressions replace elementary trees in the grammar, which the generator would otherwise have to combine with substitution. This underspecification saves us computational complexity in surface realisation, and at the same time allows us to make decisions on word choice at a later stage when we have more information on the syntax of the sentence and discourse history.

The output of the realizer is an underspecified text in the form of a sequence of lemma - feature structure pairs. Lemmas here can be underspecified – instead of an actual word, they can be an index or a sequence of indices pointing to concepts in the KB. The syntax and sentence boundaries are fully specified, and the output can be one or more sentences long. The feature structures associated with lemmas include all information necessary for referring expression generation and morphological realisation, which is performed in the next phase. To give an example, the set of relations below would produce an output with 8 underspecified referring expressions (shown as RX), distributed over two sentences:

```
(Uptake07 path   Plasma-membrane78)
(Uptake07 origin Extracellular-Side52)
```

```
(Uptake07 destination Cytoplasm39)
(Uptake07 agent Cell-Surface-Receptor79)
(Uptake07 instrument Coated-Vesicle49)
(Uptake07 object Cholesterol08)
(Uptake07 raw-material Chemical-Energy70)
(Uptake07 raw-material Free-Energy89)
```

NP(Uptake07) – RX[1] absorb RX[2] to RX[3] of RX[8] with RX[4] from RX[5] through RX[6]. This process requires RX[7].

The elementary trees selected by the realizer for this output, and the correspondences between relations and referring expressions are illustrated in Fig.3.

4.2 Referring Expression Generation

The final stage in the NLG pipeline is performing morphological realisation and spelling out the referring expressions left underspecified by the realisation module. The input to referring expression generation is a list of lemma - feature structure pairs, where lemmas are words on leaf nodes in the derived tree produced by syntactic realisation. In our system, some of the lemmas can be unspecified, i.e., there is no word associated with the leaf node, only a feature structure. For these cases, we perform lexicon lookup and referring expression generation based on the feature structure, as well as morphological realisation. To give an example, the input illustrated in the previous section will be generated as

"Uptake of cholesterol by human cell– a cell surface receptor absorbs cholesterol to the cytoplasm of a human cell with a coated vesicle from an extracellular side through a plasma membrane. This process requires chemical energy and free-energy."

Many concept labels in our ontology are very complex, often giving a description of the concept or the corresponding biology terminology, and therefore these labels can only be used for NLG under specific circumstances. To overcome this problem, we have created a lexicon that maps concept names to words, and the grammar has control over which form is used in a particular construction. Accordingly, we distinguish between two types of underspecified nodes:

- NP nodes where the lexical item for the node is derived by normalizing the concept class associated with the node (Uptake-Of-Cholesterol-By-Human-Cell → "uptake of cholesterol by human cell")
- RX (referring expression) nodes where lexical items are obtained by looking up class names in the concept-to-word mapping lexicon (Uptake-Of-Cholesterol-By-Human-Cell → "absorb")

The feature structures on RX nodes in the output of GenI describe properties of entities in the input, which were associated with that specific node during realisation. The feature structures specify three kinds of information:

- the identifier (or a list of identifiers) for the specific instances of entities the RX node refers to
- the KB class for each entity
- any cardinality constraints that were associated with each entity for the relation expressed by the tree in which the RX node appears

We define cardinality constraints as a triple (Domain, Slot, Constraint) where the Constraint itself is another triple of the form (ConstraintExpression, Number, ConstraintClass). ConstraintExpression is one of `at least`, `at most`, or `exactly` and ConstraintClass is a KB class over which the constraint holds. There is usually (but not necessarily) one or more relations associated with every cardinality constraint. We say a triple (Domain Slot Range) is associated with a cardinality constraint (Domain, Slot, (ConstraintExpression, Number, ConstraintClass)) if

- the Domain and Slot of the associated triple is equal to the Domain and Slot of the cardinality constraint and
- one of the following holds:
  - either (Range instance-of ConstraintClass) holds for the range of the triple
  - or Range is taxonomically related to ConstraintClass (via a chain of subclass relations)

We define a referring expression language (Fig. 4) which describes groups of instance names (variables) that belong to the same KB class, and the associated cardinality constraints. Groups themselves can be embedded within a larger group (an umbrella), resulting in a complex expression which gives examples of a concept (e.g., *"three atoms (a carbon and two oxygens)"*). Expressions

```
<refex>         = <umbrella> SPACE <refex> | <umbrella>
<umbrella>      = <group> ( <refex> )| <group>
<group>         = <class> <instances> <constraints>
<instances>     = :: <instance> <instances> | <instance>
<constraints> = :  <constraint> <constraints>  | <constraint>
<constraint>    = <op> : <num> | unk : <dash-delimited-string>
<op>            = ge | le | eq
```

Figure 4: Syntax of the referring expression language

in this language are constructed from triples during the input conversion stage, when we perform semantic aggregation. The groups are then passed through elementary trees by the realisation module (GenI) to appear in the output as complex feature structures on leaf nodes of the derived tree. The referring expression generation module parses these complex feature values, and constructs (possibly complex) noun phrases as appropriate.

To illustrate some examples, the following feature value shows a simple referring expression group which encodes two entities (Monomer14 and Monomer7) and two cardinality constraints (at least 2 and at most 5). This expression will be generated as "between 2 and 5 monomers":

```
Monomer::Monomer14::Monomer7:ge:2:le:5
```

We also allow more complex cardinality constraints which give the general type of an entity and specify examples of the general type, as in *"at least 3 organic molecules (2 ATPs and an ethyl alcohol)"*:

```
Organic-Molecule:ge:3
 (ATP:: ATP80938:eq:2
  Ethyl-Alcohol:: Ethyl-Alcohol80922)
```

The referring expression generation module makes three main decisions based on the referring expression, additional feature structures on the node, and discourse history: it chooses lemmas, constructs discriminators, and decides between singular/plural form. The algorithm for discriminator choice in the referring expression generation module is illustrated in Fig 5. Our referring expression generation module, including discourse history tracking and determiner choice, is made available in the Antfarm[3] open source tool.

5 Giving Domain Experts Control over Sentence Structure

By automatically associating event frames with elementary trees we are able to generate a sentence for all combinations of event-to-entity relations

[3]https://github.com/kowey/antfarm

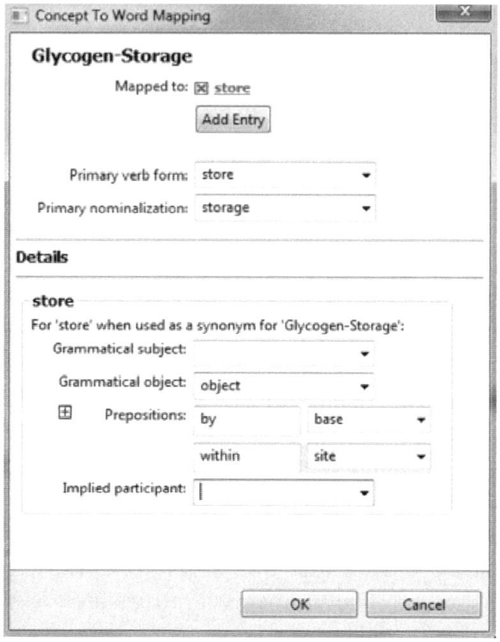

Figure 6: Parameters in the concept-to-word mapping lexicon

without having to maintain the grammar and generation lexicon of the realizer as the knowledge base evolves. However sentences generated this way are not always well-formed. Events in the KB can be realized with a wide range of verbs and nouns, which require different prepositions or syntactic constructions, and different types of events may require different participants to be their grammatical subject or object. To give an example, for events that have an agent, in the majority of the cases we get a grammatical sentence if we place the agent in subject position. If the frame lacks an agent but has an object, we can usually generate a grammatical passive sentence, with the object participant as the subject. However, it is often the case that events do not have an agent, and we get a grammatical (active) sentence by placing another relation in the subject position e.g., `base` for the event Store or `instrument` for Block. Which

for each group in the referring expression **do**
  if all members of the group are first mentions and there are no distractors in the history: **then**
    if the group has cardinality constraints: **then**
      upper bound $M \longrightarrow$ *at most M*
      lower bound $N \longrightarrow$ *at least N* (multiple group members in this case are also interpreted as lower bound)
      both bounds $\longrightarrow$ *between N and M* or *exactly N*
    else
      one group member $\longrightarrow$ generate an indefinite determiner (*a/an*)
      more than one member $\longrightarrow$ generate a cardinal
    end if
  end if
  if the group is a first mention but there are distractors in the discourse history **then**
    if the group has only one member **then**
      if the group exactly matches one previous mention $\longrightarrow$ *another*
      if the group exactly matches $N > 1$ previous mentions $\longrightarrow$ *the Nth*
      if there is a 2-member group in the history, and one of the members was mentioned by itself $\longrightarrow$ *the other*
      if the discourse history has more than one distractor $\longrightarrow$ *a(n) Nth*
    end if
    if there are multiple group members **then**
      if the group is a subset of a previously mentioned group which has no distractors $\longrightarrow$ *N of the*
    end if
  end if
  if the group is not a first mention **then**
    if the group has upper and/or lower bounds $\longrightarrow$ *the same*
    if the group has one member only $\longrightarrow$ *the*
    if the group has multiple members $\longrightarrow$ *the N*
  end if
end for

Figure 5: Algorithm for discriminator choice in our referring expression module

event participant can appear in subject and object positions depends not only on the type of the event, but also on the encoding guidelines which are continuously evolving.

In order to improve the quality of the generated output, and to give domain experts control over customizing the system without having to understand details of the grammar, we extended the concept-to-word mapping lexicon with parameters which control preposition choice, and allow customization of the position of participating entities. We developed a graphical user interface which allows encoders (biology domain experts) to add and edit these lexical parameters as they encode concepts in the KB.

To give an example, in the absence of a lexical item and any parameters for the event Glycogen-Storage, our system would produce the following default output, attempting to use the concept label as the main verb of the sentence in an automatically produced generation lexicon entry:

"Glycogen storage – glycogen is glycogened storage in a vertebrate in a liver cell and a muscle cell."

In order to improve the quality of the output, one of our biology teachers has customized the parameters in the lexicon to yield:

"Glycogen storage – glycogen is stored by a vertebrate within a liver cell and a muscle cell."

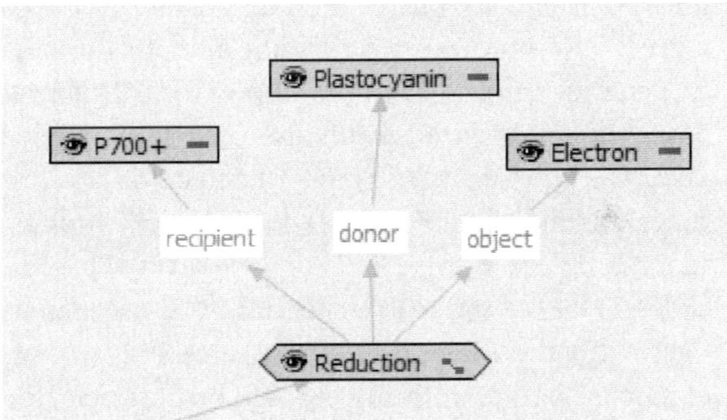

Figure 7: Concept map for the event 'Reduction'

This was achieved through a graphical user interface which is part of the tool used for knowledge encoding, and is illustrated in Fig 6. Our system allows encoders to re-generate sentences after editing the parameters to see the effect of the changes on the output. The top half of the window in in Fig 6 allows encoders to associate words or phrases with concepts, where they can add as many synonyms as they see fit. One of the synonyms has to be marked as the primary form, to be used for generation by default.[4] For events,

[4]The concept-to-word mapping lexicon is shared between the question interpretation and the NLG module, and the additional synonyms are currently only used for mapping ques-

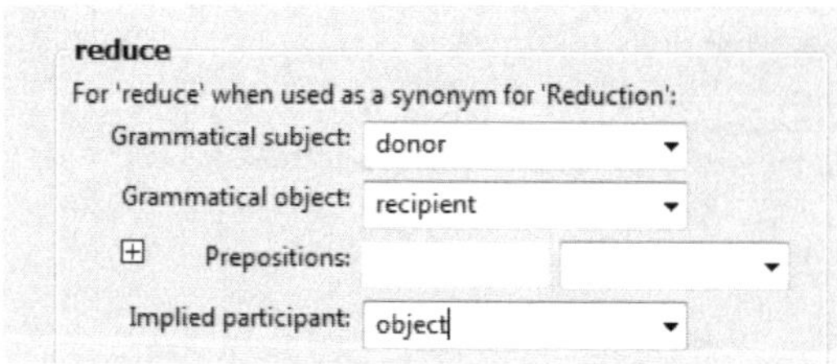

(a) "Plastocyanin reduces P700+"

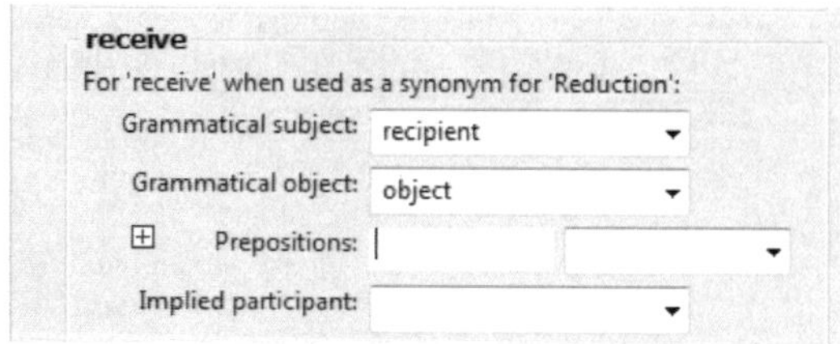

(b) "P700+ receives an electron from plastocyanin."

Figure 8: Concept-to-word mapping parameters for the two synonyms of Reduction

the primary form is a verb and its nominalization, and for entities it is a noun. The bottom half of the window shows the parameter settings for each synonym associated with the concept. Here the encoders can specify relations which link the subject and object of a verb to the event (grammatical subject/object), and assign prepositions to other event-to-entity relations for the verb, when it is used to realize the specified event. There is also an option to tell the NLG system to ignore some of the event participants when using a specific verb for the event. This functionality is used for verbs that already imply one of the participants. For example, the word polymerization already implies that the result of the event is a polymer. In these cases there is no need for the NLG system to generate the implied participant (here, result). Another example is the verb reduce, which implies that the object of the event is an electron. The editor allows the users to enter different parameter values for the synonyms of the same event. For example, the graph in Fig 7 could be described in at least three different ways:

1. P700+ is reduced by plastocyanin
2. Plastocyanin reduces P700+
3. P700+ receives an electron from plastocyanin.

Here sentences 1 and 2 make no mention of the electron involved in the process, but sentence 3 explicitly includes it. In order for the system to correctly generate sentences 1 and 2, the concept-to-word mapping parameters for "reduce" (as a synonym for Reduction) have to include an implied participant. Otherwise the system will assume that all participants should be mentioned in the sentence, and it will generate "P700+ is reduced by a plastocyanin of an electron". Fig 8. illustrates the different concept-to-word mapping parameters needed for the two synonyms for Reduction in order to generate the above sentences correctly.

tions onto concepts in the KB.

6 Conclusions

We have presented an NLG system which generates complex sentences from a biology KB. Our system includes a content selection module, which tailors the selected relations to the context in which the output is displayed, and allows the presentation module to send parameters to influence properties of generated outputs. We have developed a referring expression generation module which generates complex noun phrases from aggregated cardinality constraints and entities in the input, and keeps track of discourse history to distinguish mentions of different groups of concepts. Our system allows biology teachers to detect inconsistencies and incompleteness in the KB, such as missing cardinality constraints, errors where two instances of the concept were added unnecessarily (unification errors on entities), and missing or incorrect relations. To make the system robust, we have developed an algorithm to produce sentences and complex noun phrases for unseen combinations of event-to-entity relations in the KB by automatically generating entries in the lexicon of the GenI surface realizer. Our algorithm makes default decisions on sentence structure and ordering based on relations sent to the NLG system, expressing the event's participants. To allow domain experts to easily improve the default outputs generated by our algorithm, we have defined a framework for adding lexical parameters to concepts, which allow non-NLG-experts to customize the structure of generated sentences for events in the KB as they are encoded. Although our system currently only produces one or two possibly complex sentences, it was designed to ultimately generate paragraph-length texts. This can be achieved simply by adding more discourse-level elementary trees to the grammar of the realizer, since our system is already able to handle referring expressions across sentence boundaries.

References

E. Banik. 2010. *A Minimalist Architecture for Generating Coherent Text*. Ph.D. thesis, The Open University, UK.

K. Barker, B. Porter, and P. Clark. 2001. A library of generic concepts for composing knowledgebases. In *Proceedings K-CAP 2001*, pages 14–21.

K. Bontcheva and Y. Wilks. 2004. Automatic report generation from ontologies: the MIAKT approach. In *9th Int. Conf. on Applications of Natural Language to Information Systems*, page 324335, Manchester, UK.

K. Bontcheva. 2004. Open-source tools for creation, maintenance, and storage of lexical resources for language generation from ontologies. In *4th Conf. on Language Resources and Evaluation*, Lisbon, Portugal.

D. Galanis and I. Androutsopoulos. 2007. Generating multilingual descriptions from linguistically annotated owl ontologies: the NaturalOWL system. In *INLG07, Schloss Dagstuhl, Germany*, page 143146.

D. Gunning, V. K. Chaudhri, P. Clark, K. Barker, Shaw-Yi Chaw, M. Greaves, B. Grosof, A. Leung, D. McDonald, S. Mishra, J. Pacheco, B. Porter, A. Spaulding, D. Tecuci, and J. Tien. 2010. Project halo update - progress toward digital aristotle. *AI Magazine*, Fall:33–58.

A. K. Joshi and Y. Schabes. 1997. Tree-Adjoining Grammars. In Grzegorz Rosenberg and Arto Salomaa, editors, *Handbook of Formal Languages and Automata*, volume 3, pages 69–124. Springer-Verlag, Heidelberg.

E. Kow. 2007. *Surface realisation: ambiguity and determinism*. Ph.D. thesis, Universite de Henri Poincare, Nancy.

C. Mellish and X. Sun. 2005. The semantic web as a linguistic resource: Opportunities for natural language generation. In *Knowledge-Based Systems*.

C.L. Paris. 1988. Tailoring object descriptions to the users level of expertise. *Computational Linguistics*, 14(3):6478. Special Issue on User Modelling.

E. Reiter, R. Robertson, and L. M. Osman. 2003. Lessons from a failure: generating tailored smoking cessation letters. *Artificial Intelligence*, 144(1-2):41–58.

A. Spaulding, A. Overholtzer, J. Pacheco, J. Tien, V. K. Chaudhri, D. Gunning, and P. Clark. 2011. Inquire for ipad: Bringing question-answering ai into the classroom. In *International Conference on AI in Education (AIED)*.

G. Wilcock. 2003. Talking owls: Towards an ontology verbalizer. In *Human Lan- guage Technology for the Semantic Web and Web Services, ISWC03*, page 109112, Sanibel Island, Florida.

Enhancing the Expression of Contrast in the SPaRKy Restaurant Corpus

David M. Howcroft and **Crystal Nakatsu** and **Michael White**
Department of Linguistics
The Ohio State University
Columbus, OH 43210, USA
{howcroft,cnakatsu,mwhite}@ling.osu.edu

Abstract

We show that Nakatsu & White's (2010) proposed enhancements to the SPaRKy Restaurant Corpus (SRC; Walker et al., 2007) for better expressing contrast do indeed make it possible to generate better texts, including ones that make effective and varied use of contrastive connectives and discourse adverbials. After first presenting a validation experiment for naturalness ratings of SRC texts gathered using Amazon's Mechanical Turk, we present an initial experiment suggesting that such ratings can be used to train a realization ranker that enables higher-rated texts to be selected when the ranker is trained on a sample of generated restaurant recommendations with the contrast enhancements than without them. We conclude with a discussion of possible ways of improving the ranker in future work.

1 Introduction

To lessen the need for handcrafting in developing generation systems, Walker et al. (2007) extended the overgenerate-and-rank methodology (Langkilde and Knight, 1998; Mellish et al., 1998; Walker et al., 2002; Nakatsu and White, 2006) to complex information presentation tasks involving variation in rhetorical structure. They illustrated their approach by developing SPaRKy (Sentence Planning with Rhetorical Knowledge), a sentence planner for generating restaurant recommendations and comparisons in the context of the MATCH (Multimodal Access To City Help) system (Walker et al., 2004), and showed that SPaRKY can produce texts comparable to those of MATCH's template-based generator.

Despite the evident importance of expressing contrast clearly in making comparisons among restaurants, Nakatsu (2008) surprisingly found that most of the examples involving contrastive connectives in the SPaRKy Restaurant Corpus (SRC) received low ratings by the human judges. Even though the low ratings were not necessarily directly attributable to the use of a contrastive connective in many cases, Nakatsu conjectured that the large proportion of low-rated examples containing contrastive connectives would make it difficult to train a ranker to learn to use contrastive connectives effectively without augmenting the corpus with better examples of contrast. Subsequently, Nakatsu and White (2010) proposed a set of enhancements to the SRC intended to better express contrast—including ones employing multiple connectives in the same clause that are problematic for RST (Mann and Thompson, 1988)—and showed how they could be generated with Discourse Combinatory Categorial Grammar (DCCG), an extension of CCG (Steedman, 2000) designed to enable multi-sentence grammar-based generation. However, Nakatsu and White did not evaluate empirically whether these contrast enhancements were successful.

In this paper, we show that Nakatsu & White's (2010) proposed SRC contrast enhancements do indeed make it possible to generate better texts: in particular, we present an initial experiment that shows that the oracle best restaurant recommendations including the contrast enhancements have significantly higher human ratings for naturalness than comparable texts without these enhancements, and which suggests that even a basic n-gram ranker trained on the enhanced recommendations can select texts with higher ratings. The paper is structured as follows. In Section 2, we review Nakatsu & White's proposed enhancements to the SRC for better expressing contrast—including the use of *structural connectives* together with *discourse adverbials*—and how they can be generated with DCCG. In Section 3, we first present a validation experiment showing that naturalness ratings gathered on Amazon's Mechanical Turk (AMT) are comparable to those for the same texts in the original SRC; then, we present our method of generating and selecting a sample of new restaurant recommendation texts with and without the contrast enhancements for rating on AMT. In Section 4, we describe how we trained discriminative n-gram rankers using cross validation on the gathered ratings. In Section 5, we present the oracle and cross validation results in terms of mean scores of the top-ranked text. In Section 6, we analyze how the individual contrast enhancements affected the naturalness ratings and discuss issues that may be still hampering naturalness. Finally, in Section 7, we conclude with a summary and a discussion of possible ways of creating improved rankers in future work.

2 Enhancing Contrast with Discourse Combinatory Categorial Grammar

Figure 1 (Nakatsu, 2008) shows examples from the SRC where some of the SPaRKy realizations are clearly more natural than others. In Nakatsu's experiments, she found that the use of contrastive connectives was negatively correlated with human ratings, and that an n-gram ranker learned to disprefer texts containing these connectives. In analyzing these unexpected results, Nakatsu noted two factors that appeared to hamper the naturalness of the contrastive connective usage. First, consistent with Grote et al.'s (1995) observation that *however* and *on the other hand* (unlike *but* and *while*) signal that the clause they attach to is the more important one, we might expect realizations to be preferred when these connectives appear with the more desirable of the contrasted qualities. Such preferences do indeed appear to be present in the SRC: for example, in Figure 1, alts 8 & 13—where the better property is ordered second—are rated highly, while alts 7 & 11—where the better property is ordered first—are rated poorly. Nakatsu further observed that in human-authored comparisons, when the second clause expresses the lesser property, it is often qualified by *only* or *just*; consistent with this observation, alts 7 & 11 do seem to improve with the inclusion of these modifiers.

The second factor noted by Nakatsu that may contribute to the awkwardness of *however* and *on the other hand* is that both of these connectives seem to be rather "grand" for the rather simple contrasts in Figure 1, and may sound more natural when used with heavier arguments.

Based on these observations, Nakatsu and White (2010) proposed a set of enhancements to the SRC, all of which are exemplified in Figure 2.[1] The enhancements include (i) optional summary statements that give an overall assessment of each restaurant based on the average of their property values, thereby allowing contrasts to be expressed over larger text spans; (ii) adverbial modifiers *only*, *just* and *merely* to express a lesser value of a given property than one mentioned earlier;[2] (iii) the modifers *also* and *too* to signal the repetition of the same value for a given property (Striegnitz, 2004); and (iv) contrastive connectives for different properties of the same restaurant, exemplified here by the contrast between decent decor and mediocre food quality for Bienvenue.

In the text plan in Figure 2, <1>–<4> correspond to the propositions in the original SRC text plan and (1')–(2') are the new summary-level propositions. Following Webber et al. (2003), Nakatsu and White (2010) take *only*, *merely*, *just*, *also*, and *too* to be **discourse adverbials**, whose discourse relations are allowed to cut across the primary tree structure established by the other relations in the figure. Note that in addition to going beyond RST's limitation to tree-structured discourses, the example also contains clauses employing multiple discourse connectives, where one is a **structural connective** (such as *however* or *while*) and the other is a discourse adverbial.

To realize such texts, Nakatsu & White introduce Discourse Combinatory Categorial Grammar (DCCG), an extension of CCG (Steedman, 2000) to the discourse level. DCCG follows Discourse Lexicalized Tree Adjoining Grammar (Webber, 2004) in providing a lexicalized treatment of structural connectives and discourse adverbials, but differs in doing so in a single CCG, rather than separate sentence-level and discourse-level grammars whose interaction is not straightforward. As such, DCCG requires no changes to the OpenCCG realizer (White, 2006b; White, 2006a; White and Ra-

[1] In the text, words intended to help indicate similarities and contrasts are italicized. Note that we have added *overall* and *on the whole* to the summary statements to better indicate their summarizing role.

[2] The second value must be a less extreme one on the same side of the scale; in principle, it could be *merely poor* rather than *horrible*, but such low attribute values did not occur in the corpus.

Strategy	Alt #	Rating	Rank	Realization
C2	3	3	7	Sonia Rose has very good decor but Bienvenue has decent decor.
	7	1	16	Sonia Rose has very good decor. On the other hand, Bienvenue has decent decor.
	8	4.5	13	Bienvenue has decent decor. Sonia Rose, on the other hand, has very good decor.
	10	4.5	5	Bienvenue has decent decor but Sonia Rose has very good decor.
	11	1	12	Sonia Rose has very good decor. However, Bienvenue has decent decor.
	13	5	14	Bienvenue has decent decor. However, Sonia Rose has very good decor.
	14	5	3	Sonia Rose has very good decor while Bienvenue has decent decor.
	15	4	4	Bienvenue has decent decor while Sonia Rose has very good decor.
	17	1	15	Bienvenue's price is 35 dollars. Sonia Rose's price, however, is 51 dollars. Bienvenue has decent decor. However, Sonia Rose has very good decor.

Figure 1: Some alternative (Alt) realizations of SPaRKy sentence plans from a COMPARE2 (C2) plan, with averaged human ratings (Rating; 5 = highest rating) and ranks (Rank; 1 = top ranked) assigned by an n-gram ranker (Nakatsu, 2008)

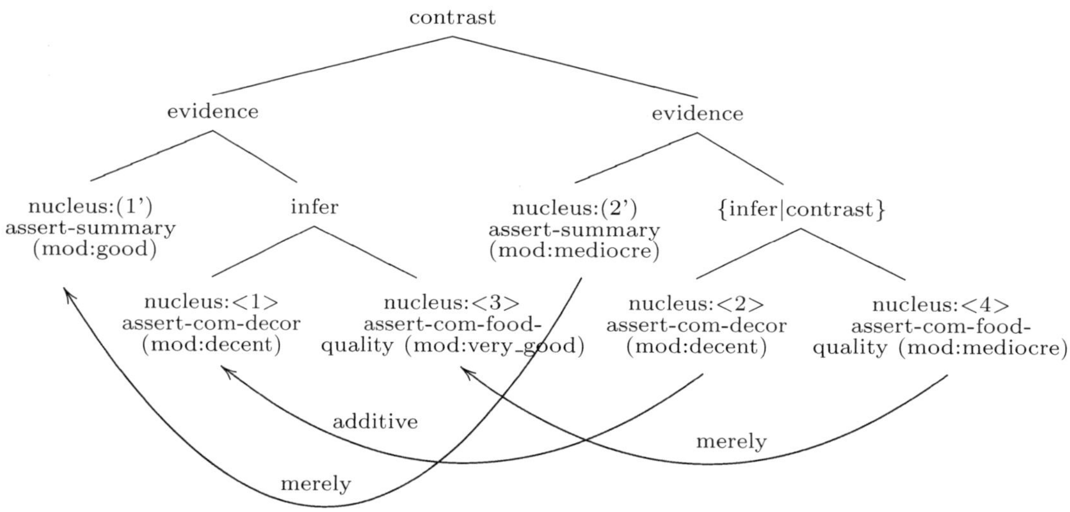

(1'): Sonia Rose is a good restaurant overall.

<1>: It has decent decor and

<3>: very good food quality.

(2'): *However*, Bienvenue is *just* a mediocre restaurant on the whole.

<2>: *While* it *also* has decent decor,

<4>: it *only* has mediocre food quality.

Figure 2: Modified SPaRKy text plan for text with new relations and summary statements intended to enhance contrast (Nakatsu and White, 2010)

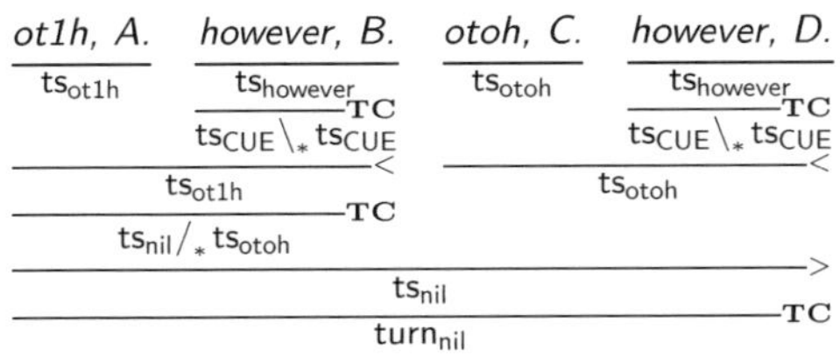

Figure 3: DCCG derivation of nested contrast relations (Nakatsu and White, 2010)

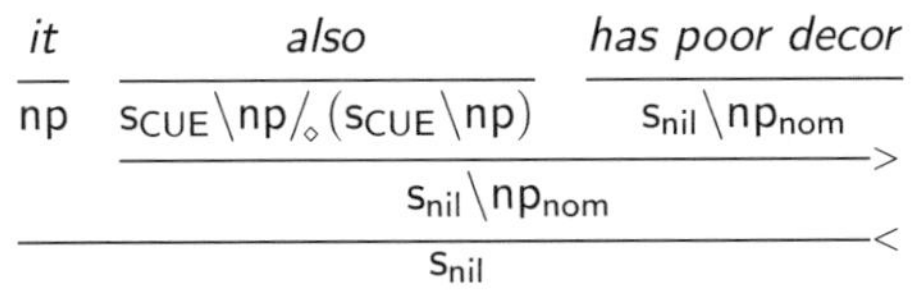

Figure 4: DCCG derivation of a clause with the discourse adverbial *also* (Nakatsu and White, 2010)

jkumar, 2009) in order to generate texts that vary in size from single sentences to entire paragraphs.

In DCCG, the technique of **cue threading** is used to allow structural connectives—including paired ones such as *on the one hand ... on the other hand*—to project beyond the sentence level, while allowing no more than one to be active at a time. In this way, structural connectives can be nested, as sketched in Figure 3, but cannot cross. In the figure, the value of the cue feature for each text segment (ts) is shown (where `ot1h` and `otoh` abbreviate *on the one hand* and *on the other hand*); these cue values can be propagated through a derivation, allowing the discourse relations to project, but must be discharged (to nil) in a complete derivation, thereby ensuring that the intended discourse relations are actually realized. By contrast, discourse adverbials introduce their relations anaphorically and are transparent to cue threading, as sketched in Figure 4, making use of typical adverb categories syntactically. See Nakatsu and White (2010) for further details.

3 Crowd Sourcing Ratings

To collect human judgements from a diverse group of speakers of US English, we used Amazon's Mechanical Turk service (AMT) to run two experiments. In the first experiment, subjects rated the naturalness of 174 passages used in Walker et al.'s (2007) study. As detailed in Section 5, this validation experiment confirmed that the judgements collected on AMT correlate with those of the raters in Walker et al.'s (2007) study. Our second experiment collected ratings on 300 passages realized with modifications for better contrast expression (WITHMODS) and 300 passages without these modifications (NOMODS), both realized using OpenCCG. While this does not admit a direct comparison to the realizations produced by Walker et al. (2007), this controls for differences between the generators other than the variable of interest: the contrastive enhancements. In addition to these materials, five passages from the SRC were seen by all subjects to control for anomalous subject behavior.

3.1 Survey Format

Each survey used demographic questions to determine the native speaker status of the subject. Instructions for completing comprehension questions and rating realizations followed the demographic questions.[3] Each subject saw fifteen stimuli, each consisting of a sample user query and the target passage as in Figure 5. After reading the stimulus, the subject answered a yes-or-no comprehension question (see §3.2). Finally the subject rated the naturalness of the passage on a seven-point Likert scale ranging from *very unnatural* to *very natural*. At the survey's conclusion, the subject could offer free-form feedback, explain their responses, or ask questions of the researchers. The average completion time across all experiments was about ten minutes.

Passage selection is detailed in §3.3 and §3.4.

3.2 Quality Control

We used three strategies to filter out low-quality responses from AMT subjects.

Comprehension Questions A template-based yes-or-no question (exemplified in Figure 5) followed each passage. Subjects who answered less than 75% of these questions correctly were rejected and not paid, in accordance with the protocol approved by our human subjects review board. Responses from three subjects were excluded from analysis on this basis.

Uniform Ratings When a subject gave the same rating for all passages in a given survey (and in disagreement with other subjects), we took this to mean that the subject was paying attention only

[3] These materials, along with the generated passages and their ratings are available at `http://www.ling.ohio-state.edu/~mwhite/data/enlg13/`.

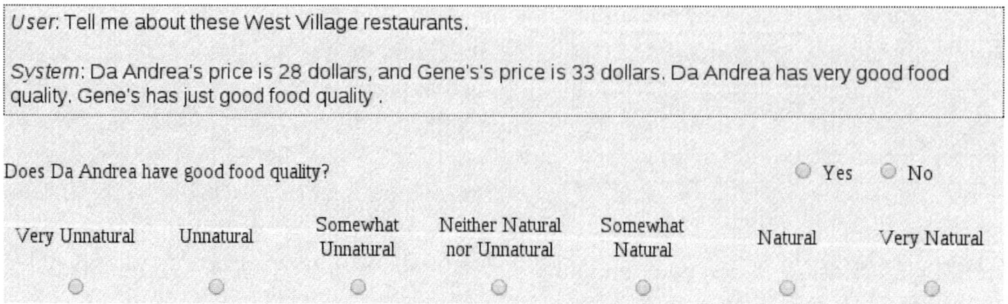

Figure 5: Sample survey stimulus and comprehension question

Method	# subjects excluded
Comprehension Questions	3
Uniform Answers	1
SAME5	0
Native Speaker Status	2

Table 1: Number of subjects excluded based on quality control measures or native language.

to the comprehension questions that ensured payment. Only one subject was excluded on this basis, though they were still paid for answering the comprehension questions correctly.

SAME5 Passages Five passages were chosen from the original SRC realizations for which the original ratings (from Walker et al. 2007) were identical for both judges. The passages were selected such that the first and third authors of this paper agreed with the general valence and relative rankings of the passages. That is, we took two unambiguously bad realizations, two unambiguously good realizations, and one realization near the middle of the spectrum to represent a gold standard for rating to compare subjects against. If any subject's ratings on these five passages were clear outliers, we could remove that subject's data for anomalous behavior, but this measure proved unnecessary for the subjects in the present study.

3.3 Validating AMT

Data Selection In this experiment, we sampled 174 of the 1757 realizations from the SRC rated by subjects A and B in Walker et al.'s (2007) experiment.

The SRC realizations were divided randomly into two groups. Within one group, realizations were labelled by subject A's rating for that realization. Subject B's rating was used for the other group. Taking the poles of the rating scale and its midpoint, the realizations were further partitioned into six sets: realizations rated 1, 3, and 5 by subject A and realizations rated 1, 3, and 5 by subject B. This division of the data ensured that the realizations used would cover the full spectrum of ratings while being representative of the SRC ratings with respect to, e.g., inter-annotator ratings correlations.

From each of these six sets, we chose 10 COMPARE2, 10 COMPARE3, and 10 RECOMMEND realizations,[4] each of these groups representing a different realization task in the SRC. The COMPARE2 and COMPARE3 tasks involved the comparison of two restaurants or three or more restaurants, respectively. In the RECOMMEND context, the sytem had to generate a recommendation for a single restaurant.

Subject Demographics Thirty-six subjects responded to this survey initially, but one was rejected based on a failure to answer the comprehension questions and data from another had to be excluded for non-native speaker status. Two additional subjects were recruited to replace their data. This resulted in a subject pool with a mean age (std. dev.) of 34.67 (9.35) years. Twenty-four subjects identified as female and twelve identified as male. Each subject received $2.50 for the survey, estimated to take approximately 20 minutes.

3.4 Rating OpenCCG Realizations

Data Selection We selected 15 content plans (CPs) from the SRC where the use of the contrastive modifiers was licensed: five COMPARE2, five COMPARE3, and five RECOMMEND CPs. Each of the 112 textplans (TPs) that produced

[4]Except that subject A used the rating '5' less than subject B. To compensate, we used as many 5-point ratings as were available from subject A and then filled in the remainder of the 10 slots with realizations rated '4'. We mirrored these selections in the data from subject B for consistency.

the SRC realizations for these CPs was then preprocessed for realization in OpenCCG both with contrast enhancements (WITHMODS) and without them (NOMODS).

Both structural choices and ordering choices are encoded in these TPs.[5] Structural choices include decisions about how to group the restaurant properties to be expressed, such as deciding whether to describe one restaurant in its entirety and then the other (i.e. a *serial* structure) or alternating between one restaurant and the other, directly contrasting particular attributes (i.e. a *back-and-forth* structure). Ordering choices fixed the order of presentation of restaurant attributes in serial plans and the order of presentation of attribute contrasts in back-and-forth plans. As discussed in §6, there turn out to be interesting interactions between these aggregation choices and the contrast enhancements, interactions which we did not explore directly in this experiment.

Processing each TP produced a different LF for each possible combination of aggregation choices and contrastive modifications, resulting in approximately 41k logical forms (LFs) for the TPs WITHMODS and 88k LFs for the TPs with NOMODS.[6]

Each realization received two language model (LM) scores, one based on the semantic classes used during realization (LM_{SC}) and one based on the Gigaword corpus (LM_{GW}). LM_{SC} used a trigram model over modified texts based on the SRC where specific entities (e.g. restaurant names like *Caffe Buon Gusto*) were replaced with their semantic class (e.g. *RESTAURANT*). The LM scores were normalized by CP, such that the scores for a given CP summed to 1 in each LM. These were then linearly combined with weights slightly preferring the LM_{SC} score to produce a combined LM score for each realization.

Sampling then proceeded without replacement, weighted by the combined LM score for each realization. For the NOMODS sample, 20 realizations were chosen this way, but, in the WITHMODS sample, a series of regular expression filters were used to ensure adequate representation of the modifications in the surveys. These filters selected (without replacement) 10 realizations such that every contrastive modification licensed by a particular CP was represented, leaving 10 realizations to be selected by weighted sampling without replacement.

This process resulted in 300 passages in each of the two conditions (WITHMODS, NOMODS): 20 realizations for each of the 15 CPs. Each survey included 5 realizations WITHMODS paired by CP with 5 realizations with NOMODS as well as the SAME5 realizations. As noted earlier, pairing realizations in this way helps to control for differences in the variety of aggregation choices and surface realizations used in the SRC as opposed to our SRC-inspired grammar for OpenCCG.

Subject Demographics Sixty-eight subjects responded to these 180 surveys initially. Subjects were allowed to complete up to six distinct surveys. One subject's data was excluded for non-native status and another's was excluded on the basis of uniform ratings (as detailed in §3.2). To compensate for the eight surveys completed by these subjects and ten surveys mistakenly administered in draft format, we recollected data for 18 of the 180 surveys. This resulted in a final pool of 80 subjects with an average (std. dev.) age 37.15 (13.5) years. Forty identified as female, thirty-nine identified as male, and one identified as non-gendered.

Because subjects in the validation study completed the survey in about 10 minutes on average with a standard deviation of about 5 minutes, we scaled the pay to $2.00 per survey in this experiment. Since subjects could participate in this experiment multiple times, they could receive up to $12.00 for their contribution.

4 Training a Text Ranker

To perform the ranking, we trained a basic n-gram ranker using SVM^{light} in preference ranking mode.[7] We used the average ratings obtained in §3 as target value.

The feature set was composed of 2 types of features. The first feature type are the two language model scores from §3.4, LM_{SC} and LM_{GW}. The second feature type consisted of n-gram counts. We indexed the unigrams and bigrams in each corpus and used each as a feature whose value was the number of times it appeared in a given realization.

We trained the ranker on, and extracted n-gram

[5]This differs from Walker et al. (2007), wherein reorderings were allowed in mapping from tp-trees to sp-trees and d-trees.

[6]In future work we will explore a probabilistic rather than exhaustive mapping algorithm to produce only LFs that are more likely to result in more fluent realizations—not unlike the weighted aggregation done by Walker et al.'s (2007) sentence plan generator.

[7]SVM^{light} is an implementation of support vector machines by (Joachims, 2002).

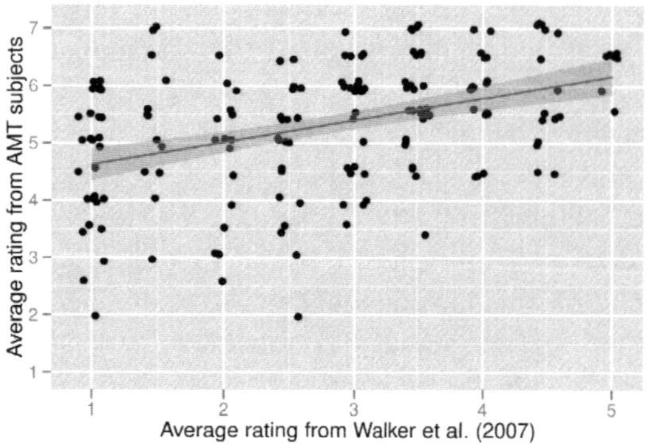

Figure 6: Average ratings from our experiment and Walker et al. (2007), accompanied by a line of best fit. Jitter (0.1) applied to each point minimizes overlap.

features from, 3 different corpora drawn from the data selection in §3.4. The first corpus contains 299 selections WITHMODS (1 selection was discarded for only being rated once), the second corpus contains 300 selections with NOMODS, and the third corpus contains BOTH of the first two corpora combined.

To train and test the ranker, we performed 15-fold cross-validation on each corpus. Within each training fold, we had 14 training examples, corresponding to 14 CPs. Each training example consisted of all of a given CP's realizations and their ratings. After training, the realizations for the remaining CP were ranked.

In order to evaluate the ranker, we used the TopRank metric (Walker et al., 2007). For each of the ranked CP realization sets, we extracted the target values (i.e. the average rating given by subjects) of the highest ranked realization. We then averaged the target scores of all of the top-ranked realizations across the 15 training folds to produce the Top Rank metric. The oracle best score is the score of the highest rated realization, as determined by the average score assigned to that realization by the subjects.

5 Results

Validation Figure 6 shows the correlation between the average ratings of our subjects on AMT and the average ratings assigned by subjects A and B in Walker et al. (2007). This correlation was 0.31 ($p < 0.01$, Kendall's tau), while the correlation between subjects A and B was only 0.28

	BOTH	WITHMODS	NOMODS
human	6.61 (0.28)	6.46 (0.43)	6.49 (0.26)
bigram	6.00 (0.58)	5.62 (0.83)	5.51 (1.02)

Table 2: TopRank scores and standard deviations for the oracle (human) & bigram (bigram) ranks.

($p < 0.01$, Kendall's tau). On this basis we conclude that using AMT workers as subjects to rate sentences for their naturalness is at least as reasonable as having two expert annotators labelling realizations for their overall quality.

SAME5 Comparison There was no significant difference ($p = 0.16$, using Welch's t-test) between the scores given to the SAME5 stimuli in the two experiments,[8] indicating that subjects used the rating scale similarly in both experiments. The mean ratings for the rest of the validation realizations was 5.31 (1.43) and the mean for the OpenCCG-based realizations in the ranking experiment was 4.96 (1.51), which is significantly lower according to Welch's t-test ($p < 0.01$). This highlights the underlying differences between the two generation systems, validating our choice to use OpenCCG for both the WITHMODS and NOMODS realizations to better examine the impact of the contrast enhancements.

Ranking Table 2 reports the oracle results, along with our ranker's results, using the TopRank metric. Most indicative of the benefit of the contrastive enhancements is the performance of the oracle score for the BOTH (6.61) condition compared to the NOMODS condition (6.49), which is significantly higher according to a paired t-test ($p = 0.01$).

We also found that the bigram ranker with the averaged raw ratings was better at predicting the top rank of the combined (BOTH) corpus (6.00 vs. oracle-best of 6.61) than either of the other two, and better on the WITHMODS condition (5.62) than on the NOMODS condition (5.51). However, a two-tailed t-test revealed that the difference was not quite signficant between BOTH and NOMODS at the conventional level ($p = 0.06$), though the p-value did meet the 0.1 threshold sometimes employed in small-scale experiments. The performance of the different rankers, as compared to the oracle scores, can be seen in Figure 7.

These preliminary results with a simple ranker

[8] Validation experiment mean (std. dev.) 4.89 (1.79) versus 5.10 (1.75) in the ranking experiment.

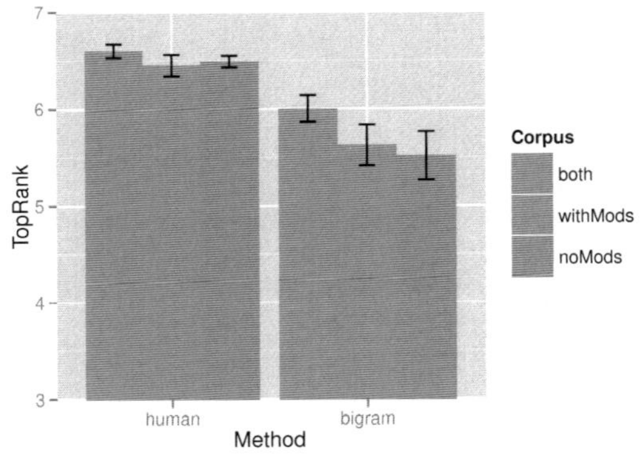

Figure 7: TopRank scores for each of the rankers with standard error bars.

are promising, motivating future work on improving the ranker in addition to enlarging the dataset.

6 Discussion

To assess the impact of the enhancement options, we performed a linear regression between the contrast-related patterns we used for data selection and the normalized ratings, with scikit-learn's implementation of the Bayesian Ridge method of regularizing weights.[9] In looking at examples, we found that the number of discourse adverbials appeared to be a factor, so we then added these counts as features. The coefficients and corpus counts appear in Table 3. The results show that the discourse adverbials were effective some of the time, especially when used sparingly and in conjunction with *while*. The "heavier" contrastive connectives *however* and *on the one/other hand* were dispreferred, perhaps in part because they ended up appearing too often with small, single-restaurant contrasts, as there were relatively few examples of summary statements, most of which were somewhat disfluent due to a medial choice for *overall / on the whole*.

Table 4 shows examples that illustrate both successes and remaining issues. At the top, two pairs of examples are given where the normalized average ratings are higher with the inclusion of *just* and *only*, and where the rating drops off greatly when *however* is used with a lesser value and no adverbial of this kind, as expected. At the bottom, the first example shows one instance where the use of multiple adverbials is dispreferred. A possible

pattern	coeff	count
$\mid$ disc advb $\mid = 1$	0.23	102
while	0.19	38
also has	0.13	47
has ... too	0.12	39
has only	0.09	43
while ... disc advb	0.09	16
contrastive ... *overall*	0.07	8
has just	0.04	46
however ... disc advb	0.03	4
but	-0.03	20
, however ,	-0.05	10
only has	-0.06	30
has merely	-0.11	46
on the whole	-0.14	33
just has	-0.16	29
merely has	-0.16	8
$\mid$ disc advb $\mid = 2$	-0.18	32
. however ,	-0.21	64
on the other hand	-0.21	40
$\mid$ disc advb $\mid >= 3$	-0.27	50
overall	-0.29	34
on the one hand	-0.36	22

Table 3: Coefficients of linear regression between contrast-related patterns and normalized ratings, along with pattern counts, where disc adv is one of *just, only, merely, also, too* and contrastive is one of *while, however, on the one/other hand*

factor here may be that in addition to there being several similar adverbials in a row, they all involve long-distance antecedents, which may be difficult to process. Finally, the last example shows a realization that receives a relatively high rating despite the use of two adverbials; note, however, that since this passage uses a back-and-forth text plan, the antecedents of the adverbials are all very local.[10]

Turning to the survey feedback, many subjects provided insightful comments regarding the task. The most frequent comment pointed out that our comprehension questions sometimes precipitated a false implicature: when asked if a restaurant had decent decor, subjects commented that they felt that answering "no" meant implying that it had terrible decor. Similar problems occurred when a restaurant had, e.g., *very good* decor and the subjects were asked if it had *good* decor. Despite occasional deviations from our intended exact-match interpretation of these questions, no subjects were excluded for scoring too low as a result of this.

[9] http://scikit-learn.org/stable/modules/linear_model.html

[10] As one reviewer points out, there's also an interaction between how attributes are aggregated and the ability to express contrast. For example, contrasting the attributes for which a restaurant scores highly with those for which it scores poorly requires the aggregation of attributes with like valence, as in "This restaurant has superb decor and very good service but only mediocre food quality." Our future work on aggregation will explore this interaction as well.

Strategy	Mods?	Rating	Realization
C2	Y	1.13	Da Andrea's price is 28 dollars. Gene's's price is 33 dollars. Da Andrea has very good food quality while Gene's has *just* good food quality.
C2	N	0.73	Da Andrea's price is 28 dollars. Gene's's price is 33 dollars. Da Andrea has very good food quality while Gene's has good food quality.
C2	Y	1.04	Da Andrea's price is 28 dollars. Gene's's price is 33 dollars. Da Andrea has very good food quality. However, Gene's has *only* good food quality.
C2	N	-0.63	Da Andrea's price is 28 dollars. Gene's's price is 33 dollars. Da Andrea has very good food quality. However, Gene's has good food quality.
C3	Y	-1.85	Daniel and Jo Jo offer exceptional value among the selected restaurants. Daniel, *on the whole*, is a superb restaurant. Daniel's price is 82 dollars. Daniel has superb decor. It has superb service and superb food quality. Jo Jo, *overall*, is an excellent restaurant. Jo Jo's price is 59 dollars. Jo Jo *just* has very good decor. It *just* has excellent service. It has *merely* excellent food quality.
C2	Y	1.12	Japonica's price is 37 dollars while Dojo's price is 14 dollars. Japonica has excellent food quality while Dojo has *merely* decent food quality. Japonica has decent decor. Dojo has *only* mediocre decor.

Table 4: Examples illustrating successful and problematic contrast enhancements

In order to elicit rankings at a variety of points on the naturalness scale, our selection included a number of realizations with lower quality overall, which subjects picked up on. For example, one subject commented that, "Repeatedly using the name of each restaurant over and over in simple sentences make[s] almost all of these excerpts sound horrifyingly awkward," while another observed, "The constant [use] of more sentences, instead of using conjunction words ... makes it seem as if the system is rambling and lost in though[t] process."

Several subjects also pointed out that it would be more natural to discuss the cost of an average meal at a restaurant than to state that a restaurant's price is some particular number of dollars. Though these domain-specific lexical preferences are tangential to the focus of this paper, they suggest that exploring options to expand the range of realizations for more naturally expressing these properties might be a fruitful direction for future work.

In addition to expressing an explicit preference for serial rather than back-and-forth text-plans, subjects also commented that higher level contrastive adverbials like *however* work better when they are used sparingly at a high level, reinforcing the findings in our regressions. We also received suggestions for future work improving the expression of contrast: some subjects suggested that using *better* and *worse* to make explicit comparisons between restaurants would improve the naturalness, and one subject suggested explicitly stating which restaurant is (say) the *cheapest* as in White et al. (2010).

7 Conclusions and Future Work

In this paper, we have shown using ratings gathered on AMT that Nakatsu & White's (2010) proposed enhancements to the SPaRKy Restaurant Corpus (Walker et al., 2007) for better expressing contrast do indeed make it possible to generate better texts, and an initial experiment suggested that even a basic n-gram ranker can do so automatically. A regression analysis further revealed that while using a few discourse adverbials sparingly was effective, using too many discourse adverbials had a negative impact, with antecedent distance potentially an important factor. In future work, we plan to improve upon this basic n-gram ranker to take these observations into account and validate these initial findings on a larger dataset. In the process we will explore the interaction between contrast expression and aggregation and seek to better model the felicity conditions for "weighty" top level adverbials such as *however*.

Acknowledgments

This work was supported in part by NSF grant IIS-1143635. Special thanks to the anonymous reviewers, the Clippers computational linguistics discussion group at Ohio State, and to Mark Dras, Francois Lareau, and Yasaman Motazedi at Macquarie University.

References

Brigitte Grote, Nils Lenke, and Manfred Stede. 1995. Ma(r)king concessions in English and German. In *Proc. of the Fifth European Workshop on Natural Language Generation*.

Thorsten Joachims. 2002. Optimizing search engines using clickthrough data. In *Proc. KDD*.

Irene Langkilde and Kevin Knight. 1998. The practical value of n-grams in generation. In *Proc. INLG-98*.

William C. Mann and Sandra A. Thompson. 1988. Rhetorical Structure Theory: Towards a functional theory of text organization. *TEXT*, 8(3):243–281.

Chris Mellish, Alistair Knott, Jon Oberlander, and Mick O'Donnell. 1998. Experiments using stochastic search for text planning. In *Proc. INLG-98*.

Crystal Nakatsu and Michael White. 2006. Learning to say it well: Reranking realizations by predicted synthesis quality. In *Proceedings of the 21st International Conference on Computational Linguistics and 44th Annual Meeting of the Association for Computational Linguistics*, pages 1113–1120, Sydney, Australia, July. Association for Computational Linguistics.

Crystal Nakatsu and Michael White. 2010. Generating with discourse combinatory categorial grammar. *Linguistic Issues in Language Technology*, 4(1):1–62.

Crystal Nakatsu. 2008. Learning contrastive connectives in sentence realization ranking. In *Proceedings of the 9th SIGdial Workshop on Discourse and Dialogue*, pages 76–79, Columbus, Ohio, June. Association for Computational Linguistics.

Mark Steedman. 2000. *The Syntactic Process*. MIT Press.

Kristina Striegnitz. 2004. *Generating Anaphoric Expressions — Contextual Inference in Sentence Planning*. Ph.D. thesis, University of Saalandes & Universit de Nancy.

Marilyn A. Walker, Owen C. Rambow, and Monica Rogati. 2002. Training a sentence planner for spoken dialogue using boosting. *Computer Speech and Language*, 16:409–433.

M. A. Walker, S. J. Whittaker, A. Stent, P. Maloor, J. D. Moore, M. Johnston, and G Vasireddy. 2004. Generation and evaluation of user tailored responses in multimodal dialogue. *Cognitive Science*, 28(5):811–840.

M. Walker, A. Stent, F. Mairesse, and Rashmi Prasad. 2007. Individual and domain adaptation in sentence planning for dialogue. *Journal of Artificial Intelligence Research (JAIR)*, 30:413–456.

Bonnie Webber, Matthew Stone, Aravind Joshi, and Alistair Knott. 2003. Anaphora and discourse structure. *Computational Linguistics*, 29(4).

Bonnie Webber. 2004. D-LTAG: Extending lexicalized TAG to discourse. *Cognitive Science*, 28(5):751–779.

Michael White and Rajakrishnan Rajkumar. 2009. Perceptron reranking for CCG realization. In *Proceedings of the 2009 Conference on Empirical Methods in Natural Language Processing*, pages 410–419, Singapore, August. Association for Computational Linguistics.

Michael White, Robert A. J. Clark, and Johanna D. Moore. 2010. Generating tailored, comparative descriptions with contextually appropriate intonation. *Computational Linguistics*, 36(2):159–201.

Michael White. 2006a. CCG chart realization from disjunctive logical forms. In *Proc. INLG-06*.

Michael White. 2006b. Efficient Realization of Coordinate Structures in Combinatory Categorial Grammar. *Research on Language and Computation*, 4(1):39–75, June.

Generating Elliptic Coordination

Claire Gardent
CNRS, LORIA, UMR 7503
Vandoeuvre-lès-Nancy, F-54500, France
claire.gardent@loria.fr

Shashi Narayan
Université de Lorraine, LORIA, UMR 7503
Villers-lès-Nancy, F-54600, France
shashi.narayan@loria.fr

Abstract

In this paper, we focus on the task of generating elliptic sentences. We extract from the data provided by the Surface Realisation (SR) Task (Belz et al., 2011) 2398 input whose corresponding output sentence contain an ellipsis. We show that 9% of the data contains an ellipsis and that both coverage and BLEU score markedly decrease for elliptic input (from 82.3% coverage for non-elliptic sentences to 65.3% for elliptic sentences and from 0.60 BLEU score to 0.47). We argue that elided material should be represented using phonetically empty nodes and we introduce a set of rewrite rules which permits adding these empty categories to the SR data. Finally, we evaluate an existing surface realiser on the resulting dataset. We show that, after rewriting, the generator achieves a coverage of 76% and a BLEU score of 0.74 on the elliptical data.

1 Introduction

To a large extent, previous work on generating ellipsis has assumed a semantically fully specified input (Shaw, 1998; Harbusch and Kempen, 2009; Theune et al., 2006). Given such input, elliptic sentences are then generated by first producing full sentences and second, deleting from these sentences substrings that were identified to obey deletion constraints.

In contrast, recent work on generation often assumes input where repeated material has already been elided. This includes work on sentence compression which regenerates sentences from surface dependency trees derived from parsing the initial text (Filippova and Strube, 2008); Surface realisation approaches which have produced results for regenerating from the Penn Treebank (Langkilde-Geary, 2002; Callaway, 2003; Zhong and Stent, 2005; Cahill and Van Genabith, 2006; White and Rajkumar, 2009); and more recently, the Surface Realisation (SR) Task (Belz et al., 2011) which has proposed dependency trees and graphs derived from the Penn Treebank (PTB) as a common ground input representation for testing and comparing existing surface realisers. In all these approaches, repeated material is omitted from the representation that is input to surface realisation.

As shown in the literature, modelling the interface between the empty phonology and the syntactic structure of ellipses is a difficult task. For parsing, Sarkar and Joshi (1996), Banik (2004) and Seddah (2008) propose either to modify the derivation process of Tree Adjoining Grammar or to introduce elementary trees anchored with empty category in a synchronous TAG to accommodate elliptic coordinations. In HPSG (Head-Driven Phrase Structure Grammar), Levy and Pollard (2001) introduce a neutralisation mechanism to account for unlike constituent coordination ; in LFG (Lexical Functional Grammar), Dalrymple and Kaplan (2000) employ set values to model coordination; in CCG (Combinatory Categorial Grammar, (Steedman, 1996)), it is the non standard notion of constituency assumed by the approach which permits accounting for coordinated structures; finally, in TLCG (Type-Logical Categorial Grammar), gapping is treated as like-category constituent coordinations (Kubota and Levine, 2012).

In this paper, we focus on how surface realisation handles elliptical sentences given an input where repeated material is omitted. We extract from the SR data 2398 input whose corresponding output sentence contain an ellipsis. Based on previous work on how to annotate and to represent ellipsis, we argue that elided material should be represented using phonetically empty nodes (Section 3) and we introduce a set of rewrite rules which permits adding these empty categories to the SR data (Section 4). We then evaluate our surface realiser (Narayan and Gardent, 2012b) on the resulting dataset (Section 5) and we show that, on this data, the generator achieves a coverage of 76% and a BLEU score, for the generated sentences, of 0.74. Section 6 discusses related work on generating elliptic coordination. Section 7 concludes.

2 Elliptic Sentences

Elliptic coordination involves a wide range of phenomena including in particular non-constituent coordination (1, NCC) i.e., cases where sequences of constituents are coordinated; gapping (2, G) i.e., cases where the verb and possibly some additional material is elided; shared subjects (3, SS) and right node raising (4, RNR) i.e., cases where a right most constituent is shared by two or more clauses[1].

(1) [It rose]$_i$ 4.8 % in June 1998 and ϵ_i 4.7% in June 1999. NCC
(2) Sumitomo bank [donated]$_i$ $500,000, Tokyo prefecture ϵ_i $15,000 and the city of Osaka ϵ_i $10,000 . *Gapping*
(3) [the state agency 's figures]$_i$ ϵ_i confirm previous estimates and ϵ_i leave the index at 178.9 . *Shared Subject*
(4) He commissions ϵ_i and splendidly interprets ϵ_i [fearsome contemporary scores]$_i$. *RNR*

We refer to the non elliptic clause as the *source* and to the elliptic clause as the *target*. In the source, the brackets indicate the element shared with the target while in the target, the ϵ_i sign indicate the elided material with co-indexing indicating the antecedent/ellipsis relation. In gapping clauses, we refer to the constituents in the gapped clause, as *remnants*.

3 Representing and Annotating Elided Material

We now briefly review how elided material is represented in the literature.

Linguistic Approaches. While Sag (1976), Williams (1977), Kehler (2002), Merchant (2001) and van Craenenbroeck (2010) have argued for a structural approach i.e., one which posits syntactic structure for the elided material, Keenan (1971), Hardt (1993), Dalrymple et al. (1991), Ginzburg and Sag (2000) and Culicover and Jackendoff (2005) all defend a non structural approach. Although no consensus has yet been reached on these questions, many of these approaches do postulate an abstract syntax for ellipsis. That is they posit that elided material licenses the introduction of phonetically empty categories in the syntax or at some more abstract level (e.g., the logical form of generative linguistics).

Treebanks. Similarly, in computational linguistics, the treebanks used to train and evaluate parsers propose different means of representing ellipsis.

For phrase structure syntax, the Penn Treebank Bracketing Guidelines extensively describe how to annotate coordination and missing material in English (Bies et al., 1995). For shared complements (e.g., shared subject and right node raising constructions), these guidelines state that the elided material licenses the introduction of an empty *RNR* category co-indexed with the shared complement (cf. Figure 1) while gapping constructions are handled by labelling the gapping remnants (i.e., the constituents present in the gapping clause) with the index of their parallel element in the source (cf. Figure 2).

```
(S
 (VP (VB Do)(VP (VB avoid)
   (S (VP (VPG puncturing(NP *RNR*-5))
   (CC or)
   (VP (VBG cutting)(PP (IN into)
       (NP *RNR*-5)))
    (NP-5 meats)))))
```

Figure 1: Penn Treebank annotation for Right Node Raising "*Do avoid puncturing ϵ_i or cutting into ϵ_i [meats]$_i$.*"

```
(S
  (S (NP-SBJ-10 Mary)
     (VP (VBZ likes) (NP-11 potatoes)))
  (CC and)
  (S (NP-SBJ=10 Bill)
     (, ,) (NP=11 ostriches)))
```

Figure 2: Penn Treebank annotation for gapping "*Mary [likes]$_i$ potatoes and Bill ϵ_i ostriches.*"

In dependency treebanks, headless elliptic constructs such as gapping additionally raise the is-

[1] Other types of elliptic coordination include sluicing and Verb-Phrase ellipsis. These will not be discussed here because they can be handled by the generator by having the appropriate categories in the grammar and the lexicon e.g., in a Tree Adjoining Grammar, an auxiliary anchoring a verb phrase for VP ellipsis and question words anchoring a sentence for sluicing.

sue of how to represent the daughters of an empty head. Three main types of approaches have been proposed. In dependency treebanks for German (Daum et al., 2004; Hajič et al., 2009) and in the Czech treebank (Čmejrek et al., 2004; Hajič et al., 2009), one of the dependents of the headless phrase is declared to be the head. This is a rather undesirable solution because it hides the fact that there the clause lacks a head. In contrast, the Hungarian dependency treebank (Vincze et al., 2010) explicitly represents the elided elements in the trees by introducing phonetically empty elements that serve as attachment points to other tokens. This is the cleanest solution from a linguistic point of view. Similarly, Seeker and Kuhn (2012) present a conversion of the German Tiger treebank which introduces empty nodes for verb ellipses if a phrase normally headed by a verb is lacking a head. They compare the performance of two statistical dependency parsers on the canonical version and the CoNLL 2009 Shared Task data and show that the converted dependency treebank they propose yields better parsing results than the treebank not containing empty heads.

In sum, while some linguists have argued for an approach where ellipsis has no syntactic representation, many have provided strong empirical evidence for positing empty nodes as place-holders for elliptic material. Similarly, in devising treebanks, computational linguists have oscillated between representations with and without empty categories. In the following section, we present the way in which elided material is represented in the SR data; we show that it underspecifies the sentences to be generated; and we propose to modify the SR representations by making the relationship between ellipsis and antecedent explicit using phonetically empty categories and co-indexing.

4 Rewriting the SR Data

The SR Task 2011 made available two types of data for surface realisers to be tested on: shallow dependency trees and deep dependency graphs. Here we focus on the shallow dependency trees i.e., on syntactic structures.

The input data provided by the SR Task were obtained from the Penn Treebank. They were derived indirectly from the LTH Constituent-to-Dependency Conversion Tool for Penn-style Treebanks (Pennconverter, (Johansson and Nugues, 2007)) by post-processing the CoNLL data to remove word order, inflections etc. It consists of a set of unordered labelled syntactic dependency trees whose nodes are labelled with word forms, part of speech categories, partial morphosyntactic information such as tense and number and, in some cases, a sense tag identifier. The edges are labelled with the syntactic labels provided by the Pennconverter. All words (including punctuation) of the original sentence are represented by a node in the tree. Figures 3, 4, 5 and 6 show (simplified) input trees from the SR data.

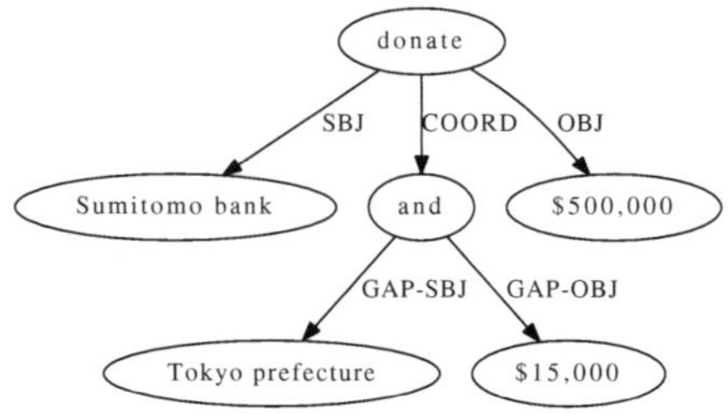

Figure 3: Gapping in the SR data. "*Sumitomo bank [donated]*$_i$ \$500, 000 *and Tokyo prefecture* ϵ_i \$15, 000."

In the SR data, the representation of ellipsis adopted in the Penn Treebank is preserved modulo some important differences regarding co-indexing.

Gapping is represented as in the PTB by labelling the remnants with a marker indicating the source element parallel to each remnant. However while in the PTB, this parallelism is made explicit by co-indexing (the source element is marked with an index i and its parallel target element with the marker $= i$), in the SR data this parallelism is approximated using functions. For instance, if the remnant is parallel to the source subject, it will be labelled GAP-SBJ (cf. Figure 3).

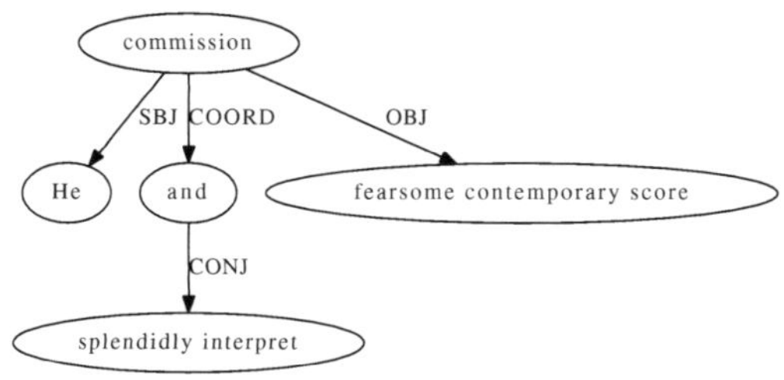

Figure 4: Subject Sharing and RNR in the SR data. "*[He]*$_j$ ϵ_j *commissions* ϵ_i *and* ϵ_j *splendidly interprets* ϵ_i *[fearsome contemporary scores]*$_i$."

For right-node raising and shared subjects, the coindexation present in the PTB is dropped in the SR data. As a result, the SR representation under-

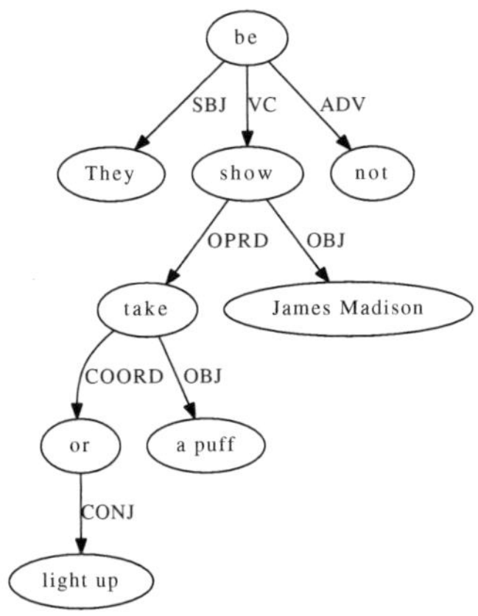

Figure 5: Non shared Object "*They aren't showing James Madison taking a puff or lighting up*"

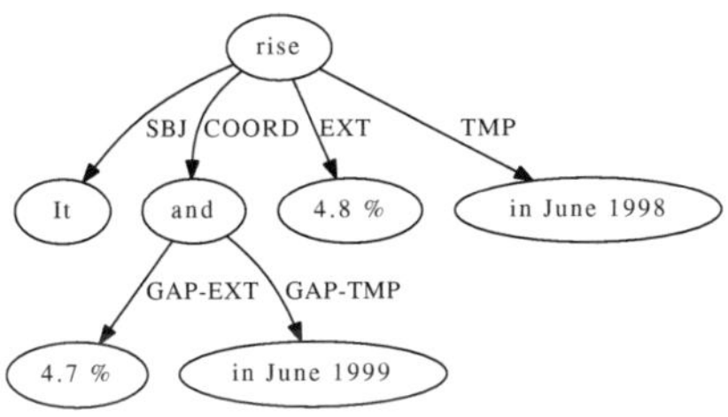

Figure 6: NCC in the SR data. "*It rose 4.8 % in June 1998 and 4.7% in June 1999.*"

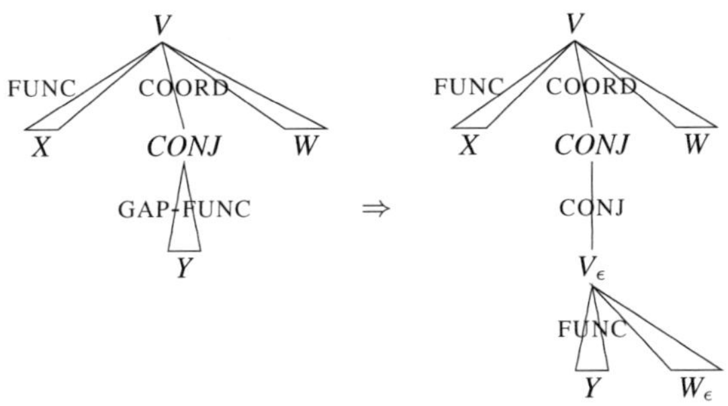

Figure 7: Gapping and Non Constituent Coordination structures rewriting (*V*: a verb, *CONJ*: a conjunctive coordination, *X*, *Y* and *W* three sets of dependents). The antecedent verb (*V*) and the source material without counterpart in the gapping clause (*W*) are copied over to the gapping clause and marked as phonetically empty.

specifies the relation between the object and the coordinated verbs in RNR constructions: the object could be shared as in *He commissions* ϵ_i *and splendidly interprets* ϵ_i *[fearsome contemporary scores]*$_i$. (Figure 4) or not as in *They aren't showing James Madison taking a puff or lighting up* (Figure 5). In both cases, the representation is the same i.e., the shared object (*fearsome contemporary scores*) and the unshared object (*a puff*) are both attached to the first verb.

Finally, NCC structures are handled in the same way as gapping by having the gapping remnants labelled with a GAP prefixed function (e.g., GAP-SBJ) indicating which element in the source the gapping remnant is parallel to (cf. Figure 6).

Summing up, the SR representation schema underspecifies ellipsis in two ways. For gapping and non-constituent coordination, it describes parallelism between source and target elements rather than specifying the syntax of the elided material. For subject sharing and right node raising, it fails to explicitly specify argument sharing.

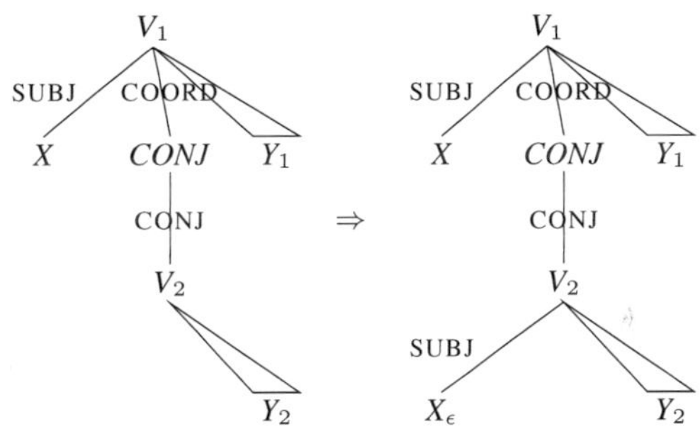

Figure 8: Subject sharing: the subject dependent is copied over to the target clause and marked as phonetically empty.

To resolve this underspecification, we rewrite the SR data using tree rewrite rules as follows.

In Gapping and NCC structures, we copy the source material that has no (GAP- marked) counterpart in the target clause to the target clause marking it to indicate a phonetically empty category (cf. Figure 7).

For Subject sharing, we copy the shared subject of the source clause in the target clause and mark it to be a phonetically empty category (cf. Figure 8).

For Right-Node-Raising, we unfold the ambiguity producing structures where arguments present in the source but not in the target are optionally copied over to the target (cf. Figure 9).

These rewrite rules are implemented efficiently

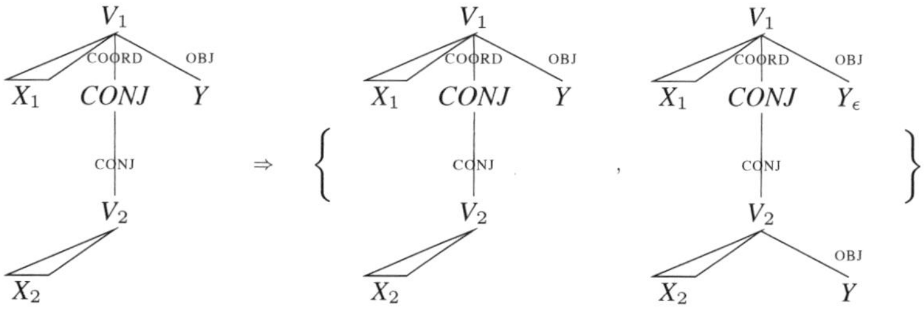

Figure 9: Right-Node-Raising: the object dependent is optionally copied over to the target clause and marked as phonetically empty in the source clause.

using GrGen, an efficient graph rewriting system (Geißet al., 2006).

5 Generating Elliptic Coordination

5.1 The Surface Realiser

To generate sentences from the SR data, we use our surface realiser (Narayan and Gardent, 2012b), a grammar-based generator based on a Feature-Based Lexicalised Tree Adjoining Grammar (FB-LTAG) for English. This generator first selects the elementary FB-LTAG trees associated in the lexicon with the lemmas and part of speech tags associated with each node in the input dependency tree. It then attempts to combine the selected trees bottom-up taking into account the structure of the input tree (only trees that are selected by nodes belonging to the same local input tree are tried for combination). A language model is used to implement a beam search letting through only the n most likely phrases at each bottom up combination step. In this experiment, we set n to 5. The generator thus outputs at most 5 sentences for each input.

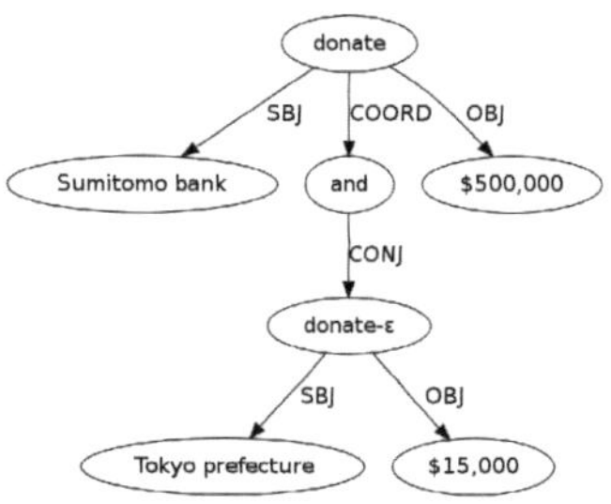

Figure 10: Gapping after rewriting "*Sumitomo bank [donated]$_i$* $500,000 *and Tokyo prefecture* ϵ_i $15,000."

As mentioned in the introduction, most computational grammars have difficulty accounting for ellipses and FB-LTAG is no exception.

The difficulty stems from the fact that in elliptical sentences, there is meaning without sound. As a result, the usual form/meaning mappings that in non-elliptic sentences allow us to map sounds onto their corresponding meanings, break down. For instance, in the sentence *John eats apples and Mary pear*, the Subject-Verb-Object structure which can be used in English to express a binary relation is present in the source clause but not in the elided one. In practice, the syntax of elliptical sentences often leads to a duplication of the grammatical system, one system allowing for non elliptical sentences and the other for their elided counterpart.

For parsing with TAG, two main methods have been proposed for processing elliptical sentences. (Sarkar and Joshi, 1996) introduces an additional operation for combining TAG trees which yields derivation graphs rather than trees. (Seddah, 2008) uses Multi-Component TAG and proposes to associate each elementary verb tree with an elliptic tree with different pairs representing different types of ellipses.

We could use either of these approaches for generation. The first approach however has the drawback that it leads to a non standard notion of derivation (the derivation trees become derivation graphs). The second on the other hand, induces a proliferation of trees in the grammar and impacts efficiency.

Instead, we show that, given an input enriched with empty categories as proposed in the previous section, neither the grammar nor the tree combination operation need changing. Indeed, our FB-LTAG surface realiser directly supports the generation of elliptic sentences. It suffices to assume that an FB-LTAG elementary tree may be anchored by the empty string. Given an input node marked as phonetically empty, the generator will then select all FB-LTAG rules that are compatible with the lexical and the morpho-syntactic features labelling that node. Generation will then proceed as usual by composing the trees selected on the basis of the input using substitution and adjunction; and by retrieving from the generation forest those sentences whose phrase structure tree covers the input.

For instance, given the rewritten input shown in Figure 10, the TAG trees associated in the lexicon with *donate* will be selected; anchored with the empty string and combined with the TAG trees built for *Tokyo Prefecture* and *$15,000* thus yielding the derivation shown in Figure 11.

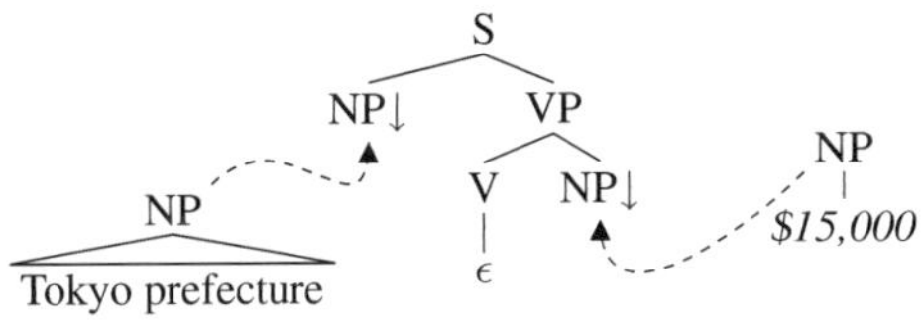

Figure 11: Derivation for "Tokyo prefecture ε $15,000"

5.2 The Data

We use both the SR test data (2398 sentences) and the SR training data (26604 sentences) to evaluate the performance of the surface realiser on elliptic coordination. Since the realiser we are using is not trained on this data (the grammar was written manually), this does not bias evaluation. Using the training data allows us to gather a larger set of elliptic sentences for evaluation while evaluating also on the test data allows comparison with other realisers.

To focus on ellipses, we retrieve those sentences which were identified by our rewrite rules as potentially containing an elliptic coordination. In essence, these rewrite rules will identify all cases of non-constituent coordination and gapping (because these involve GAP-X dependencies with "X" a dependency relation and are therefore easily detected) and of shared-subjects (because the tree patterns used to detect are unambiguous i.e., only apply if there is indeed a shared subject). For RNR, as discussed in the previous section, the SR format is ambiguous and consequently, the rewrite rules might identify as object sharing cases where in fact the object is not shared. As noted by one of our reviewers, the false interpretation could be dropped out by consulting the Penn Treebank[2]. The approach would not generalise to other data however.

In total, we retrieve 2398 sentences[3] potentially containing an elliptic coordination from the SR training data. The number and distribution of these sentences in terms of ellipsis types are given in Table 1. From the test data, we retrieve an additional 182 elliptic sentences.

Elliptic Coordination Data				
Elliptic Coordination		Pass	BLEU Scores	
			COV	ALL
RNR (384)	Before	66%	0.68	0.45
	After	81%	0.70	0.57
	Delta	+15	+0.02	+0.12
SS (1462)	Before	70%	0.74	0.52
	After	75%	0.75	0.56
	Delta	+5	+0.01	+0.04
SS + RNR (456)	Before	61%	0.71	0.43
	After	74%	0.73	0.54
	Delta	+13	+0.02	+0.11
Gapping (36)	Before	3%	0.53	0.01
	After	67%	0.74	0.49
	Delta	+64	+0.21	+0.48
NCC (60)	Before	5%	0.68	0.03
	After	73%	0.74	0.54
	Delta	+68	+0.06	+0.51
Total (2398)	Before	65%	0.72	0.47
	After	76%	0.74	0.56
	Delta	**+11**	+0.02	+0.09

Table 1: Generation results on elliptical data before and after input rewriting (SS: Shared Subject, NCC: Non Constituent Coordination, RNR: Right Node Raising). The number in brackets in the first column is the number of cases. Pass stands for the coverage of the generator. COV and ALL in BLEU scores column stand for BLEU scores for the covered and the total input data.

5.3 Evaluation

We ran the surface realiser on the SR input data both before and after rewriting elliptic coordinations; on the sentences estimated to contain ellipsis; on sentences devoid of ellipsis; and on all sentences. The results are shown in Table 2. They indicate coverage and BLEU score before and after rewriting. BLEU score is given both with respect to covered sentences (COV) i.e., the set of input for which generation succeeds; and for all sentences (ALL). We evaluate both with respect to the SR test data and with respect to the SR training

[2]The Penn Treebank makes the RNR interpretations explicit (refer to Figure 1).

[3]It is just a coincidence that the size of the SR test data and the number of extracted elliptic sentences are the same.

SR Data			Pass	BLEU Scores	
				COV	ALL
Test	+E (182)	Before	58%	0.59	0.34
		After	67%	0.59	0.40
		Delta	+9	+0.00	+0.06
	-E (2216)	Before	80%	0.59	0.47
		After	80%	0.59	0.48
		Delta	+0	+0.00	+0.01
	T (2398)	Before	78%	0.58	0.46
		After	79%	0.59	0.47
		Delta	+1	+0.01	+0.01
Training	+E (2398) (Table 1)	Before	65%	0.72	0.47
		After	76%	0.74	0.56
		Delta	**+11**	+0.02	+0.09
	-E (24206)	Before	82%	0.73	0.60
		After	82%	0.73	0.60
		Delta	+0	+0.00	+0.00
	T (26604)	Before	81%	0.72	0.58
		After	**82%**	**0.73**	0.60
		Delta	**+1**	+0.01	+0.02

Table 2: Generation results on SR test and SR training data before and after input rewriting (+E stands for elliptical data, -E for non elliptical data and T for total.)

data. We use the SR Task scripts for the computation of the BLEU score.

The impact of ellipsis on coverage and precision. Previous work on parsing showed that coordination was a main source of parsing failure (Collins, 1999). Similarly, ellipses is an important source of failure for the TAG generator. Ellipses are relatively frequent with 9% of the sentences in the training data containing an elliptic structure and performance markedly decreases in the presence of ellipsis. Thus, before rewriting, coverage decreases from 82.3% for non-elliptic sentences to 80.75% on all sentences (elliptic and non elliptic sentences) and to 65.3% on the set of elliptic sentences. Similarly, BLEU score decreases from 0.60 for non elliptical sentences to 0.58 for all sentences and to 0.47 for elliptic sentences. In sum, both coverage and BLEU score decrease as the number of elliptic input increases.

The impact of the input representation on coverage and precision. Recent work on treebank annotation has shown that the annotation schema adopted for coordination impacts parsing. In particular, Maier et al. (2012) propose revised annotation guidelines for coordinations in the Penn Treebank whose aim is to facilitate the detection of coordinations. And Dukes and Habash (2011) show that treebank annotations which include phonetically empty material for representing elided material allows for better parsing results.

Similarly, Table 2 shows that the way in which ellipsis is represented in the input data has a strong impact on generation. Thus rewriting the input data markedly extends coverage with an overall improvement of 11 points (from 65% to 76%) for elliptic sentences and of almost 1 point for all sentences.

As detailed in Table 1 though, there are important differences between the different types of elliptic constructs: coverage increases by 68 points for NCC and 64 points for gapping against only 15, 13 and 5 points for RNR, mixed RNR-Shared Subject and Shared Subject respectively. The reason for this is that sentences are generated for many input containing the latter types of constructions (RNR and Shared Subject) *even without rewriting*. In fact, generation succeeds on the non rewritten input for a majority of RNR (66% PASS), Shared Subject (70% PASS) and mixed RNR-Shared Subject (61% PASS) constructions whereas it fails for almost all cases of gapping (3% PASS) and of NCC (5% PASS). The reason for this difference is that, while the grammar cannot cope with headless constructions such as gapping and NCC constructions, it can often provide a derivation for shared subject sentences by using the finite verb form in the source sentence and the corresponding infinitival form in the target. Since the infinitival does not require a subject, the target sentence is generated. Similarly, RNR constructions can be generated when the verb in the source clause has both a transitive and an intransitive form: the transitive form is used to generate the source clause and the intransitive for the target clause. In short, many sentences containing a RNR or a shared subject construction can be generated without rewriting because the grammar overgenerates i.e., it produces sentences which are valid sentences of English but whose phrase structure tree is incorrect.

Nevertheless, as the results show, rewriting consistently helps increasing coverage even for RNR (+15 points), Shared Subject (+5 points) and mixed RNR-Shared Subject (+13 points) constructions because (i) not all verbs have both a transitive and an intransitive verb form and (ii) the input for the elliptic clause may require a finite form for the target verb (e.g., in sentences such as "*[they]$_i$ weren't fired but instead ϵ_i were neglected*" where the target clause includes an auxiliary requiring a past participial which in this context requires a subject).

Precision is measured using the BLEU score. For each input, we take the best score obtained within the 5 derivations[4] produced by the generator. Since the BLEU score reflects the degree to which a sentence generated by the system matches the corresponding Penn Treebank sentence, it is impacted not just by elliptic coordination but also by all linguistic constructions present in the sentence. Nonetheless, the results show that rewriting consistently improves the BLEU score with an overall increase of 0.09 points on the set of elliptic sentences. Moreover, the consistent improvement in terms of BLEU score for generated sentences (COV column) shows that rewriting simultaneously improves both coverage and precision that is, that for those sentences that are generated, rewriting consistently improves precision.

Analysing the remaining failure cases. To better assess the extent to which rewriting and the FB-LTAG generation system succeed in generating elliptic coordinations, we performed error mining on the elliptic data using our error miner described in (Narayan and Gardent, 2012a). This method permits highlighting the most likely sources of error given two datasets: a set of successful cases and a set of failure cases. In this case, the successful cases is the subset of rewritten input data for elliptic coordination cases for which generation succeeds . The failure cases is the subset for which generation fails. If elliptic coordination was still a major source of errors, input nodes or edges labelled with labels related to elliptic coordination (e.g., the COORD and the GAP-X dependency relations or the CONJ part of speech tag) would surface as most suspicious forms. In practice however, we found that the 5 top sources of errors highlighted by error mining all include the DEP relation, an unknown dependency relation used by the Pennconverter when it fails to assign a label to a dependency edge. In other words, most of the remaining elliptic cases for which generation fails, fails for reasons unrelated to ellipsis.

Comparison with other surface realisers There is no data available on the performance of surface realisers on elliptic input. However, the performance of the surface realiser can be compared with those participating in the shallow track of the SR challenge. On the SR training data, the TAG surface realiser has an average run time of 2.78 seconds per sentence (with an average of 20 words per sentence), a coverage of 82% and BLEU scores of 0.73 for covered and 0.60 for all. On the SR test data, the realiser achieves a coverage of 79% and BLEU scores of 0.59 for covered and 0.47 for all. In comparison, the statistical systems in the SR Tasks achieved 0.88, 0.85 and 0.67 BLEU score on the SR test set and the best symbolic system 0.25 (Belz et al., 2011).

6 Related work

Previous work on generating elliptic sentences has mostly focused on identifying material that could be elided and on defining procedures capable of producing input structures for surface realisation that support the generation of elliptic sentences.

Shaw (1998) developed a sentence planner which generates elliptic sentences in 3 steps. First, input data are grouped according to their similarities. Second, repeated elements are marked. Third, constraints are used to determine which occurrences of a marked element should be deleted. The approach is integrated in the PLANDoc system (McKeown et al., 1994) and shown to generate a wide range of elliptic constructs including RNR, VPE and NCC using FUF/SURGE (Elhadad, 1993), a realisation component based on Functional Unification Grammar.

Theune et al. (2006) describe how elliptic sentences are generated in a story generation system. The approach covers conjunction reduction, right node raising, gapping and stripping and uses dependency trees connected by rhetorical relations as input. Before these trees are mapped to sentences, repeated elements are deleted and their antecedent (the*source element*) is related by a SUBORROWED relation to their governor in the elliptic clause and a SUIDENTICAL relation to their governor in the antecedent clause. This is then interpreted by the surface realiser to mean that the repeated element should be realised in the source clause, elided in the target clause and that it licenses the same syntactic structure in both clauses.

Harbusch and Kempen (2009) have proposed a module called Elleipo which takes as input unreduced, non-elliptic, syntactic structures annotated with lexical identity and coreference relationships

[4]The language model used in the generator allows only 5 likely derivations (refer to section 5.1).

between words and word groups in the conjuncts; and returns as output structures annotated with elision marks indicating which elements can be elided and how (i.e., using which type of ellipsis). The focus is on developing a language independent module which can mediate between the unreduced input syntactic structures produced by a generator and syntactic structures that are enriched with elision marks rich enough to determine the range of possible elliptic and non elliptic output sentences.

In CCG, grammar rules (type-raising and composition) permit combining non constituents into a functor category which takes the shared element as argument; and gapping remnants into a clause taking as argument its left-hand coordinated source clause. White (2006) describes a chart based algorithm for generating with CCG and shows that it can efficiently realise NCC and gapping constructions.

Our proposal differs from these approaches in that it focuses on the surface realisation stage (assuming that the repeated elements have already been identified) and is tested on a large corpus of newspaper sentences rather than on hand-made document plans and relatively short sentences.

7 Conclusion

In this paper, we showed that elliptic structures are frequent and can impact the performance of a surface realiser. In line with linguistic theory and with some recent results on treebank annotation, we argued that the representation of ellipsis should involve empty categories and we provided a set of tree rewrite rules to modify the SR data accordingly. We then evaluated the performance of a TAG based surface realiser on 2398 elliptic input derived by the SR task from the Penn Treebank and showed that it achieved a coverage of 76% and a BLEU score of 0.74 on generated sentences. Our approach relies both on the fact that the grammar is lexicalised (each rule is associated with a word from the input) and on TAG extended domain of locality (which permits using a rule anchored with the empty string to reconstruct the missing syntax in the elided clause thereby making it grammatical).

We will release the 2398 input representations we gathered for evaluating the generation of elliptic coordination so as to make it possible for other surface realisers to be evaluated on their ability to generate ellipsis. In particular, its would be interesting to examine how other grammar based generators perform on this dataset such as White's CCG based generator (2006) (which eschews empty categories by adopting a more flexible notion of constituency) and Carroll and Oepen's HPSG based generator (2005) (whose domain of locality differs from that of TAG).

Acknowledgments

We would like to thank Anja Belz and Mike White for providing us with the evaluation data and the evaluation scripts. The research presented in this paper was partially supported by the European Fund for Regional Development within the framework of the INTERREG IV A Allegro Project.

References

Eva Banik. 2004. Semantics of VP coordination in LTAG. In *Proceedings of the 7th International Workshop on Tree Adjoining Grammars and Related Formalisms (TAG+)*, volume 7, pages 118–125, Vancouver, Canada.

Anja Belz, Michael White, Dominic Espinosa, Eric Kow, Deirdre Hogan, and Amanda Stent. 2011. The first surface realisation shared task: Overview and evaluation results. In *Proceedings of the 13th European Workshop on Natural Language Generation (ENLG)*, Nancy, France.

Ann Bies, Mark Ferguson, Katz Katz, Robert MacIntyre, Victoria Tredinnick, Grace Kim, Marry Ann Marcinkiewicz, and Britta Schasberger. 1995. Bracketing guidelines for treebank II style penn treebank project. *University of Pennsylvania.*

Aoife Cahill and Josef Van Genabith. 2006. Robust pcfg-based generation using automatically acquired lfg approximations. In *Proceedings of the 21st International Conference on Computational Linguistics (COLING) and the 44th annual meeting of the Association for Computational Linguistics (ACL)*, pages 1033–1040, Sydney, Australia.

Charles B Callaway. 2003. Evaluating coverage for large symbolic nlg grammars. In *Proceedings of the 18th International joint conference on Artificial Intelligence (IJCAI)*, volume 18, pages 811–816, San Francisco, CA, USA. Morgan Kaufmann Publishers Inc.

John Carroll and Stephan Oepen. 2005. High efficiency realization for a wide-coverage unification grammar. In *Proceedings of the 2nd International Joint Conference on Natural Language Processing (IJCNLP)*, pages 165–176, Jeju Island, Korea. Springer.

M. Čmejrek, J. Hajič, and V. Kuboň. 2004. Prague czech-english dependency treebank: Syntactically annotated resources for machine translation. In *Proceedings of the 4th International Conference on Language Resources and Evaluation (LREC)*, Lisbon, Portugal.

Michael Collins. 1999. *Head-Driven Statistical Models for Natural Language Parsing*. Ph.D. thesis, University of Pennsylvania.

Peter W. Culicover and Ray Jackendoff. 2005. *Simpler Syntax*. Oxford University Press.

Mary Dalrymple and Ronald M. Kaplan. 2000. Feature indeterminacy and feature resolution. *Language*, pages 759–798.

Mary Dalrymple, Stuart M. Sheiber, and Fernando C. N. Pereira. 1991. Ellipsis and higher-order unification. *Linguistics and Philosophy*.

Michael Daum, Kilian Foth, and Wolfgang Menzel. 2004. Automatic transformation of phrase treebanks to dependency trees. In *Proceedings of the 4th International Conference on Language Resources and Evaluation (LREC)*, Lisbon, Portugal.

Kais Dukes and Nizar Habash. 2011. One-step statistical parsing of hybrid dependency-constituency syntactic representations. In *Proceedings of the 12th International Conference on Parsing Technologies*, pages 92–103, Dublin, Ireland. Association for Computational Linguistics.

Michael Elhadad. 1993. *Using argumentation to control lexical choice: a functional unification implementation*. Ph.D. thesis, Columbia University.

Katja Filippova and Michael Strube. 2008. Dependency tree based sentence compression. In *Proceedings of the Fifth International Natural Language Generation Conference (INLG)*, pages 25–32, Salt Fork, Ohio, USA. Association for Computational Linguistics.

Rubino Geiß, Gernot Veit Batz, Daniel Grund, Sebastian Hack, and Adam M. Szalkowski. 2006. Grgen: A fast spo-based graph rewriting tool. In *Proceedings of the 3rd International Conference on Graph Transformation*, pages 383–397. Springer. Natal, Brasil.

Jonathan Ginzburg and Ivan Sag. 2000. *Interrogative investigations*. CSLI Publications.

J. Hajič, M. Ciaramita, R. Johansson, D. Kawahara, M.A. Martí, L. Màrquez, A. Meyers, J. Nivre, S. Padó, J. Štěpánek, et al. 2009. The conll-2009 shared task: Syntactic and semantic dependencies in multiple languages. In *Proceedings of the 13th Conference on Computational Natural Language Learning: Shared Task*, pages 1–18.

Karin Harbusch and Gerard Kempen. 2009. Generating clausal coordinate ellipsis multilingually: A uniform approach based on postediting. In *Proceedings of the 12th European Workshop on Natural Language Generation*, pages 138–145, Athens, Greece. Association for Computational Linguistics.

Daniel Hardt. 1993. *Verb phrase ellipsis: Form, meaning and processing*. Ph.D. thesis, University of Pennsylvania.

Richert Johansson and Pierre Nugues. 2007. Extended constituent-to-dependency conversion for english. In *Proceedings of the 16th Nordic Conference of Computational Linguistics (NODALIDA)*, pages 105–112, Tartu, Estonia.

Edward Keenan. 1971. Names, quantifiers, and the sloppy identity problem. *Papers in Linguistics*, 4:211–232.

Andrew Kehler. 2002. *Coherence in discourse*. CSLI Publications.

Yusuke Kubota and Robert Levine. 2012. Gapping as like-category coordination. In *Proceedings of the 7th international conference on Logical Aspects of Computational Linguistics (LACL)*, pages 135–150, Nantes, France. Springer-Verlag.

Irene Langkilde-Geary. 2002. An empirical verification of coverage and correctness for a general-purpose sentence generator. In *Proceedings of the 12th International Natural Language Generation Workshop*, pages 17–24.

Roger Levy and Carl Pollard. 2001. Coordination and neutralization in HPSG. *Technology*, 3:5.

Wolfgang Maier, Erhard Hinrichs, Julia Krivanek, and Sandra Kübler. 2012. Annotating coordination in the Penn Treebank. In *Proceedings of the 6th Linguistic Annotation Workshop (LAW)*, pages 166–174, Jeju, Republic of Korea. Association for Computational Linguistics.

Kathleen McKeown, Karen Kukich, and James Shaw. 1994. Practical issues in automatic documentation generation. In *Proceedings of the fourth conference on Applied natural language processing (ANLC)*, pages 7–14, Stuttgart, Germany. Association for Computational Linguistics.

Jason Merchant. 2001. *The syntax of silence: Sluicing, islands, and the theory of ellipsis*. Oxford University Press.

Shashi Narayan and Claire Gardent. 2012a. Error mining with suspicion trees: Seeing the forest for the trees. In *Proceedings of the 24th International Conference on Computational Linguistics (COLING)*, Mumbai, India.

Shashi Narayan and Claire Gardent. 2012b. Structure-driven lexicalist generation. In *Proceedings of the 24th International Conference on Computational Linguistics (COLING)*, Mumbai, India.

Ivan Sag. 1976. *Deletion and logical form*. Ph.D. thesis, Massachusetts Institute of Technology, Cambridge, Massachusetts.

Anoop Sarkar and Arvind Joshi. 1996. Coordination in tree adjoining grammars: Formalization and implementation. In *Proceedings of the 16th conference on Computational linguistics-Volume 2*, pages 610–615, Copenhagen, Denmark. Association for Computational Linguistics.

Djamé Seddah. 2008. The use of mctag to process elliptic coordination. In *Proceedings of The Ninth International Workshop on Tree Adjoining Grammars and Related Formalisms (TAG+ 9)*, volume 1, page 2, Tübingen, Germany.

Wolfgang Seeker and Jonas Kuhn. 2012. Making ellipses explicit in dependency conversion for a german treebank. In *Proceedings of the 8th International Conference on Language Resources and Evaluation (LREC)*, Istanbul, Turkey.

James Shaw. 1998. Segregatory coordination and ellipsis in text generation. In *Proceedings of the 36th Annual Meeting of the Association for Computational Linguistics and 17th International Conference on Computational Linguistics*, pages 1220–1226, Montreal, Quebec, Canada.

Mark Steedman. 1996. *Surface Structure and Interpretation*, volume 30. MIT press Cambridge, MA.

Mariët Theune, Feikje Hielkema, and Petra Hendriks. 2006. Performing aggregation and ellipsis using discourse structures. *Research on Language & Computation*, 4(4):353–375.

Jeoren van Craenenbroeck. 2010. *The syntax of ellipsis: Evidence from Dutch dialects*. Oxford University Press.

V. Vincze, D. Szauter, A. Almási, G. Móra, Z. Alexin, and J. Csirik. 2010. Hungarian dependency treebank. In *Proceedings of the 7th International Conference on Language Resources and Evaluation (LREC)*, Valletta, Malta.

Michael White and Rajakrishnan Rajkumar. 2009. Perceptron reranking for ccg realization. In *Proceedings of the 2009 Conference on Empirical Methods in Natural Language Processing (EMNLP)*, pages 410–419, Singapore. Association for Computational Linguistics.

Michael White. 2006. Efficient realization of coordinate structures in combinatory categorial grammar. *Research on Language & Computation*, 4(1):39–75.

Edwin Williams. 1977. Discourse and logical form. *Linguistic Inquiry*.

Huayan Zhong and Amanda Stent. 2005. Building surface realizers automatically from corpora. In *Proceedings of the Workshop on Using Corpora for Natural Language Generation (UCNLG)*, volume 5, pages 49–54.

Using Integer Linear Programming for Content Selection, Lexicalization, and Aggregation to Produce Compact Texts from OWL Ontologies

Gerasimos Lampouras and **Ion Androutsopoulos**
Department of Informatics
Athens University of Economics and Business
Patission 76, GR-104 34 Athens, Greece
http://nlp.cs.aueb.gr/

Abstract

We present an Integer Linear Programming model of content selection, lexicalization, and aggregation that we developed for a system that generates texts from OWL ontologies. Unlike pipeline architectures, our model jointly considers the available choices in these three text generation stages, to avoid greedy decisions and produce more compact texts. Experiments with two ontologies confirm that it leads to more compact texts, compared to a pipeline with the same components, with no deterioration in the perceived quality of the generated texts. We also present an approximation of our model, which allows longer texts to be generated efficiently.

1 Introduction

Concept-to-text natural language generation (NLG) generates texts from formal knowledge representations (Reiter and Dale, 2000). With the emergence of the Semantic Web (Berners-Lee et al., 2001; Shadbolt et al., 2006; Antoniou and van Harmelen, 2008), interest in concept-to-text NLG has been revived and several methods have been proposed to express axioms of OWL ontologies (Grau et al., 2008), a form of description logic (Baader et al., 2002), in natural language (Bontcheva, 2005; Mellish and Sun, 2006; Galanis and Androutsopoulos, 2007; Mellish and Pan, 2008; Schwitter et al., 2008; Schwitter, 2010; Liang et al., 2011; Williams et al., 2011).

NLG systems typically employ a pipeline architecture. They usually start by selecting the logical facts (axioms, in the case of an OWL ontology) to be expressed. The purpose of the next stage, text planning, ranges from simply ordering the facts to be expressed to making more complex decisions about the rhetorical structure of the text. Lexicalization then selects the words and syntactic structures that will realize each fact, specifying how each fact can be expressed as a single sentence. Sentence aggregation may then combine shorter sentences to form longer ones. Another component generates appropriate referring expressions, and surface realization produces the final text.

Each stage of the pipeline is treated as a local optimization problem, where the decisions of the previous stages cannot be modified. This arrangement produces texts that may not be optimal, since the decisions of the stages have been shown to be co-dependent (Danlos, 1984; Marciniak and Strube, 2005; Belz, 2008). For example, decisions made during content selection may maximize importance measures, but may produce facts that are difficult to turn into a coherent text; also, content selection and lexicalization may lead to more or fewer sentence aggregation opportunities. Some of these problems can be addressed by overgenerating at each stage (e.g., producing several alternative sets of facts at the end of content selection, several alternative lexicalizations etc.) and employing a final ranking component to select the best combination (Walker et al., 2001). This overgenerate and rank approach, however, may also fail to find an optimal solution, and it generates an exponentially large number of candidate solutions when several components are pipelined.

In this paper, we present an Integer Linear Programming (ILP) model that combines content selection, lexicalization, and sentence aggregation. Our model does not consider directly text planning, nor referring expression generation, which we hope to include in future work, but it is combined with an external simple text planner and an external referring expression generation component; we also do not discuss surface realization. Unlike pipeline architectures, our model jointly examines the possible choices in the three NLG stages it considers, to avoid greedy local decisions.

Given an individual (entity) or class of an OWL ontology and a set of facts (axioms) about the individual or class, we aim to produce a compact text that expresses as many facts in as few words as possible. This is desirable when space is limited or expensive, e.g., when displaying product descriptions on smartphones, or when including advertisements in Web search results. If an importance score is available for each fact, our model can take it into account to prefer expressing important facts, again using as few words as possible. The model itself, however, does not produce importance scores, i.e., we assume that the scores are produced by a separate process (Barzilay and Lapata, 2005; Demir et al., 2010), not included in our content selection. In the experiments of this article, we treat all the facts as equally important.

Although the search space of our model is very large and ILP problems are in general NP-hard, off-the-shelf ILP solvers can be used, which can be very fast in practice and guarantee finding a global optimum. Experiments with two ontologies show that our ILP model outperforms, in terms of expressed facts per word, an NLG system that uses the same components connected in a pipeline, with no deterioration in perceived text quality; the ILP model may actually lead to texts of higher quality, compared to those of the pipeline, when there are many facts to express. We also present an approximation of our ILP model, which is more efficient when larger numbers of facts need to be expressed.

Section 2 discusses previous related work. Section 3 defines our ILP model. Section 4 presents our experimentals. Section 5 concludes.

2 Related work

Marciniak and Strube (2005) propose a general ILP approach for language processing applications where the decisions of classifiers that consider particular, but co-dependent, subtasks need to be combined. They also show how their approach can be used to generate multi-sentence route directions, in a setting with very different inputs and processing stages than the ones we consider.

Barzilay and Lapata (2005) treat content selection as an optimization problem. Given a pool of facts and scores indicating their importance, they select the facts to express by formulating an optimization problem similar to energy minimization. The problem is solved by applying a minimal cut partition algorithm to a graph representing the pool of facts and the importance scores. The importance scores of the facts are obtained via supervised machine learning (AdaBoost) from a dataset of (sports) facts and news articles expressing them.

In other work, Barzilay and Lapata (2006) consider sentence aggregation. Given a set of facts that a content selection stage has produced, aggregation is viewed as the problem of partitioning the facts into optimal subsets. Sentences expressing facts of the same subset are aggregated to form a longer sentence. The optimal partitioning maximizes the pairwise similarity of the facts in each subset, subject to constraints that limit the number of subsets and the number of facts in each subset. A Maximum Entropy classifier predicts the semantic similarity of each pair of facts, and an ILP model is used to find the optimal partitioning.

Althaus et al. (2004) show that ordering a set of sentences to maximize local coherence is equivalent to the traveling salesman problem and, hence, NP-complete. They also show an ILP formulation of the problem, which can be solved efficiently in practice using branch-and-cut with cutting planes.

Kuznetsova et al. (2012) use ILP to generate image captions. They train classifiers to detect the objects in each image. Having identified the objects of a given image, they retrieve phrases from the captions of a corpus of images, focusing on the captions of objects that are similar (color, texture, shape) to the ones in the given image. To select which objects of the image to report and in what order, Kuznetsova et al. maximize (via ILP) the mean of the confidence scores of the object detection classifiers and the sum of the co-occurrence probabilities of the objects that will be reported in adjacent positions in the caption. Having decided which objects to report and their order, Kuznetsova et al. use a second ILP model to decide which phrases to use for each object and to order the phrases. The second ILP model maximizes the confidence of the phrase retrieval algorithm and the local cohesion between subsequent phrases.

Joint optimization ILP models have also been used in multi-document text summarization and sentence compression (McDonald, 2007; Clarke and Lapata, 2008; Berg-Kirkpatrick et al., 2011; Galanis et al., 2012; Woodsend and Lapata, 2012), where the input is text, not formal knowledge represetations. Statistical methods to jointly perform content selection, lexicalization, and surface realization have also been proposed in NLG (Liang et al., 2009; Konstas and Lapata, 2012a; Konstas and Lapata, 2012b), but they are currently limited to generating single sentences from flat records, as opposed to ontologies. Our method is the first one to consider content selection, lexicalization, and sentence aggregation as an ILP joint optimization problem in the context of multi-sentence concept-to-text generation.

3 Our ILP model of NLG

Let $F = \{f_1, \ldots, f_n\}$ be the set of all the facts f_i (OWL axioms) about the individual or class to be described. OWL axioms can be represented as sets of RDF triples of the form $\langle S, R, O \rangle$, where S is an individual or class, O is another individual, class, or datatype value, and R is a relation (property) that connects S to O.[1] Hence, we can assume that each fact f_i is a triple $\langle S_i, R_i, O_i \rangle$.[2]

For each fact f_i, a set $P_i = \{p_{i1}, p_{i2}, \ldots\}$ of alternative sentence plans is available. Each sentence plan p_{ik} specifies how to express $f_i = \langle S_i, R_i, O_i \rangle$ as an alternative single sentence. In our work, a sentence plan is a sequence of slots, along with instructions specifying how to fill the slots in; and each sentence plan is associated with the relations it can express. For example, ⟨`exhibit12`, `foundIn`, `athens`⟩ could be expressed using a sentence plan like "[*ref*(S)] [find$_{past}$] [in] [*ref*(O)]", where square brackets denote slots, *ref*(S) and *ref*(O) are instructions requiring referring expressions for S and O in the corresponding slots, and "find$_{past}$" requires the simple past form of "find". In our example, the sentence plan would lead to a sentence like "Exhibit 12 was found in Athens". We call *elements* the slots with their instructions, but with "S" and "O" accompanied by the individuals, classes, or datatype values they refer to; in our example, the elements are "[*ref*(S: `exhibit12`)]", "[find$_{past}$]", "[in]", "[*ref*(O: `athens`)]".

Different sentence plans may lead to more or fewer aggregation opportunities; e.g., sentences with the same verb are easier to aggregate. We use aggregation rules similar to those of Dalianis (1999), which operate on sentence plans and usually lead to shorter texts, as in the example below.

> Bancroft Chardonnay is a kind of Chardonnay. It is made in Bancroft. ⇒ Bancroft Chardonnay is a kind of Chardonnay made in Bancroft.

Let $s_1, \ldots, s_m$ be disjoint subsets of F, each containing 0 to n facts, with $m < n$. A single sentence is generated for each subset s_j by aggregating the sentences (more precisely, the sentence plans) expressing the facts of s_j.[3] An empty s_j generates no sentence, i.e., the resulting text can be at most m sentences long. Let us also define:

$$a_i = \begin{cases} 1, & \text{if fact } f_i \text{ is selected} \\ 0, & \text{otherwise} \end{cases} \tag{1}$$

$$l_{ikj} = \begin{cases} 1, & \text{if sentence plan } p_{ik} \text{ is used to express fact } f_i \text{, and } f_i \text{ is in subset } s_j \\ 0, & \text{otherwise} \end{cases} \tag{2}$$

$$b_{tj} = \begin{cases} 1, & \text{if element } e_t \text{ is used in subset } s_j \\ 0, & \text{otherwise} \end{cases} \tag{3}$$

and let B be the set of all the distinct elements (no duplicates) from all the available sentence plans that can express the facts of F. The length of an aggregated sentence resulting from a subset s_j can be roughly estimated by counting the distinct elements of the sentence plans that have been chosen to express the facts of s_j; elements that occur more than once in the chosen sentence plans of s_j are counted only once, because they will probably be expressed only once, due to aggregation.

Our objective function (4) maximizes the total importance of the selected facts (or simply the number of selected facts, if all facts are equally important), and minimizes the number of distinct elements in each subset s_j, i.e., the approximate length of the corresponding aggregated sentence; an alternative explanation is that by minimizing the number of distinct elements in each s_j, we favor subsets that aggregate well. By a and b we jointly denote all the a_i and b_{tj} variables. The two parts of the objective function are normalized to $[0, 1]$ by dividing by the total number of available facts $|F|$ and the number of subsets m times the total number of distinct elements $|B|$. We assume that the importance scores $imp(f_i)$ are provided by a separate component (Barzilay and Lapata, 2005; Demir et al., 2010) and range in $[0, 1]$. The parameters λ_1, λ_2 are used to tune the priority given to expressing many important facts vs.

[1] See `www.w3.org/TR/owl2-mapping-to-rdf/`.

[2] We actually convert the RDF triples to simpler *message triples*, so that each message triple can be easily expressed by a simple sentence, but we do not discuss this conversion here.

[3] All the sentences of every possible subset s_j can be aggregated, because all the sentences share the same subject, the class or individual being described. If multiple aggregation rules apply, we use the one that leads to a shorter text.

generating shorter texts; we set $\lambda_1 + \lambda_2 = 1$.

$$\max_{a,b} \lambda_1 \cdot \sum_{i=1}^{|F|} \frac{a_i \cdot imp(f_i)}{|F|} - \lambda_2 \cdot \sum_{j=1}^{m} \sum_{t=1}^{|B|} \frac{b_{tj}}{m \cdot |B|} \tag{4}$$

subject to:

$$a_i = \sum_{j=1}^{m} \sum_{k=1}^{|P_i|} l_{ikj}, \text{for } i = 1, \ldots, n \tag{5}$$

$$\sum_{e_t \in B_{ik}} b_{tj} \geq |B_{ik}| \cdot l_{ikj}, \text{for } \begin{array}{l} i = 1, \ldots, n \\ j = 1, \ldots, m \\ k = 1, \ldots, |P_i| \end{array} \tag{6}$$

$$\sum_{p_{ik} \in P(e_t)} l_{ikj} \geq b_{tj}, \text{for } \begin{array}{l} t = 1, \ldots, |B| \\ j = 1, \ldots, m \end{array} \tag{7}$$

$$\sum_{t=1}^{|B|} b_{tj} \leq B_{max}, \text{for } j = 1, \ldots, m \tag{8}$$

$$\sum_{k=1}^{|P_i|} l_{ikj} + \sum_{k'=1}^{|P_{i'}|} l_{i'k'j} \leq 1, \text{for } \begin{array}{l} j = 1, \ldots, m, \ i = 2, \ldots, n \\ i' = 1, \ldots, n-1; i \neq i' \\ section(f_i) \neq section(f_i') \end{array} \tag{9}$$

Constraint 5 ensures that for each selected fact, only one sentence plan in only one subset is selected; if a fact is not selected, no sentence plan for the fact is selected either. $|\sigma|$ denotes the cardinality of a set σ. In constraint 6, B_{ik} is the set of distinct elements e_t of the sentence plan p_{ik}. This constraint ensures that if p_{ik} is selected in a subset s_j, then all the elements of p_{ik} are also present in s_j. If p_{ik} is not selected in s_j, then some of its elements may still be present in s_j, if they appear in another selected sentence plan of s_j.

In constraint 7, $P(e_t)$ is the set of sentence plans that contain element e_t. If e_t is used in a subset s_j, then at least one of the sentence plans of $P(e_t)$ must also be selected in s_j. If e_t is not used in s_j, then no sentence plan of $P(e_t)$ may be selected in s_j. Lastly, constraint 8 limits the number of elements that a subset s_j can contain to a maximum allowed number B_{max}, in effect limiting the maximum length of an aggregated sentence.

We assume that each relation R has been manually mapped to a single *topical section*; e.g., relations expressing the color, body, and flavor of a wine may be grouped in one section, and relations about the wine's producer in another. The section of a fact $f_i = \langle S_i, R_i, O_i \rangle$ is the section of its relation R_i. Constraint 9 ensures that facts from different sections will not be placed in the same subset s_j, to avoid unnatural aggregations.

4 Experiments

We used NaturalOWL (Galanis and Androutsopoulos, 2007; Galanis et al., 2009; Androutsopoulos et al., 2013), an NLG system for OWL ontologies that relies on a pipeline of content selection, text planning, lexicalization, aggregation, referring expression generation, and surface realization components.[4] We modified the content selection, lexicalization, and aggregation components to use our ILP model, maintaining the aggregation rules of the original system. For referring expressions and surface realization, the new system, called ILPNLG, invokes the corresponding components of the original system. We use branch-and-cut to solve the ILP problems.[5]

The original system, hereafter called PIPELINE, assumes that each relation has been mapped to a topical section, as in ILPNLG. It also assumes that a manually specified order of the sections and the relations of each section is available, which is used by the text planner to order the selected facts (by their relations). The subsequent components of the pipeline are not allowed to change the order of the facts, and aggregation operates only on sentence plans of adjacent facts from the same section. In ILPNLG, the manually specified order of sections and relations is used to order the sentences of each subset s_j (before aggregating them), the aggregated sentences in each section (each aggregated sentence inherits the minimum order of its constituents), and the sections (with their sentences).

4.1 Experiments with the Wine Ontology

In a first set of experiments, we used the Wine Ontology, which had also been used in previous experiments with PIPELINE (Androutsopoulos et al., 2013). The ontology contains 63 wine classes, 52 wine individuals, a total of 238 classes and individuals (including wineries, regions, etc.), and 14 properties.[6] We kept the 2 topical sections, the ordering of sections and relations, and the sentence plans of the previous experiments, but we added more sentence plans to ensure that 3 sentence plans were available per relation. We generated English texts for the 52 wine individuals

[4] All the software and data that we used will be freely available from http://nlp.cs.aueb.gr/software.html. We use version 2 of NaturalOWL.

[5] We use the branch-and-cut implementation of GLPK with mixed integer rounding, mixed cover, and clique cuts; see sourceforge.net/projects/winglpk/.

[6] See www.w3.org/TR/owl-guide/wine.rdf.

of the ontology; we did not experiment with texts describing classes, because we could not think of multiple alternative sentence plans for many of their axioms. For each wine individual, there were 5 facts on average and a maximum of 6 facts. We set the importance scores $imp(f_i)$ of all the facts f_i to 1, to make the decisions of PIPELINE and ILPNLG easier to understand; both systems use the same importance scores. PIPELINE does not provide any mechanism to estimate the importance scores, assuming that they are provided manually.

PIPELINE has a parameter M specifying the maximum number of facts it is allowed to report per text. When M is smaller than the number of available facts ($|F|$) and all the facts are treated as equally important, as in our experiments, it selects randomly M of the available facts. We repeated the generation of PIPELINE's texts for the 52 individuals for $M = 2, 3, 4, 5, 6$. For each M, the texts of PIPELINE for the 52 individuals were generated three times, each time using one of the different alternative sentence plans of each relation. We also generated the texts using a variant of PIPELINE, dubbed PIPELINESHORT, which always selects the shortest (in elements) sentence plan among the available ones. In all cases, PIPELINE and PIPELINESHORT were allowed to form aggregated sentences containing up to $B_{max} = 22$ distinct elements, which was the number of distinct elements of the longest aggregated sentence in the previous experiments (Androutsopoulos et al., 2013), where PIPELINE was allowed to aggregate up to 3 original sentences.[7]

With ILPNLG, we repeated the generation of the texts of the 52 individuals using different values of λ_1 ($\lambda_2 = 1 - \lambda_1$), which led to texts expressing from zero to all of the available facts. We set the maximum number of fact subsets to $m = 3$, which was the maximum number of (aggregated) sentences in the texts of PIPELINE and PIPELINESHORT. Again, we set $B_{max} = 22$.

We compared ILPNLG to PIPELINE and PIPELINESHORT by measuring the average number of facts they reported divided by the average text length (in words). Figure 1 shows this ratio as a function of the average number of reported facts, along with 95% confidence intervals (of sample means). PIPELINESHORT achieved better results than PIPELINE, but the differences were small.

For $\lambda_1 < 0.2$, ILPNLG produces empty texts,

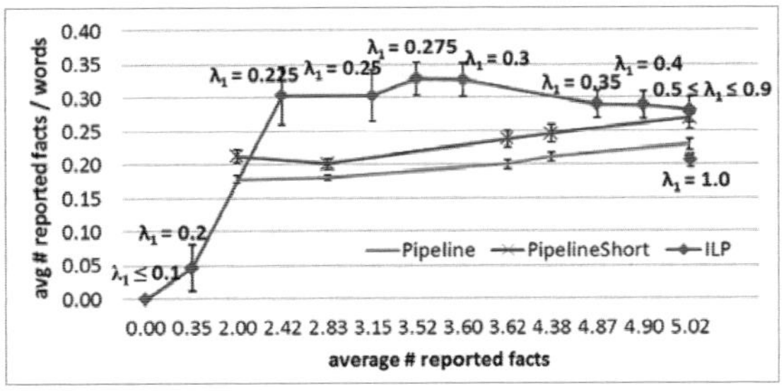

Figure 1: Facts/words of Wine Ontology texts.

because it focuses on minimizing the number of distinct elements of each text. For $\lambda_1 \geq 0.225$, it performs better than the other systems. For $\lambda_1 \approx 0.3$, it obtains the highest fact/words ratio by selecting the facts and sentence plans that lead to the most compressive aggregations. For greater values of λ_1, it selects additional facts whose sentence plans do not aggregate that well, which is why the ratio declines. For small numbers of facts, the two pipeline systems select facts and sentence plans that offer few aggregation opportunities; as the number of selected facts increases, some more aggregation opportunities arise, which is why the facts/words ratio of the two systems improves. In all the experiments, the ILP solver was very fast (average: 0.08 sec, worst: 0.14 sec per text).

We show below texts produced by PIPELINE ($M = 4$) and ILPNLG ($\lambda_1 = 0.3$).

PIPELINE: This is a strong Sauternes. It is made from Semillon grapes and it is produced by Chateau D'ychem.

ILPNLG: This is a strong Sauternes. It is made from Semillon grapes by Chateau D'ychem.

PIPELINE: This is a full Riesling and it has moderate flavor. It is produced by Volrad.

ILPNLG: This is a full sweet moderate Riesling.

In the first pair, PIPELINE uses different verbs for the grapes and producer, whereas ILPNLG uses the same verb, which leads to a more compressive aggregation; both texts describe the same wine and report 4 facts. In the second pair, ILPNLG has chosen to express the sweetness instead of the producer, and uses the same verb ("be") for all the facts, leading to a shorter sentence; again both texts describe the same wine and report 4 facts. In both examples, some facts are not aggregated because they belong in different sections.

We also wanted to investigate the effect that the higher facts/words ratio of ILPNLG has on the perceived quality of the generated texts, compared to the texts of the pipeline. We were concerned that the more compressive aggregations of ILPNLG

[7] We modified the two pipeline systems to count elements.

Criteria	PIPELINESHORT	ILPNLG
Sentence fluency	4.75 ± 0.21	**4.85** ± 0.10
Text structure	**4.94** ± 0.06	4.88 ± 0.14
Clarity	**4.77** ± 0.18	4.75 ± 0.15
Overall	4.52 ± 0.20	**4.60** ± 0.18

Table 1: Human scores for Wine Ontology texts.

might lead to sentences that sound less fluent or unnatural, though aggregation often helps produce more natural texts. We were also concerned that the more compact texts of ILPNLG might be perceived as being more difficult to understand (less clear) or less well-structured. To investigate these issues, we showed the $52 \times 2 = 104$ texts of PIPELINESHORT ($M = 4$) and ILPNLG ($\lambda_1 = 0.3$) to 6 computer science students not involved in the work of this article; they were all fluent, though not native, English speakers. Each one of the 104 texts was given to exactly one student. Each student was given approximately 9 randomly selected texts of each system. The OWL statements that the texts were generated from were not shown, and the students did not know which system had generated each text. Each student was shown all of his/her texts in random order, regardless of the system that generated them. The students were asked to score each text by stating how strongly they agreed or disagreed with statements S_1–S_3 below. A scale from 1 to 5 was used (1: strong disagreement, 3: ambivalent, 5: strong agreement).

(S_1) *Sentence fluency*: The sentences of the text are fluent, i.e., each sentence *on its own* is grammatical and sounds natural. When two or more smaller sentences are combined to form a single, longer sentence, the resulting longer sentence is also grammatical and sounds natural.

(S_2) *Text structure*: The order of the sentences is appropriate. The text presents information by moving reasonably from one topic to another.

(S_3) *Clarity*: The text is easy to understand, provided that the reader is familiar with basic wine terms.

The students were also asked to provide an overall score (1–5) per text. We did not score referring expressions, since both systems use the same component to generate them.

Table 1 shows the average scores of the two systems with 95% confidence intervals (of sample means). For each criterion, the best score is shown in bold. The sentence fluency and overall scores of ILPNLG are slightly higher than those of PIPELINESHORT, whereas PIPELINESHORT obtained a slightly higher score for text structure and clarity. The differences, however, are very small, especially in clarity, and there is no statistically significant difference between the two systems in any of the criteria.[8] Hence, there was no evidence in these experiments that the highest facts/words ratio of ILPNLG comes at the expense of lower perceived text quality. We investigated these issues further in a second set of experiments, discussed next, where the generated texts were longer.

4.2 Consumer Electronics experiments

In the second set of experiments, we used the Consumer Electronics Ontology, which had also been used in previous work with PIPELINE. The ontology comprises 54 classes and 441 individuals (e.g., printer types, paper sizes), but no information about particular products.[9] In previous work, 30 individuals (10 digital cameras, 10 camcorders, 10 printers) were added to the ontology; they were randomly selected from a publicly available dataset of 286 digital cameras, 613 camcorders, and 58 printers, whose instances comply with the Consumer Electronics Ontology.[10] We kept the 6 topical sections, the ordering of sections and relations, and the sentence plans of the previous work, but we added more sentence plans to ensure that 3 sentence plans were available for almost every relation; for some relations we could not think of enough sentence plans. Again, we set the importance scores of all the facts to 1.

We generated texts with PIPELINE and PIPELINESHORT for the 30 individuals, for $M = 3, 6, 9, \ldots, 21$. Again for each M, the texts of PIPELINE were generated three times, each time using one of the different alternative sentence plans of each relation. PIPELINE and PIPELINESHORT were allowed to form aggregated sentences containing up to $B_{max} = 39$ distinct elements, which was the number of distinct elements of the longest aggregated sentence in the previous work with this ontology, where PIPELINE was allowed to aggregate up to 3 original sentences. We also set $B_{max} = 39$ in ILPNLG.

There are 14 facts (F) on average and a maximum of 21 facts for each one of the 30 individuals, compared to the 5 facts on average and the maximum of 6 facts of the experiments with the Wine Ontology. Hence, the texts of the Consumer

[8]The confidence intervals do not overlap, and we also performed paired two-tailed t-tests ($\alpha = 0.05$) to check for statistical significance. In previous work, where judges were asked to score texts using the same criteria, inter-annotator agreement was strong (sample Pearson correlation $r \geq 0.91$).

[9]Ontology available from `www.ebusiness-unibw.org/ontologies/consumerelectronics/v1`.

[10]See `rdf4ecommerce.esolda.com/`.

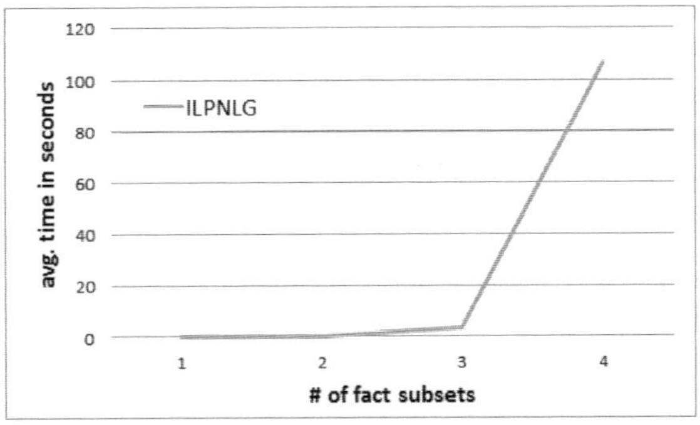

Figure 2: Average solver times for ILPNLG for different maximum numbers of fact subsets (m).

Electronics Ontology are much longer, when they report all the available facts. To generate texts for the 30 individuals with ILPNLG, we would have to set the maximum number of fact subsets to $m = 10$, which was the maximum number of (aggregated) sentences in the texts of PIPELINE and PIPELINESHORT. The number of variables of our ILP model, however, grows exponentially to m and the number of available facts $|F|$. Figure 2 shows the average time the ILP solver took for different values of m in the experiments with the Consumer Electronics ontology; the results are also averaged for $\lambda_1 = 0.4, 0.5, 0.6$ ($\lambda_2 = 1 - \lambda_1$). For $m = 4$, the solver took 1 minute and 47 seconds on average per text; recall that $|F|$ is also much larger now, compared to the experiments of the previous section. For $m = 5$, the solver was so slow that we aborted the experiment. Figure 3 shows the average solver time for different numbers of available facts $|F|$, for $m = 3$; in this case, we modified the set of available facts (F) of every individual to contain $3, 6, 9, 12, 15, 18, 21$ facts; the results are averaged for $\lambda_1 = 0.4, 0.5, 0.6$. Although the times of Fig. 3 also grow exponentially, they remain under 4 seconds, showing that the main problem for ILPNLG is m, the number of fact subsets, which is also the maximum allowed number of (aggregated) sentences of each text.

To be able to efficiently generate texts with larger m values, we use a variant of ILPNLG, called ILPNLGAPPROX, which considers each fact subset separately. ILPNLGAPPROX starts with the full set of available facts (F) and uses our ILP model (Section 3) with $m = 1$ to produce the first (aggregated) sentence of the text. It then removes the facts expressed by the first (aggregated) sentence from F, and uses the ILP model, again with

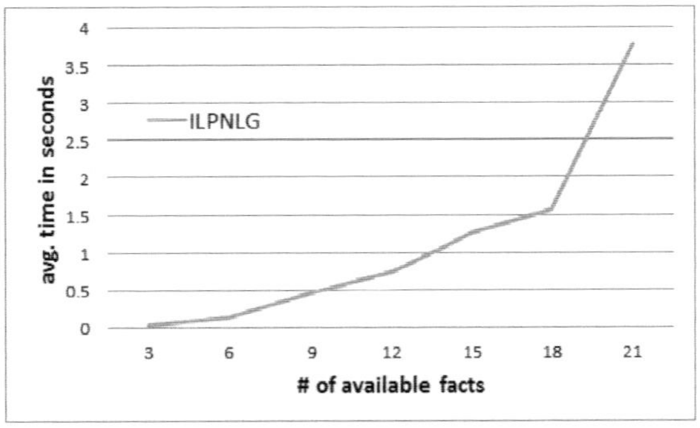

Figure 3: Average solver times for ILPNLG for different numbers of available facts ($|F|$) and $m = 3$.

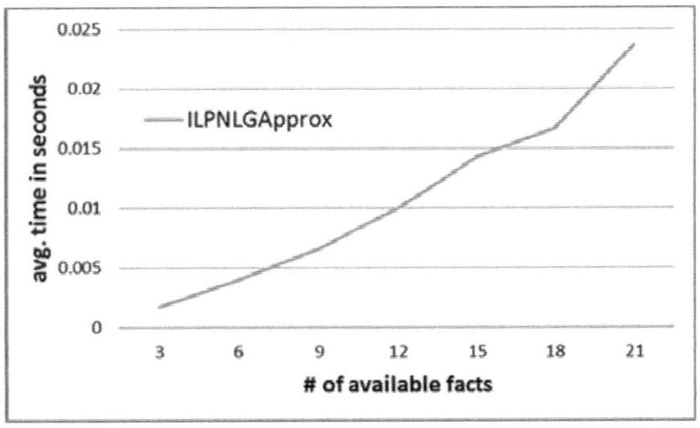

Figure 4: Avg. solver times for ILPNLGAPPROX for different max. numbers of fact subsets (m).

$m = 1$, to produce the second (aggregated) sentence etc. This process is repeated until we produce the maximum number of allowed aggregated sentences, or until we run out of facts. ILPNLGAPPROX is an approximation of ILPNLG, in the sense that it does not consider all the fact subsets jointly and, hence, does not guarantee finding a globally optimal solution for the entire text. Figures 4–5 show the average solver times of ILPNLGAPPROX for different values of m and $|F|$; all the other settings are as in Figures 2–3. The solver times of ILPNLGAPPROX grow approximately linearly to m and $|F|$ and are under 0.3 seconds in all cases.

Figure 6 shows the average facts/words ratio of ILPNLGAPPROX ($m = 10$), PIPELINE and PIPELINESHORT, along with 95% confidence intervals (of sample means), for the texts of the 30 individuals. Again, PIPELINESHORT achieves slightly better results than PIPELINE, but the differences are now smaller (cf. Fig. 1). ILPNLGAPPROX behaves very similarly to ILPNLG in the Wine Ontology experiments (cf. Fig. 1); for $\lambda_1 \leq 0.35$, it produces empty texts, while for $\lambda_1 \geq 0.4$ it performs better than the other systems. ILPNLGAPPROX obtains

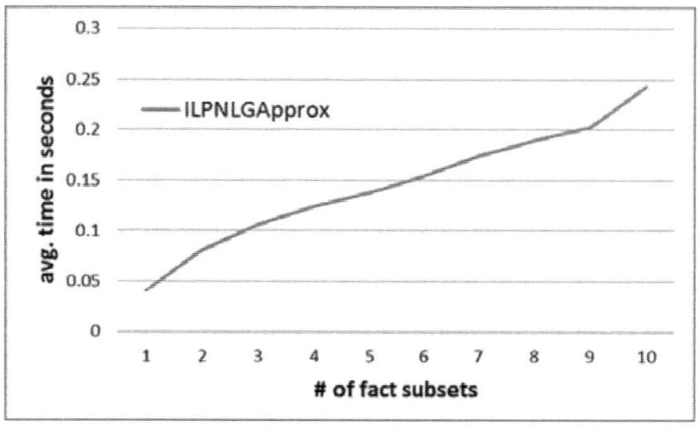

Figure 5: Avg. solver times for ILPNLGAPPROX for different $|F|$ values and $m = 3$.

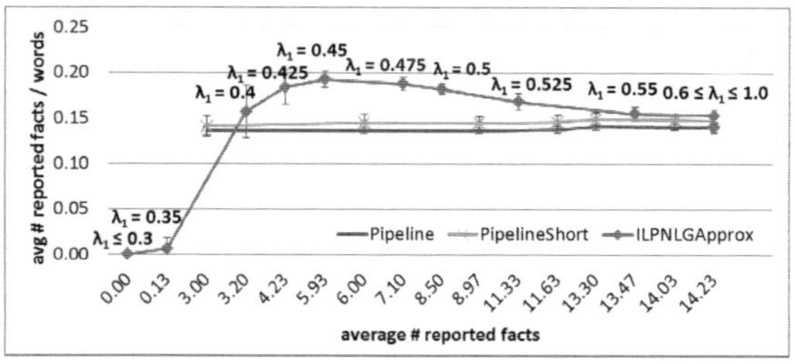

Figure 6: Facts/words for Consumer Electronics.

the highest facts/words ratio for $\lambda_1 = 0.45$, where it selects the facts and sentence plans that lead to the most compressive aggregations. For greater values of λ_1, it selects additional facts whose sentence plans do not aggregate that well, which is why the ratio declines. The two pipeline systems select facts and sentence plans that offer very few aggregation opportunities; as the number of selected facts increases, some more aggregation opportunities arise, which is why the facts/words ratio of the two systems improves slightly, though the improvement is now hardly noticeable.

We show below two example texts produced by PIPELINE ($M = 6$) and ILPNLGAPPROX ($\lambda_1 = 0.45$). Both texts report 6 facts, but ILPNLGAPPROX has selected facts and sentence plans that allow more compressive aggregations. Recall that we treat all the facts as equally important.

PIPELINE: Sony DCR-TRV270 requires minimum illumination of 4.0 lux and its display is 2.5 in. It features a sports scene mode, it includes a microphone and an IR remote control. Its weight is 780.0 grm.

ILPNLGAPPROX: Sony DCR-TRV270 has a microphone and an IR remote control. It is 98.0 mm high, 85.0 mm wide, 151.0 mm deep and it weighs 780.0 grm.

We showed the $30 \times 2 = 60$ texts of PIPELINESHORT ($M = 6$) and ILPNLGAPPROX ($\lambda_1 = 0.45$) to the same 6 students, as in Section 4.1. Again, each text was given to exactly one student. Each student was given approximately 5 randomly selected texts of each system. The OWL statements that the texts were generated from were not shown, and the students did not know which system had generated each text. Each student was shown all of his/her texts in random order, regardless of the system that generated them. The students were asked to score each text by stating how strongly they agreed or disagreed with statements S_1–S_3, as in Section 4.1. They were also asked to provide an overall score (1–5) per text.

Criteria	PIPELINESHORT	ILPNLGAPPROX
Sentence fluency	4.50 ± 0.30	$\mathbf{4.87} \pm 0.12$
Text structure	4.33 ± 0.36	$\mathbf{4.73} \pm 0.22$
Clarity	4.53 ± 0.29	$\mathbf{4.97 \pm 0.06}$
Overall	4.10 ± 0.31	$\mathbf{4.73 \pm 0.16}$

Table 2: Human scores for Consumer Electronics.

Table 2 shows the average scores of the two systems with 95% confidence intervals (of sample means). For each criterion, the best score is shown in bold; the confidence interval of the best score is also shown in bold, if it does not overlap with the confidence interval of the other system. Unlike the Wine Ontology experiments, the scores of our ILP approach are now higher than those of the pipeline in all of the criteria, and the differences are also larger, though the differences are statistically significant only for clarity and overall quality.[11] We attribute these differences to the fact that the texts are now longer and the sentence plans more varied, which often makes the texts of the pipeline sound verbose and, hence, more difficult to follow, compared to the more compact texts of ILPNLGAPPROX, which sound more concise.

Overall, the human scores of the experiments with the two ontologies suggest that the higher facts/words ratio of our ILP approach does *not* come at the expense of lower perceived text quality. On the contrary, the texts of the ILP approach may be perceived as clearer and overall better than those of the pipeline, when the texts are longer.

5 Conclusions

We presented an ILP model of content selection, lexicalization, and aggregation that jointly considers the possible choices in the three stages, to

[11] When two confidence intervals do not overlap, the difference is statistically significant. When they overlap, the difference may still be statistically significant; we performed additional paired two-tailed t-tests ($\alpha = 0.05$) in those cases.

avoid greedy local decisions and produce more compact texts. The model has been embedded in NaturalOWL, a NLG system for OWL ontologies, which used a pipeline architecture in its original form. Experiments with two ontologies confirmed that our approach leads to expressing more facts per word, with no deterioration in the perceived text quality; the ILP approach may actually lead to texts perceived as clearer and overall better, compared to the pipeline, when there are many facts to express. We also presented an approximation of our ILP model, which allows longer texts to be generated efficiently. We plan to extend our model to include text planning, referring expression generation, and mechanisms to obtain importance scores.

Acknowledgments

This research has been co-financed by the European Union (European Social Fund – ESF) and Greek national funds through the Operational Program "Education and Lifelong Learning" of the National Strategic Reference Framework (NSRF) – Research Funding Program: Heracleitus II. Investing in knowledge society through the European Social Fund.

References

E. Althaus, N. Karamanis, and A. Koller. 2004. Computing locally coherent discourses. In *42nd Annual Meeting of ACL*, pages 399–406, Barcelona, Spain.

I. Androutsopoulos, G. Lampouras, and D. Galanis. 2013. Generating natural language descriptions from OWL ontologies: the NaturalOWL system. Technical report, Natural Language Processing Group, Department of Informatics, Athens University of Economics and Business.

G. Antoniou and F. van Harmelen. 2008. *A Semantic Web primer*. MIT Press, 2nd edition.

F. Baader, D. Calvanese, D.L. McGuinness, D. Nardi, and P.F. Patel-Schneider, editors. 2002. *The Description Logic Handbook*. Cambridge Univ. Press.

R. Barzilay and M. Lapata. 2005. Collective content selection for concept-to-text generation. In *HLT-EMNLP*, pages 331–338, Vancouver, BC, Canada.

R. Barzilay and M. Lapata. 2006. Aggregation via set partitioning for natural language generation. In *HLT-NAACL*, pages 359–366, New York, NY.

A. Belz. 2008. Automatic generation of weather forecast texts using comprehensive probabilistic generation-space models. *Natural Language Engineering*, 14(4):431–455.

T. Berg-Kirkpatrick, D. Gillick, and D. Klein. 2011. Jointly learning to extract and compress. In *49th Meeting of ACL*, pages 481–490, Portland, OR.

T. Berners-Lee, J. Hendler, and O. Lassila. 2001. The Semantic Web. *Scientific American*, May:34–43.

K. Bontcheva. 2005. Generating tailored textual summaries from ontologies. In *2nd European Semantic Web Conf.*, pages 531–545, Heraklion, Greece.

J. Clarke and M. Lapata. 2008. Global inference for sentence compression: An integer linear programming approach. *Journal of Artificial Intelligence Research*, 1(31):399–429.

H. Dalianis. 1999. Aggregation in natural language generation. *Comput. Intelligence*, 15(4):384–414.

L. Danlos. 1984. Conceptual and linguistic decisions in generation. In *10th COLING*, pages 501–504, Stanford, CA.

S. Demir, S. Carberry, and K.F. McCoy. 2010. A discourse-aware graph-based content-selection framework. In *6th Int. Nat. Lang. Generation Conference*, pages 17–25, Trim, Co. Meath, Ireland.

D. Galanis and I. Androutsopoulos. 2007. Generating multilingual descriptions from linguistically annotated OWL ontologies: the NaturalOWL system. In *11th European Workshop on Natural Lang. Generation*, pages 143–146, Schloss Dagstuhl, Germany.

D. Galanis, G. Karakatsiotis, G. Lampouras, and I. Androutsopoulos. 2009. An open-source natural language generator for OWL ontologies and its use in Protégé and Second Life. In *12th Conf. of the European Chapter of ACL (demos)*, Athens, Greece.

D. Galanis, G. Lampouras, and I. Androutsopoulos. 2012. Extractive multi-document summarization with ILP and Support Vector Regression. In *COLING*, pages 911–926, Mumbai, India.

B.C. Grau, I. Horrocks, B. Motik, B. Parsia, P. Patel-Schneider, and U. Sattler. 2008. OWL 2: The next step for OWL. *Web Semantics*, 6:309–322.

I. Konstas and M. Lapata. 2012a. Concept-to-text generation via discriminative reranking. In *50th Annual Meeting of ACL*, pages 369–378, Jeju Island, Korea.

I. Konstas and M. Lapata. 2012b. Unsupervised concept-to-text generation with hypergraphs. In *HLT-NAACL*, pages 752–761, Montréal, Canada.

P. Kuznetsova, V. Ordonez, A. Berg, T. Berg, and Y. Choi. 2012. Collective generation of natural image descriptions. In *50th Annual Meeting of ACL*, pages 359–368, Jeju Island, Korea.

P. Liang, M. Jordan, and D. Klein. 2009. Learning semantic correspondences with less supervision. In *47th Meeting of ACL and 4th AFNLP*, pages 91–99, Suntec, Singapore.

S.F. Liang, R. Stevens, D. Scott, and A. Rector. 2011. Automatic verbalisation of SNOMED classes using OntoVerbal. In *13th Conf. AI in Medicine*, pages 338–342, Bled, Slovenia.

T. Marciniak and M. Strube. 2005. Beyond the pipeline: Discrete optimization in NLP. In *9th Conference on Computational Natural Language Learning*, pages 136–143, Ann Arbor, MI.

R. McDonald. 2007. A study of global inference algorithms in multi-document summarization. In *European Conference on Information Retrieval*, pages 557–564, Rome, Italy.

C. Mellish and J.Z. Pan. 2008. Natural language directed inference from ontologies. *Artificial Intelligence*, 172:1285–1315.

C. Mellish and X. Sun. 2006. The Semantic Web as a linguistic resource: opportunities for nat. lang. generation. *Knowledge Based Systems*, 19:298–303.

E. Reiter and R. Dale. 2000. *Building Natural Language Generation Systems*. Cambridge Univ. Press.

R. Schwitter, K. Kaljurand, A. Cregan, C. Dolbear, and G. Hart. 2008. A comparison of three controlled nat. languages for OWL 1.1. In *4th OWL Experiences and Directions Workshop*, Washington DC.

R. Schwitter. 2010. Controlled natural languages for knowledge representation. In *23rd COLING*, pages 1113–1121, Beijing, China.

N. Shadbolt, T. Berners-Lee, and W. Hall. 2006. The Semantic Web revisited. *IEEE Intell. Systems*, 21:96–101.

M.A. Walker, O. Rambow, and M. Rogati. 2001. Spot: A trainable sentence planner. In *2nd Annual Meeting of NAACL*, pages 17–24, Pittsburgh, PA.

S. Williams, A. Third, and R. Power. 2011. Levels of organization in ontology verbalization. In *13th European Workshop on Natural Lang. Generation*, pages 158–163, Nancy, France.

K. Woodsend and M. Lapata. 2012. Multiple aspect summarization using ILP. In *EMNLP-CoNLL*, pages 233–243, Jesu Island, Korea.

Generating and Interpreting Referring Expressions as Belief State Planning and Plan Recognition *

Dustin A. Smith
MIT Media Lab
E15-358; 20 Ames St.
Cambridge, MA USA
dustin@media.mit.edu

Henry Lieberman
MIT Media Lab
E15-320F; 20 Ames St.
Cambridge, MA USA
lieber@media.mit.edu

Abstract

Planning-based approaches to reference provide a uniform treatment of linguistic decisions, from content selection to lexical choice. In this paper, we show how the issues of lexical ambiguity, vagueness, unspecific descriptions, ellipsis, and the interaction of subsective modifiers can be expressed using a belief-state planner modified to support context-dependent actions. Because the number of distinct denotations it searches grows doubly-exponentially with the size of the referential domain, we present representational and search strategies that make generation and interpretation tractable.

1 Introduction

Planning-based approaches[1] to reference are appealing because they package a broad range of linguistic decisions into actions that can be used for both generation and interpretation. In section 2, we present linguistic issues and discuss their implications for designing planning domains and search algorithms. In section 3, we describe AIGRE,[2] our belief space planner, and explain how it efficiently handles the issues from section 2. Lastly, we demonstrate AIGRE's output for a suite of generation and interpretation tasks, and walk through a trace of an interpretation task.

1.1 The two linguistic reference tasks

A linguistic act of **referring** aims to communicate the identity of an object, agent, event or collection thereof to an audience. Depending on the agent's dialogue role, referring involves one of two tasks. The speaker completes a **referring expression generation (REG)** task: given a *context set* and a designated member of it called the *target set*, he produces a *referring expression* that allows the listener to isolate the target from the rest of the elements in the context set, called the *distractors* (Dale and Reiter, 1995). A listener completes a **referring expression interpretation (REI)** task: given a referring expression and an assumed context set, her goal is to infer the targets that the speaker intended.

1.2 Reference generation as planning

Many approaches to REG (see (Krahmer and van Deemter, 2012) for an overview) have focused exclusively on the sub-task of **content determination**: given context and target sets, they search for content that distinguishes the targets from the distractors. This content is then passed to the next module in an NLG pipeline (c.f. (Reiter, 1994)) to ultimately become a noun phrase embedded in a larger construct.

These "pipeline" architectures prevent information from being shared between different layers of linguistic analysis, contrary to evidence that the layers interact (Altmann and Steedman, 1988; Danlos and Namer, 1988; Stone and Webber, 1998; Krahmer and Theune, 2002; Horacek, 2004). As an alternative, one can take an integrated "lexicalized approach," following (Stone et al., 2003; Koller and Stone, 2007; Garoufi and Koller, 2010; Koller et al., 2010), in which each lexical unit's syntactic, semantic, and pragmatic contributions are represented as a *lexical entry*.

Lexicalized approaches presume that lexical entries can be designed to contain all of the syntactic and semantic ingredients required to synthesize a phrase or sentence. As such, the REG problem is reduced to choosing (i.e., content selection *and* lexical choice) and serializing lexical

We thank Nicolas Bravo and Yin Fu Chen for their contributions to AIGRE; the three anonymous reviewers for their comments; and the sponsors of the MIT Media lab.

[1]Throughout this paper planning is framed as a heuristic search problem.

[2]**A**utomatic **i**nterpretation and **g**eneration of **r**eferring **e**xpressions. In French, it means "sour".

units (putting them into a flat sequence), which bears strong similarities to **automated planning** (Ghallab et al., 2004). Automated planners try to find *plans* (sequences of actions), given (1) a fixed *planning domain* that describes how the relevant aspects of the world are changed by actions, and (2) a *problem instance*: a description of the initial state and the desired goal states.

For planning-based approaches to reference, the set of actions defined by the planning domain is analogous to a *lexicon*: each action corresponds to a lexical unit and is responsible for defining its semantic effects, along with the local syntactic and compositional constraints that are relevant to the lexical unit (Appelt, 1985; Heeman and Hirst, 1995; Koller and Stone, 2007; Koller et al., 2010; Garoufi and Koller, 2011).

1.3 Automated planning as heuristic search

When solving an instance of a planning problem, planners internally generate a directed graph called a **planning graph**, where the nodes represent hypothetical states and the labeled edges correspond to actions that represent valid transitions between the states. A planning domain and an initial state thus characterize an *implicit* graph of all the possible states and transitions between them, which is usually infeasible to enumerate. To avoid constructing parts of the planning graph that are irrelevant to particular problem, planning tasks are often solved using heuristic search (Bonet and Geffner, 2001), which is the same framework underlying popular approaches to content selection (Bohnet and Dale, 2005).[3] Heuristic search is useful for balancing costs (e.g. the cost of a given word) against benefits (e.g. meeting the communication goals): lower-cost[4] solutions are inherently preferred. The effectiveness of heuristic search is determined by the search algorithm and **heuristic function**, which gives a numerical estimation of a given state's distance to a goal state, $h(\mathsf{s}) \rightarrow [0, 1]$, that guides the search algorithm toward states that have a lower estimated distance to a goal.

The automated planning community has developed domain-independent techniques for automatically deriving a heuristic function from the structure of a planning domain, provided it is encoded a certain way. These approaches solve a simplified version of the original planning problem, calculate each generated state's minimal distance to a goal, and then use that distance as a lower-bound estimate in the heuristic function for the original problem (Bonet et al., 1997; Hoffmann, 2001).

(Koller and Petrick, 2011; Koller and Hoffmann, 2010) applied domain-independent planners toward REG, but found them "too slow to be useful in real NLG applications." It is important to note, however, that their results were for a specific implementation of a planning domain and set of heuristic search techniques, of which there are many variations (Edelkamp and Schroedl, 2011). For example, (Koller and Hoffmann, 2010) later reported being able to speed a planner by making its action proposal function more restrictive.

1.4 Interpretation as plan recognition

If generating a sentence can be modeled as a planning problem, then interpretation can be modeled as **plan recognition** (Heeman and Hirst, 1995; Geib and Steedman, 2006). Plan recognition can be seen as an "inversion" the planning problem, and solved using planning techniques (Baker et al., 2007; Ramírez and Geffner, 2010): Given an initial state (context set), a sequence of partially observed actions (words), what are the most likely goals (interpretations)?

Moreover, addressing both generation and interpretation in tandem places a strong constraint on how the lexicon can be designed—an otherwise underconstrained knowledge engineering problem. Because the same planning domain (lexicon) is used for multiple problem instances, a relevant evaluation of a planning-based approach is its **coverage** of a range of various linguistic input (for REI tasks) and output (for REG tasks). One goal of this paper is to analyze several problematic referring expressions and draw conclusions from how they can be used to guide planning-based approaches to REG and REI.

2 Problems for Referring Expressions

In this section, we describe several linguistic issues using example referring expressions that are applied to two visual referential domains: KINDLE (Figure 1) and CIRCLE (Figure 2).

Imagine you are a clerk selling the *Amazon Kindles* in Figure 1. Three separate customers ask you

[3]FULL BREVITY ALGORITHM is simply breadth-first search; GREEDY ALGORITHM is best-first search; and the INCREMENTAL ALGORITHM is a best-first where actions are sorted by preferences (Bohnet and Dale, 2005)

[4]If a plan's cost is just its length, heuristic search will bake-in the brevity sub-maxim of Grice's Cooperative Principle (Dale and Reiter, 1995).

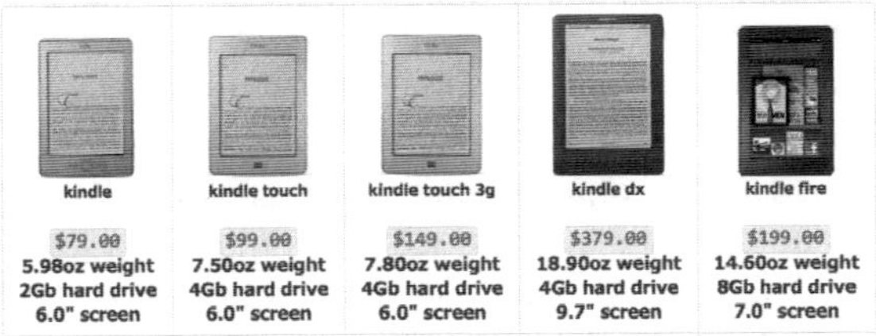

Figure 1: The KINDLE referential domain containing 5 items: k_1, k_2, k_3, k_4 and k_5.

to pass them:

(R1) *the big one*

(R2) *the inexpensive ones*

(R3) *a kindle touch*

2.1 The problem of lexical ambiguity

The problem with the referring expression (R1) is that it contains **lexical ambiguity**: did the customer intend the sense *big*$_1$, which modifies the size attribute, or *big*$_2$, which modifies the hard_drive.size attribute? Although one is much more likely, they are both mutually exclusive possibilities $[\![the\ big\ one]\!] = \{k_4\} \oplus \{k_5\}$.

What does this mean for planning-based approaches to REG and REI? For generation, it means that some words can cause the listener to draw multiple interpretations—but only in certain contexts (which provides an example of how word meanings draw from the context set). For interpretation, this means that we need a way to represent conflicting interpretations; and, if there are multiple interpretations for a given observed plan, we need a way to pick among the alternative interpretations.

2.2 The problem of gradable adjectives

Referring expression (R2) does not contain lexical ambiguity; however, it does suffer from **vagueness** as a result of having a gradable adjective, "inexpensive," in the positive form modifying a plural noun, "ones." Vagueness is problematic because it can lead to different interpretations depending on how the listener determines whether a referent is/a cluster of referents are INEXPENSIVE or $\neg$INEXPENSIVE (van Deemter, 2010). If we assume vagueness comes down to the interpreter inferring the speaker's implicit *standard*—a specific value of Price as a cut off, we can exhaust all possibilities by considering all unique prices. At one extreme, *only* the cheapest Kindle is inexpensive, at the other extreme *all* of the Kindles are inexpensive (i.e. the comparison class is a proper superset of the KINDLE domain): (R2) has four distinct denotations: $[\![the\ inexpensive\ ones]\!] = \{k_1, k_2\} \oplus \{k_1, k_2, k_3\} \oplus \{k_1, k_2, k_3, k_5\} \oplus \{k_1, k_2, k_3, k_5, k_4\}$. Like ambiguity, the use of a vague lexical unit can cause multiple distinct interpretations, and these outcomes are a function of the available options in the context set at the time the lexical unit is used.

2.3 The problem of unspecific descriptions

Referring expression (R3) is problematic because there are two possible denotations $[\![a\ kindle\ touch]\!] = \{k_2\} \vee \{k_3\}$[5] but in a way that differs subtly from having two mutex interpretations like in (R1). The indefinite article *"a"* indicates that the speaker has not only communicated a description that matches multiple targets, but also the authority to choose on his behalf. Either $\{k_2\}$ or $\{k_3\}$ is acceptable. For planning-based approaches, this means that we should be able to represent *a choice* between multiple alternative targets in an interpretation, and distinguish it from the mutex alternatives created by vagueness and ambiguity.

2.4 The problem of word ordering

This and the next problem use this CIRCLE reference domain for their examples:

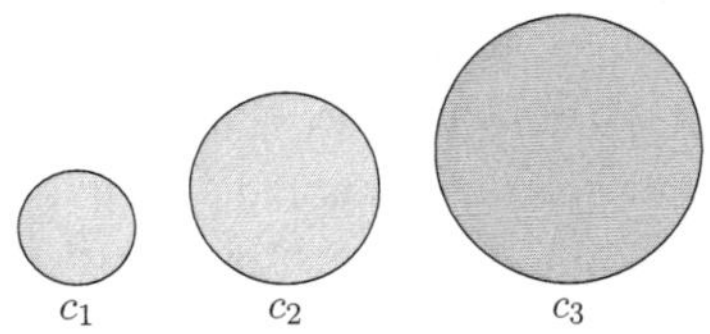

Figure 2: The CIRCLE referential domain.

Given the visual scene above, how would you interpret the following referring expressions?

(R4) *the biggest green shape*

(R5) *the second biggest green circle*

(R6) *the biggest*

(R7) *the first one*

[5] Our use of the disjunction operator here is non-standard, but we are not familiar of alternative notation for this distinction.

By incrementally evaluating each word in the sequence (R4), at the second word we have (R6) $[\![$*"the biggest"*$]\!] = \{c_3\}$. If every word's meanings were combined by intersecting their denotations, adding the next word, $[\![$*"green"*$]\!] = \{c_1\} \vee \{c_2\} \vee \{c_1, c_2\}$, would denote nothing: $[\![$*"the biggest"*$]\!] \cap [\![$*"green"*$]\!] = \emptyset$.

An incremental planning system should be able to handle the non-monotonicity created by these so-called subsective[6] adjectives: (R4) should yield an interpretation that is not included in (R6), even though (R6) is a prefix of (R4). If the model of REI aims to reflect human abilities, it should be able to incrementally process the words and switch between disjoint interpretations in real time, as the psycholinguistic research suggests (Altmann and Steedman, 1988; Tanenhaus, 2007).

Now, consider when multiple subsective adjectives occur before a noun, as in (R5). Does "second biggest"[7] modify both $[\![$*"green circle"*$]\!]$ or just $[\![$*"circle"*$]\!]$? This depends on who is interpreting: when we asked 108 self-reported native English speakers on Mechanical Turk to interpret (R5) *"the second biggest green circle"* the uncertainty was high, but $\{c_1\}$ was favored over $\{c_2\}$ by 3:2 odds. An REI must decide whether it interprets on behalf of an individual or population; and REG approaches may want to avoid such expressions that can lead to conflicting interpretations.

The issues raised by subsective adjectives can be seen as symptoms of a more general problem: that of deciding how to combine the meanings of individual lexical units. This is the responsibility of a syntactic theory; its duty is to describe how the combinatoric constraints on surface forms relates to the "evaluation order" of their semantic parts. For planning-based approaches, the syntactic theory should be *incremental*, capable of producing an interpretation at any stage of processing, and *invertible*, capable of being used in generation and interpretation.

2.5 The problem of ellipsis

(R6) is missing a noun, and in (R7), *"the first one,"* the ordinal "first" appears without a gradable adjective. We take these to be instances of **ellipsis**: when the meaning of a word is present but its surface form is omitted. In our view, these expressions should be interpreted as:

(R6') *the biggest [one$_{NN}$]*

(R7') *the first [leftmost$_{JJS}$] one*

For planning-based approaches to REI, accommodating the phenomenon of ellipsis involves inferring missing actions—interleaving the partially[8] observed actions of the speaker with abductively inferred actions of the listener (Hobbs et al., 1993; Benotti, 2010). For a REG, this means that the speaker can decide to elide some surface forms under certain conditions—such as if the listener is expected to infer it from context.

3 AIGRE: a belief-state planning approach to REI and REG

We used these problematic referring expressions to guide the design of our belief-state planner, AIGRE. Both REG and REI tasks begin with an *initial belief state* about a referential domain. In addition, the REI task is given a *referring expression* as input, and the REG task is given a *target set*.

3.1 Representing states (interpretations) as beliefs

We draw an analogy between the representation for an interpretation in a reference task and the concept of a belief state from artificial intelligence. A **belief state** characterizes a state of uncertainty about some lower layer, such as the world or another belief state. The standard representation of a belief state is the power set of the states in the lower layer, $b = \mathcal{P}(\mathcal{W})$, containing $2^{|\mathcal{W}|}$ members, or more generally as a probability distribution, $b = p(\mathcal{W})$, representing degree of belief.

Given a referential domain, R, REG systems that can refer to sets (van Deemter, 2000; Stone, 2000; Horacek, 2004) explore a hypothesis space containing $2^{|R|} - 1$ denotations, which is representationally equivalent to a belief state about the hypothesis space of only singleton referents. In our

[6] Characterizing adjectives set-theoretically, (Siegel, 1976; Partee, 1995) contrasted **intersective** and **subsective** meanings. Unlike intersective adjectives, the subsective adjectives cannot be defined independently of their nouns.

[7] The two words *"second biggest"* are treated as a single modifier: just as adjectives can modify nouns, ordinals like "second" modify superlatives like "biggest," changing its meaning so that it skips over the first biggest.

[8] The actions are not fully observed because of ellipsis and, as we have seen with vagueness and ambiguity, different *senses* of a word can produce the same surface form of the lexical unit.

case, we want to be able to represent multiple interpretations about sets (due to unspecific descriptions, vagueness and ambiguity) so our hypothesis space contains $2^{2^{|R|-1}} - 1$ interpretations. This state-space grows large quick: for the CIRCLE domain, where $|R| = 3$, there are 127 denotations; while for KINDLE, where $|R| = 5$, there are over two billion.

Fortunately, there are ways to avoid this double-exponent. First, a belief state uses *lazy evaluation* to generate its contents: the members of the power set of the referential domain that are consistent with its intensional description and arity constraints (more details in section 3.1.1).

Second, the base exponent is avoided altogether, as we derive it by aggregating states from the planning graph. The initial belief state, one of complete uncertainty, implicitly represents $2^{|R|} - 1$ possible target sets: it is the branching of non-deterministic actions that gives rise to the first exponent (due to lexical ambiguity and vagueness; see 3.2). This gives a clear way to distinguish unspecific interpretations (when the listener has a choice over multiple targets) from the other mutually exclusive targets (choices that were artifacts of the interpretation process): If two candidate target sets belong to the same belief state, then they are the result of unspecificity; whereas, if they are in different belief states, then they are mutually exclusive. For example, a REI procedure may produce two belief states as results: $b_x = \{t_1\} \vee \{t_2\} \vee \{t_3\}$ and $b_y = \{t_1, t_2, t_3\}$. From this, we conclude its denotation is: $(\{t_1\} \vee \{t_2\} \vee \{t_3\}) \oplus \{t_1, t_2, t_3\}$.

In the field of automated planning, belief-state planning using heuristic search (Bonet and Geffner, 2000; Hoffmann and Brafman, 2005) has been used to relax some assumptions of classical planning, such as the requirement that the problem instance contains a single (known) initial state, and that each action in the planning domain only changes the state in a single (deterministic) way. Belief state planners allow one action to have multiple effects, and instead of finding linear plans, they output plan trees that describe which action the agent should take contingent upon each action's possible outcomes.

Furthermore, because a belief state represents an interpretation, we can stop and inspect the search procedure at any point and we will have a complete interpretation; thus, achieving the incremental property we desired.

3.1.1 Belief state implementation details

The key responsibilities of a belief state are to represent and detect equivalent or inconsistent information at the intensional level. Its function is to aggregate all actions' informational content and detect whether a partial information update is inconsistent or would cause the interpretation to be invalid (i.e., have no members). In AIGRE, belief states are represented as a collection of objects, called `cells`,[9] which hold partial information and manage the consistency of information updates. AIGRE's belief states contain the following components:

- target an attribute-value matrix describing properties that a referent in the domain must entail to be considered consistent with the belief state.
- distractor an attribute-value matrix describing properties that a referent in the domain *must not* entail to be considered consistent with the belief state. This allows AIGRE to represent negative assertions, such as *"the not big one"* or *"all but the left one."*
- target_arity an interval (initially $[0, \infty)$) representing the valid sizes of a target set.
- contrast_arity an interval (initially $[0, \infty)$) representing the valid sizes of the difference in the sizes of a target set and the set containing all consistent referents.
- part_of_speech a symbol (initially S) representing the previous action's part of speech.
- deferred_effects a list (initially empty) that holds effect functions and the trigger part_of_speech symbol that indicates when the function will be executed on the belief state.

A belief state does not have to store all $2^{|R|} - 1$ target sets; it can lazily produce its full denotation only when needed. It does this by generating the power set of all elements in the referential domain that entail the target description, do not entail the distractor, and are consistent with two arity constraints: The target_arity property requires the target set's size to be within its interval, and it is used to model number agreement and cardinal modifiers. The contrast_arity requires that the *difference* between a given target set and the largest target set in the belief state (the number of consistent referents) is a size within its interval, and is used to model the semantics of determiners and qualifiers.

Actions operate on AIGRE's belief states, yet the belief state influences much of the behavior of

[9]The idea behind `cells` comes from the *propagator framework* of (Radul and Sussman, 2009) and our Python library is available from `http://eventteam.github.io/beliefs/`

the action's effects. As we will see in the next section, the contents of a belief state determine the number of effects an action will yield, the specific values within the effect's belief (using late binding), and whether or not the update is valid.

3.2 Representing context-dependent actions

AIGRE's lexicon is comprised of lexical units—actions that can change belief states. Each action/word is an instantiation of an action class and has (1) a syntactic category (part of speech), (2) a lexical unit, (3) a specific semantic contribution—determined in part by its syntactic category, (4) a fixed lexical cost, and (5) a computed effect cost. Actions are defined by instantiating class instances, for example:

```
GradableAdj('big', attr='size')
CrispAdj('big', attr='size', val=[5,∞))
```

When instantiating an action, the first argument is its lexeme in its *root form*; the class' initialization method uses the root lexeme to also instantiate variant actions for each derivative lexical unit (e.g. plural, comparative, superlative, etc).

3.2.1 Actions yield effect functions, not states

Actions in AIGRE receive a belief state as input and lazily generate 0 or more effect functions as output, depending on the contents of the belief state. Unlike conventional planners, actions produce effect functions rather than successor states because (1) it allows us to defer the execution of an effect, as we describe in 3.2.3, (2) generating effect functions is fast; copying belief states is slow, and (3) actions can annotate the yielded effect functions with an *estimated cost*, giving the search process an additional degree of control over what successor state is created next. We view an action that does not yield any effects to be analogous to a traditional planning domain's action that does not having its preconditions satisfied; unlike traditional domains, an action's behavior is opaque until it is explicitly applied to a belief state.

3.2.2 Ambiguity and vagueness using non-deterministic actions

Gradable adjectives yield an effect for each same-named attribute[10] (lexical ambiguity) for each value (vagueness) in the parent belief state's consistent referents. For example, given the action BIG_{JJ} applied to an initial belief state about the KINDLE referential domain, b_0, the action yields a separate effect for each unique value of each unique attribute-path that terminates with size for all consistent referents. In this case, the referents have two size properties, size and hard_drive.size, each with 3 distinct values, so the BIG_{JJ} action applied to b_0 yields 6 effects in total: $\text{BIG}(b_0) \rightarrow e_0, e_1 \ldots e_6$. When executed on a belief state, e_0 would add the nested property size to its target property (if it doesn't already exist) and then attempt to merge it with an interval beginning at the largest size value[11] of a referent consistent with b_0: $[7, \infty)$.

Effects for vague and ambiguous actions proliferate: if the adjective BIG has s senses, and there are r referents compatible with the belief state, then it can yield as many as $s \times r$ effect functions. In section 3.3.1, we will show how the search algorithm can mitigate this complexity by conservatively generating effects.

3.2.3 Effects can be deferred until a trigger

We view subsective adjectives (see 2.4) as having their context-specific meaning evaluated within the scope of the noun's meaning (i.e., after evaluating the noun). To achieve this without changing the words' surface orderings, each adjective's effects are deferred until a syntactic trigger: when the belief state's part_of_speech indicates it has reached a noun state. Deferred effect functions are stored in the belief state's deferred_effects queue along with a trigger. This solution makes the search harder: deferred actions have no immediate effect on the belief state, and so (in the eyes of the search algorithm) they do not move the belief toward the search goal.

3.3 Controlling search through belief states

A heuristic search planner must specify how to determine which state to expand next, and how to determine when a search process has succeeded, i.e., a **goal test function**. AIGRE approaches the first issue in a variety of ways: by (a) using a **heuristic function** to rank the candidate nodes so that the most promising nodes are expanded first (b) using an **action proposal function** to restrict the actions used to expand the current node (c) using a greedy **search algorithm** that does not generate all successor nodes.

Note that although both REG and REI tasks involve choosing belief-changing actions that map

[10] Ordered by breadth-first traversal of targets' properties.

[11] Gradable (vague) values are represented with intervals, where one extreme is the *standard*.

an initial belief state onto a target belief state, the two search processes are subject to very different constraints. With generation, the desired semantic content is fixed and the linguistic choices are open; while for interpretation, the linguistic contents are relatively fixed and the semantic possibilities are open. We use these differences to create task-specific heuristics, action proposal mechanisms, and goal-test functions; and find that the interpretation task tends to search a much smaller space than that of generation.

3.3.1 Heuristic functions

For REI, the action proposal function is so restrictive that we can generate and test the entire search space; therefore, no heuristic is necessary.

For REG, the heuristic function characterizes its communicational objective: to describe the target(s) and none of the distractors. For this we use the **F1** score (*F-measure*) from information retrieval, because it rewards inclusion of targets (recall) and penalizes inclusion of distractors (precision). Given a belief state, s, and the intended target set, $\dot{\mathsf{t}}$:

$$h(\mathsf{s}) = \max \mathbf{F1}(\dot{\mathsf{t}}, \mathsf{t}) \; \forall \, \mathsf{t} \in \mathsf{s} \qquad (1)$$

This heuristic iterates over each target set, t, in a belief state to find the biggest set difference according to the F1 score. By taking the worst possible score of any target, it always is greater than or equal to the true distance.

3.3.2 Goal test functions

For REI, a goal state is one in which all observations have been accounted for, and the belief state's part of speech is a noun. For REG, a goal state is one in which only the targets are described (i.e. its heuristic, Equation 1, returns 0), and the belief state's part of speech is a noun.

Both goal test functions impose a syntactic constraint: the requirement that plans terminate in a noun state. This all-or-nothing constraint, along with the language model in the action proposal function, forces the generated expressions to be syntactically well-formed English expressions.

3.3.3 Action proposal functions

While expanding a search state, instead of generating effects for every action in the lexicon, the action proposal restricts the set of actions that are considered. It is passed the parent belief state, whose part_of_speech property tells the syntactic category of the last action that changed it. Actions are proposed only if they are consistent with a **language model** that describes valid transitions between syntactic categories. Our (limited) language model is expressed in a regular language: `DT? CD? (ORD? JJS)* JJ* (NN|NNS)+`.

For the problem of REI, we are licensed to make the action proposal function even more restrictive. AIGRE restricts those whose lexical units can produce the text that appears in the remaining observation sequence.

In addition to enforcing syntactic constraints, the action proposal function gives us a nice way to handle omitted actions. During interpretation, AIGRE allows **default actions**, representing elided words or conventional implictures, to be inferred at a cost, but only under rare circumstances. A designated subset of actions are marked as default actions, indicating that they can be assumed even though their lexical unit is not present. A default action is only suggested if (1) none of the other actions have matched the remaining observed input text and (2) its precondition is met.

For example, the language model forbids the ORD→NN transition and the goal test function requires that all noun phrases terminate with a noun. Consequently, *"the second"* is interpreted as *"the$_{DT}$ second$_{ORD}$ [leftmost$_{JJS}$] [one$_{NN}$]"*, assuming the default actions LEFTMOST$_{JJS}$ and ONE$_{NN}$. For (R6), the requirement of ending with a noun allows the subsective meaning of *"biggest"* to be evaluated: its deferred effect is triggered after ONE$_{NN}$.

3.3.4 Search strategies

Because the action proposal function is so restrictive for REI, the *entire* search space can be explored usually under a second. For REG, expanding the complete planning graph to a depth of 5 using ≈ 100 actions takes several minutes.

To complete the REG task efficiently, we have experimented with search strategies and found optimal **A* search** to be too slow. Although they give up guarantees of optimality and completeness, hillclimbing-based approaches rescue the REG task from having to expand every relevant action's effect by committing to the first effect whose successor shows an improvement over the current state. Because we do not want the same results each time (non-deterministic output is characteristic of human reference generation (van Deemter et al., 2011)), AIGRE randomly chooses effects with a probability inversely proportional to the action's lexical cost, which is a kind of **stochastic hillclimbing**. The results are promising: non-deterministic outputs can be generated in usually less than a second (see Figure 4).

4 AIGRE's Output for REI and REG

In lieu of a formal evaluation, we have included examples of AIGRE's output for several tasks involving the CIRCLE and KINDLE reference domains: see Table 1 for output of the REG task; and Figures 5 and 6 for outputs of REI tasks.

AIGRE's word costs were derived from their inverse token frequencies in the Open American National Corpus (Ide and Macleod, 2001). They are only a approximation and clearly do not accurately quantify the costs of human linguistic decisions. With this in mind, the referring expression's denotations' relative likelihoods, which are derived from costs, should not be given much credence. Our point here is that this large hypothesis space can be represented and searched efficiently.

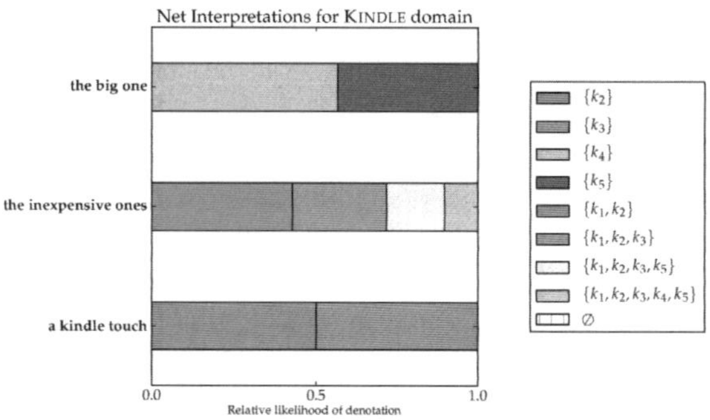

Figure 3: REI results for R1, R2 and R3 in the KINDLE domain. Each color represents a different target set, and more than one color in a bar indicates the interpretation is *uncertain*.

5 An example trace of a REI task

The interpretation task begins with an initial state containing the belief state b_0 about the KINDLE referring domain[12] (figure 1) and the referring expression, *"any two cheap ones."* The search procedure begins by selecting actions to transform b_0 into successor states. The actions are sorted by how much of the prefix of the observed text they match; and for *"any two cheap ones,"* the first action is ANY_{DT} and it transforms b_0 into b_1:

[12]To AIGRE, each Kindle is an attribute-values matrix rather than a visual image.

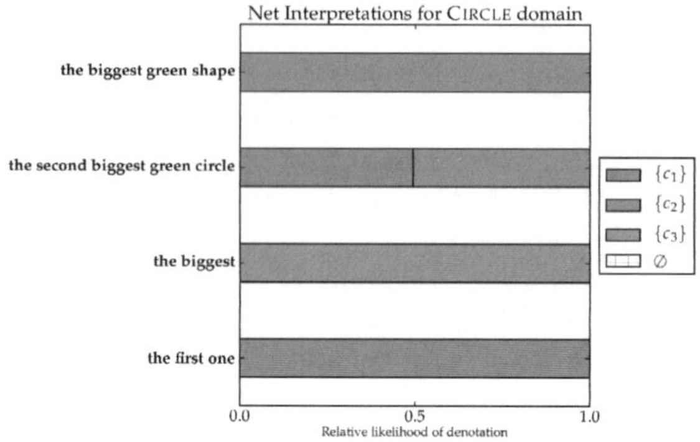

Figure 4: REI for R4-R7 in the CIRCLE domain.

$$b_0 = \begin{bmatrix} \text{TARGET\_ARITY} & [0,\infty) \\ \text{CONTRAST\_ARITY} & [0,\infty) \\ \text{TARGET} & [] \\ \text{DISTRACTOR} & [] \\ \text{PART\_OF\_SPEECH} & \text{S} \\ \text{DEFERRED\_EFFECTS} & [] \end{bmatrix}$$

(Note: For lack of space, we just show the parts of the belief state that change)

$$b_1 = \begin{bmatrix} \text{CONTRAST\_ARITY} & [1,\infty) \\ \text{PART\_OF\_SPEECH} & \text{DT} \end{bmatrix}$$

The contrast_arity property allows AIGRE to represent the notion of conveying a choice from alternatives, as with the indefinite meanings of *"some"* or *"any,"* as well as the fact that definite descriptions take the maximal set.[13]

Applying the effect of the action, TWO_{CD}, for the word *"two"* transforms b_1 into b_2:

$$b_2 = \begin{bmatrix} \text{TARGET\_ARITY} & [2,2] \\ \text{PART\_OF\_SPEECH} & \text{CD} \end{bmatrix}$$

To be concrete, the initial belief state, b_0, models all 31 groupings of referents: $b_0 \models \{k_1\}, \{k_3, k_5\} \ldots$; the belief state b_1 contains 30 sets—all but the set containing all 5 kindles; and b_2 represents $\binom{5}{2} = 10$ alternative sets.

The action CHEAP_{JJ} corresponding to the gradable adjective *"cheap"* is non-deterministic: it yields a different effect for each distinct attributes' values, starting with the lowest price, \$79.00. This

[13]The power set of the belief state's referents forms a lattice under the subset operator, and for the definite article *"the"* we only want the top row. We model its meaning with a deferred effect that sets contrast_arity to [0,0] after a noun. The indefinite article *"a"* sets contrast_arity to [1,∞) and target_arity to 1; *"a"* has the same meaning as *"any one."*

TARGET	SECONDS	REFERRING EXPRESSIONS (AND COSTS)
$\{c_1\}$	0.66 ± 0.3	the small one (2.3), the left one (2.4), the smaller one (2.4), the smallest one (2.4), the leftmost one (2.4) ...
$\{c_2\}$	1.05 ± 0.5	the center one (2.4), the medium-sized one (2.4), the center circle (2.4), the green big one (3.4)
$\{c_3\}$	1.63 ± 1.1	the blue one (2.3), the right one (2.3), the big one (2.3), the large one (2.4), the larger one (2.4)...
$\{c_1, c_2\}$	0.37 ± 0.1	the green ones (2.3), the green circles (2.3), the 2 green ones (3.4), **the small ones** (3.4)
$\{c_1, c_3\}$	0.52 ± 0.1	the 2 not center ones (4.5), the 2 not center circles (4.5), the 2 not medium-sized ones (4.5)
$\{c_2, c_3\}$	0.41 ± 0.1	**the right ones** (3.4), the 2 right ones (4.4), the 2 right circles (4.4), the 2 big ones (4.5)
$\{c_1, c_2, c_3\}$	0.19 ± 0.1	the ones (1.2), the circles (1.2), the 3 ones (2.3)
$\{k_1\}$	3.24 ± 2.0	the left one (2.4), the light one (2.4), the small cheap one (3.5), the small cheapest one (3.5)
$\{k_2\}$	0.94 ± 0.2	the left touch (3.4), **the small center one** (3.5), **the small center touch** (3.6), **the small center cheap one** (4.7)
$\{k_3\}$	1.11 ± 1.0	the center one (2.4), **the small heavy one** (3.5), **the small heavier one** (3.5), the small heaviest touch (3.6) ...
$\{k_4\}$	0.20 ± 0.2	the kindle dx (1.2), **the big one** (2.3), the big kindle dx (2.4)
$\{k_5\}$	0.19 ± 0.1	the kindle fire (1.2), the right one (2.3), the right kindle fire (2.4)

Table 1: AIGRE's outputs for REG tasks (each repeated for 20 trials). If the output is **bold**, it means that when we fed the referring expression back to AIGRE as a REI task, it was able to derive multiple alternative interpretations and the referring expression is uncertain.

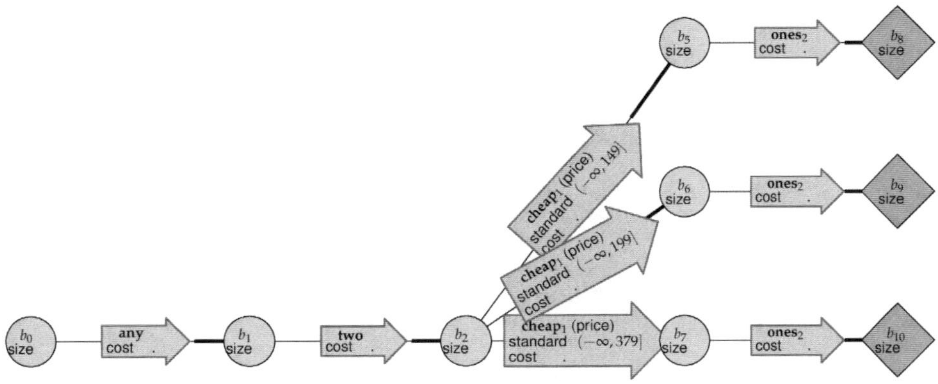

Figure 5: The **planning graph** for interpreting, *"any two cheap ones."* Search proceeds from the initial state b_0 rightward toward goal states (diamonds). The labeled edges represent the actions, and contain the cumulative path costs. Only intermediate states that lead to a goal are shown—even though CHEAP$_{JJ}$ initially had 5 successors, two were *invalid* belief states because they had 0 members.

effect *adds* a new attribute target.price to the belief state and sets its value to be the open interval $(-\infty, 79.00]$. The action's next effect creates a separate belief state for the second lowest price from the referents, \$99.00, and so on, all the way up to the most expensive price, \$379.00.

$$b_3 = \begin{bmatrix}\text{TARGET} & \begin{bmatrix}\text{PRICE} & (-\infty, 79.00]\end{bmatrix}\end{bmatrix}$$

$$b_4 = \begin{bmatrix}\text{TARGET} & \begin{bmatrix}\text{PRICE} & (-\infty, 99.00]\end{bmatrix}\end{bmatrix}$$

$$b_5 = \begin{bmatrix}\text{TARGET} & \begin{bmatrix}\text{PRICE} & (-\infty, 149.00]\end{bmatrix}\end{bmatrix}$$

...

The last word, *"ones,"* invokes an action ONES$_{NNS}$ whose effect adds the target.type=*entity* property to the belief state and then merges targetset_arity with $[2, \infty)$ because it is plural (though its value doesn't change).

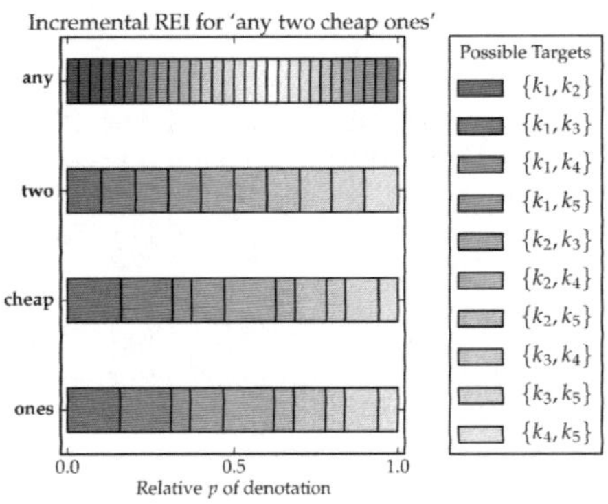

Figure 6: All denotation's relative likelihoods. Each row corresponds to a column of the planning graph in Figure 5: the first row, "any," is just node b_1 and the last row is the aggregate of the belief states b_8, b_9 and b_{10}—derived by summing all the denotations' inverted costs.

References

Gerry Altmann and Mark Steedman. 1988. Interaction with context during human sentence processing. *Cognition*.

Douglas E Appelt. 1985. Planning English referring expressions. *Artificial Intelligence*.

Chris L Baker, Joshua B Tenenbaum, and Rebecca R Saxe. 2007. Goal inference as inverse planning. *Proceedings of the 29th annual meeting of the cognitive science society*.

Luciana Benotti. 2010. Implicature as an Interactive Process. *Ph.D. Thesis*.

Bernd Bohnet and Robert Dale. 2005. Viewing referring expression generation as search. *Proc. IJCAI-05*.

Blai Bonet and Hector Geffner. 2000. Planning with Incomplete Information as Heuristic Search in Belief Space. *AIPS 2000: Proceedings of the Conference on Artificial Intelligence Planning Systems*.

Blai Bonet and Hector Geffner. 2001. Planning as heuristic search: New results. *Artificial Intelligence*.

Blai Bonet, Gábor Loerincs, and Hector Geffner. 1997. A Robust and Fast Action Selection Mechanism for Planning. In *Proceedings of AAAI-1997*.

Robert Dale and Ehud Reiter. 1995. Computational interpretations of the Gricean maxims in the generation of referring expressions. *Cognitive Science*.

Laurence Danlos and Fiammetta Namer. 1988. Morphology and cross dependencies in the synthesis of personal pronouns in Romance languages. In *COLING '88: Proceedings of the 12th conference on Computational linguistics*.

Stefan Edelkamp and Stefan Schroedl. 2011. *Heuristic Search*. Morgan Kaufmann.

Konstantina Garoufi and Alexander Koller. 2010. Automated planning for situated natural language generation. *Proceedings of the 48th Annual Meeting of the Association for Computational Linguistics*.

Konstantina Garoufi and Alexander Koller. 2011. Combining symbolic and corpus-based approaches for the generation of successful referring expressions. In *ENLG '11: Proceedings of the 13th European Workshop on Natural Language Generation*.

Christopher W Geib and Mark Steedman. 2006. On Natural Language Processing and Plan Recognition. *Proceedings of the 20th International Joint Conference on Artificial Intelligence*.

Malik Ghallab, Dana Nau, and Paolo Traverso. 2004. *Automated Planning*. Morgan Kaufmann.

Peter A Heeman and Graeme Hirst. 1995. Collaborating on referring expressions. *Computational Linguistics*.

Jerry R Hobbs, Mark E Stickel, Douglas E Appelt, and Paul Martin. 1993. Interpretation as abduction. *Artificial Intelligence*.

Jörg Hoffmann and Ronen Brafman. 2005. Contingent Planning via Heuristic Forward Search with Implicit Belief States .

Joerg Hoffmann. 2001. FF: The Fast-Forward Planning System. *AI Magazine*.

Helmut Horacek. 2004. On Referring to Sets of Objects Naturally. In *Natural Language Generation*.

Nancy Ide and Catherine Macleod. 2001. The american national corpus: A standardized resource of american english. In *Proceedings of Corpus Linguistics 2001*, volume 3.

Alexander Koller and Jörg Hoffmann. 2010. Waking up a sleeping rabbit: On natural-language sentence generation with FF. In *Proceedings of AAAI 2010*.

Alexander Koller and Ronald P A Petrick. 2011. Experiences with planning for natural language generation. *Computational Intelligence*.

Alexander Koller and Matthew Stone. 2007. Sentence generation as a planning problem. *Annual Meeting of the Association of Computational Linguistics*.

Alexander Koller, Andrew Gargett, and Konstantina Garoufi. 2010. A scalable model of planning perlocutionary acts. In *Proceedings of the 14th Workshop on the Semantics nd Pragmatics of Dialogue*.

Emiel Krahmer and Mariët Theune. 2002. Efficient generation of descriptions in context. *Proceedings of the ESSLLI workshop on the generation of nominals*.

Emiel Krahmer and Kees van Deemter. 2012. Computational Generation of Referring Expressions: A Survey. *Computational Linguistics*.

Barbara Partee. 1995. Lexical semantics and compositionality. *An invitation to cognitive science: Language*.

Alexey Radul and Gerald Jay Sussman. 2009. The Art of the Propagator. *Technical Report MIT-CSAIL-TR-2009-002, MIT Computer Science and Artificial Intelligence Laboratory*.

Miquel J Ramírez and Hector Geffner. 2010. Probabilistic plan recognition using off-the-shelf classical planners. *Proceedings of the Conference of the Association for the Advancement of Artificial Intelligence (AAAI 2010)*.

Ehud Reiter. 1994. Has a consensus NL generation architecture appeared, and is it psycholinguistically plausible? *Proceedings of the Seventh International Workshop on Natural Language Generation (INLG 1994)*.

Muffy E A Siegel. 1976. Capturing the adjective. *PhD. Thesis. University of Massachusetts Amherst.*

Matthew Stone and Bonnie Webber. 1998. Textual Economy through Close Coupling of Syntax and Semantics. *arXiv.org*.

Matthew Stone, Christine Doran, Bonnie L. Webber, Tonia Bleam, and Martha Palmer. 2003. Microplanning with communicative intentions: The spud system. *Computational Intelligence*, 19(4):311–381.

Matthew Stone. 2000. On identifying sets. In *INLG '00: Proceedings of the first international conference on Natural language generation*.

Michael K Tanenhaus. 2007. Spoken language comprehension: Insights from eye movements. *Oxford handbook of psycholinguistics*.

Kees van Deemter, Albert Gatt, Roger P G van Gompel, and Emiel Krahmer. 2011. Toward a Computational Psycholinguistics of Reference Production. *Topics in Cognitive Science*.

Kees van Deemter. 2000. Generating vague descriptions. In *INLG '00: Proceedings of the first international conference on Natural language generation*.

Kees van Deemter. 2010. Not Exactly: In Praise of Vagueness. *Oxford University Press*.

Graphs and Spatial Relations in the Generation of Referring Expressions

Jette Viethen
h.a.e.viethen@uvt.nl
TiCC
University of Tilburg
Tilburg, The Netherlands

Margaret Mitchell
m.mitchell@jhu.edu
HLT Centre of Excellence
Johns Hopkins University
Baltimore, USA

Emiel Krahmer
e.j.krahmer@uvt.nl
TiCC
University of Tilburg
Tilburg, The Netherlands

Abstract

When they introduced the Graph-Based Algorithm (GBA) for referring expression generation, Krahmer et al. (2003) flaunted the natural way in which it deals with relations between objects; but this feature has never been tested empirically. We fill this gap in this paper, exploring referring expression generation from the perspective of the GBA and focusing in particular on generating human-like expressions in visual scenes with spatial relations. We compare the original GBA against a variant that we introduce to better reflect human reference, and find that although the original GBA performs reasonably well, our new algorithm offers an even better match to human data (77.91% Dice). Further, it can be extended to capture speaker variation, reaching an 82.83% Dice overlap with human-produced expressions.

1 Introduction

Ten years ago, Krahmer et al. (2003) published the Graph-Based Algorithm (GBA) for referring expression generation (REG). REG has since become one of the most researched areas within Natural Language Generation, due in a large part to the central role it plays in communication: referring allows humans and language generation systems alike to invoke the entities that the discourse is about in the mind of a listener or reader.

Like most REG algorithms, the GBA is focussed on the task of selecting the semantic content for a referring expression, uniquely identifying a target referent among all objects in its visual or linguistic context. The framework used by the GBA is particularly attractive because it provides fine-grained control for finding the 'best' referring expression, encompassing several previous approaches. This control is made possible by defining a desired cost function over object properties to guide the construction of the output expression and using a search mechanism that does not stop at the first solution found.

One characteristic of the GBA particularly emphasized by Krahmer et al. (2003), advancing from research on algorithms such as the Incremental Algorithm (Dale and Reiter, 1995) and the Greedy Algorithm (Dale, 1989), was the treatment of relations between entities. Relations such as *on top of* or *to the left of* fall out naturally from the graph-based representation of the domain, a facet missing in earlier algorithms. We believe that this makes the GBA particularly well-suited for generating language in spatial visual domains.

In the years since the inception of the GBA, the REG community has become increasingly interested in evaluating algorithms against human-produced data in visual domains, aiming to mimic human references to objects. This interest has manifested most prominently in the 2007-2009 REG Challenges (Belz and Gatt, 2007; Gatt et al., 2008; Gatt et al., 2009) based on the TUNA Corpus (van Deemter et al., 2012). The GBA performed among the best algorithms in all three of these challenges. However, in particular its ability to analyze relational information could not be assessed, because the TUNA Corpus does not contain annotated relational descriptions.

We rectify this omission in the current work by testing the GBA on the GRE3D3 Corpus, which was designed to study the use of spatial relations in referring expressions (Viethen and Dale, 2008). We compare against a variant of the GBA that we introduce to build longer referring expressions, following the observation that humans tend to overspecify (i.e., not be maximally brief) in their referring expressions (Sonnenschein, 1985; Pechmann, 1989; Engelhardt et al., 2006; Arts et al., 2011). For both algorithms, we experiment with cost functions defined at different granularities to produce the best match to human data. We find that we can match human data better than the original GBA with the variant that encourages overspecification.

With this model, we aim to further advance towards human-like reference by developing a method to capture speaker-specific variation. Speaker variation cannot easily be modeled by the classic input variables of REG algorithms, but a number of authors have shown that system output can be improved by using speaker identity as an additional feature; this has often been accompanied by the observation that commonalities can be found in the reference behaviour of different speakers (Bohnet, 2008; Di Fabbrizio et al., 2008a; Mitchell et al., 2011b), particularly for spatial relations (Viethen and Dale, 2009). In the second experiment reported in this paper, we combine these insights by automatically clustering groups of speakers with similar behaviour and then defining separate cost functions for each group to better guide the algorithms.

Before we assess the ability of the GBA and our variant to produce human-like referring expressions containing relations (Sections 5 and 6), we will give an overview of the relevant background to the treatment of relations in REG, a short history of the GBA, and the relevance of individual variation (Section 2). We introduce our new variant graph-based algorithm, LongestFirst, in Section 3.

2 Relations, Graphs and Individual Variation

2.1 Relations in REG

In the knowledge representation underlying most work in REG, each object in a scene is modeled as a set of attribute-value pairs describing the object's properties, such as $\langle\mathsf{size}, \mathsf{large}\rangle$. Such a representation is used in the two of the classic algorithms, the Greedy Algorithm (Dale, 1989) and the Incremental Algorithm (IA) (Dale and Reiter, 1995). Neither of these was originally intended to process relations between objects.

Several attempts have been made to adapt the traditional REG algorithms to include relations between objects in their output, but all of them suffer from problems with the knowledge representation not being suited to relations. Dale and Haddock (1991) use a constraint network and a recursive loop to extend the Greedy Algorithm, which uses the discriminatory power of an attribute as the main selection criterion. They treat relations the same as other attributes; but in most cases a certain spatial relation to a particular other object is fully distinguishing, which easily leads to strange chains of relations in the output omitting most other attributes (Viethen and Dale, 2006).

Krahmer and Theune (2002) suggest a similar adjustment for the IA by introducing a recursive loop if a relation to another object is introduced to the referring expression under construction. They treat relations as fundamentally different from other attributes in order to recognize when to enter the recursive loop, however, they fail to address the problem of infinite regress, whereby the objects in a domain might be described in a circular manner by the relations holding between them. Another relational extension to the IA has been proposed by Kelleher and Kruijff (2006), treating relations as a completely different class from other attributes. Both extensions of the IA make the simplifying assumption that relations should only be considered if it is not possible to fully distinguish the target referent from the surrounding objects in any other way, with the idea that it takes less effort to consider and describe only one object (Krahmer and Theune, 2002; Viethen and Dale, 2008).

2.2 A Short History of the GBA

A new approach to REG was proposed by Krahmer et al. (2003). In this approach, a scene is represented as a labeled directed graph (see Figure 1(b)), and content selection is a subgraph construction problem. Assuming a scene graph G = $\langle V_G, E_G \rangle$, where vertices V_G represent objects and edges E_G represent the properties and relations of these objects with associated costs, their algorithm returns the cheapest distinguishing subgraph that uniquely refers to the target object $v \in V_G$. Relations between objects (i.e., edges between different vertices) are a natural part of this representation, without requiring special computational mechanisms. In addition to cost functions, the GBA requires a preference ordering (PO) over the edges to arbitrate between equally cheap descriptions (Viethen et al., 2008).

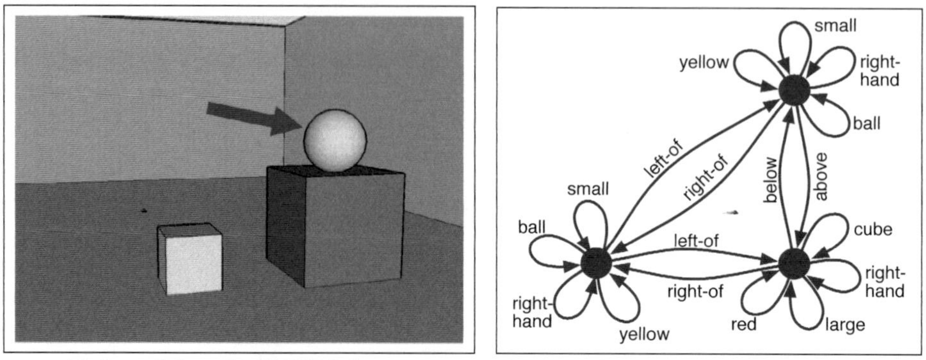

(a) Scene 7 from the GRE3D3 Corpus. (b) A graph representing the scene to the left.

Figure 1: An example scene from the GRE3D3 Corpus and the corresponding domain graph.

As the cost functions and preference orders are specified over edges (i.e., properties), they allow much more fine-grained control over which properties to generate for a target referent than the attribute-based preference orders employed by the IA and its descendants. The cost functions can be used to give preference to a commonly used size value, such as large, over a rarely used color value, such as mauve, although in general color is described more often than size. This process is aided by a branch-and-bound search that guarantees to find the cheapest (i.e., 'best') referring expression.

Since its inception, the GBA has been shown to be useful for several referential phenomena. Krahmer and van der Sluis (2003) combined verbal descriptions with pointing gestures by modelling each such gesture as additional looping edges on all objects that it might be aimed at. While the authors confirmed the ideas implemented in the algorithm in psycholinguistic studies (van der Sluis, 2005), they never assessed its output in an actual domain.

van Deemter and Krahmer (2007) demonstrated how the GBA could be used to generate reference to sets as well as to negated and gradable properties by representing implicit information as explicit edges in domain graphs. They also presented a simple way to account for discourse salience based on restricting the distractor set. Its ability to cover such a breadth of referential phenomena makes the GBA a reasonably robust algorithm for further exploring the generation of human-like reference.

The GBA was systematically tested against human-produced referring expressions for the first time in the ASGRE Challenge 2007 (Belz and Gatt, 2007). This entry is described in detail in (Viethen et al., 2008) and was very successful as well in the following 2008 and 2009 REG Challenges (Gatt et al., 2008; Gatt et al., 2009) with a *free-naïve* cost function. This cost function assigns 0 cost to the most common attributes, 2 to the rarest, and 1 to all others. By making the most common attributes free, it became possible to include these attributes redundantly in a referring expression, even if they were not strictly necessary for identifying the target. The cost functions used in the challenges were attribute-based, and did therefore not make use of the refined control capabilities of the GBA.

Theune et al. (2011) used k-means clustering on the property frequencies in order to provide a more systematic method to transfer the FREE-NAÏVE cost function to new domains. They found that using only two clusters (a high frequency and a low frequency group with associated costs of 0 and 1) achieves the best results, with no significant differences to the FREE-NAÏVE cost function on the TUNA Corpus. Subsequently they showed that on this corpus, a training set of only 20 descriptions suffices to determine a 2-means cost function that performs as well as one based on 165 descriptions. In (Koolen et al., 2012), the same authors extended these experiments to a Dutch version of the TUNA Corpus (Koolen and Krahmer, 2010) and came to a similar conclusion. Neither of the corpora used in these experiments included relations between objects.

2.3 Individual Variation in REG

A number of authors have argued that to be able to produce human-like referring expressions, an algorithm must account for speaker variation: Different speakers will refer to the same object in different ways, and modeling this variation can bring us closer to generating the rich variety of expressions that people produce. Several approaches have been made in this direction.

Although this was not explicitly discussed in (Jordan and Walker, 2005), the machine-learned models presented there performed significantly better at replicating human-produced referring expressions when a feature set was used that included information about the identity of the speaker. In (Viethen and Dale, 2010), the impact of speaker identity as a machine-learning feature is more systematically tested. They show that exact knowledge about which speaker produced a referring expression boosts performance, but also find many commonalities between different speakers' strategies for content selection. Mitchell et al. (2011b) used participant identity in a machine learner to successfully predict the kind of size modifier to be used in a referring expression. Additionally, various submissions to the REG challenges, particularly by Bohnet and Fabbrizio et al. (Bohnet, 2008; Bohnet, 2009; Di Fabbrizio et al., 2008a; Di Fabbrizio et al., 2008b) used speaker-specific POs to increase performance in their adaptations of the IA.

All of these systems used the exact speaker identity as input, although many of the authors noted that groups of speakers behave similarly (Viethen and Dale, 2010; Mitchell et al., 2011b). We build off of this idea by clustering similar speakers together before learning parameters, and then generate for speaker-specific clusters. This method results in a significant improvement in performance.

3 LongestFirst: a New Search Strategy

The GBA guarantees to return the cheapest possible subgraph that fully distinguishes the target. However, many distinguishing subgraphs can have the same cost, for example, if a target can be identified either by its color or by its size, and color and size have the same cost. Viethen et al. (2008) discuss some examples in more detail.

In the case that more than one cheapest subgraph exists, the original GBA will generate the first it encountered. Due to its branch-and-bound search strategy, this is also the smallest subgraph, corresponding to the shortest possible description that can be found at the cheapest cost. Because its pruning mechanism does not allow further expansion of a graph once it is distinguishing, the number of attributes that the algorithm can include redundantly is limited, in particular if relations are involved. Attributes of visually salient nearby landmark objects that are introduced to the referring subgraph by a relation are only considered after all other attributes of the target object. This is the case even if these attributes are free and feature early in the preference order.

The GBA is therefore not able to replicate many overspecified descriptions that human speakers may use: if a subgraph containing a relation is already distinguishing before the attributes of a landmark object are considered, the algorithm will not include any information about the landmark. Not only is it unlikely that a landmark object should be included in a description without any further information about it, it also seems intuitive that speakers with a preference for certain attributes (such as color) would include these attributes not only for the target referent, but for a landmark object as well.

We solve this problem by amending the search algorithm in a way that finds the *longest* of all the cheapest subgraphs, and call the resulting algorithm *LongestFirst*. This search strategy results in a much larger number of subgraphs to check, in particular, when used with cost functions that involve a lot of free edges. In order to keep our systems tractable, we therefore limit the number of attributes the LongestFirst algorithm can include to four, based on the finding from (Mitchell et al., 2011a) that people rarely include more than four modifiers in a noun phrase. In Experiment 2 we additionally test a setting in which the maximum number of attributes is determined on the basis of the average description length in the training data.

4 Implementation Note

The original implementation of the GBA did not provide a method to specify the order in which edges were tried, although the edge order determines the order in which distinguishing subgraphs are found by the algorithm (Krahmer et al., 2003). This was fixed in (Viethen et al., 2008) by adding a PO as parameter to the GBA to arbitrate between equally cheap solutions.

A further issue arose in this implementation when tested on the GRE3D3 domain, because there was no simple way to specify which object each property belonged to; for the TUNA domain where the GBA has traditionally been evaluated, it is safe to always assume a property belongs to the target referent. We have therefore provided additional functionality to the GBA that requires that not only ⟨attribute, value⟩ pairs are specified, but ⟨entity1, attribute, value, entity2⟩ tuples, which can be translated directly into graph edges. For example the tuple ⟨tg:relation:above:lm⟩ represents the edge labelled above between the yellow ball and the red cube in Figure 1. For direct attributes, such as size or color, entity1 and entity2 in these tuples are identical, resulting in loop edges. This Java implementation of the GBA and the Python implementation of the LongestFirst algorithm are available at `www.m-mitchell.com/code`.

5 Experiment 1: Relational Descriptions

In our first experiment, we evaluate how well the GBA produces human-like reference in a corpus that uses spatial relations. We compare against the LongestFirst variant that encourages overspecification.

5.1 Material

To evaluate the different systems, we use the GRE3D3 Corpus. It consists of 630 distinguishing descriptions for objects in simple 3D scenes. Each of the 20 scenes contains three objects in different spatial relations relative to one another (see Figure 1). The target referent, marked by an arrow, was always in a direct adjacency relation (on – top – of or in – front – of) to one of the other two objects, while the third object was always placed at a small distance to the left or right. The objects are either spheres or cubes and differ in size and color. In addition to these attributes, the 63 human participants who contributed to the corpus used the objects' location as well as the spatial relation between the target referent and the closest landmark object. Each participant described one of two sets of 10 scenes. The scenes in the two sets are not identical, but equivalent, so the sets can be conflated for most analyses. Spatial relations were used in 36.6% (232) of the descriptions, although they were never necessary to distinguish the target object. Further details about the corpus may be found in (Viethen and Dale, 2008).

5.2 Approaches to Parameter Settings

As discussed above, the GBA behaves differently depending on the PO and the cost functions over its edges. To find the best match with human data, we explore several different approaches to setting these two parameters. An important distinction between the approaches we try hinges on the difference between *attributes* and *properties*. Attributes correspond to, e.g., color, size, or location, while properties are attribute-value pairs, e.g., ⟨color, red⟩, ⟨size, large⟩, ⟨location, middle⟩.

Previous evaluations of the GBA typically used parameter settings based on either attribute frequency (Viethen et al., 2008) or property frequency (Koolen et al., 2012). We compare both methods for setting the parameters. Because the scenes on which the corpus is based were not balanced for the different attribute-values, the frequency of a property is calculated as the proportion of descriptions in which it was used for those scenes where the target actually possessed this property. For our evaluation, the trainable costs and the POs are determined using cross-validation (see Section 5.3). We use the following approaches:

0-COST-PROP: All edges have 0 cost, and the PO is based on property frequency. Each property is included (regardless of how distinguishing it is) until a distinguishing subgraph is found.

0-COST-ATT: As 0-COST-PROP, but the PO is based on attribute frequency.

FREE-NAÏVE-PROP: Properties that occur in more than 75% of descriptions where they could be used cost 0, properties with a frequency below 20% cost 2, and all others cost 1 (Viethen et al., 2008). The PO is based on property frequency.

FREE-NAÏVE-ATT: As FREE-NAÏVE-PROP:, but costs and PO are based on attribute frequency.

K-PROP: Costs are assigned using k-means clustering over property frequencies with k=2 (Theune et al., 2011). The PO is based on property frequency.

K-ATT: As K-PROP, but the k-means clustering and the PO are based on attribute frequency.

5.3 Evaluation Setup

We evaluate the version of the GBA used by Viethen et al. (2008), with additional handling for relations between entities (see Section 4). We compare against our LongestFirst algorithm from Section 3 on all approaches described in Section 5.2. As baselines, we compare against the Incremental Algorithm (Dale and Reiter, 1995) and a simple informed approach that includes attributes/properties seen in more than 50% of the training descriptions. We do not use the IA's relational extensions (Krahmer and Theune, 2002; Kelleher and Kruijff, 2006), because these would deliver the same relation-free output as the basic IA (relations are never necessary for identifying the target in GRE3D3). These two baselines are tried with an attribute-based PO and a property-based one. We do not expect a difference between the attribute- and the property-based PO on the IA, as this difference would only come to the fore in a situation where a choice has to be made between two values of the same attribute. In the IA's analysis of the GRE3D3 domain, this can only happen with relations, which it will not use in this domain.

We use Accuracy and Dice, the two most common metrics for human-likeness in REG (Gatt and Belz, 2008; Gatt et al., 2009), to assess our systems. Accuracy reports the relative frequency with which the generated attribute set and the human-produced attribute set match exactly. Dice measures the overlap between the two attribute sets. For details, see, for example, Krahmer and van Deemter's (2012) survey paper. We train and test our systems using 10-fold cross-validation.

		Original GBA	Longest First
0-COST-PROP	Acc	39.21	0.16
	Dice	73.40	68.75
0-COST-ATT	Acc	39.21	0.00
	Dice	73.40	64.34
FREE-NAÏVE-ATT	Acc	39.21	**46.51**
	Dice	73.40	**77.91**
FREE-NAÏVE-PROP	Acc	39.21	38.10
	Dice	73.40	74.99
K-PROP	Acc	39.21	35.08
	Dice	73.40	74.66
K-ATT	Acc	39.21	35.08
	Dice	73.40	74.56
		50%-Base	IA
prop-based PO	Acc	27.30	37.14
	Dice	72.17	72.21
att-based PO	Acc	24.92	37.14
	Dice	71.16	72.21

Table 1: Experiment 1: System performance in %. We used χ^2 on Accuracy and paired t-tests on Dice to check for statistical significance. The best performance is highlighted in boldface. It is statistically significantly different from all other systems (Acc: $p < 0.02$, Dice: $p < 0.0001$).

5.4 Results

The original version of the Graph-Based Algorithm shows identical performance for all approaches (See Table 1). All use a preference order starting with type, followed by color and size, and a cost function that favors the same attributes. As these attributes always suffice to distinguish the intended referent, the algorithm stops before spatial relations are considered. For the scene in Figure 1 it includes the minimal content ⟨tg:type:ball⟩, but for a number of scenes it overspecifies the description.

The LongestFirst/0-COST systems and the LongestFirst/K-PROP system are the only systems that include relations in their output. The LongestFirst/0-COST systems both include a relation in every description; however, not always the one that was included in the human-produced reference, resulting in 521 false-positives for the attribute-based version and 398 for the property-based one. For the scene in Figure 1 they include ⟨tg:color:yellow, tg:size:small, tg:type:ball, tg:right_of:obj3⟩ and ⟨tg:color:yellow, tg:size:small, tg:type:ball, tg:on_top_of:lm⟩, respectively. The first one of these two attribute sets (produced by LongestFirst/0-COST-ATT) includes the relation between the target and the third object to the right, which was almost never included in the human-produced references, leading to many false-positives. The LongestFirst/K-PROP system results in only 45 true-positives and 81 false-positives. It includes the attribute set ⟨tg:color:yellow, tg:type:ball⟩ for Figure 1. One of its relational descriptions (for Scene 5) contains the set ⟨tg:size:small, tg:color:blue, tg:on_top_of:lm⟩.

The 50%-baseline system outperforms the LongestFirst/0-COST systems, which illustrates the utility of cost functions in combination with a PO. It includes the attribute set ⟨tg:color:yellow, tg:type:ball⟩ for the scene in Figure 1. The best performing system is the LongestFirst algorithm with the attribute-based FREE-NAÏVE approach, although this system produces no spatial relations.

6 Experiment 2: Individual Variation

We now extend our methods to take into account individual variation in the content selection for referring expressions, and evaluate whether we have better success at reproducing participants' relational descriptions. Rather than using speaker identity as an input parameter to the system (Section 2.3), we automatically find groups of people who behave similarly to each other, but significantly different to speakers in the other groups.

6.1 Evaluation Setup

We use k-means clustering to group the speakers in the GRE3D3 Corpus based on the number of times they used each attribute and the average length of their descriptions. We tried values between 2 and 5 for k, but found that any value above 2 resulted in two very large clusters accompanied by a number of extremely small clusters. As these small clusters would not be suitable for x-fold cross-validation, we proceed with two clusters, one consisting of speakers preferring relatively long descriptions that often contain spatial relations (Cluster CL0, 16 speakers, 160 descriptions), and one consisting of speakers preferring short, non-relational descriptions (Cluster CL1, 47 speakers, 470 descriptions).

We train cost functions and POs separately for the two clusters in order to capture the different behaviour patterns they are based on. We use the FREE-NAÏVE cost functions for this experiment, which outperformed all others in Experiment 1. We again use 10-fold cross-validation for the evaluation. In this experiment, we vary the maximum length setting for the LongestFirst algorithm. In Experiment 1, the maximum length for a referring expression was set to 4 based on previous empirical findings. Here we additionally test setting it to the rounded average length for each training fold. On Cluster CL0 this average length is 6 in all folds, on Cluster CL1 it is 3.

6.2 Results

As shown in Table 2, the LongestFirst algorithm performs best at generating human-like spatial relations (Cluster CL0), with property-based parameters and a maximum description length determined by the training set. It produces the attribute set ⟨lm:type:cube, tg:on_top_of:lm, tg:type:ball, tgcolouryellow, lm:colour:red⟩ for Figure 1. The difference to the other systems is statistically significant for both Accuracy (χ^2>15, p<0.0001) and Dice (t>13, p<0.0001). The attribute-based parameters and the original GBA perform very badly on this cluster. For participants who do not tend to use spatial relations (Cluster CL1), the maximum length setting has no influence, but attribute-based parameters perform better than property-based ones. The attribute-based LongestFirst systems also outperform the original GBA

			CL0	CL1	avg
LongestFirst -max-av	FN-PROP	Acc	**19.38**	48.94	**41.43**
		Dice	**75.61**	80.27	**79.08**
	FN-ATT	Acc	0.00	**60.00**	**44.76**
		Dice	55.74	**85.28**	77.78
LongestFirst -max4	FN-PROP	Acc	0.63	48.94	36.67
		Dice	72.15	80.21	78.17
	FN-ATT	Acc	0.00	**60.00**	**44.76**
		Dice	59.01	**85.28**	**78.61**
Original GBA	FN-PROP	Acc	5.00	48.30	37.30
		Dice	49.36	80.77	72.79
	FN-ATT	Acc	5.00	50.85	**39.21**
		Dice	49.36	81.58	73.40

Table 2: Experiment 2: Performance in % of the LongestFirst and OriginalGraph algorithms on the two speaker clusters and overall using the FREE-NAÏVE (FN) approaches. We used χ^2 on Accuracy and paired t-tests on Dice to check for statistical significance. The best performance in each column and those that are statistically not significantly different are highlighted in boldface.

on CL1, but interestingly none of the differences are as large as on CL0. For the scene in Figure 1 they produce the attribute set ⟨tg:type:ball, tg:colour:yellow⟩.

The average results over both clusters (shown in the last column Table 2) are not conclusive as to which setting should be used overall, although it is clear that the LongestFirst version is preferable when evaluated by Dice. The different result patterns on the two clusters suggest that the different referential behaviour of the participants in the two clusters are ideally modeled using different parameters. In particular, it appears that *property*-based costs are useful for replicating descriptions containing relations to other objects, while *attribute*-based costs are useful for replicating shorter descriptions. The best overall performance, achieved by combining the best performing systems on each cluster (LongestFirst-max-av/FN-PROP on CL0 and LongestFirst/FN-ATT with either maximum length setting on CL1), lies at 49.68% Accuracy and 82.83% Dice. The Dice score in this combined model is significantly higher than the best achieved by LongestFirst-max-av/FN-PROP and from the best Dice score achieved on the unclustered data in Experiment 1 (t=8.2, p<0.0001). The difference in Accuracy is not significant (χ^2=1.2, p> 0.2).

To get an idea of how successful the new LongestFirst approach is at replicating the use of relations on the clustered data, we take a closer look at the output of the best-performing systems on the two clusters. On CL0, the cluster of participants who produce longer descriptions containing more spatial relations, the best match to the human data comes from LongestFirst-max-av/FN-PROP. 147 of the 160 descriptions in this cluster contain a relation, and the system includes the correct relation for all 147. It falsely also includes a relation for the remaining 13 descriptions. This shows that with the appropriate parameter settings the LongestFirst algorithm is able to replicate human relational reference behaviour, but personal speaker preferences are the main driving factor for the human use of relations.

CL1, the cluster with shorter descriptions, contains only 85 (18%) relational descriptions. The best performing system on this cluster (LongestFirst/FN-ATT) does not produce any relations. This is not surprising as the cost functions and POs for this cluster are necessarily dominated by the non-relational attributes used more regularly. The cases in which relations are used stem from participants who do not show a clear preference for or against relations and would therefore be hard to model in any system. With more data it might be possible to group these participants into a third cluster and find suitable parameter settings for them. This would only be possible if their use of relations is influenced by other factors available to the algorithm, such as the spatial configuration of the scene. Viethen and Dale's (2008) analysis of the GRE3D3 Corpus suggests that this is the case at least to some extent.

7 Conclusions and Future Work

We have evaluated the Graph-Based Algorithm for REG (Krahmer et al., 2003) as well as a novel search algorithm, LongestFirst, that functions on the same graph-based representation, to assess their ability to generate referring expressions that contain spatial relations. We coupled the search algorithms with a number of different approaches to setting the cost functions and preference orders that guide the search.

In Experiment 1, we found that ignoring the cost function (our 0-cost approaches) is not helpful; but the LongestFirst algorithm, which produces longer descriptions, leads to more human-like output for the visuospatial domain we evaluate on than the original Graph-Based Algorithm or the Incremental Algorithm (Dale and Reiter, 1995). However, in order for spatial relations to be included in a human-like way, it was necessary to take into account speaker preferences. We modeled these in Experiment 2 by clustering the participants who had contributed to the evaluation corpus based on their referential behaviour. By training separate cost functions and preference orders for the different clusters, we enabled the LongestFirst algorithm to correctly reproduce 100% of relations used by people who regularly mentioned relations.

Our findings suggest that the graph-based representation proposed by Krahmer et al. (2003) can be used to successfully generate relational descriptions, however their original search algorithm needs to be amended to allow more overspecification. Furthermore, we have shown that variation in the referential behaviour of individual speakers has to be taken into account in order to successfully model the use of relations in referring expressions. We have proposed a clustering approach to advance this goal based directly on the referring behaviour of speakers rather than speaker identity. We have found that the best models use fine-grained property-based parameters for speakers who tend to use spatial relations, and coarser attribute-based parameters for speakers who tend to use shorter descriptions.

In future work, we hope to expand to more complex domains, beyond the simple properties available in the GRE3D3 Corpus. We also aim to explore further graph-based representations and search strategies, modeling non-spatial properties as separate vertices, similar to the approach by Croitoru and van Deemter (2007).

8 Acknowledgements

Viethen and Krahmer received financial support from The Netherlands Organization for Scientific Research, (NWO, Vici grant 277-70-007), and Mitchell received financial support from the Scottish Informatics and Computer Science Alliance (SICSA), which is gratefully acknowledged.

References

Anja Arts, Alfons Maes, Leonard Noordman, and Carel Jansen. 2011. Overspecification in written instruction. *Linguistics*, 49(3):555–574.

Anja Belz and Albert Gatt. 2007. The Attribute Selection for GRE Challenge: Overview and evaluation results. In *Proceedings of the Workshop on Using Corpora for NLG: Language Generation and*

Machine Translation (UCNLG+MT), pages 75–83, Copenhagen, Denmark.

Bernd Bohnet. 2008. The fingerprint of human referring expressions and their surface realization with graph transducers. In *Proceedings of the 5th International Conference on Natural Language Generation*, pages 207–210, Salt Fork OH, USA.

Bernd Bohnet. 2009. Generation of referring expression with an individual imprint. In *Proceedings of the 12th European Workshop on Natural Language Generation*, pages 185–186, Athens, Greece.

Madalina Croitoru and Kees van Deemter. 2007. A conceptual graph approach to the generation of referring expressions. In *Proceedings of the 20th International Joint Conference on Artificial Intelligence*, pages 2456–2461, Hyderabad, India.

Robert Dale and Nicholas Haddock. 1991. Generating referring expressions involving relations. In *Proceedings of the 5th Conference of the European Chapter of the Association for Computational Linguistics*, pages 161–166, Berlin, Germany.

Robert Dale and Ehud Reiter. 1995. Computational interpretations of the Gricean maxims in the generation of referring expressions. *Cognitive Science*, 19(2):233–263.

Robert Dale. 1989. Cooking up referring expressions. In *Proceedings of the 27th Annual Meeting of the Association for Computational Linguistics*, pages 68–75, Vancouver BC, Canada.

Giuseppe Di Fabbrizio, Amanda Stent, and Srinivas Bangalore. 2008a. Referring expression generation using speaker-based attribute selection and trainable realization (ATTR). In *Proceedings of the 5th International Conference on Natural Language Generation*, pages 211–214, Salt Fork OH, USA.

Giuseppe Di Fabbrizio, Amanda J. Stent, and Srinivas Bangalore. 2008b. Referring expression generation using speaker-based attribute selection and trainable realization. In *Twelfth Conference on Computational Natural Language Learning*, Manchester, UK.

Paul E. Engelhardt, Karl D. Bailey, and Fernanda Ferreira. 2006. Do speakers and listeners observe the gricean maxim of quantity? *Journal of Memory and Language*, 54:554–573.

Albert Gatt and Anja Belz. 2008. Attribute selection for referring expression generation: New algorithms and evaluation methods. In *Proceedings of the 5th International Conference on Natural Language Generation*, pages 50–58, Salt Fork OH, USA.

Albert Gatt, Anja Belz, and Eric Kow. 2008. The TUNA Challenge 2008: Overview and evaluation results. In *Proceedings of the 5th International Conference on Natural Language Generation*, pages 198–206, Salt Fork OH, USA.

Albert Gatt, Anja Belz, and Eric Kow. 2009. The TUNA-REG Challenge 2009: Overview and evaluation results. In *Proceedings of the 12th European Workshop on Natural Language Generation*, pages 174–182, Athens, Greece.

Pamela W. Jordan and Marilyn Walker. 2005. Learning content selection rules for generating object descriptions in dialogue. *Journal of Artificial Intelligence Research*, 24:157–194.

John Kelleher and Geert-Jan Kruijff. 2006. Incremental generation of spatial referring expressions in situated dialog. In *Proceedings of the 21st International Conference on Computational Linguistics and the 44th Annual Meeting of the Association for Computational Linguistics*, pages 1041–1048, Sydney, Australia.

Ruud Koolen and Emiel Krahmer. 2010. The D-TUNA Corpus: A dutch dataset for the evaluation of referring expression generation algorithms. In *Proceedings of the 7th International Conference on Language Resources and Evaluation*, Valetta, Malta.

Ruud Koolen, Emiel Krahmer, and Mariët Theune. 2012. Learning preferences for referring expression generation: Effects of domain, language and algorithm. In *Proceedings of the 7th International Natural Language Generation Conference*, pages 3–11, Starved Rock, IL, USA.

Emiel Krahmer and Mariët Theune. 2002. Efficient context-sensitive generation of referring expressions. In Kees van Deemter and Rodger Kibble, editors, *Information Sharing: Reference and Presupposition in Language Generation and Interpretation*, pages 223–264. CSLI Publications, Stanford CA, USA.

Emiel Krahmer and Kees van Deemter. 2012. Computational generation of referring expressions: A survey. *Computational Linguistics*, 38(1):173–218.

Emiel Krahmer and Ielka van der Sluis. 2003. A new model for generating multimodal referring expressions. In *Proceedings of the 9th European Workshop on Natural Language Generation*, pages 47–57, Budapest, Hungary.

Emiel Krahmer, Sebastiaan van Erk, and André Verleg. 2003. Graph-based generation of referring expressions. *Computational Linguistics*, 29(1):53–72.

Margaret Mitchell, Aaron Dunlop, and Brian Roark. 2011a. Semi-supervised modeling for prenominal modifier ordering. In *Proceedings of the 49th Annual Meeting of the Association for Computational Linguistics: Human Language Technologies*, pages 236–241, Portland OR, USA.

Margaret Mitchell, Kees van Deemter, and Ehud Reiter. 2011b. Applying machine learning to the choice of size modifiers. In *Proceedings of the 2nd Workshop on the Production of Referring Expressions*, Boston MA, USA.

Thomas Pechmann. 1989. Incremental speech production and referential overspecification. *Linguistics*, 27:89–110.

Susan Sonnenschein. 1985. The development of referential communication skills: Some situations in which speakers give redundant messages. *Journal of Psycholinguistic Research*, 14(5):489–508.

Mariët Theune, Ruud Koolen, Emiel Krahmer, and Sander Wubben. 2011. Does size matter - how much data is required to train a REG algorithm? In *Proceedings of the 49th Annual Meeting of the Association for Computational Linguistics: Human Language Technologies*, pages 660–664, Portland OR, USA.

Kees van Deemter and Emiel Krahmer. 2007. Graphs and Booleans: On the generation of referring expressions. In Harry C. Bunt and Reinhard Muskens, editors, *Computing Meaning*, volume 3, pages 397–422. Kluwer, Dordrecht, The Netherlands.

Kees van Deemter, Albert Gatt, Ielka van der Sluis, and Richard Power. 2012. Generation of referring expressions: Assessing the incremental algorithm. *Cognitive Science*, 36(5):799–836.

Ielka van der Sluis. 2005. *Multimodal Reference, Studies in Automatic Generation of Multimodal Referring Expressions*. Ph.D. thesis, Tilburg University, The Netherlands.

Jette Viethen and Robert Dale. 2006. Algorithms for generating referring expressions: Do they do what people do? In *Proceedings of the 4th International Conference on Natural Language Generation*, pages 63–70, Sydney, Australia.

Jette Viethen and Robert Dale. 2008. The use of spatial relations in referring expression generation. In *Proceedings of the 5th International Conference on Natural Language Generation*, pages 59–67, Salt Fork OH, USA.

Jette Viethen and Robert Dale. 2009. Referring expression generation: What can we learn from human data? In *Proceedings of the 2009 Workshop on Production of Referring Expressions: Bridging the Gap Between Computational and Empirical Approaches to Reference*, Amsterdam, The Netherlands.

Jette Viethen and Robert Dale. 2010. Speaker-dependent variation in content selection for referring expression generation. In *Proceedings of the 8th Australasian Language Technology Workshop*, pages 81–89, Melbourne, Australia.

Jette Viethen, Robert Dale, Emiel Krahmer, Mariët Theune, and Pascal Touset. 2008. Controlling redundancy in referring expressions. In *Proceedings of the 6th International Conference on Language Resources and Evaluation*, Marrakech, Morocco.

What and where: An empirical investigation of pointing gestures and descriptions in multimodal referring actions

Albert Gatt
Institute of Linguistics
University of Malta
albert.gatt@um.edu.mt

Patrizia Paggio
Institute of Linguistics
University of Malta
patrizia.paggio@um.edu.mt

Abstract

Pointing gestures are pervasive in human referring actions, and are often combined with spoken descriptions. Combining gesture and speech naturally to refer to objects is an essential task in multimodal NLG systems. However, the way gesture and speech should be combined in a referring act remains an open question. In particular, it is not clear whether, in planning a pointing gesture in conjunction with a description, an NLG system should seek to minimise the redundancy between them, e.g. by letting the pointing gesture indicate locative information, with other, non-locative properties of a referent included in the description. This question has a bearing on whether the gestural and spoken parts of referring acts are planned separately or arise from a common underlying computational mechanism. This paper investigates this question empirically, using machine-learning techniques on a new corpus of dialogues involving multimodal references to objects. Our results indicate that human pointing strategies interact with descriptive strategies. In particular, pointing gestures are strongly associated with the use of locative features in referring expressions.

1 Introduction

Referring Expression Generation (REG) is considered a core task in many NLG systems (Krahmer and van Deemter, 2012). Typically, the REG task is defined in terms of identification: a referent needs to be unambiguously identified in a discourse, enabling the reader or listener to pick it out from among its potential distractors. Most work in this area has focused on algorithms that select the content for definite descriptions (Dale, 1989; Dale and Reiter, 1995), or on the best form for a referring expression given the discourse context, for example, whether it should be a full definite description, a reduced one, or a pronoun (McCoy and Strube, 1999; Callaway and Lester, 2002; Krahmer and Theune, 2002).

Less attention has been payed to the role of gestures in referring actions and the way these can be coupled with discursive strategies for referent identification. This question becomes particularly important in the context of multimodal systems, for example, those involving embodied conversational agents, where the 'naturalness' of an interaction hinges in part on the appropriate use of embodied actions, including referring actions. Multimodal strategies can also make communication more efficient. For example, Louwerse and Bangerter (2010) found that the use of pointing gestures resulted in significantly faster resolution of ambiguous referring expressions; crucially, this result was replicated when the pointing gesture was artificially generated, rather than made by a human.

Like human communicators, embodied agents need the ability to plan multimodal referring acts, combining both linguistic reference and pointing. An important question is whether these two components of a referring act should be planned in order to minimise redundancy between them or not. For example, given that a pointing gesture can efficiently locate a target referent in a visual domain, should an accompanying description avoid mentioning locative properties, thereby minimising redundancy? This question is the main focus of this paper. However, it bears on a deeper issue, of relevance to the architecture of multimodal systems (and the cognitive architectures whose behaviours such systems seek to emulate): Should gestural and descriptive strategies be viewed as separate (implying that a REG module can plan its linguistic referring expressions more or less independently of whether a pointing gesture is also used) or should they be viewed as tightly coupled? If they are indeed coupled, are there any features of a linguistic description (for example, an object's location) which are excluded when a pointing gesture is used, or are linguistic features always redundant with pointing?

The present paper addresses these questions in a data-driven fashion, using a multimodal corpus of dialogues collected specifically to study referring actions at both the linguistic and gestural levels. We focus on pointing (that is, *deictic*) gestures directed at an intended referent (as opposed to, say, iconic gestures) and investigate the extent to which pointing interacts with linguistic means for referent identification. Following an overview of previous work on pointing and reference (Section 2) and a description of the corpus (Section 3), we describe a number of machine-learning experiments that address the main empirical question (Section 4), concluding with a discussion.

2 Background: Pointing and describing

There is a growing consensus in the psycholinguistic literature, especially following the work of McNeill (McNeill, 1985), that gesture and language share a number of underlying mental processes and are therefore coupled to a significant degree. This view is in part based on the observation that gestures are temporally coupled with speech and contribute meaningfully to the achievement of a communicative intention (McNeill and Duncan, 2000). For instance, in the example below, extracted from our corpus (see Section 3), a speaker identifies a landmark (composed of a collection of five circles) on a map through a combination of a pointing gesture and the mention of the size and colour of the elements making up the landmark.

(1) there's a group of five large red ones [points]

In this case, the pointing gesture further contributes to the communicative aim of identifying the cluster of five objects, in tandem with the visual features mentioned in the description. McNeill's proposal (McNeill and Duncan, 2000) is that speech and gesture should be considered as the joint outcome of the language production process, rather than as outcomes of separate processes. Various models have been proposed which are more or less congruent with this view. For example, de Ruiter (2000) proposes that the two modalities are planned together at early stages of conceptualisation during speech production, while Kita and Özyürek (2003) suggest that gestures are planned by spatio-motoric processes which differ from the planning of speech production, but interact with it at particular points.

Recent computational work has also taken these ideas on board. For example, Kopp et. al. (2008) describe a system for the concurrent planning and generation of gesture and speech, whose architecture is inspired by Kita and Özyürek (2003) and which makes use of 'multimodal concepts' (inspired by McNeill's 'growth points') combining both propositional and visuo-spatial properties. This contrasts with earlier architectures, such as that proposed by André and Rist (1996), where generation of text and gesture is undertaken by separate modules communicating with a central planner.

The idea that the planning of language is tightly coupled with that of gesture raises the possibility that the two modalities may overlap to different degrees. Gesture may be completely redundant with speech, or may encode aspects of the communicative intention that are not included in the linguistic message itself. This raises an interesting question for multimodal REG: are there features of objects that tend to be mentioned in tandem with a pointing gesture; if so, which are they? For example, the reference in (1) mentions the size and colour of the landmark, but not its location, possibly suggesting that the speaker relied on pointing to convey the 'where' of the target referent, as opposed to the 'what', which is conveyed by the description. This, however, is not the case in the example below, where pointing is accompanied by a mention of the referent's location.

(2) [...] the red ones directly to the left [...] [points]

There are at least two views on the relationship between pointing and describing (de Ruiter et al., 2012). On the one hand, the *trade-off* hypothesis holds that the decision to use a pointing gesture depends on the effort or 'cost' involved (the further away from the speaker and the smaller a referent is, the more costly it would be to point at it), compared to the effort involved in describing a referent linguistically.

On the other hand, pointing and (some aspects of) describing might proceed hand in hand, so that there is some degree of redundancy between the two modalities. Under this view, pointing may be chosen not based on (low) cost assessment but as part of a specifically multimodal cognitive strategy.

Evidence for the trade-off hypothesis is reported by Bangerter (2004), who found that, as pointing became easier in a task-oriented dialogue (because the distance between the speaker and the referent was shorter), there was a decrease in verbal effort, as measured by the number of words produced, as well as a decrease in the use of locative and visual features such as colour. Piwek (2007) also found that referring acts accompanied by pointing tended to include descriptions containing fewer properties than those which were not. These results are compatible with a view of the speaker/generator as essentially seeking to minimise effort in the communicative act, adopting the easiest available strategy that will not compromise communicative success (Beun and Cremers, 1998).

Similar results are reported by van der Sluis and Krahmer (2007), who model the trade-off hypothesis in a multimodal REG algorithm based on the graph-based framework of Krahmer et. al. (2003). The algorithm chooses to use pointing gestures, with various degrees of precision, depending on their cost relative to that of features that can be used in a linguistic description.

There is also evidence against the trade-off model. Recent experimental work by de Ruiter et. al. (2012) showed that the tendency for speakers to point was unaffected by the difficulty of referring to an object using linguistic features, although pointing did decrease with repeated reference to the same entities. Interestingly, the authors observed a correlation between the rate of pointing and the use of locative properties of objects. This would appear to favour a model in which the linguistically describable features of objects are differentiated: speakers may be using locative properties and pointing together as part of a strategy to identify the 'where' of an object. This is in line with the observation by Louwerse and Bangerter (2010) that, in visual domains, using pointing gestures with locative expressions increases the speed with which references are resolved.

The evidence from de Ruiter et. al would seem to contradict the assumptions underlying current multimodal REG models. As we have seen, van der Sluis and Krahmer (van der Sluis and Krahmer, 2007) assume a trade-off between speech and gesture. A similar assumption is made by Kranstedt and Wachsmuth (2005), who view pointing gesturs as mainly concerned with the 'where' of an object. Their algorithm, which underlies the planning of multimodal references by a virtual agent, extends the Incremental Algorithm (Dale and Reiter, 1995) as follows. Given an object in a 3D space, the algorithm first considers the possibility of producing an unambiguous pointing gesture; failing this, a pointing gesture covering the intended referent and some of its surrounding distractors may be planned. In the latter case, the algorithm then integrates other features of the object (e.g. its colour), in an effort to exclude the distractors that remain within the scope of the ambiguous point. One of the claims underlying this model is that 'absolute' location, which is covered by pointing, is given first preference after pointing itself, with other features of a referent being considered afterwards, in a preference order that will only use relative location if all other options (such as colour) are exhausted.

In summary, the empirical evidence for the relationship between pointing and describing is mixed. While the view that the planning of language in different modalities should be tightly coupled has proven useful and productive, the precise way in which the two interact in a referring act is still an open question, especially where the relationship between location and the other features of a target referent is concerned. In the remainder of this paper, we report on an empirical study that used machine learning methods with a view to establishing the relationship between descriptive features and pointing in multimodal references. Our study is not committed to a specific architecture for multimodal reference planning; rather, our aim is to establish whether pointing and describing can partly overlap in the information that they convey about a referent. Specifically, we are interested in whether the use of a description that includes spatial or locative information excludes a pointing gesture.

3 Corpus and data

The data used in this study comes from the MREDI (Multimodal REference in DIalogue) corpus (van der Sluis et al., 2008)[2], a new collection of dia-

[2]We intend to make this corpus publicly available in the near future.

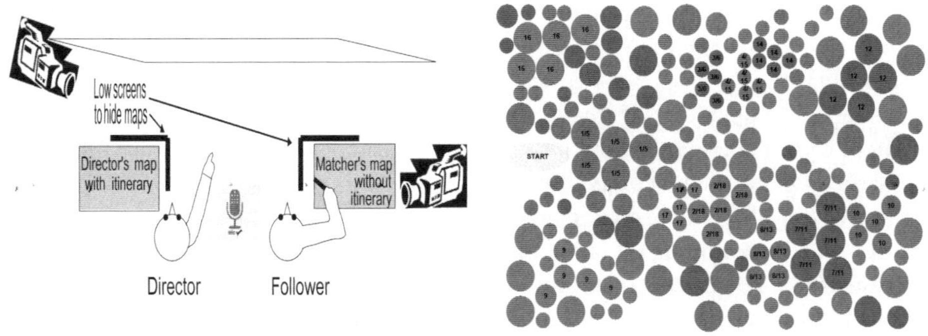

(a) Experiment setup

(b) Group circles map (numbers indicate the order in which landmarks are visited along the itinerary)

Figure 1: MREDI dialogue setup

	Feature	Name	Definition	Example
Visual	S	Size	mention of the target size	*the group of small circles*
	Sh	Shape	mention of the target shape	*the circles at the bottom*
	C	Colour	mention of the target colour	*The blue square near the red square*
Deictic/anaphoric	I	Identity	Statement of identity between the current and a previous or later target	*the red square, the same one we saw at number 5*
	D	Deixis	Use of a deictic reference	*those squares*
Locative	RP	Relative position	Position of the target landmark relative to another object on the map	*the blue square just below the red square*
	AP	Absolute position	Target position based on absolute frame of reference	*The blue circle down at the bottom*
	FP	Path references	References to non-targets on the path leading to the target.	*go east to the first tiny square, past the blue one*
	DIR	Directions	Direction-giving.	*take a right, go across and straight down*
Action	GZ	Gaze	Gaze at the shared map (boolean).	
	Point	Pointing	Use of a pointing gesture (boolean).[1]	

Table 1: Features annotated in the dialogues. All features have frequency values, except for the Action features, which are boolean.

logues elicited using a task similar to the Map-Task (Anderson et al., 1991), in which a director and a follower talked about a map displayed on a wall in front of them, approximately 1 metre away. Each also had a private copy of the map; the director's map had an itinerary on it, and her task was to communicate the itinerary to the follower, who marked it on his own private map. Participants were free to interact using speech and gesture, without touching the shared map or standing up. They could see each other, but could not see each other's private maps. Figure 1(a) displays the basic experimental setup.

The maps consisted of shapes (squares or circles), with a sequence of landmarks constituting the itinerary (initially known only to the director). The maps were designed to manipulate a number of independent variables, in a balanced design:

- **Cardinality** The target destinations in the itineraries were either individual landmarks (in 2 of the maps) or sets of 5 landmarks with the same attributes (e.g., all green squares);
- **Visual Attributes:** Targets on the itinerary differed from their distractors – the objects in their immediate vicinity (the *focus area*) – in colour, or in size, or in both colour and size. The focus area was defined as the set of objects immediately surrounding a target;
- **Prior reference:** Some of the targets were visited twice in the itinerary;
- **Shift of domain focus:** Targets were located near to or far away from the previous target. Note that if two targets t_1 and t_2 were in the *near* condition, then t_1 is one of the distractors of t_2 and vice versa.

Each participant dyad did all four maps (singleton squares and circles; group squares and circles), in a pseudo-random order, alternating in the director/matcher role so that each was director for two of the maps. Figure 1(b) displays the director's map consisting of group circles. Note that the itinerary is marked by numbering the target landmarks. Landmarks with two numbers are visited twice (for example, the first landmark is marked 1, but is also marked 5, meaning that it is the first and the fifth landmark in the itinerary). During the experiment, the map was mounted on a wall and blown up to A0 size; this significantly reduced the impression of visual clutter.

Data was collected from 8 pairs of participants[3]. In the present study, we focus exclusively on the directors' utterances. These were transcribed and split up according to the landmark to which they corresponded. In case a landmark was described over multiple turns in the dialogue, each turn was annotated as a separate utterance. Utterances were annotated with the features displayed in Table 1. Broadly, features are divided into four types: (a) *Deictic/Anaphoric*, pertaining to the use of deictic demonstratives, and/or references to previously identified entities; (ii) *Visual*, that is, corresponding to a landmark's perceptual properties; (iii) *Locative*, involving a description of the object's location; and (iv) *Action*, pertaining to gesture and gaze. All features are frequencies per utterance, except for Action features, which are boolean.

Feature	Frequency	Mean	SD
S	510	0.23	0.48
Sh	252	0.10	0.40
C	603	0.30	0.50
I	249	0.10	0.40
D	375	0.17	0.43
RP	529	0.13	0.40
AP	293	0.13	0.40
FP	989	0.40	0.70
DIR	251	0.11	0.37
GZ	836		
Point	370		

Table 2: Descriptive statistics for features in the corpus

The corpus consists of a total of 2255 director's utterances. The frequency of each feature in the corpus, as well as the per-utterance mean and standard deviation (where relevant), are indicated in Table 2; note that, with the exception of Action features, all feature values are frequencies per utterance.

Type	No point (#)	Point (#)	Total
Group	907	201	1108
Singleton	978	169	1147
Total	1885	370	2255

Table 3: Frequency of occurrence of pointing gestures relative to different object types.

As expected, linguistic features are much more frequent than pointing gestures. In fact only 16.4% of the utterances in the corpus are accompanied by pointing gestures. Previous studies, such as that by Beun and Cremers (Beun and Cremers, 1998) report a higher incidence of pointing (48% overall). Note, however, that Beun and Cremers focussed exclusively on first mention descriptions (which numbered 145 in all), while our corpus includes subsequent mentions, as well as multiple consecutive references to the same object divided over several utterances (which are counted separately in our totals).

Table 3 shows frequency figures for the pointing gestures in the corpus relative to the type of object they refer to (group vs. singleton): in accordance with the trade-off theory, which predicts that larger objects should be easier to point at, we see a significant difference ($\chi^2(1) = 4.769$, $p = 0.028$) between the two types, with more pointing occurring with group objects (that is, in group maps).

4 Experiments

In much of the work discussed in Section 2, the generation of pointing gestures is viewed as dependent on physical characteristics of the referents, in other words on their being suitable for pointing. This is especially true of work related to the trade-off hypothesis, in which the costs of pointing gestures are calculated as a function of the referent object's size and its distance from the speaker. In the present paper, by contrast, we are interested in investigating the relation between pointing and linguistic means of referent identification. More specifically, we address the question to what degree the different linguistic expressions used by the speaker to refer to objects in

[3] A number of other dialogues were recorded, but were not included in the corpus because participants focused on their own private maps and never used pointing gestures, making it impossible to study the conditions under which such gestures are produced.

the MREDI dialogues, can be used to predict the occurrence of pointing gestures. Note that this question addresses the *correlation* between properties in a description and the occurrence of pointing, rather than the issue of *how* pointing and describing should be planned. Nevertheless, as we have emphasised in Section 2, the question of co-occurrence of the two referential strategies does have a bearing on architectural issues.

A first set of experiments were run in order to test the general trade-off hypothesis. We tested a number of classifiers on the task of classifying the binary feature *point*, given all the linguistic features in the corpus. More specifically, the attributes used for the classification were *MapConfl, DIR, RP, AP, FP, S, Sh, C, D, I, Point*. They are all explained and exemplified in Table 1 with the exception of *MapConfl*, which indicates whether a specific case in the data comes from a group or a singleton map. This feature was included because, as noted in the previous section, whether a target landmark was a singleton or a group made a difference, presumably because groups are larger and more visually salient. Note further that one of the Action features, *GZ* (gaze), is ignored in the experiments because it is an almost univocal predictor of pointing. Indeed, gazing is involved roughly every time *Point* has the value *y* (yes) (but not the other way round).

The experiments were run using the Weka (Witten and Frank, 2005) tool, which gives access to many different algorithms, and 10-fold cross-validation was used throughout. The results are shown in Table (4) in terms of Precision, Recall and F-measure for each of the classifiers.

Classifier	**P**	**R**	**F**
Baseline 1 (ZeroR)	0.699	0.836	0.761
Baseline 2 (OneR)	0.762	0.834	0.765
SMO	*0.699*	0.836	*0.761*
NaiveBayes	0.795	0.811	0.802
Logistic	0.806	0.84	0.808
J48	**0.829**	**0.85**	**0.833**

Table 4: Predicting pointing gestures given all the linguistic features in the corpus: classification results.

Two baselines were created to evaluate the results. The first one is provided by the ZeroR classifier, which always chooses the most frequent class, in this case *n* (no pointing gesture). The F-measure obtained by this method is somewhat high at 0.761, because there are relatively few pointing gestures in the data. The second baseline, which provides a slightly more interesting result against which to evaluate the other classifiers, is provided by OneR. It achieves an F-measure of 0.765 by predicting a pointing gesture if DIR >= 2.5, in other words if there are at least 2.5 occurrences of direction expressions in the utterance. Using this rule has the effect of predicting a few of the pointing gestures, with an F-measure on the *y* class (occurrence of pointing gestures) of 0.031.

The other four sets of results were obtained by running four different classification algorithms with the same set of attributes. Apart from SMO (an algorithm using support vector machines), all the classifiers perform better than the baseline. The best results are produced by the decision tree classifier J48, which obtains an overall F-measure of 0.833, and an F-measure of 0.421 on the *y* class. The confusion matrix generated by J48 on this data-set is shown in Table (5)

a	**b**	← classified as
1794	91	a = n
247	123	b = y

Table 5: Predicting pointing given all the linguistic features in the corpus: confusion matrix.

The model created by the decision tree classifier (J48) is quite complex (size=57 and no. of leaves=29). The first branching, which corresponds to no *AP* (Absolute Position) and no *C* (Colour), assigns *n* to as many as 1571 instances (with 115 errors). The tree is shown in Figure (2). The tree also shows that certain combinations of features are more likely to be associated with pointing gestures. These are predominantly combinations including occurrences of *AP*, or, in the absence of absolute position, combinations including positive values for *FP* (Frequency of reference on Path) and *DIR* (Direction).

The maximum entropy model, built by the logistic regression algorithm (Logistic), shows similar tendencies in that the attributes that are assigned the highest weights are *AP*, *C* and *DIR*.

These results confirm the general hypothesis that there is a strong relationship between linguistic features used in a description and pointing gestures. Indeed, it is possible to predict pointing gestures on the basis of the linguistic features used.

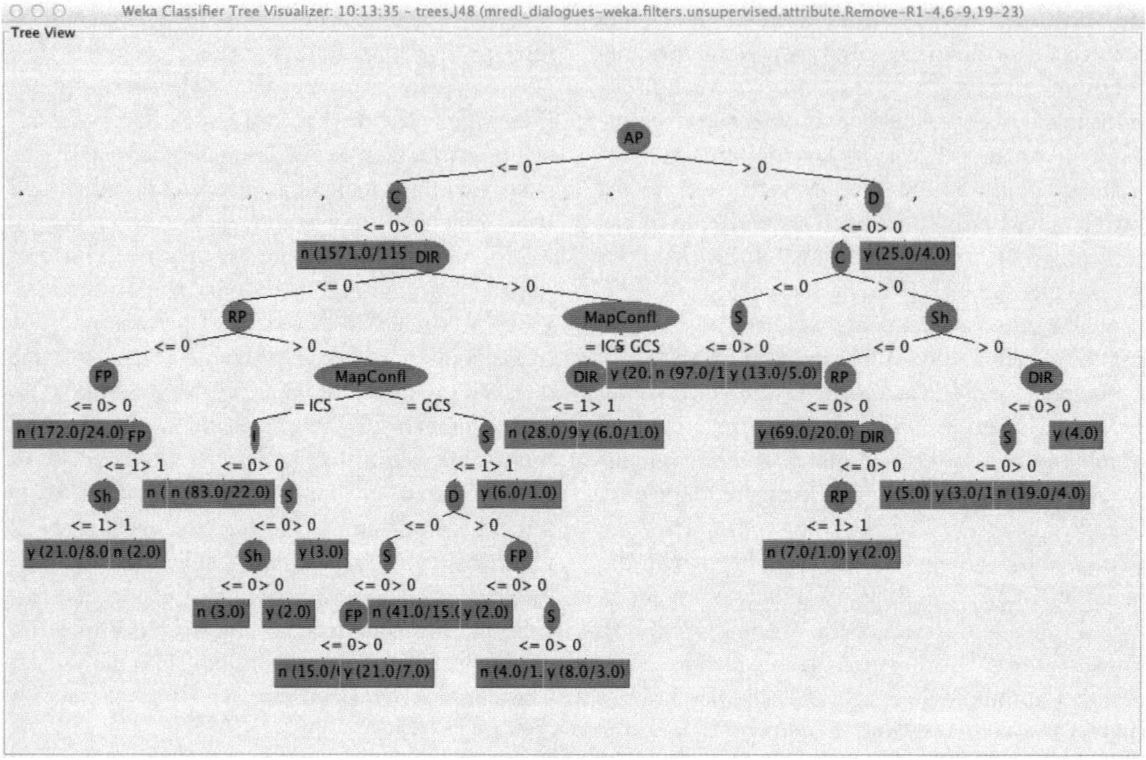

Figure 2: J48 decision tree

Classifier	P	R	F	Features
Exp1: J48	0.829	0.85	0.833	All features
Exp3: Logistic	0.806	0.84	0.808	Loc+D+I
Exp2: J48	0.835	0.851	0.806	MapConfl+Loc+D+I
Exp6: NaiveBayes	0.793	0.825	0.802	Loc
Exp4: NaiveBayes	0.764	0.804	0.779	MapConfl+Visual+D+I
Exp5: J48	0.761	0.808	0.777	MapConfl+Visual
Exp8: NaiveBayes	0.761	0.808	0.777	Visual
Exp9: NaiveBayes	0.761	0.801	0.775	Visual+D+I
Baseline 2: OneR	0.762	0.834	0.765	Dir
Exp7: F48	0.699	0.836	0.761	MapConfl+D+I
Baseline 1: ZeroR	0.699	0.836	0.761	Most freq class

Table 6: Predicting pointing gestures with different feature combinations: classification results.

In particular, the results suggest a difference between features that express locative properties and those having to do with the visual description of the same object (its colour, size and shape). More specifically, it would seem that locative features are more useful to the classifiers than visual properties.

To test this second hypothesis, we ran a series of experiments where the task was still to predict pointing gestures, but different subsets of the linguistic features were tested one at the time. For each feature combination, we run the classification using J48, Naive Bayes and the Logistic regression algorithm. In Table (6), we show the best result obtained for each feature combination. The classifiers are ordered from the most accurate to the least accurate, and the combination of features used by each of them is listed in the last column. The best results and the two baselines from the previous set of experiments are included for the sake of comparison. Note that the term *Loc* is used to refer to all the locative attributes *AP, DIR, RP, AP* and *FP*, while *Visual* refers to *S*, *Sh* and *C*.

The best results are those obtained when the complete feature set is used in the training. However, the next best results are achieved by the classifiers using the locative features, either alone or together with features concerning the map type, identity with a previously mentioned object and deictic reference, with an F-measure in the range 0.802–0.808. If visual features are used instead, the F-measure is in the range 0.775–0.779. The worst results are obtained if neither location nor visual description are used. Thus, although the differences between the best and the worst classifiers are not dramatic, in this data we see a tendency for the locative features to be slightly better predictors of pointing gestures than features corresponding to visual descriptions.

5 Discussion and conclusions

The automatic classification experiments described above show that to a certain extent, the pointing gestures occurring in the MREDI corpus can be predicted based on the linguistic expressions used by the speaker in conjunction with pointing. More precisely, linguistic descriptions can be used to predict about one third of the pointing gestures that speakers have produced in the corpus. This is an interesting and novel result, which not only supports the general notion that gestures and speech should be seen as tightly coupled, but also suggests that this coupling does not result in a minimisation of redundancy between the two modalities. Rather, it appears that a number of pointing gestures accompanied descriptions containing locative properties, something that contradicts the predictions of models based on the trade-off hypothesis (Kranstedt and Wachsmuth, 2005; van der Sluis and Krahmer, 2007).

There are a number of limitations of the present study, which we plan to address in future work. First, pointing gestures in our corpus were relatively scarce (16.4% of utterances were accompanied by pointing). This in part explains the relative accuracy of our baselines: predicting the majority class (that is, no pointing) in every case will clearly yield reasonable results given that the size of the class is so large. On the other hand, the relative scarcity of pointing may also indicate that pointing is somewhat more costly than linguistic description, in cognitive and physical terms. In fact, the difference we see in the number of pointing gestures between singleton and group maps also seems to confirm this assumption: in the group maps, where objects are larger, and thus more easily pointed at according to the trade-off model, there are in fact significantly more pointing gestures. The incidence of pointing may also have been affected by the nature of the domains used: although the shared maps in the experiments were large and quite close to the interlocutors, the presence of objects of the same shape may have added to the general visual clutter of the maps, making pointing less likely.

Another aspect of the data that we have not investigated is the presence of individual strategies. We know that speakers differ a lot in their use of gesturing as regards e.g. frequency, type of gesture and representation techniques. Recent models of gesture production for embodied agents are taking such differences into account (Neff et al., 2008; Bergmann and Kopp, 2009). Similarly, some speakers might have a greater preference for pointing than others. For example, Beun and Cremers (1998) note that certain speakers in their corpus explicitly stated that they had attempted to perform the task in their dialogues without pointing, in spite of their having been told that they could point. Recent data-driven experiments on referential descriptions by Dale and Viethen (Dale and Viethen, 2010), In a domain quite similar to the one used here, suggest that speakers do indeed cluster according to their preferred referential strategy. Similar assumptions have informed REG algorithms trained on the TUNA Corpus, in the context of the Generation Challenges (Gatt and Belz, 2010) (Bohnet, 2008; Di Fabbrizio et al., 2008). In future work, we plan to address this question in a multimodal context, where results by Piwek (2007) have already suggested that such individual strategies may play an important role.

The hypothesis that specific combinations of pointing and linguistic descriptions (for example, an object's colour or size) can be excluded, is clearly not borne out by the data. There is, however, a tendency for locative features to act as stronger predictors of pointing gestures. Although the trend is not very strong, it is an interesting one since it confirms the experimental results by de Ruiter et. al. reviewed earlier (de Ruiter et al., 2012). This may suggest that a pointing gesture may ultimately be planned within the same system as locative features (i.e. the decision of whether or not to point is not dependent on the decision of whether or not to describe inherent, visual properties of the object, but on whether the object's location is to be indicated). Another feature that is worth exploring further is deixis, specifically the difference between proximal and distal deictic expressions and their interaction with pointing gestures. For example, Piwek et al. (2007) found that proximal deictic expressions tend to be associated with a more intensive attentional focusing mechanism, while Bangerter (2004) also observes an association between pointing and the use of deictic expressions.

From an NLG perspective, our results suggest that decisions to generate a pointing gesture and those to select visual attributes might take place independently (perhaps in parallel, perhaps in different modules). From a cognitive perspective, it suggests two types of interaction between attention/vision and language/gesture, related to the description of the 'what' of an object and its 'where' (Landau and Jackendoff, 1993).

Finally, our study focused on the relationship between the two modalities involved in a referential act, addressing the question of redundancy between them. We have not addressed the impact of the visual properties of a target referent in relation to its surrounding objects, on the choices speakers make in these two modalities. This is a priority for future work, given that the corpus was designed to balance the presence or absence of various visual properties of an object (see Section 3). Taking this even further, it remains to be investigated, for example, whether there would be interesting differences in the relationship betwene pointing and describing between 2D scenes of the kind used here, and 3D environments of the sort used by Kranstedt and Wachsmuth (2005). Another priority is to take into account the interactive nature of the dialogues, with particular focus on the follower's feedback to the director, as an indicator of the success of referential expressions. This is another aspect of the dialogue situation that may have an impact on planning multimodal referential acts.

Acknowledgements

Special thanks are due to Ielka van der Sluis, Adrian Bangerter and Paul Piwek, who were involved in every step of the design, collection and annotation of the MREDI corpus, and who also commented on preliminary drafts of this paper.

References

A. Anderson, M. Bader, E. Bard, E. Boyle, G. M. Doherty, S. Garrod, S. Isard, J. Kowtko, J. McAllister, J. Miller, C. Sotillo, H. S. Thompson, and R. Weinert. 1991. The HCRC Map Task corpus. *Language and Speech*, 34:351–366.

E. André and T. Rist. 1996. Coping with temporal constraints in multimedia presentation planning. In *Proceedings of the 13th National Conference on Artificial Intelligence (AAAI'96)*.

A. Bangerter. 2004. Using pointing and describing to achieve joint focus of attention in dialogue. *Psychological Science*, 15(6):415–419.

K. Bergmann and S. Kopp. 2009. GNetIc - using bayesian decision networks for iconic gesture generation. In A. Nijholt and H. Vilhjálmsson, editors, *Proceedings of the 9th International Conference on Intelligent Virtual Agents (LNAI 5773)*, pages 76–89. Springer.

R.J. Beun and A. Cremers. 1998. Object reference in a shared domain of conversation. *Pragmatics and Cognition*, 6(1-2):121–152.

B. Bohnet. 2008. The fingerprint of human referring expressions and their surface realization with graph transducers. In *Proceedings of the 5th International Conference on Natural Language Generation (INLG'08)*.

C. Callaway and J. C. Lester. 2002. Pronominalization in generated discourse and dialogue. In *Proceedings of the 40th Annual Meeting of the Association for Computational Linguistics (ACL'02)*.

R. Dale and E. Reiter. 1995. Computational interpretation of the Gricean maxims in the generation of referring expressions. *Cognitive Science*, 19(8):233–263.

R. Dale and J. Viethen. 2010. Attribute-centric referring expression generation. In E. Krahmer and M. Theune, editors, *Empirical Methods in Natural Language Generation*, volume 5790 of *LNAI*. Springer, Berlin and Heidelberg.

R. Dale. 1989. Cooking up referring expressions. In *Proceedings of the 27th annual meeting of the Association for Computational Linguistics (ACL'89)*, pages 68–75.

J.P. de Ruiter, A. Bangerter, and P. Dings. 2012. The interplay between gesture and speech in the production of referring expressions: Investigating the tradeoff hypothesis. *Topics in Cognitive Science*, 4:232–248.

J.P. de Ruiter. 2000. The production of gesture and speech. In D. McNeill, editor, *Language and Gesture*, pages 284–311. Cambridge University Press.

G. Di Fabbrizio, A. J. Stent, and S. Bangalore. 2008. Trainable speaker-based referring expression generation. In *Proceedings of the 12th Conference on Computational Natural Language Learning (CONLL'08)*, pages 151–158.

A. Gatt and A. Belz. 2010. Introducing shared task evaluation to nlg: The TUNA shared task evaluation challenges. In E. Krahmer and M. Theune, editors, *Empirical Methods in Natural Language Generation*. Springer.

S. Kita and A. Özyürek. 2003. What does cross-linguistic variation in semantic coordination of speech and gesture reveal?: Evidence for an interface representation of spatial thinking and speaking. *Journal of Memory and Language*, 48:16–32.

S. Kopp, K. Bergmann, and I. Wachsmuth. 2008. Multimodal communication from multimodal thinking: Towards an integrated model of speech and gesture production. *International Journal of Semantic Computing*, 2(1):115–136.

E. Krahmer and M. Theune. 2002. Efficient context-sensitive generation of referring expressions. In K. van Deemter and R. Kibble, editors, *Information Sharing: Reference and Presupposition in Language Generation and Interpretation*. CSLI Publications, Stanford.

E. Krahmer and K. van Deemter. 2012. Computational generation of referring expressions: A survey. *Computational Linguistics*, 38(1):173–218.

E. Krahmer, S. van Erk, and A. Verleg. 2003. Graph-based generation of referring expressions. *Computational Linguistics*, 29(1):53–72.

A. Kranstedt and I. Wachsmuth. 2005. Incremental generation of multimodal deixis referring to objects. In *Proceedings of the 10th European Workshop on Natural Language Generation (ENLG'05)*.

B. Landau and R. Jackendoff. 1993. what and where in spatial language and spatial cognition. *Behavioral and Brain Sciences*, 16:217–238.

M. Louwerse and A. Bangerter. 2010. Effects of ambiguous gestures and language on the time-course of reference resolution. *Cognitive Science*, 34:1517–1529.

K.F. McCoy and M. Strube. 1999. Generating anaphoric expressions: Pronoun or definite description? In *Proceedings of the Workshop on the Relation of Discourse/Dialogue Structure and Reference*.

D. McNeill and S.D. Duncan. 2000. Growth points in thinking for speaking. In D. McNeill, editor, *Language and Gesture*, pages 141–161. Cambridge University Press.

D. McNeill. 1985. So you think gestures are nonverbal? *Psychological Review*, 92(3):350–371.

M. Neff, M. Kipp, I. Albrecht, and H.-P. Seidel. 2008. Gesture modeling and animation based on a probabilistic recreation of speaker style. *ACM Transactions on Graphics*, 27(1):1–24.

P. Piwek, R-J. Beun, and A. Cremers. 2007. proximal and distal in language and cognition: Evidence from deictic demonstratives in dutch. *Journal of Pragmatics*, 40(4):694–718.

P. Piwek. 2007. Modality choice for generation of referring acts: Pointing vs describing. In *Proceedings of the Workshop on Multimodal Output Generation (MOG'07).*, pages 129–139.

I. van der Sluis and E. Krahmer. 2007. Generating multimodal referring expressions. *Discourse Processes*, 44(3):145–174.

I. van der Sluis, P. Piwek, A. Gatt, and A. Bangerter. 2008. Towards a balanced corpus of multimodal referring expressions in dialogue. In *Proceedings of the Symposium on Multimodal Output Generation (MOG'08)*.

I.H. Witten and E. Frank. 2005. *Data Mining: Practical machine learning tools and techniques*. Morgan Kaufmann, San Francisco, second edition.

Natural Language Generation and Summarization at RALI

Guy Lapalme
RALI - DIRO
Université de Montréal
C.P. 6128, Succ. Centre-Ville
Montréal, Québec, Canada, H3C 3J7
lapalme@iro.umontreal.ca

Processing language in written or spoken form, in a mother tongue or in another language is a very complex and important problem. Hence the idea of building automatic or semi-automatic tools to support people during their attempt to understand what they read or to translate a given message into an adequate linguistic form. Since the eighties, I have worked with my students on many NLP projects, this talk focusses on some of them, past and present, dealing with generation and summarization.

We have always thrived to produce *working* systems that deal with *real* texts or use data to produce texts that can be easily understood by humans. This fundamental motivation imposes some challenging constraints but also produces interesting payoffs. Given the fact that our lab is in French speaking university in a mostly English speaking country, we have often worked in either of these languages and often in both.

1 Generation

PRÉTEXTE (Gagnon and Lapalme, 1996) was a system for generating French texts conveying temporal information. Temporal information and localization expressed by temporal adverbial and verbal phrases was represented with DRT. Systemic Grammar Theory was used to translate the DRT representation into a syntactic form to produce the final text.

SPIN (Kosseim and Lapalme, 2000) deals with a fundamental problem in natural language generation: how to organize the content of a text in a coherent and natural way. From a corpus analysis of French instructional texts, we determined 9 senses typically communicated in these texts and 7 rhetorical relations used to present them. We then developed presentation heuristics to determine how the senses should be organized rhetorically to create a coherent and natural text.

POSTGRAPHE (Fasciano and Lapalme, 2000) generated a report integrating graphics and text from a set of writer's intentions. The system was given data in tabular form and a declaration of the types of values in the columns of the table. Also indicated were intentions to be conveyed in the graphics (e.g., compare two variables or show the evolution of a set of variables) and the system generated a report in LaTeX. PostGraphe also generated the accompanying text to help the reader focus on the important points of the graphics.

SIMPLENLG-EN-FR (Vaudry and Lapalme, 2013) is a bilingual adaptation of the English realizer SimpleNLG. Its French grammatical coverage is equivalent to the English one and covers the essential notions that are taught to learners of French as a second language as defined by *Le français fondamental (1er Degré)*. The French lexicon contains a commonly used French vocabulary, including function words. JSREAL is a work in progress describing a French text realizer in Javascript that can be easily embedded in a web browser. Its main originality is the fact that it produces DOM elements and not text strings so that they can easily produce parts of web pages from JSON inputs sent by the server for example.

In a project of interactive generation, we develop a cognitively inspired methodology to assist people during the production process, as the route between input and output can be full of hurdles and quite long. For each step, we want to develop web based applications that address a specific problem and help induce some pattern reaction in the production of language. For the moment we have produced two prototypes: DRILLTUTOR (Zock and Lapalme, 2010) which is goal-oriented multilingual phrasebook and WEBREG (Zock et al., 2012) to practice the generation of appropriate referring expressions.

2 Summarization

Summarization is *in principle* strongly related to NLG because it implies reading and understanding one or many documents in order to produce a short text describing the main ideas of the original. Summarization approaches are often classified as either abstractive or extractive, the former being the selection of the most important sentences from the original documents.

In much the same way as NLG has *suffered* from the fact that it is often possible to trick the readers with canned text or formatted templates, abstractive summarization had to compete with acceptable results produced by scorers of sentences, the ones with the best scores being then concatenated to produce a summary. In our group, we tried to stay away from such approaches that in our view did not give any new insights even though it did not always allow us to *win* the summarization competitions at DUC or TAC.

SUMUM (Saggion and Lapalme, 2002) explored the idea of dynamic summarization by taking a raw technical text as input and produced an indicative-informative summary. The indicative part of the summary identifies the topics of the document, and the informative part elaborates on some of these topics according to the reader's interest. SumUM motivates the topics, describes entities, and defines concepts. This is accomplished through a process of shallow syntactic and semantic analysis, concept identification, and text regeneration.

LETSUM (Farzindar and Lapalme, 2004) developed an approach for the summarization of legal documents by helping a legal expert determine the key ideas of a judgment. It is based on the exploration of the document's architecture and its thematic structures in order to build a table style summary for improving coherency and readability of the text. Although LetSUM extracted full sentences from the original document, it reorganized, merged and displayed different parts in order to better give an idea of the document and focus the reader, a legal expert, to the important parts.

ABSUM (Genest and Lapalme, 2013) introduces a flexible and scalable methodology for abstractive summarization that analyzes the source documents using a knowledge base to identify patterns in the the source documents and generate summary text from them. This knowledge-based approach allows for implicit understanding and transformation of the source documents' content because it is carefully crafted for the summarization task and domain of interest.

3 Conclusion

These examples illustrate some links that we have established between generation and summarization over the last few years and that are promising for the future of these two research areas.

References

Atefeh Farzindar and Guy Lapalme. 2004. Legal texts summarization by exploration of the thematic structures and argumentative roles. In Stan Szpakowicz Marie-Francine Moens, editor, *Text Summarization Branches Out: Proceedings of the ACL-04 Workshop*, pages 27–34, Barcelona, Spain, July. Association for Computational Linguistics.

M. Fasciano and G. Lapalme. 2000. Intentions in the coordinated generation of graphics and text from tabular data. *Knowledge and Information Systems*, 2(3):310–339, Aug.

M. Gagnon and G. Lapalme. 1996. From conceptual time to linguistic time. *Computational Linguistics*, 22(1):91–127, March.

Pierre-Etienne Genest and Guy Lapalme. 2013. Absum: a knowledge-based abstractive summarizer. *Computational Linguistics*, page 30 pages, July. In preparation.

L. Kosseim and G. Lapalme. 2000. Choosing rhetorical structures to plan instructional texts. *Computational Intelligence*, 16(3):408–445, Aug.

Horacio Saggion and Guy Lapalme. 2002. Generating informative and indicative summaries with SumUM. *Computational Linguistics*, 28(4):497–526, Dec.

Pierre-Luc Vaudry and Guy Lapalme. 2013. Adapting SimpleNLG for bilingual English-French realisation. In *14th European Conference on Natural Language Generation*, Sofia, Bulgaria, Aug. This volume.

Michael Zock and Guy Lapalme. 2010. A generic tool for creating and using multilingual phrasebooks. In Bernadette Sharp and Michael Zock eds., editors, *Proceedings of NLPCS 2010 (Natural Language Processing and Cognitive Science)*, pages 79–89, Funchal, Madeira - Portugal, Jun.

Michael Zock, Guy Lapalme, and Mehdi Yousfi-Monod. 2012. Learn to speak like normal people do: the case of object descriptions. In *9th International Workshop on Natural Language Processing and Cognitive Science (NLPCS 2012)*, pages 120–129, Wraclow, jun.

The KBGen Challenge

Eva Banik
Computational Linguistics Ltd
London, UK
ebanik@comp-ling.com

Claire Gardent
CNRS, LORIA
Nancy, France
claire.gardent@loria.fr

Eric Kow*
Computational Linguistics Ltd
London, UK
kowey@comp-ling.com

1 Introduction

The KBGen 2013 natural language generation challenge[1] was intended to survey and compare the performance of various systems which perform tasks in the content realization stage of generation (Banik et al., 2012). Given a set of relations which form a coherent unit, the task is to generate complex sentences which are grammatical and fluent in English. The relations for this year's challenge were selected from the AURA knowledge base (KB) (Gunning et al., 2010). In this paper we give an overview of the KB, describe our methodology for selecting sets of relations from the KB to provide input-output pairs for the challenge, and give details of the development and test data set that was provided to participating teams. Three teams have submitted system outputs for this year's challenge. In this paper we show BLEU and NIST scores for outputs generated by the teams. The full results of our evaluation, including human judgements, as well as the development and test data set are available at http://www.kbgen.org.

2 The AURA Knowledge Base

The AURA knowledge base (Gunning et al., 2010) encodes information from a biology textbook (Reece et al., 2010). It was developed to support a question answering system, to help students understand biological concepts by allowing them to ask questions about the material while reading the textbook. AURA is a frame-based KB which encodes events, the entities that participate in events, properties, and roles that the entities play in an event. The relations in the KB include relations between these types, including event-to-entity, event-to-event, event-to-property, entity-to-property. The KB is built on top of the CLIB generic library of concepts (Barker et al., 2001). As part of the encoding process, concepts in CLIB are specialized and/or combined to encode biology-specific information. AURA is organized into a set of concept maps, where each concept map corresponds to a biological entity or process. The KB was encoded by biology teachers and contains around 5,000 concept maps. It is available for download for academic purposes in various formats including OWL[2].

3 The Content Selection Process for KBGen 2012

The input provided to the participants consisted of a set of content units extracted from the KB, and a sentence corresponding to each content unit. The content units were semi-automatically selected from AURA such that:

- the set of relations in each content unit formed a connected graph
- each content unit can be verbalised by a single, possibly complex sentence which is grammatical and meaningful
- the set of content units contain as many different relations and concepts of different semantic types (events, entities, properties, etc) as possible.

To produce these inputs we first asked biology teachers to provide coherent content units using the AURA graphical interface. The basic assumption behind this approach was that, since every content unit can be expressed by a coherent sentence, each set of relations will exhibit a "coherence pattern". We then created a search space of candidate content units by extracting patterns from the KB which were similar to the patterns given by the biologists. Finally, we manually selected coherent content units.

*The work reported in this paper was supported by funding from Vulcan, Inc.

[1] http://www.kbgen.org

[2] http://www.ai.sri.com/halo/halobook2010/exported-kb/biokb.html

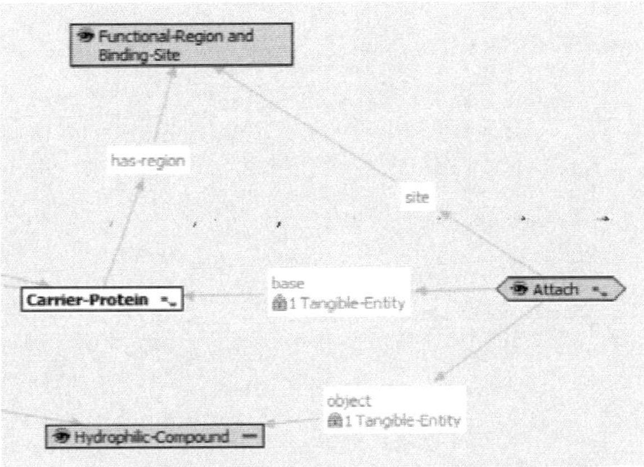

Figure 1: " A hydrophobic compound attaches to a carrier protein at a region called the binding site."

3.1 Manual Selection of Content Units

In the first step of our process, biology teachers manually selected parts of concept maps which represented educationally useful information for biology students by searching for specific concepts in AURA's graph-based user interface. For each content unit they wrote a sentence verbalising the selected relations (Fig. 1). The biology teachers who identified these coherent, sentence-sized chunks of information were familiar with the encoding practices in AURA, the underlying biology textbook, and had experience with the Inquire e-book application (Spaulding et al., 2011) which displays educationally useful content from the KB.

3.2 From Graphs to Queries

In the second step, the graphical representations produced by the biologists were manually translated to specific knowledge base queries which were run in AURA to retrieve the instances satisfying the queries. Queries consist of two parts: a set of triples whose domain and range are variables, and a set of `instance-of` triples stating type constraints on the variables. The graph shown in Figure 1 was translated to the following query:

Type constraints:

```
(?CP  instance-of Carrier-Protein)
(?A  instance-of Attach)
(?BS  instance-of Binding-Site)
(?HP  instance-of Hydrophilic-Compound)
```

Relation constraints:

```
(?A object ?HP)
(?A base ?CP)
(?A site ?BS)
(?CP has-region ?BS)
```

3.3 From Queries to Generalized Query Patterns

After checking that it returns an answer, each query was generalized to a query pattern in order to find other queries which involved different concepts and relations; but still exhibited the same general coherence pattern. To derive generalized query patterns, specific queries were modified in two ways: 1) by removing type constraints on concepts, and 2) by replacing specific relations with generalized relation types.

Removing type constraints

Manually specified queries were extended by removing type constraints on variables. In the above example, types were generalised to Event or Entity:

```
(?CP  instance-of Entity)
(?A  instance-of Event)
(?BS  instance-of Entity)
(?HP  instance-of Entity)
```

Other generalized types we used from the ontology were Property-Values and Roles.

Generalizing relations

Each query was generalized by defining equivalence classes over semantically similar relations and replacing the specific relation in the query with its equivalence class. The basic assumption behind this was that if a set of relations is coherent, we should be able to replace a relation with another, semantically similar relation in the set, and still have a coherent content unit. For example, whether two entities are connected by `has-part` or `has-region` is unlikely to make a difference to the coherence of a content unit.

Following this approach we identified groups of semantically similar relations within each relation type (Event-to-Event, Event-to-Entity, etc). The equivalence classes over relations were straightforwardly derived from distinctions made in CLIB (Barker et al., 2001), the upper ontology and library of general concepts that AURA is built on, although there was some manual fine-tuning required to exclude relations which were not reliably encoded in the KB. For example, we divided Entity-to-Entity relations into three categories, based on whether they had a spatial or meronymic sense, or expressed a specific relation between two chemicals:

en2en-spatial: abuts is-above is-along is-at is-inside is-opposite is-outside is-over location is-across is-on is-parallel-to is-perpendicular-to is-under is-between is-facing is-below is-beside is-near

en2en-part: possesses has-part has-region encloses has-basic-structural-unit has-structural-part has-functional-part

en2en-chemical: has-solute has-solvent has-atom has-ion has-oxidized-form has-reduced-form has-isomer

Here the distinction between spatial relations and meronymic relations was given by CLIB. Relations in the third group were specific to our domain and added during the process of encoding.

Event-to-entity relations were divided into "aux-participant" relations, which express the spatial orientation of an event, and "core-participant" relations which describe ways in which entities participate in the event. Here we used the categories of spatial relations and "participant" relations from CLIB. Our terminology reflects the fact that entities connected to an event by a core-participant relation are typically expressed as obligatory arguments of the verb in a sentence, whereas aux-participants would be expressed as optional modifiers:

core-participants: agent object donor base instrument raw-material recipient result

aux-participants: away-from destination origin path site toward

With these definitions, the specific query illustrated above in section 3.2 was translated to the following query pattern:

```
(?A core-participant ?X)
(?A core-participant ?CP)
(?A aux-participant ?BS)
(?CP en2en-part ?BS)
```

3.4 From Query Results to Content Units

Query patterns were expanded by producing all valid instantiations of the pattern in order to create a search space of candidate content units, and we ran each expanded query in AURA. The last step was filtering the results returned by satisfiable queries to obtain content units which can be verbalised in a single sentence. We used the following selection criteria to do this:

- A meaningful and grammatical sentence could be formed by verbalising all concepts, relations and properties present in the query result.

```
(KBGEN-INPUT :ID "ex03c.99-1"
:TRIPLES (
(|Secretion21994| |object| |Mucus21965|)
(|Secretion21994| |base|  |Earthworm21974|)
(|Secretion21994| |site| |Alimentary-Canal21978|)
(|Earthworm21974| |has-region|
                  |Alimentary-Canal21978|))
:INSTANCE-TYPES (
(|Mucus21965|      |instance-of| |Mucus|)
(|Secretion21994| |instance-of| |Secretion|)
(|Earthworm21974| |instance-of| |Earthworm|)
(|Alimentary-Canal21978| |instance-of|
                         |Alimentary-Canal|))
:ROOT-TYPES (
(|Secretion21994| |instance-of| |Event|)
(|Mucus21965|      |instance-of| |Entity|)
(|Earthworm21974| |instance-of| |Entity|)
(|Alimentary-Canal21978| |instance-of| |Entity|)
))
```

Figure 2: Input for the sentence *"Mucus is secreted in the alimentary canal of earthworms."*

- The set of content units should be as varied as possible. In particular, we did not keep a content unit if another very similar content unit was present in the selected units. For instance, if two content units contain identical relations (modulo concept labels), only one of these two units would be kept.

Given the pattern shown in Fig. 1 for instance, we obtained 27 coherent content units. Each content unit was verbalized as a sentence to provide development data for the content realization challenge. The following sentences illustrate the variation in the resulting content units:

- Polymers are digested in the lysosomes of eukaryotic cells.
- Mucus is secreted in the alimentary canal of earthworms.
- Lysosomal enzymes digest proteins and polymers at the lysosome of a eukaryotic cell.
- A chemical is attached to the active site of a protein enzyme with an ionic bond.
- An enzyme substrate complex is formed when a chemical attaches to the active site of a protein enzyme with a hydrogen bond.
- Starch is stored in the lateral root of carrots.

4 Development Data Set

The development data set provided to participants contained 207 input-output pairs. These inputs were based on 19 different coherence patterns. Fig. 2 shows an input-output pair based on the pattern illustrated above. We also provided two lexicons: a lexicon for events which gave a mapping from events to verbs, their inflected forms and nominalizations and a lexicon for entities, which provided a noun and its plural form. The relevant entries in these lexicons for the input in Fig. 2 were:

```
Secretion,secretes,secrete,secreted,secretion
Mucus, mucus, mucus
Earthworm,earthworm,earthworms
Alimentary-Canal,alimentary canal,alimentary canals
```

5 Test Set

Our test data set contained 72 inputs in the same format (and corresponding lexical resources as above), which were divided into three categories:
(1) **seen patterns, seen relations:** inputs that have exactly the same relations as some of the inputs in the development data set, but different concepts
(2) **seen patterns, unseen relations:** these inputs are derived from patterns in the development data set. They have similar structure, but contain slightly different combinations of relations.
(3) **unseen patterns:** inputs extracted from a previously unused pattern, containing combinations of relations not seen in the development data set.

6 Evaluation

Participants submitted two sets of outputs:
(1) outputs generated by their system as is (modulo including the lexicon provided in the test data set) (2) outputs generated 6 days later, during which time teams had a chance to make improvements.
Each team was allowed to submit a set of 5 ranked outputs for each input. We have evaluated all of the submitted outputs using BLEU and NIST scores and we are currently in the process of collecting human judgements for the final system outputs that were ranked first. Table 1 shows the overall results of automatic evaluation on both the initial and final data sets for our three teams[3], as well as the coverage of the individual systems over the 72 test inputs. More detail including the full results of our evaluation can be found at `http://www.kbgen.org`, along with a link to download the development and test data set used in the challenge, and more information about AURA and related resources.

[3]IMS: Stuttgart University Institute for Computational Language Processing, LOR: LORIA, University of Nancy, UDEL: University of Delaware, Computer and Information Science Department

	NIST	BLEU	coverage
HUMAN-1	10.0098	1.0000	100%
UDEL-final-1	5.9749	0.3577	97%
UDEL-initial-1	5.6030	0.3165	100%
LOR-final-1	4.8569	0.3053	84%
LOR-final-3	4.7238	0.2993	100%
LOR-final-2	4.6711	0.2945	100%
LOR-final-5	4.5720	0.2812	100%
LOR-final-4	4.4889	0.2781	100%
IMS-final-2	3.9649	0.1107	100%
IMS-final-4	3.8813	0.1140	100%
IMS-final-1	3.8670	0.1111	100%
IMS-final-3	3.7765	0.1023	100%
IMS-initial-2	3.6726	0.1117	100%
IMS-initial-3	3.6608	0.1181	100%
IMS-initial-1	3.6384	0.1173	100%
IMS-initial-4	3.5817	0.1075	100%
LOR-initial-1	0.1206	0.0822	30%
LOR-initial-3	0.1091	0.0751	100%
LOR-initial-4	0.0971	0.0732	100%
LOR-initial-2	0.0948	0.0757	100%
LOR-initial-5	0.0881	0.0714	100%

Table 1: BLEU and NIST scores of initial and final system outputs. The digit behind the team names refer to the output rank

References

E. Banik, C. Gardent, D. Scott, N. Dinesh, and F. Liang. 2012. Kbgen text generation from knowledge bases as a new shared task. In *INLG 2012, Starved Rock State Park, Illinois, USA*.

K. Barker, B. Porter, and P. Clark. 2001. A library of generic concepts for composing knowledgebases. In *Proceedings K-CAP 2001*, pages 14–21.

D. Gunning, V. K. Chaudhri, P. Clark, K. Barker, Shaw-Yi Chaw, M. Greaves, B. Grosof, A. Leung, D. McDonald, S. Mishra, J. Pacheco, B. Porter, A. Spaulding, D. Tecuci, and J. Tien. 2010. Project halo update - progress toward digital aristotle. *AI Magazine*, Fall:33–58.

Jane B. Reece, Lisa A. Urry, Michael L. Cain, Steven A. Wasserman, Peter V. Minorsky, and Robert B. Jackson. 2010. *Campbell Biology*. Pearson Publishing.

A. Spaulding, A. Overholtzer, J. Pacheco, J. Tien, V. K. Chaudhri, D. Gunning, and P. Clark. 2011. Inquire for iPad: Bringing question-answering AI into the classroom. In *International Conference on AI in Education (AIED)*.

Overview of the First Content Selection Challenge from Open Semantic Web Data

Nadjet Bouayad-Agha[1]
Gerard Casamayor[1]
Leo Wanner[1,2]
[1]DTIC, University Pompeu Fabra
[2]Institució Catalana de Recerca i Estudis Avançats
Barcelona, Spain
firstname.lastname@upf.edu

Chris Mellish
Computing Science
University of Aberdeen
Aberdeen AB24 3UE, UK
c.mellish@abdn.ac.uk

Abstract

In this overview paper we present the outcome of the first content selection challenge from open semantic web data, focusing mainly on the preparatory stages for defining the task and annotating the data. The task to perform was described in the challenge's call as follows: given a set of RDF triples containing facts about a celebrity, select those triples that are reflected in the target text (i.e., a short biography about that celebrity). From the initial nine expressions of interest, finally two participants submitted their systems for evaluation.

1 Introduction

In (Bouayad-Agha et al., 2012), we presented the NLG challenge of content selection from semantic web data. The task to perform was described as follows: given a set of RDF triples containing facts about a celebrity, select those triples that are reflected in the target text (i.e., a short biography about that celebrity). The task first required a data preparation stage that involved the following two subtasks: 1) *data gathering and preparation*, that is, deciding which data and texts to use, then downloading and pairing them, and 2) *working dataset selection and annotation*, that is, defining the criteria/guidelines for determining when a triple is marked as selected in the target text, and producing a corpus of triples annotated for selection.

There were initially nine interested participants (including the two organizing parties). Five of which participated in the (voluntary) triple annotation rounds.[1] In the end, only two participants submitted their systems:

UA: Roman Kutlak, Chris Mellish and Kees van Deemter. Department of Computing Science , University of Aberdeen, Scotland (UK).

UIC: Hareen Venigalla and Barbara Di iEugenio. Department of Computer Science, University of Illinois at Chicago (USA).

Before the presentation of the baseline evaluation of the submitted systems and the discussion of the results (Section 4), we outline the two data preparation subtasks (Sections 2 and 3). In Section 5, we then sketch some conclusions with regard to the achievements and future of the content selection task challenge. More details about the data, annotation and resources described in this overview, as well as links for downloading the data and other materials (e.g., evaluation results, code, etc.) are available on the challenge's website.[2]

2 Data gathering and preparation

We chose Freebase as our triple datastore.[3,4] We obtained the triple set for each person in the Turtle format (ttl) by grepping the official Freebase RDF dump released on the 30th of December 2012 for all triples whose subject is the person's URI; certain meta-data and irrelevant triples (i.e., triples with specific namespaces such as "base" or "common") have been filtered out.

Each triple set is paired with the person's summary biography typically available in Wikipedia, which consists of the first paragraph(s) preceding the page's table of contents[5]

Our final corpus consists of 60000+ pairs, all of which follow two restrictions that are supposed to

[1]We would like to thank Angelos Georgaras and Stasinos Konstantopoulos from NCSR (Greece) for their participation in the annotation rounds.

[2]http://www.taln.upf.edu/cschallenge2013/

[3]http://www.freebase.com

[4]For a comparison between Freebase and DBPedia, see http://wiki.freebase.com/wiki/DBPedia.

[5]For example, the first four paragraphs in the following page constitute the summary biography of that person: http://en.wikipedia.org/wiki/George_Clooney.

maximize the chances of having interesting pairs with sufficient original and selected input triples for the challenge. Firstly, the number of unique predicates in the input ttl must be greater than 10. The number 10 is estimated based on the fact that a person's nationality, date and place of birth, profession, type and gender are almost always available and selected, such that we need a somewhat large set to select content from in order to make the task minimally challenging. Secondly, the Wikipedia-extracted summary biography must contain more than 5 anchors and at least 20% of the available anchors, where an anchor is a URI in the text (i.e., external href attribute value in the html) pointing to another Wikipedia article which is directly related to that person. Given that most Freebase topics have a corresponding DBPedia entity with a Wikipedia article, anchors found in the introductory text are an indicator of potential relevant facts available in Freebase and are communicated in the text. In other words, the anchor threshold restriction is useful to discard pairs with very few triples to annotate. We found this criterion more reliable than the absolute length of the text which is not necessarily proportional with the number of triples available for that person.

3 Working Dataset selection and annotation

The manual annotation task consisted in emulating the content selection task of a Natural Language Generation system, by marking in the triple dataset associated with a person the triples predicated in the summary biography of that person according to a set of guidelines. We performed two rounds of annotations. In the first round, participants were asked to select content for the same three celebrities. The objectives of this annotation, in which five individuals belonging to four distinct institutions participated, were 1) for participants to get acquainted with the content selection task envisaged, the domain and guidelines, 2) to validate the guidelines, and 3) to formally evaluate the complexity of the task by calculating inter-annotator agreement. For the latter we used free-marginal multi-rater Kappa, as it seemed suited for the annotation task (i.e. independent ratings, discrete categories, multiple raters, annotators are not restricted in how they distribute categories across cases) (Justus, 2005). We obtained an average Kappa of 0.92 across the three pairs for the 5 annotators and 2 categories (selected, not selected), which indicates a high level of agreement and therefore validates our annotation guidelines.

Our objective for the second round of annotations was to obtain a dataset for participants to work with. In the end, we gathered 344 pairs from 5 individuals of 5 distinct institutions. It should be noted that although both rounds of annotations follow the anchor restriction presented in Section 2, the idea to set a minimum number of predicates for the larger corpus of 60000+ pairs came forth after analysing the results of the second round and noting the data sparsity in some pairs. In what follows, we detail how the triples were presented to human annotators and what were the annotation criteria set forth in the guidelines.

3.1 Data presentation

A machine-readable triple consists of a subject which is a Freebase machine id (mid), a predicate and an object which can either be a Freebase mid or a literal, as shown in the following two triples:

```
ns:m.0dvld
  ns:people.person.spouse_s
    ns:m.02kknf3 .

ns:m.0dvld
  ns:people.person.date_of_birth
    "1975-10-05"^^xsd:datetime .
```

Triples were transformed into a human-readable form. In particular, each mid in object position (e.g., 02kknf3) was automatically mapped onto an abbreviated description of the Freebase topic it refers to. Thus, the triples above have been mapped onto a tabular form consisting of (1) predicate, (2) object description, (3) object id, and (4) object types (for literals):

```
(1) /people/person/spouse_s
(2) "1998-11-22 - Jim Threapleton -
     2001-12-13 - Marriage -
     Freebase Data Team - Marriage"
(3) /m/02kknf3

(1) /people/person/date_of_birth
(2) value
(3) "1975-10-05"
(4) "datetime"
```

For each triple thus presented, annotators were asked to mark 1) whether it was selected, 2) in which sentence(s) of the text did it appear, and 3) which triples, if any, are its coreferents. Two triples are coreferent if their overlap in meaning is such that either of them can be selected to represent the content communicated by the same text fragment and as such should not count as two separate triples in the evaluation. Thus, the same text might say *He is probably best known for his stint with heavy metal band Godsmack* and *He has also toured and recorded with a number of other bands including Detroit based metal band Halloween 'The Heavy Metal Horror Show'* ..., thus referring in two different sentences to near-equivalent triples `/music/artist/genre ''Heavy metal''` and `/music/artist/genre ''Hard rock''`.

3.2 Annotation criteria

Annotators were asked to first read the text carefully, trying to identify propositional units (i.e., potential triples) and then to associate each identified propositional unit with zero, one or more (coreferent) triples according to the following rules:

Rule 1. One cannot annotate facts that are not predicated and cannot be inferred from predicates in the text. In other words, all facts must be grounded in the text. For example, in the sentence *He starred in Annie Hall*, the following is predicated: `W.H.has_profession actor` and `W.H. acted_in film Annie Hall`. The former fact can be inferred from the latter. However, the following is not predicated: (1) `Person has_name W.H.`, (2) `W.H. is Male`, and (3) `W.H. is Person`.

Rule 2. In general, one can annotate more generic facts if they can be inferred from more specific propositions in the text, but one cannot annotate specific facts just because a more general proposition is found in the text. In the example *He was a navigator*, we can mark the triples `Person has_profession Sailor` as well as `Person has_profession Navigator` (we would also mark them as coreferent). However, given the sentence *He was a sailor*, we cannot mark the triple `Person has_profession Navigator`, unless we can infer it from the text or world knowledge.

Rule 3. One can annotate specific facts from a text where the predicate is too vague or general if the facts can be inferred from the textual context, from the available data, or using world knowledge. This rule subsumes four sub-cases:

Rule 3.1. The predicate in the proposition is too vague or general and can be associated with multiple, more specific triples. In this case, do not select any triple. In the example *Film A was a great commercial success*, we have several triples associating the celebrity with Film A, as director, actor, writer, producer and composer and none of them with a predicate resembling "commercial success". In this case there are no triples that can be associated with the text.

Rule 3.2. The predicate in the proposition is too vague or general, but according to the data there is just one specific triple it can be associated with. In this case, select that triple. In the example *Paris released Confessions of an Heiress*, the term `released` could be associated with *authored*, *wrote* or *published*. However, there is only one triple associating that subject with that object, which matches one of the interpretations (i.e., *authoring*) of the predicate. Therefore that triple can be selected.

Rule 3.3. The predicate in the proposition is too vague or general, but one or more specific triples can be inferred using world knowledge. In this case, select all. The sentence *He is also a jazz clarinetist who performs regularly at small venues in Manhattan*, can be associated with the available triples `W.H. profession Clarinetist` and `W.H. music/group_member/instruments_played Clarinet`, even though for this latter triple the person being in a group is not mentioned explicitly. However, this can be inferred from basic world knowledge.

Rule 3.4. The predicate in the proposition is too vague or general, but one or more specific triples can be inferred using the textual context. In this case, select all. In the example *By the mid-1960s Allen was writing and directing films ... Allen often stars in his own films ... Some of the best-known of his over 40 films are Annie Hall (1977)* ..., the relations of the person with the film `Annie Hall` are that of writer, director and actor, as supported by the previous text. Therefore we would annotate facts stating that the person wrote, directed and starred in `Annie Hall`. However, we wouldn't annotate composer or producer triples if they existed.

Rule 4. A proposition can be associated with multiple facts with identical or overlapping meanings. In the example, *Woody Allen is a musician*, we have the triples `W.H occupation musician` and `W.H profession musician`, which have near identical meanings. Therefore, we mark both triples and indicate that they co-refer. The sentence *Woody Allen won prize as best director for film Manhattan*, on the other hand, can be associated with non-coreferring triples `W.H won prize` and `W.H. directed Manhattan`.

Rule 5. If the text makes reference to a set of facts but it does not enumerate them explicitly, and there is no reason to believe it makes reference to any of them in particular, then do not annotate individual facts. Thus, sentence *Clint Eastwood has seven children* does not warrant marking each of the seven children triples as selected, given that they are not enumerated explicitly.

Rule 6. If the text makes a clear and unambiguous reference to a fact, do not annotate any other facts, even though they can be inferred from it. In other words, as explained in Rule 1, all annotated triples must be grounded in the text. In the sentence *For his work in the films Unforgiven (1992) and Million Dollar Baby (2004), Eastwood won Academy Awards for Best Director and Producer of the Best Picture*, we can infer from world knowledge that the celebrity was nominated prior to winning the award in those categories. However, the text makes a clear reference only to the fact that he won the award and there is no reason to believe that it is also predicating the fact that the celebrity was nominated.

4 Baseline evaluation

Briefly speaking, the UA system uses a general heuristic based on the cognitive notion of *communal common ground* regarding each celebrity, which is approximated by scoring each lexicalized triple (or property) associated with a celebrity according to the number of hits of the Google search API. Only the top-ranked triples are selected (Kutlak et al, 2013). The UIC system uses a small set of rules for the conditional inclusion of predicates that was derived offline from the statistical analysis of the co-occurrence between predicates that are about the same topic or that share some shared arguments; only the best performing rules tested against a subset of the development set are included (Venigalla and Di Eugenio, 2013).

For the baseline evaluation, we used the development set obtained in the second round annotation (see Section 3). However, we only consider pairs obtained during the second round annotation that 1) follow both restrictions presented in Section 2, and 2) have no coreferring triples. This last restriction was added to minimize errors because we observed that annotators were not always consistent in their annotation of triple coreference.[6] We therefore considered 188 annotations from the 344 annotations of the development set. Of these, we used 40 randomly selected annotations for evaluating the systems and 144 for estimating a baseline that only considers the top 5 predicates (i.e., the predicates most often selected) and the type-predicate.[7].

	Baseline	UIC	UA
Precision	49	64	47
Recall	67	50	39
F1	51	51	42

Table 1: Baseline evaluation results (%)

The evaluation results of the three systems (baseline, UIC and UA) are presented in Table 1. The figures in the table were obtained by comparing the triples selected and rejected by each system against the manual annotation. The performance of the baseline is quite high. The UA system based on a general heuristic scores lower than the baseline, whilst the UIC system has a better precision than the baseline, albeit a lower recall. This might be due, as the UA authors observe in their summary (Venigalla and Di Eugenio, 2013), to "the large number of predicates that are present only in a few files ... [which] makes it harder to decide whether we have to include these predicates or not."

5 Conclusions

We have given an overview of the first content selection challenge from open semantic web data, focusing on the rather extensive and challenging technological and methodological work involved in defining the task and preparing the data. Unfortunately, despite agile participation in these early

[6]Type-predicate triples were filtered out of the annotated files in the development set whilst they were included in the large corpus made available to the candidates. Therefore, we added type-predicate triples in the development set a posteriori for this evaluation. These type-predicate triples might be coreferring with other triples, say `ns:m.08rd51 ns:type.object.type ns:film.actor` and `ns:m.08rd5 people/person/profession "Actor" /m/02hrh1q .` Nonetheless, this was not taken into account in the evaluation.

[7]The top 5 predicates were (in descending order of frequency): music track, film actor, profession, date of birth and nationality

preparatory stages, the number of submitted systems was limited. Both of the presented systems were data-intensive in that they usedeither a pool of textual knowledge or the corpus of triple data provided by the challenge in order to select the most relevant data.

Unlike several previous challenges that involve more traditional NLG tasks (e.g., surface realization, referring expression generation), content selection from large input semantic data is a relatively new research endeavour in the NLG community that coincides with the rising interest in statistical approaches to NLG and dates back, to the best of our knowledge, to (Duboue and McKeown, 2003). Furthermore, although we had initially planned to produce a training set for the task, the cost of manual annotation turned out to be prohibitive and the resulting corpus was only fit for development and baseline evaluation. Despite these setbacks, we believe that open semantic web data is a promising test-bed and application field for NLG-oriented content selection (Bouayad-Agha et al., 2013) and trust that this first challenge has prepared the ground for follow up challenges with a larger participation. We would also like to encourage researchers from NLG and Semantic Web research fields to exploit the framework and materials developed during the course of this challenge to advance research in content selection.

References

Nadjet Bouayad-Agha, Gerard Casamayor, and Leo Wanner. 2013. Natural Language Generation in the Context of the Semantic Web. *Submitted to the Semantic Web Journal.*

Nadjet Bouayad-Agha, Gerard Casamayor, Chris Mellish, and Leo Wanner. 2012. Content Selection from Semantic Web Data. *INLG '12 Proceedings of the Seventh International Natural Language Generation Conference.* Pages 146-149.

Pablo A. Duboue and Kathleen R. McKeown. 2003. Statistical Acquisition of Content Selection Rules for Natural Language Generation *Proceedings of the Conference on Empirical Methods for Natural Language Processing (EMNLP).* Pages 121–128.

Randolph, Justus J. 2005. Free-marginal multirater kappa (multirater κfree): An alternative to fleiss fixed-marginal multirater kappa. *Presented as the Joensuu University Learning and Instruction Symposium.*

Roman Kutlak, Chris Mellish and Kees van Deemter 2013. Content Selection Challenge University of Aberdeen entry *Proceedings of the 14th European Natural Language Generation (ENLG) Workshop.*

Hareen Venigalla and Barbara Di Eugenio. 2013. UIC-CSC: The Content Selection Challenge Entry from the University of Illinois at Chicago *Proceedings of the 14th European Natural Language Generation (ENLG) Workshop.*

Narrative Composition: Achieving the Perceived Linearity of Narrative

Pablo Gervás
Universidad Complutense de Madrid, Ciudad Universitaria, 28040 Madrid, Spain
pgervas@sip.ucm.es

The last few years have seen an increased interest in narrative within the field of Natural Language Generation (Reiter et al., 2008; Elson and McKeown, 2010; Siddharthan et al., 2012; Lester, 2012). Narrative is generally acknowledged as a fundamental mode of presenting and communicating information between humans, with different manifestations across media but with a very significant presence in textual form. Yet efforts in Natural Language Generation research have generally side stepped the issue. Aside from the pioneering work of (Callaway, 2002) and an early attempt to bridge the gap between narratology and natural language generation (Lönneker, 2005), the field had mostly avoided narrative until recent times. Two possible arguments may be considered as an explanation of this: one based on the need to restrict initial work within a field to the simpler challenges before tackling the difficult ones, and another based on an assumption that the peculiarities of narrative have already been covered by existing work. Both arguments can be shown to be inappropriate.

With respect to the first argument, the field of natural language generation has for many years operated under the tacit assumption that state of the art technology can only aspire to generating texts within a limited range of domains and genres. These have over the years been defined in different ways, but in spite of changes, literary texts have usually been considered to be outside the range of possible candidates. From an engineering point of view, this kind of restriction made sense when the field was starting, for two important reasons. One, the technological solutions available at the time for the various tasks involved in natural language generation were in their infancy, and the linguistic complexity of literary text might have been beyond their scope. Two, natural language generation arose from a desire to extend the studies that had been carried out for computational analysis of language to the task of generation, and what was known about language from a computational point of view concerned simple texts. Most of the studies on language and computation had applied similar simplifying assumptions. However, such restricting assumptions are no longer necessary and may be inhibiting progress. In terms of technology, the field has matured significantly over the intervening years. The current state of the art provides a wide range of solutions that may be well suited to address some of the more complex phenomena involved in literary text. Additional objections may be made on the grounds that we do not know enough about these phenomena. Such objections, however valid they might have been originally, are no longer valid either. Many of the phenomena that were considered beyond computational treatment (metaphor, emotion, temporal reasoning, dialogue...) have been the subject of serious and sustained study over the same time period. Many approaches to their computational modelling and treatment have become available. More to the point, the last few years have seen a rise of interest on literary text within the natural language processing community. This is evidenced by the number of workshops addressing topics related to literature: Workshop on Computational Approaches to Linguistic Creativity at NAACL HLT 2009 and 2010, Computational Linguistics for Literature Workshop at NAACL HLT 2012 and 2013, Computational Models of Narrative events held as AAAI Fall symposium in 2010, as LREC workshop in 2012, and as satellite workshop of CogSci 2013, just to name a few.

With respect to the second argument, the recent reappearance of narrative as a research topic for NLG should be enough to dispel the notion that all its problems have already been solved. Narrative has many peculiarities that set it apart from other kinds of text, and the body of work addressing narrative as a research topic within NLG has at most uncovered and staked out a set of problems and challenges that area waiting further exploration. Of these various open problems in the treatment of narrative, my talk will focus on the problem of narrative composition.

Research on narrative is plagued by the difficulty of establishing a definition of the term that is both sufficiently formal to act as foundation for scientific rigour, and sufficiently rich to cover the fundamental aspects that people associate with the term. At the present stage of development, tentative definition need to be established, to be later confirmed on the basis of empirical work and succesful evaluation of results. The talk will outline some of the possibilities that must be considered (arising from established definitions in the field of narratology) and some of the restrictions that arise from the computational nature of the task. From the combination of these constraints, a working model of narrative structure will be outlined. However, it is clear that such a model must document the relation between a semantic description of the content of the narrative (what is usually termed the *fabula*) and its rendition as a sequential discourse. The task of *narrative composition* will be specified as the task of constructing such a discourse (or discourse plan) for a given semantic description of fabula. This discourse should be susceptible of being converted into text and it should appropriately conveys the set of events in the fabula in such a way that satifies a number of traditionally accepted requirements (like having an identifiable theme, a certain temporal and causal coherence, a recognisable set of characters...). A number of basic narratological concepts will be described where they provide tools for breaking down the task into computationally tractable subproblems. Of particular interest is the concept of *focalization*, which is used by narratologists to describe the way certain segments of a narrative follow a particular character, and which provides a useful computational representation of both the granularity and the shift in focus employed during the process of converting the semantics of the fabula into a linear discourse.

As part of the talk, narrative composition will be framed in terms of the accepted task breakdown for natural language generation, considering that it may involve a combination of content determination and discourse planning that cannot be segregated into separate subtasks. The talk will also discuss the relation of the task of narrative composition with a number of existing research problems such as story generation (which could correspond to the construction of fabula but is sometimes simplified down to construction of a discourse directly) and creativity (which has been addressed with respect to story generation but may also constitute a fundamental ingredient of the composition task).

Acknowledgments

The work on which this talk is based was partially supported by the Ministerio de Educación y Ciencia (TIN2009-14659-C03-01).

References

Charles B. Callaway. 2002. Narrative prose generation. *Artificial Intelligence*, 139(2):213–252.

David K. Elson and Kathleen R. McKeown. 2010. Tense and aspect assignment in narrative discourse. In *Proceedings of the 6th International Natural Language Generation Conference*, INLG '10, pages 47–56, Stroudsburg, PA, USA. Association for Computational Linguistics.

James Lester. 2012. Expressive nlg for next-generation learning environments: language, affect, and narrative. In *Proceedings of the Seventh International Natural Language Generation Conference*, INLG '12, pages 2–2, Stroudsburg, PA, USA. Association for Computational Linguistics.

Birte Lönneker. 2005. Narratological Knowledge for Natural Language Generation. In Graham Wilcock, Kristiina Jokinen, Chris Mellish, and Ehud Reiter, editors, *Proceedings of the 10th European Workshop on Natural Language Generation (= ENLG 2005)*, pages 91–100, Aberdeen, Scotland, August.

Ehud Reiter, Albert Gatt, François Portet, and Marian van der Meulen. 2008. The importance of narrative and other lessons from an evaluation of an nlg system that summarises clinical data. In *Proceedings of the Fifth International Natural Language Generation Conference*, INLG '08, pages 147–156, Stroudsburg, PA, USA. Association for Computational Linguistics.

Advaith Siddharthan, Matthew Green, Kees van Deemter, Chris Mellish, and René van der Wal. 2012. Blogging birds: generating narratives about reintroduced species to promote public engagement. In *Proceedings of the Seventh International Natural Language Generation Conference*, INLG '12, pages 120–124, Stroudsburg, PA, USA. Association for Computational Linguistics.

Generating Natural Language Questions to Support Learning On-Line

David Lindberg **Fred Popowich**
School of Computing Science
Simon Fraser University
Burnaby, BC, CANADA
dll4,popowich@sfu.ca

John Nesbit **Phil Winne**
Faculty of Education
Simon Fraser University
Burnaby, BC, CANADA
nesbit,winne@sfu.ca

Abstract

When instructors prepare learning materials for students, they frequently develop accompanying questions to guide learning. Natural language processing technology can be used to automatically generate such questions but techniques used have not fully leveraged semantic information contained in the learning materials or the full context in which the question generation task occurs. We introduce a sophisticated template-based approach that incorporates semantic role labels into a system that automatically generates natural language questions to support online learning. While we have not yet incorporated the full learning context into our approach, our preliminary evaluation and evaluation methodology indicate our approach is a promising one for supporting learning.

1 Introduction

Ample research (e.g., Callender and McDaniel, 2007) shows that learners learn more, and more deeply, if they are prompted to examine their learning materials while and after they study. Often, these prompts consist of questions related to the learning materials. After reading a given passage or section of text, learners are familiar with learning exercises which consist of questions they need to answer.

Questioning is one of the most common and intensively studied instructional strategies used by teachers (Rus and Graesser, 1989). Questions embedded in text, or presented while learners are studying text, are hypothesized to promote self-explanation which is known to increase comprehension and enhance transfer of learning (e.g., Rittle-Johnson, 2006).

Traditionally, these questions have been constructed by educators. Recent research, though, has investigated how natural language processing techniques can be used to automatically generate these questions (Kalady et al., 2010; Varga and Ha, 2010; Ali et al., 2010; Mannem et al., 2010). While the automated approaches have generally focussed on syntactic features, we propose an approach that also takes semantic features into account, in conjunction with domain dependent and domain independent templates motivated by educational research. After introducing our question generation system, we will provide a preliminary analysis of the performance of the system on educational material, and then outline our future plans to tailor the questions to the needs of specific learners and specific learning outcomes.

2 Question Generation from Text

The task of question generation (QG) from text can be broadly divided into three (not entirely disjoint) categories: syntax-based, semantics-based, and template-based. Systems in the syntactic category often use elements of semantics and vice-versa. A system we would call template-based must to some extent use syntactic and/or semantic information. Regardless of the approach taken, systems must perform at least four tasks:

1. content selection: picking spans of source text (typically single sentences) from which questions can be generated
2. target identification: determining which specific words and/or phrases should be asked about
3. question formulation: determining the appropriate question(s) given the content identified
4. surface form generation: producing the final surface-form realization

Task 2 need not always precede task 3; target identification can drive question formulation and vice-versa. A system constrained to generating specific kinds of questions will select only the targets appropriate for those kinds of questions. Conversely, a system with broader generation capabilities might pick targets more freely and (ideally) generate only the questions that are appropriate for those targets. We consider the methods used in performing tasks 2 and 4 to be the primary discriminators in determining the category into which a given method is best placed. This is not the only way one might classify a QG system. However, we believe this method allows us to best compare and contrast our approach with previous approaches.

Syntax-based methods comprise a large portion of the existing literature. Kalady et al. (2012), Varga and Ha (2010), Wolfe (1976), and Ali et al. (2010) provide a sample of these methods. Although each of these efforts has differed on a few details, they have followed the same basic strategy: parse sentences using a syntactic parser, simplify complex sentences, identify key phrases, and apply syntactic transformation rules and question word replacement.

The methods we have labeled "semantics-based" use method(s) of target identification (task 2) that are primarily semantic, using techniques such as semantic role labeling (SRL). Given a sentence, a semantic role labeler identifies the predicates (relations and actions) along with the semantic entities associated with each predicate. Semantic roles, as defined in PropBank (Palmer et al., 2005), include Arg0, Arg1, ..., Arg5, and ArgA. A set of modifiers is also defined and includes ArgM-LOC (location), ArgM-EXT (extent), ArgM-DIS (discourse), ArgM-ADV (adverbial), ArgM-NEG (negation), ArgM-MOD (modal verb), ArgM-CAU (cause), ArgM-TMP (time), ArgM-PNC (purpose), ArgM-MNR (manner), and ArgM-DIR (direction). We adopt the shorter CoNLL SRL shared task naming conventions (Carreras and Màrquez, 2005) (e.g., A0 and AM-LOC).

Mannem et al. (2010), for example, introduce a semantics-based system that combines SRL with syntactic transformations. In the content selection stage, a single sentence is first parsed with a semantic role labeler to identify potential targets. Targets are selected using simple selection criteria. Any of the predicate-specific semantic arguments (A0-A5), if present, are considered valid targets. Mannem et al. further identify modifiers AM-MNR, AM-PUNC, AM-CAU, AM-TMP, AM-LOC, and AM-DIS as potential targets. These roles are used to generate additional questions that cannot be attained using only the A0-A5 roles. For example, AM-LOC can be used to generate a *where* question, and an AM-TMP can be used to generate a *when* question. After targets have been identified, these, along with the complete SRL parse of the sentence are passed to the question formulation stage. Two heuristics are used to rank the generated questions. Questions are ranked first by the depth of their predicate in the dependency parse of the original question. This is based on the assumption that questions arising from main clauses are more desirable than those generated from deeper predicates. In the second stage, questions with the same rank are re-ranked according to the number of pronouns they contain, with questions with fewer pronouns having higher rank.

One limitation of the syntax and semantics-based methods is that they generate questions by rearranging the surface form of sentences. Question templates offer the ability to ask questions that are not so tightly-coupled to the exact wording of the source text. A question template is any predefined text with placeholder variables to be replaced with content from the source text. Question templates allow question generation systems to leverage human expertise in language generation.

The template-based system of Cai et al. (2006) uses Natural Language Generation Markup Language (NLGML), a language that can be used to generate not only questions but any natural language expression. NLGML uses syntactic pattern matching and semantic features for content selection and question templates to guide question formulation and surface-form realization. Note that a pattern need not specify a complete syntax tree. Additionally, patterns can impose semantic constraints. However, simple "copy and paste" templates are not a panacea for surface-form realization. Mechanisms for changing capitalization of words and changing verb conjugation (when source sentence verbs are to appear in the output text) need to be provided: NLGML provides some such functions.

3 Our Approach

We develop a template-based framework for QG. The primary motivation for this decision is the ability of a template-based approach to generate questions that are not merely declarative to interrogative transformations. We aim to address some of the limitations of the existing approaches outlined in the previous section while leveraging some of their strengths in novel ways. We combine the benefits of a semantics-based approach, the most important of which is not being tightly-constrained by syntax, with the surface-form flexibility of a template-based approach.

The data used to develop our approach was obtained from a collection of 25 documents prepared for educational research purposes within the Faculty of Education at SFU. All hand-coded rules we describe below were motivated by patterns observed in this development data. This collection was modeled after a high-school science curriculum on global warming, with vocabulary and discourse appropriate for learners in that age group. Although the collection included a glossary of key terms and their definitions, this resource was used only for evaluation purposes as described in Section 4.

3.1 Semantic-based templates

Previous template-based methods have used syntactic pattern matching, which does provide a great deal of flexibility in specifying sentences appropriate for generating certain types of questions. However, this flexibility comes at the expense of generality. As seen in Wyse and Piwek (2009), who use Stanford Tregex (Levy and Andrew, 2006) for pattern matching, the specificity of syntactic patterns can make it difficult to specify a syntactic pattern of the desired scope. Furthermore, semantically similar entities can span different syntactic structures, and matching these requires either multiple patterns (in the case of Cai et al., 2006) or a more complicated pattern (in the case of Wyse and Piwek, 2009).

If we want to develop templates that are semantically motivated, more flexible in terms of the content they successfully match, and more approachable for non-technical users, we need to move away from syntactic pattern matching. Instead, we match *semantic patterns*. We define a *semantic pattern* as the SRL parse of a sentence and the named entities (if any) contained within the span of each semantic role. We use Stanford NER (Finkel et al., 2005) for named entity recognition. Figure 1 shows a sentence and its corresponding semantic pattern. Notice this sentence has two predicates, each with its own semantic arguments. Each of these predicate-argument structures is a distinct *predicate frame*.

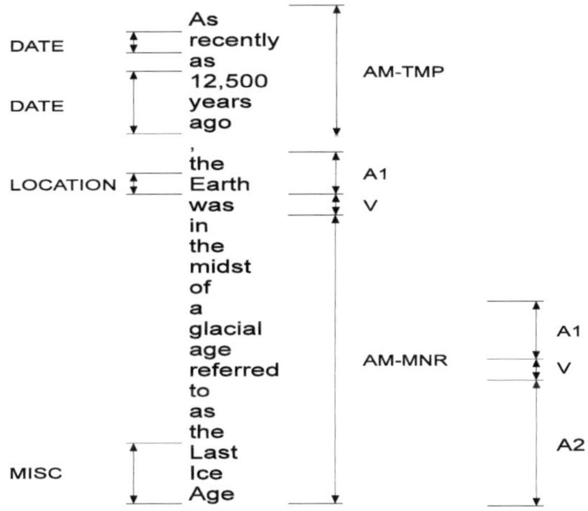

Figure 1: A sentence and its semantic pattern

Even the shallow semantics of SRL can identify the semantically interesting portions of a sentence, and these semantically-meaningful substrings can span a range of syntactic patterns. Figure 2 shows a clear example of this phenomenon. In this example, we see two sentences expressing the same semantic relationship between two concepts, namely, the fact that trapped heat causes the Earth's temperature to increase. In one case, this causation is expressed in an adjective phrase, while the other uses a sentence-initial prepositional phrase. The parse trees are generated using the Stanford Parser (Klein and Manning, 2003). The AM-CAU semantic role captures the cause in both sentences. It is impossible to accomplish the same feat with a single NLGML pattern. However, it is possible to capture both with a single Tregex pattern.

The principle advantage of semantic pattern matching is that a single semantic pattern casts a narrow semantic net while casting a large syntactic net. This means fewer patterns need to be defined by the template author, and the patterns are more compact.

Our templates have three components: plaintext, slots, and slot options. Plaintext forms the

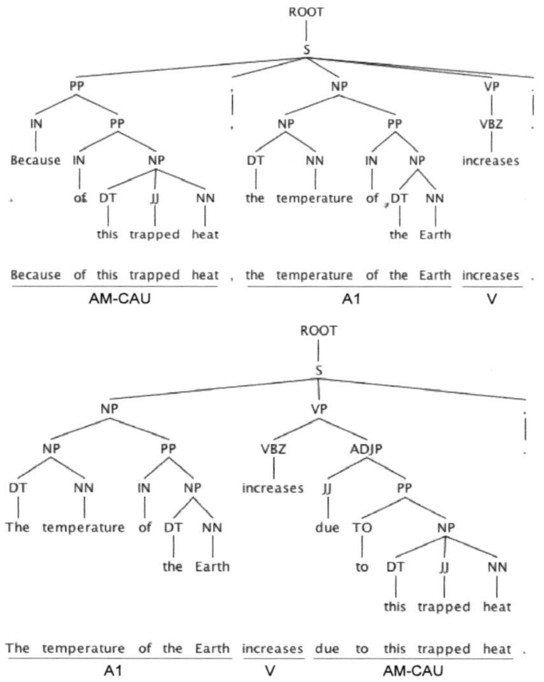

Figure 2: Two different syntax subtrees subsumed by a single semantic role

skeleton into which semantically-meaningful substrings of a source sentence are inserted to create a question. The only restrictions on the plaintext is that it cannot contain any text that looks like a slot but is not intended as one, and it cannot contain the character sequence used to delineate the plaintext from the slots appearing outside the plaintext. Aside from these restrictions, any desired text is valid.

Slots facilitate sentence and template matching. They accept specific semantic arguments, and can appear inside or outside the plaintext. These provide the semantic pattern against which a source sentence is matched. A slot inside the plaintext acts as a variable to be replaced by the corresponding semantic role text from a matching sentence, while any slots appearing outside the plaintext serve only to provide additional pattern matching criteria. The template author does not need to specify the complete semantic pattern in each template. Instead, only the portions relevant to the desired question need to be specified. This is an important point of contrast between our template-based approach vs. syntax and semantics-based approaches. We can choose to generate questions that do not include any predicates from the source sentence but instead ask more abstract or general questions about other semantic constituents. We believe these kinds of questions are better able to escape the realm of the factoid, because they are not constrained to the actions and relations described by predicates.

Slot options function much like NLGML functions and are of two types: modifiers and filters. Modifiers apply transformations to the role text inserted into a slot, and filters enforce finer-grained matching criteria. Predicate slots have their own distinct set of options, while the other semantic roles share a common set of options. A template's slots and filters describe the necessary conditions for the template to be matched with a source sentence semantic pattern.

3.2 Predicate slot options

The predicate filter options restrict the predicates that can match a predicate slot. With no filter options specified, any predicate is considered a match. Table 1 shows the complete list of filters.

Filter	Description
be	predicate lemma must not be "be"
!be	predicate lemma must be "be"
!have	predicate lemma must not be "have"

Table 1: Predicate filters

The selection of predicate filters might at first seem oddly limited. Failing to consider the functional differences between various types of verbs (particularly auxiliary and copula) would indeed produce low-quality questions and should in fact be ignored in most cases. For example, consider the sentence "Dinosaurs, along with many other animals, became extinct approximately 65 million years ago." A question such as "What did dinosaurs, along with many other animals, become?" is not particularly useful. We can recognize copula predicates by their surrounding semantic pattern, so in the broad sense, we do not need to adopt any copula-specific rules.

The one exception to the above rule is any copula whose lemma is *be*. The `be` and `!be` filters allow the presence or absence of such a predicate to be detected. This capability is useful for two reasons. First, the presence of such a predicate gives us an inexpensive way to generate definition questions, even if the source text is not written in the form of a definition. Although this will over-generate definition questions, non-predicate filters can be used to add additional mitigating constraints. Second, requiring the absence of such a predicate allows us to actively avoid generating certain kinds of ungrammatical or meaningless questions. Whether using one of these predicates results in ungrammatical questions depends on the wording of the underlying template, so we provide the `!be` filter for the template author to use as needed. Consider the sentence "El Nino is caused when the westerly winds are unusually weak." Without the `!be` filter, one of our templates would generate the question "When can El Nino be?" Applying the `!be` filter prevents this question from being generated.

Like copula, auxiliary verbs are often not suitable for question generation. Fortunately, many auxiliary verbs are also modal and are assigned the label AM-MOD and so do not form predicate frames of their own. Instead, they are included in the frame of the predicate they modify. In other cases auxiliary verbs are not modal, such as in the sentence "So far, scientists have not been able to predict the long term effects of this wobble." In this case, the auxiliary *have* is treated as a separate predicate, but importantly, the span of its A1 includes the predicate *been*. We provide a non-predicate filter to prevent generation when this overlap is present.

The `!have` filter is motivated by the observation that the predicate *have* can appear as a full, non-copula predicate (with an A0 and A1) but often does not yield high-quality questions. For example, consider the sentence "This effect can have a large impact on the Earth's climate." Without the `!have` filter, one of our templates would generate the question "What can this effect have?" With the `!have` filter, that template does not yield any questions from the given sentence.

Predicate modifiers allow the template author to explicitly force a change in conjugation. See Table 2 for the complete set of predicate modifiers, where fps is an abbreviation for first person singular, sps for second person singular, and so on. The `lemma` modifier can appear on its own. However, all other conjugation changes must specify both a *tense* and a *person*. If no modifiers are used, the predicate is copied as-is from the source sentence. Although *perfect* is an aspect rather than a tense, MorphAdorner[1], which we use to conjugate predicates, defines it as a tense, so we have implemented it as a tense filter.

[1] http://morphadorner.northwestern.edu

Modifier	Tense	Modifier
lemma	lemma (dictionary form)	fps
pres	present	sps
prespart	present participle	tps
past	past	fpp
pastpart	past participle	spp
perf	perfect	tpp
pastperf	past perfect	
pastperfpart	past perfect participle	

Table 2: Predicate modifiers

3.3 Non-predicate slot options

The filters for non-predicate slots impose additional syntactic and named entity restrictions on any matching role text. As with predicates, the absence of any non-predicate filters results in the mere presence of the corresponding semantic role being sufficient for matching. See Table 3 for the complete list of non-predicate filters describing restrictions on the role text (RT), role span (RS), and predicate frame (PF) in terms of the semantic type of named entities (and in some cases in terms of non-semantic features).

Filter	Description
null	PF must not contain this semantic role.
!nv	RS must not contain a predicate
dur	RT must contain DURATION
date	RT must contain DATE
!date	RT must not contain a DATE
loc	RT must contain a LOCATION.
ne	RT must contain a named entity
misc	RT must contain a MISC
comp	RT must contain a comparison
!comma	RT must not contain a comma
singular	RT must be singular
plural	RT must be plural

Table 3: Non-predicate filters

The choice of filters again requires some explanation. The `null` and `!nv` filters were foreshadowed above. For slots appearing outside the template's plaintext, the `null` filter explicitly requires that the corresponding semantic role not be present in a source sentence semantic pattern. An A0 slot paired with the `null` filter is the mechanism alluded to earlier that allows for the recognition of copula predicates without the need to examine the predicate itself. The `!nv` filter can be used to prevent ungrammatical questions. We observe that if a role span does include a predicate, resulting questions are often ungrammatical due to the conjugation of that predicate. Applying this filter to the A1 of a predicate prevents generation from a predicate frame whose predicate is a non-modal auxiliary verb.

The named entity filters (`dur`, `!dur`, `date`, `loc`, `ne`, and `misc`) are those most relevant to the corpus we have used to evaluate our approach and thus the easiest to experiment with effectively. Because named entities are used only for filtering, expanding the set of named entity filters is a trivial task.

The filters `comp`, `!comma`, `singular`, and `plural` are syntax-based filters. With the exception of `!comma`, these filters force the examination of the part-of-speech (POS) tags to detect the desired features. The `singular` and `plural` filters let templates be tailored to singular and plural arguments in any desired way, beyond simply selecting appropriate auxiliary verbs. The type of comparison we search for when the `comp` filter is used is quite specific. We search for phrases that describe conditions that are atypical. These can be seen in phrases such "unusually weak," "unseasonably warm," "strangely absent," and so on. These phrases are present when a word whose POS tag is RB (adverb) is followed by a word whose tag is JJ (adjective). Consider a sentence such as "El Nino is caused when the westerly winds are unusually weak." The `comp` filter allows us to generate questions such as "What data would indicate El Nino?" or "How do the conditions that cause El Nino differ from normal conditions?" Although this heuristic does produce both false positives and false negatives, other syntactic features such as comparative adverbs and comparative adjectives are less semantically constrained. Further investigation is needed to determine more flexible ways to recognize descriptions of atypical conditions.

We see two situations in which a comma appears within the span of a single semantic role. The first situation occurs when a list of nouns is serving the role, such as in "Climate change includes changes in precipitation, temperature, and pressure." Here, "changes in precipitation, temperature, and pressure" is the A1 of the predicate *includes*. In cases where a question is only appropriate for single concept (e.g. temperature) rather than a set of concepts, the `!comma` filter prevents such a question from being generated from the sentence above. This has implications for role text containing appositives, the second situation in which a comma appears within a single role span. Such roles are rejected when `!comma` is used. This is not ideal, as removing appositives does not cause semantic roles to be lost from a semantic pattern. Future work will address this problem.

The non-predicate modifiers (Table 4) serve two purposes: to create more fluent questions and to remove non-essential text. Note that the `-tpp`, which forces the removal of trailing prepositional phrases, can have undesired results when applied to certain modifier roles, such as AM-LOC, AM-MNR, and AM-TMP, when they appear in the template plaintext. These modifiers often contain only a prepositional phrase, and in such cases, `-tpp` will result in an empty string being placed into the template.

Modifier	Effect
-lp	If initial token is prep, remove it
-tpp	If RT ends with PP, remove PP
-ldt	If initial token is determiner, remove it

Table 4: Non-predicate modifiers

3.4 Our QG system

Figure 3 shows the architecture and data flow of our QG system. One of the most important things to observe about this architecture is that the templates are an external input. They are in no way coupled to the system and can be modified as needed without any system modifications.

Compared to most other approaches, we perform very little pre-processing. Syntax-based methods in particular have been motivated to perform sentence simplification, because their methods are more likely to generate meaningful questions from short, succinct sentences. We have chosen not to perform any sentence simplification. This decision was motivated by the observation that common methods of sentence simplification can eliminate useful semantic content. For example, Kalady et al. (2010) claim that prepositional phrases are often not fundamental to the meaning of a sentence, so they remove them when simplifying a sentence. However, as Figure 4 shows, a prepositional phrase can contain important semantic information. In that example, removing the prepositional phrase causes temporal information to be lost.

One pre-processing step we do perform is pronominal anaphora resolution (Charniak and Elsner, 2009). Even though we do not split com-

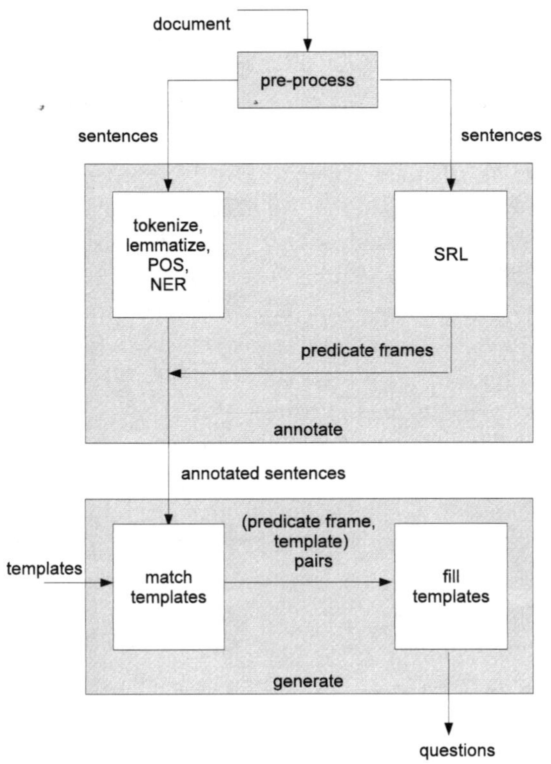

Figure 3: System architecture and data flow

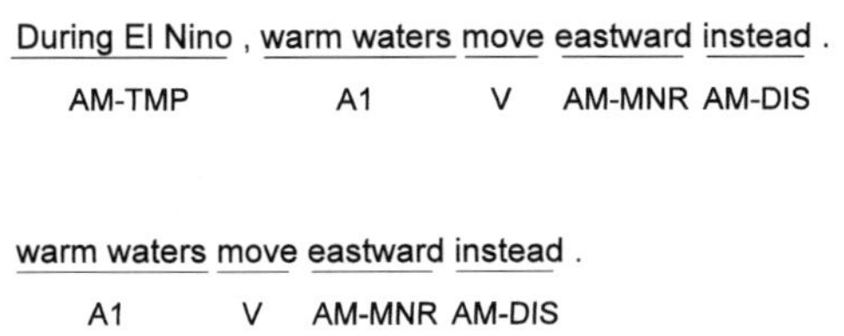

Figure 4: Semantic information can be lost during sentence simplification. Removing the prepositional phrase from the first sentence leaves the simpler second sentence, but the AM-TMP modifier is lost.

plex sentences and therefore do not create new sentences in which pronouns are separated from their antecedents, this kind of anaphora resolution remains an important step in limiting the number of vague questions.

Each source sentence is tokenized and annotated with POS tags, named entities, lemmata, and its SRL parse. SRL is the cornerstone of our approach. We generate the SRL parse (Collobert et al., 2011) in order to extract a set of predicate frames. Questions are generated from individual predicate frames rather than entire sentences (unless the sentence contains only one predicate frame). Given a sentence, the semantic pattern of each of its predicate frames is compared against that of each template. Algorithm 1 describes the process of matching a single predicate frame (*pf*) to a single template (*t*). Although it is not stated in Algorithm 1, the sentence-level tokenization, lemmata, named entities and POS tags are checked as needed according to the template's slot filters. If a predicate frame and template are matched, they are passed to Algorithm 2, which fills template slots with role text to produce a question. Even in the absence of modifiers, all role text receives some additional processing before being inserted into its corresponding slot. These additional steps include the removal of colons and the things they introduce and the removal of text contained in parentheses. We observe that these extra steps lead to questions that are more meaningful.

Algorithm 1 patternsMatch(pf,t)

for all $slot \in t$ **do**
  if pf does not have $slot.role$ **then**
    if $null \notin slot.filters$ **then**
      return $false$
    end if
  else
    for all $filter \in slot.filters$ **do**
      if $pf.role$ does not match $filter$ **then**
        return $false$
      end if
    end for
  end if
end for
return $true$

Because we generate questions from predicate frames rather than entire sentences, two sentences describing the same semantic entities might result in duplicate questions. To avoid duplicates we keep only the first occurrence of a question.

Using slots and filters, we can now create some interesting templates and see the questions they

Algorithm 2 fillTemplate(t,pf)

```
question_text ← t.plaintext
for all slot ∈ t.plaintext_slots do
    role_text ← pf.role(slot.role).text
    for all modifier ∈ slot.modifiers do
        applyModifier(role_text,modifier)
    end for
    In question_text, replace slot with role_text
end for
return question_text
```

yield. Table 5 shows some templates (**T**) that match the sentence in Figure 1 and the questions (**Q**) that result. Although the questions that are generated are not answerable from the original sentence, they were judged answerable from the source document in our evaluation. The full set of templates is provided in (Lindberg, 2013).

As recently as 12,500 years ago, the Earth was in the midst of a glacial age referred to as the Last Ice Age.
T: How would you describe [A2 -lp misc]? **Q**: How would you describe the Last Ice Age?
T: Summarize the influence of [A1 -lp !comma !nv] on the environment. **Q**: Summarize the influence of a glacial age on the environment.
T: What caused [A2 -lp !nv misc]? ## [A0 null] **Q**: What caused the Last Ice Age?

Table 5: A few sample templates and questions

4 Evaluation

There remains no standard set of evaluation metrics for assessing the quality of question generation output. Some present no evaluation at all (Wyse and Piwek, 2009; Stanescu et al., 2008). Among those who do perform an evaluation, there does appear to be a consensus that some form of human evaluation is necessary. Despite this agreement in principle, approaches tend to diverge thereafter. There are differences in the evaluation criteria and the evaluation procedure.

Most previous efforts in QG have not gone beyond manual evaluation. While some have gone a step further and built models for ranking based on the probability of a question being *acceptable* (Heilman and Smith, 2010), these models have not had a strong basis in pedagogy. While a question that is both syntactically and semantically well-formed is considered acceptable in some evaluation schemes, such questions can greatly outnumber the questions that we can reasonably expect a student would want or have time to answer. We implement a classifier that attempts to identify the questions that are the most pedagogically useful.

For our initial evaluation of the performance of our QG system, we selected a subset of 10 documents from the collection described in the previous section. On average, each document contained 25 sentences. From the 10 documents, our system generated 1472 questions in total, an average of 5.9 questions per sentence. Due to the educational nature of this material, we needed evaluators with educational training rather than naive ones. Accordingly, the questions we generated were evaluated by a graduate student from the Faculty of Education. She was asked to give binary judgements for grammaticality, semantic validity, vagueness, answerability, and learning value. For each question, two aspects of answerability were evaluated. The first aspect was whether the question was answerable from the source sentence from which it was generated. The second was whether the question was answerable given the source document as a whole. The evaluator was given no predetermined guidelines regarding the relationships among the evaluation criteria (e.g., the influence of vagueness and answerability on learning value). This aspect of the evaluation was left to her discretion as an educator. She found that 85% of the questions were grammatical, with 66% of them actually *making sense*. It was determined that 14% of the questions were answerable from the sentence used to generate them, while 20% of them were answerable from the document. Finally, she determined that 17% of the questions had *learning value* according to the prescribed learning outcomes for the curriculum being modeled. Aside from performing this evaluation, the evaluator was not involved in this research.

Given this evaluation, we then built a classifier which used logistic regression (L2 regularized log-likelihood) to classify on learning value. We used length, language model, SRL, named entity, glossary, and syntax features. Length and language model features measure the token count and grammaticality of a question and the sentence from which it was generated. SRL features include the token count of each semantic role in the generating predicate frame, whether each role is required by the matching template, and whether each role's text is used. Named entity features indicate the presence of each of nine named entity types in both the source sentence and generated question. Glossary features note the number of glossary terms that appear in a sentence and question and a measure of the average importance of each term, which we calculated from a simple *in-terms-of* graph (Winne and Hadwin, 2013) we constructed from the glossary. This graph has directed edges between each glossary term and the terms that appear in its gloss. Syntax features identify the depth of the generating predicate frame in the source sentence and the POS tag of its predicate. Without adding noise, the training set had 217 questions with learning value and 1101 questions without learning value. The classifier obtained precision and recall scores of 0.47 and 0.22 respectively for questions with learning value, along with scores of 0.79 and 0.92 for questions with no learning value. We then added *noise* to the training set by relabelling any grammatical question that *made sense* as having *learning value*. This relabelling resulted in a training set of 778 questions with learning value and only 540 questions without learning value. The classifier trained on this noisy set showed a precision score on learning value questions decreased to 0.29 but a dramatic increase in recall to 0.81. For questions with no learning value, the precision increased slightly to 0.86 which was offset by a dramatic decrease in recall to 0.38. So when the system generates a poor quality question, we have a high probability of knowing that it is a poor question which allows us to then filter or discard it.

5 Conclusions

We have shown how a template-based method, using predominately semantic information, can be used to generate natural language questions for use in an on-line learning system. Our templates are based on semantic patterns, which cast a wide syntactic net and a narrow semantic net. The template mechanism supports rich selectional and generational capabilities, generating a large pool from which questions for learners can be selected. A simple automated technique for selecting questions with learning value was introduced. Although this automated technique shows promise for some applications, future investigation into what constitutes a *useful question* in the context of a specific task and an individual learner is needed. Some might argue that it is risky to generate questions that cannot be answered from the source sentence from which they were generated. Although some questions are generated that are not answered elsewhere in a document, there is a benefit in learners being able to recognize that a particular question is not answerable. Our future work will expand both on the types of potential questions generated, and on the selection from the set of potential questions based on the information an individual learner (a) knows, (b) has available in a "library" of saved sources, (c) has operated on while studying online (e.g., tagged), and (d) might find in the Internet. To facilitate this further research, we will be integrating question generation into the nStudy system (Hadwin et al., 2010; Winne and Hadwin, 2013). We will also be performing thorough user studies which will evaluate the generated questions from the learner's perspective in addition to the educator's perspective.

Acknowledgments

This research was supported by an Insight Development Grant (#430-2012-044) from the Social Sciences and Humanities Research Council of Canada and a Discovery Grant from the Natural Sciences and Engineering Research Council of Canada. The authors are extremely grateful to Kiran Bisra from the Faculty of Education for providing information for the evaluation. Finally, special thanks to the reviewers for their comments and suggestions.

References

Husam Ali, Yllias Chali, and Sadid A Hasan. 2010. Automation of question generation from sentences. In *Proceedings of QG2010: The Third Workshop on Question Generation*, pages 58–67.

Zhiqiang Cai, Vasile Rus, Hyun-Jeong Joyce Kim, Suresh C. Susarla, Pavan Karnam, and Arthur C. Graesser. 2006. Nlgml: A markup language for question generation. In Thomas Reeves and Shirley Yamashita, editors, *Proceedings of World Conference on E-Learning in Corporate, Government, Healthcare, and Higher Education 2006*, pages 2747–2752, Honolulu, Hawaii, USA, October. AACE.

Aimee A. Callender and Mark A. McDaniel. 2007. The benefits of embedded question adjuncts for low and high structure builders. *Journal Of Educational Psychology (2007)*, pages 339–348.

Xavier Carreras and Lluís Màrquez. 2005. Introduction to the conll-2005 shared task: Semantic role labeling. In *Proceedings of the Ninth Conference on Computational Natural Language Learning*, pages 152–164. Association for Computational Linguistics.

Eugene Charniak and Micha Elsner. 2009. Em works for pronoun anaphora resolution. In *Proceedings of the 12th Conference of the European Chapter of the Association for Computational Linguistics*, pages 148–156. Association for Computational Linguistics.

Ronan Collobert, Jason Weston, Léon Bottou, Michael Karlen, Koray Kavukcuoglu, and Pavel Kuksa. 2011. Natural language processing (almost) from scratch. *The Journal of Machine Learning Research*, 12:2493–2537.

Jenny Rose Finkel, Trond Grenager, and Christopher Manning. 2005. Incorporating non-local information into information extraction systems by gibbs sampling. In *Proceedings of the 43rd Annual Meeting on Association for Computational Linguistics*, pages 363–370. Association for Computational Linguistics.

A.F. Hadwin, M. Oshige, C.L.Z. Gress, and P.H. Winne. 2010. Innovative ways for using nstudy to orchestrate and research social aspects of self-regulated learning. *Computers in Human Behaviour (2010)*, pages 794–805.

Michael Heilman and Noah A Smith. 2010. Good question! statistical ranking for question generation. In *Human Language Technologies: The 2010 Annual Conference of the North American Chapter of the Association for Computational Linguistics*, pages 609–617. Association for Computational Linguistics.

Saidalavi Kalady, Ajeesh Elikkottil, and Rajarshi Das. 2010. Natural language question generation using syntax and keywords. In *Proceedings of QG2010: The Third Workshop on Question Generation*, pages 1–10.

Dan Klein and Christopher D Manning. 2003. Accurate unlexicalized parsing. In *Proceedings of the 41st Annual Meeting on Association for Computational Linguistics-Volume 1*, pages 423–430. Association for Computational Linguistics.

Roger Levy and Galen Andrew. 2006. Tregex and tsurgeon: tools for querying and manipulating tree data structures. In *LREC 2006*.

David Lindberg. 2013. Automatic question generation from text for self-directed learning. Master's thesis, Simon Fraser University, Canada.

Prashanth Mannem, Rashmi Prasad, and Aravind Joshi. 2010. Question generation from paragraphs at upenn: Qgstec system description. In *Proceedings of QG2010: The Third Workshop on Question Generation*, pages 84–91.

Martha Palmer, Daniel Gildea, and Paul Kingsbury. 2005. The proposition bank: An annotated corpus of semantic roles. *Computational Linguistics*, 31(1):71–106.

Bethany Rittle-Johnson. 2006. Promoting transfer: Effects of self-explanation and direct instruction. *Child Development (2006)*, pages 1–15.

Vasile Rus and Arthur C Graesser. 1989. Classroom questioning. In *School improvement research series*.

Liana Stanescu, Cosmin Stoica Spahiu, Anca Ion, and Andrei Spahiu. 2008. Question generation for learning evaluation. In *Computer Science and Information Technology, 2008. IMCSIT 2008. International Multiconference on*, pages 509–513. IEEE.

Andrea Varga and Le An Ha. 2010. Wlv: A question generation system for the qgstec 2010 task b. In *Proceedings of QG2010: The Third Workshop on Question Generation*, pages 80–83.

Philip H Winne and Allyson F Hadwin. 2013. nstudy: Tracing and supporting self-regulated learning in the internet. In *International handbook of metacognition and learning technologies*, pages 293–308. Springer.

John H Wolfe. 1976. Automatic question generation from text-an aid to independent study. In *ACM SIGCUE Outlook*, volume 10, pages 104–112. ACM.

Brendan Wyse and Paul Piwek. 2009. Generating questions from openlearn study units. In *AIED 2009 Workshop Proceedings Volume 1: The 2nd Workshop on Question Generation, 6-9 July 2009, Brighton, UK.*

Generating student feedback from time-series data using Reinforcement Learning

Dimitra Gkatzia, Helen Hastie, Srinivasan Janarthanam and Oliver Lemon
Department of Mathematical and Computer Sciences
Heriot-Watt University
Edinburgh, Scotland
{dg106, h.hastie, sc445, o.lemon} @hw.ac.uk

Abstract

We describe a statistical Natural Language Generation (NLG) method for summarisation of time-series data in the context of feedback generation for students. In this paper, we initially present a method for collecting time-series data from students (e.g. marks, lectures attended) and use example feedback from lecturers in a data-driven approach to content selection. We show a novel way of constructing a reward function for our Reinforcement Learning agent that is informed by the lecturers' method of providing feedback. We evaluate our system with undergraduate students by comparing it to three baseline systems: a rule-based system, lecturer-constructed summaries and a Brute Force system. Our evaluation shows that the feedback generated by our learning agent is viewed by students to be as good as the feedback from the lecturers. Our findings suggest that the learning agent needs to take into account both the student and lecturers' preferences.

1 Introduction

Data-to-text generation refers to the task of automatically generating text from non-linguistic data (Reiter and Dale, 2000). The goal of this work is to develop a method for summarising time-series data in order to provide continuous feedback to students across the entire semester. As a case study, we took a module in Artificial Intelligence and asked students to fill out a very short diary-type questionnaire on a weekly basis. Questions included, for example, number of deadlines, number of classes attended, severity of personal issues. These data were then combined with the marks from the weekly lab reflecting the students' performance. As data is gathered each week in the lab, we now have a set of time-series data and our goal is to automatically create feedback. The goal is to present a holistic view through these diary entries of how the student is doing and what factors may be affecting performance.

Feedback is very important in the learning process but very challenging for academic staff to complete in a timely manner given the large number of students and the increasing pressures on academics' time. This is where automatic feedback can play a part, providing a tool for teachers that can give insight into factors that may not be immediately obvious (Porayska-Pomsta and Mellish, 2013). As reflected in NSS surveys[1], students are not completely satisfied with how feedback is currently delivered. The 2012 NSS survey, for all disciplines reported an 83% satisfaction rate with courses, with 70% satisfied with feedback. This has improved from recent years (in 2006 this was 60% for feedback) but shows that there is still room for improvement in how teachers deliver feedback and its content.

In the next section (Section 2) a discussion of the related work is presented. In Section 3, a description of the methodology is given as well as the process of the data collection from students, the template construction and the data collection with lecturers. In Section 4, the Reinforcement Learning implementation is described. In Section 5, the evaluation results are presented, and finally, in Sections 6 and 7, a conclusion and directions for future work are discussed.

2 Related Work

Report generation from time-series data has been researched widely and existing methods have been used in several domains such as weather forecasts (Belz and Kow, 2010; Angeli et al., 2010; Sripada et al., 2004), clinical data summarisation (Hunter

[1] http://www.thestudentsurvey.com/

et al., 2011; Gatt et al., 2009), narrative to assist children with communication needs (Black et al., 2010) and audiovisual debriefs from sensor data from Autonomous Underwater Vehicles missions (Johnson and Lane, 2011).

The two main challenges for time-series data summarisation are what to say (Content Selection) and how to say it (Surface Realisation). In this work we concentrate on the former. Previous methods for content selection include Gricean Maxims (Sripada et al., 2003); collective content selection (Barzilay and Lapata, 2004); and the Hidden Markov model approach for content selection and ordering (Barzilay and Lee, 2004). NLG systems tend to be very domain-specific and data-driven systems that seek to simultaneously optimize both content selection and surface realisation have the potential to be more domain-independent, automatically optimized and lend themselves to automatic generalization (Angeli et al., 2010; Rieser et al., 2010; Dethlefs and Cuayahuitl, 2011). Recent work on report generation uses statistical techniques from Machine Translation (Belz and Kow, 2010), supervised learning (Angeli et al., 2010) and unsupervised learning (Konstas and Lapata, 2012).

Here we apply Reinforcement Learning methods (see Section 4 for motivation) which have been successfully applied to other NLG tasks, such as Temporal Expressions Generation (Janarthanam et al., 2011), Lexical Choice (Janarthanam and Lemon, 2010), generation of adaptive restaurant summaries in the context of a dialogue system (Rieser et al., 2010) and generating instructions (Dethlefs and Cuayahuitl, 2011).

3 Methodology

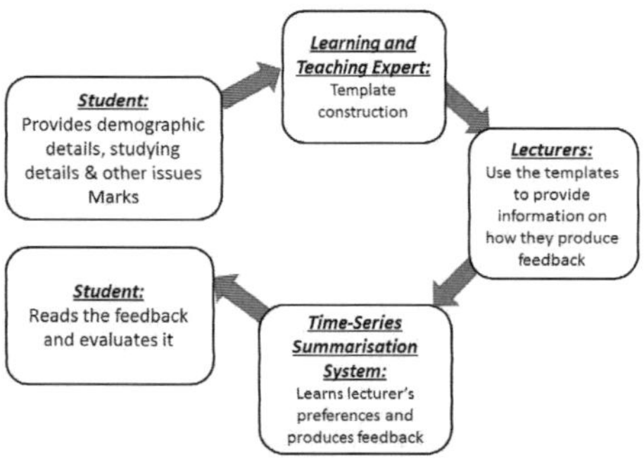

Figure 1: Methodology for data-driven feedback report generation

Figure 1 shows graphically our approach to the development of a generation system. Firstly, we collected data from students including marks, demographic details and weekly study habits. Next, we created templates for surface realisation with the help of a Teaching and Learning expert. These templates were used to generate summaries that were rated by lecturers. We used these ratings to train the learning agent. The output of the learning agent (i.e. automatically generated feedback reports) were finally evaluated by the students. Each of these steps are discussed in turn.

3.1 Time-series Data Collection from Students

The data were collected during the weekly lab sessions of a Computer Science module which was taught to third year Honours and MSc students over the course of a 10 week semester. We recruited 26 students who were asked to fill in a web-based diary-like questionnaire. Initially, we asked students to provide some demographic details (age, nationality, level of study). In addition, students provided on a weekly basis, information for nine factors that could influence their performance. These nine factors were motivated from the literature and are listed here in terms of effort (Ames, 1992), frustration (Craig et al., 2004) , difficulty (Person et al., 1995; Fox, 1993) and performance (Chi et al., 2001). *Effort* is measured by three factors: (1) how many hours they studied; (2) the level of revision they have done; (3) as well as the number of lectures (of this module) they attended. *Frustration* is measured by (4) the level of understandability of the content; (5) whether they have had other deadlines; and whether they faced any (6) health and/or (7) personal issues and at what severity. The *difficulty of the lab exercises* is measured by (8) the students' perception of difficulty. Finally, (9) marks achieved by the students in each weekly lab was used as a measure of their *performance*.

3.2 Data Trends

Initially, the data were processed so as to identify the existing trend of each factor during the semester, (e.g. number of lectures attending decreases). The tendencies of the data are estimated using linear least-squares regression, with each factor annotated as INCREASING, DECREASING or STABLE. In addition, for each student we perform a comparison between the average of each

Type	Description	Examples
AVERAGE	describes the factor data by either averaging the values given by the student, or by comparing the student's average with the class average (e.g. if above the mean value for the class, we say that the material is challenging).	"You spent 2 hours studying the lecture material on average". (HOURS STUDIED) "You found the lab exercises very challenging". (DIFFICULTY)
TREND	discusses the trend of the data, e.g. increasing, decreasing or stable.	"Your workload is increasing over the semester". (DEADLINES)
WEEKS	talks about specific events that happened in one or more weeks.	"You have had other deadlines during weeks 5, 6 and 9". (DEADLINES)
OTHER	all other expressions that are not directly related to data.	"Revising material during the semester will improve your performance". (REVISION)

Table 1: The table explains the different template types.

factor and the class average of the same factor.

3.3 Template Generation

The wording and phrasing used in the templates to describe the data were derived from working with and following the advice of a Learning and Teaching (L&T) expert. The expert provided consultation on how to summarise the data. We derived 4 different kinds of templates for each factor: AVERAGE, TREND, WEEKS and OTHER based on time-series data on plotted graphs. A description of the template types is shown in Table 1.

In addition, the L&T expert consulted on how to enhance the templates so that they are appropriate for communicating feedback according to the guidelines of the Higher Education Academy (2009), for instance, by including motivating phrases such as "You may want to plan your study and work ahead".

3.4 Data Collection from Lecturers

The goal of the Reinforcement Learning agent is to learn to generate feedback at least as well as lecturers. In order to achieve this, a second data collection was conducted with 12 lecturers participating.

The data collection consisted of three stages where lecturers were given plotted factor graphs and were asked to:

1. write a free style text summary for 3 students (Figure 2);
2. construct feedback summaries using the templates for 3 students (Figure 3);
3. rate random feedback summaries for 2 students (Figure 4).

We developed the experiment using the Google Web Toolkit for Web Applications, which facilitates the development of client-server applications. The server side hosts the designed tasks and stores the results in a datastore. The client side is responsible for displaying the tasks on the user's browser.

In Task 1, the lecturers were presented with the factor graphs of a student (one graph per factor) and were asked to provide a free-text feedback summary for this student. The lecturers were encouraged to pick as many factors as they wanted and to discuss the factors in any order they found useful. Figure 2 shows an example free text summary for a high performing student where the lecturer decided to talk about lab marks and understandability. Each lecturer was asked to repeat this task 3 times for 3 randomly picked students.

In Task 2, the lecturers were again asked to construct a feedback summary but this time they were given a range of sentences generated from the templates (as described in Section 2.3). They were asked to use these to construct a feedback report. The number of alternative utterances generated for each factor varies depending on the factor and the given data. In some cases, a factor can have 2 generated utterances and in other cases up to 5 (with a mean of 3 for each factor) and they differentiate in the style of trend description and wording. Again the lecturer was free to choose which factors to talk about and in which order, as well as to decide on the template style he/she prefers for the realisation through the template options. Figure 3 shows an example of template selection for the same student as in Figure 2.

In Task 3, the lecturers were presented with the plotted factor graphs plus a corresponding feedback summary that was generated by randomly choosing n factors and their templates, and were asked to rate it in a scale between 0-100 (100 for the best summary). Figure 4 shows an example of

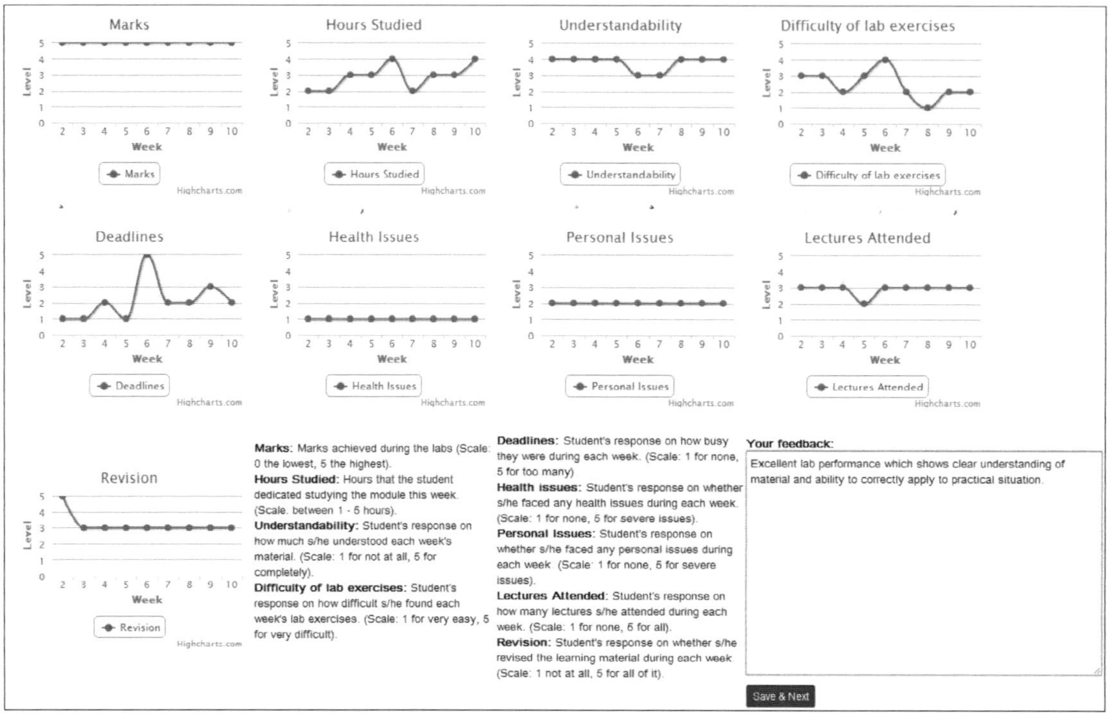

Figure 2: The interface of the 1st task of the data collection: the lecturer consults the factor graphs and provides feedback in a free text format.

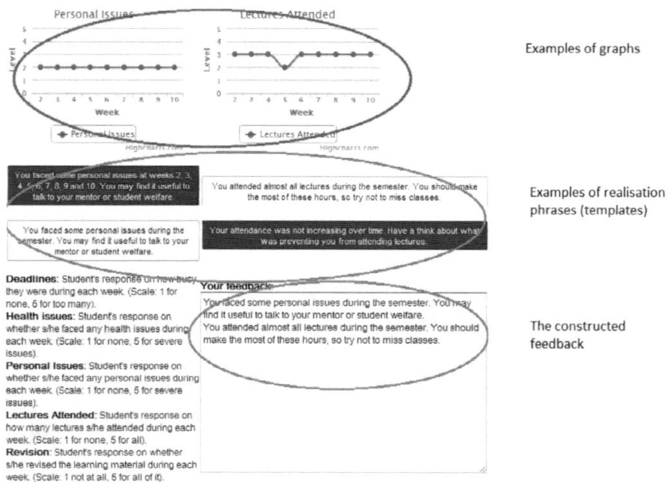

Figure 3: The interface of the 2nd task of data collection: the lecturer consults the graphs and constructs a feedback summary from the given templates (this graph refers to the same student as Figure 2).

a randomly generated summary for the same student as in Figure 2.

4 Learning a Time-Series Generation Policy

Reinforcement Learning (RL) is a machine learning technique that defines how an agent learns to take optimal actions in a dynamic environment so as to maximize a cumulative reward (Sutton and Barto, 1998). In our framework, the task of content selection of time-series data is presented as a Markov Decision problem. The goal of the agent is to learn to choose a sequence of actions that obtain the maximum expected reward in the long run. In this section, we describe the Reinforcement Learning setup for learning content selection

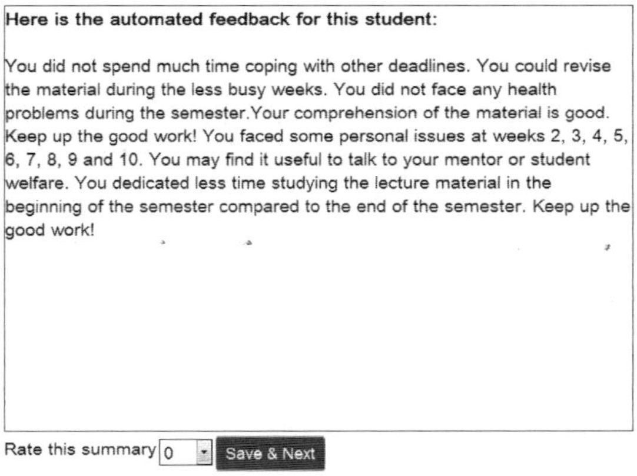

Figure 4: The interface of the 3rd task of data collection: the lecturer consults the graphs and rates the randomly generated feedback summary (this graph refers to the same student as Figures 2 and 3).

from time-series data for feedback report generation. Summarisation from time-series data is an open challenge and we aim to research other methods in the future, such as supervised learning, evolutionary algorithms etc.

4.1 Actions and States

In this learning setup, we focused only on selecting the correct content, i.e. which factors to talk about. The agent selects a factor and then decides whether to talk about it or not. The state consists of a description of the factor trends and the number of templates that have been selected so far. An example of the initial state of a student can be:

<marks_increased, lectures_attended_stable, hours_studied_increased, understandability_stable, difficulty_increased, health_issues_stable, personal_issues_stable, revision_increased, 0>

The agent explores the state space by selecting a factor and then by deciding whether to talk about it or not. If the agent decides to talk about the selected factor, it chooses the template in a greedy way, i.e. it chooses for each factor the template that results in a higher reward. After an action has been selected, it is deleted from the action space.

4.1.1 Ordering

In order to find out in which order the lecturers describe the factors, we transformed the feedback summaries into n-grams of factors. For instance, a summary that talks about the student's performance, the number of lectures that he/she attended, potential health problems and revision done can be translated into the following ngram: start, marks, lectures_attended, health_issues, revision, end. We used the constructed n-grams to compute the bigram frequency of the tokens in order to identify which factor is most probable to be referred to initially, which factors follow particular factors and which factor is usually talked about in the end. It was found that the most frequent ordering is: start, marks, hours_studied, understandability, difficulty, deadlines, health_issues, personal_issues, lectures_attended, revision, end.

4.2 Reward Function

The goal of the reward function is to optimise the way lecturers generate and rate feedback. Given the expert annotated summaries from Task 1, the constructed summaries from Task 2 and the ratings from Task 3, we derived the multivariate reward function:

$$Reward = a + \sum_{i=1}^{n} b_i * x_i + c * length$$

where $X = \{x_1, x_2, ..., x_n\}$ represents the combinations between the data trends observed in the time-series data and the corresponding lecturers' feedback (i.e. whether they included a factor to be realised or not and how). The value x_i for factor i is defined by the function:

$$x_i = \begin{cases} 1, & \text{the combination } i \text{ of a factor trend} \\ & \text{and a template type is included in} \\ & \text{the feedback} \\ 0, & \text{if not.} \end{cases}$$

For instance, the value of x_1 is 1 if marks were increased and this trend is realised in the feedback, otherwise it is 0. In our domain $n = 90$ in order to cover all the different combinations. The $length$ stands for the number of factors selected, a is the intercept, b_i and c are the coefficients for x_i and $length$ respectively.

In order to model the reward function, we used linear regression to compute the weights from the data gathered from the lecturers. Therefore, the reward function is fully informed by the data provided by the experts. Indeed, the intercept a, the vector weights b and the weight c are learnt by making use of the data collected by the lecturers from the 3 tasks discussed in Section 3.4.

The reward function is maximized (Reward = 861.85) for the scenario (i.e. each student's data), content selection and preferred template style shown in Table 2 (please note that this scenario was not observed in the data collection).

Factor	Trend	Template
difficulty	stable	NOT_MENTIONED
hours studied	stable	TREND
understandability	stable	NOT_MENTIONED
deadlines	increase	WEEKS
health issues	stable	WEEKS
personal issues	stable	WEEKS
lectures att.	stable	WEEKS
revision	stable	OTHER
marks	increase	TREND

Table 2: The table shows the scenario at which the reward function is maximised.

The reward function is minimized (Reward = -586.0359) for the scenario shown in Table 3 (please note that this scenario also was not observed in the data collection).

Factor	Trend	Template
difficulty	increase	AVERAGE
hours studied	stable	NOT_MENTIONED
understandability	decrease	AVERAGE
deadlines	*	*
health issues	increase	TREND
personal issues	stable	TREND
lectures att.	stable	NOT_MENTIONED
revision	stable	AVERAGE
marks	stable	TREND

Table 3: The table shows the scenario at which the reward function is minimised (* denotes multiple options result in the same minimum reward).

4.3 Training

We trained a time-series generation policy for 10,000 runs using the Tabular Temporal-Difference Learning (Sutton and Barto, 1998). During the training phase, the learning agent generated feedback summaries. When the construction of the summary begins, the length of the summary is 0. Each time that the agent adds a template (by selecting a factor), the length is incremented, thus changing the state. It repeats the process until it decides for all factors whether to talk about them or not. The agent is finally rewarded at the end of the process using the Reward function described in Section 3.2. Initially, the learning agent selects factors randomly, but gradually learns to identify factors that are highly rewarding for a given data scenario. Figure 5 shows the learning curve of the agent.

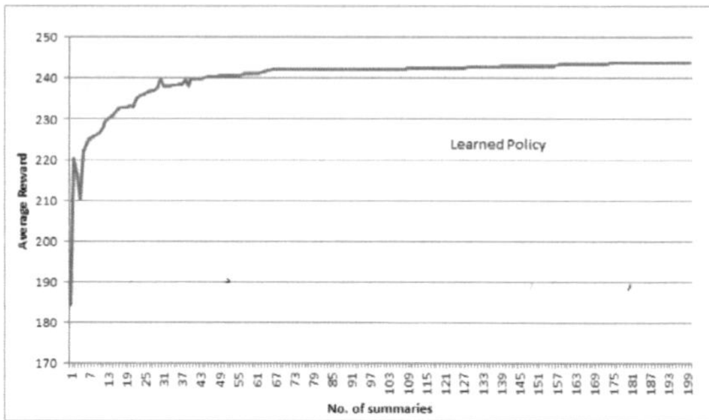

Figure 5: Learning curve for the learning agent. The x-axis shows the number of summaries produced and y- axis the total reward received for each summary.

5 Evaluation

We evaluated the system using the reward function and with students. In both these evaluations, we compared feedback reports generated using our Reinforcement Learning agent with four other baseline systems. Here we present a brief description of the baseline systems.

Baseline 1: Rule-based system. This system selects factors and templates for generation using a set of rules. These hand-crafted rules were derived from a combination of the L&T expert's advice and a student's preferences and is therefore a challenging baseline and represents a middle ground between the L&T expert's advice and a student's preferences. An example rule is: if the mark average is less than 50% then refer to revision.

Baseline 2: Brute Force system. This system performs a search of the state space, by exploring randomly as many different feedback summaries as possible. The Brute Force algorithm is shown below:

Algorithm 1 Brute Force algorithm

```
Input data: D
for n=0...10,000
 construct randomly feedback[n]
 assign getReward[n]
   if getReward[n]>getReward[n-1]
      bestFeedback = feedback[n]
   else
      bestFeedback = feedback[n-1]
return bestFeedback
```

In each run the algorithm constructs a feedback summary, then it calculates its reward, using the same reward function used for the Reinforcement Learning approach, and if the reward of the new feedback is better than the previous, it keeps the new one as the best. It repeats this process for 10,000 times for each scenario. Finally, the algorithm returns the summary that scored the highest ranking.

Baseline 3: Lecturer-produced summaries. These are the summaries produced by the lecturers, as described in Section 2.4, for Task 2 using template-generated utterances.

Baseline 4: Random system: The Random system constructs feedback summaries by selecting factors and templates randomly as described in Task 3 (in Section 3.4).

5.1 Evaluation with Reward Function

Table 4 presents the results of the evaluation performed using the Reward Function, comparing the learned policy with the four baseline systems. Each system generated 26 feedback summaries. On average the learned policy scores significantly higher than any other baseline for the given scenarios ($p < 0.05$ in a paired t-test).

Time-Series Summarisation Systems	Reward
Learned	**243.82**
Baseline 1: Rule-based	107.77
Baseline 2: Brute Force	241.98
Baseline 3: Lecturers	124.62
Baseline 4: Random	43.29

Table 4: The table summarises the average rewards that are assigned to summaries produced from the different systems.

5.2 Evaluation with Students

A subjective evaluation was conducted using 1st year students of Computer Science as participants. We recruited 17 students, who were all English native speakers. The participants were shown 4 feedback summaries in a random order, one generated by the learned policy, one from the rule-based system (Baseline 1), one from the Brute Force system (Baseline 2) and one summary produced by a lecturer using the templates (Baseline 3). Given the poor performance of the Random system in terms of reward, Baseline 4 was omitted from this study.

Overall there were 26 different scenarios, as described in Section 3.1. All summaries presented to a participant were generated from the same scenario. The participants then had to rank the summaries in order of preference: 1 for the most preferred and 4 for the least preferred. Each participant repeated the process for 4.5 scenarios on average (the participant was allowed to opt out at any stage). The mode values of the rankings of the preferences of the students are shown in Table 5. The web-based system used for the evaluation is shown in Figure 6.

System	Mode of Rankings
Learned	3rd
Baseline 3: Lecturers	3rd
Baseline 1: Rule-based	1st
Baseline 2: Brute Force	4th

Table 5: The table shows the mode value of the rankings of the preference of the students.

We ran a Mann-Whitney's U test to evaluate the difference in the responses of our 4-point Likert Scale question between the Learned system and the other three baselines. It was found that, for the given data, the preference of students for the feedback generated by the Learned system is as good as the feedback produced by the experts, i.e. there is no significant difference between the mean value of the rankings of the Learned system and the lecturer-produced summaries ($p = 0.8$) (Baseline 3).

The preference of the users for the Brute Force system does not differ significantly from the summaries generated by the Learned system ($p = 0.1335$). However, the computational cost of the Brute Force is higher because each time that the algorithm sees a new scenario it has to run approximately 3k times to reach a good summary (as seen in Figure 7) and about 10k to reach an optimal one, which corresponds to 46 seconds. This delay would prohibit the use of such a system in time-critical situations (such as defence) and in live systems such as tutoring systems. In addition, the processing time would increase with more complicated scenarios and if we want to take into account the ordering of the content selection and/or if we have more variables. In contrast, the RL method needs only to be trained once.

Finally, the users significantly preferred the summaries produced by the Rule-based system (Baseline 1) to the summaries produced by the Learned system. This is maybe because of the fact that in the rule-based system some knowledge of the end user's preferences (i.e. students) was taken into account in the rules which was not the case in the other three systems. This fact suggests that

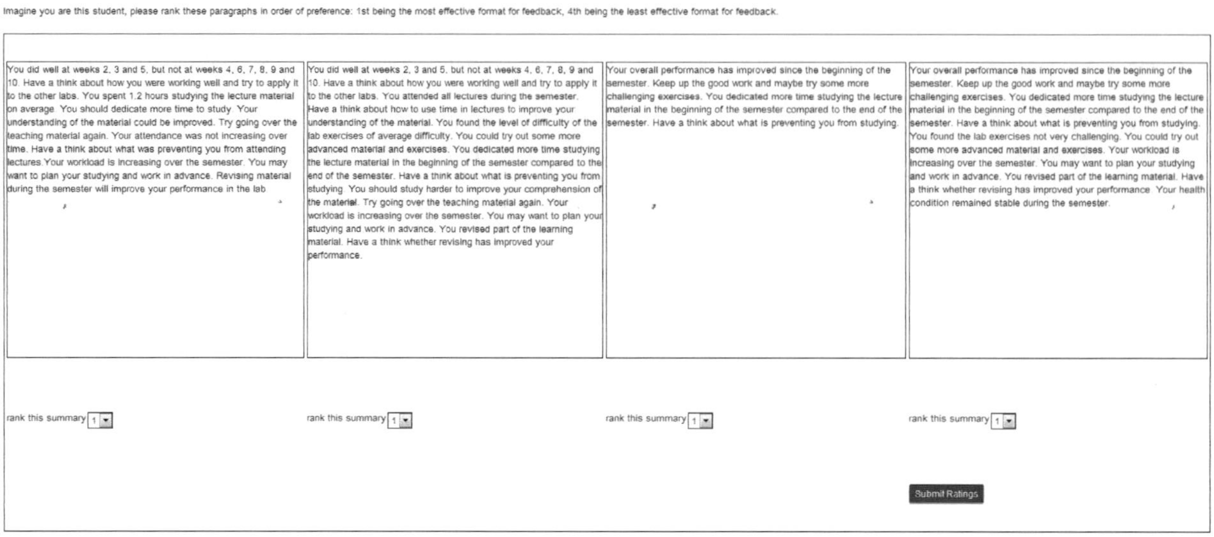

Figure 6: The interface for the evaluation: the students viewed the four feedback summaries and ranked them in order of preference. From left to right, the summaries as generated by: an Expert (Baseline 3), the Rule based system (Baseline 1), the Brute Force algorithm (Baseline 2), the Learned system.

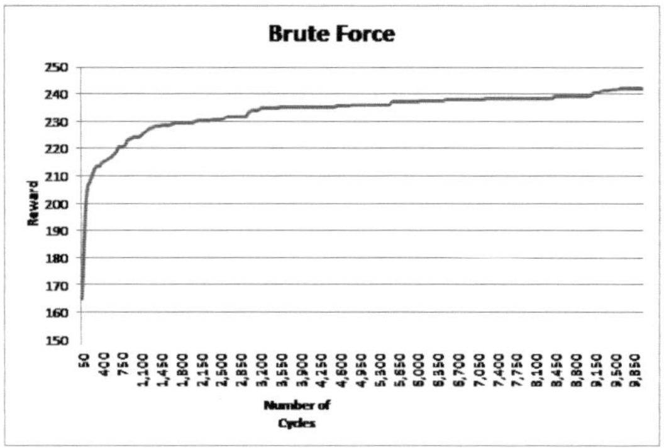

Figure 7: The graphs shows the number of cycles that the Brute Force algorithm needs to achieve specific rewards.

students' preferences should be taken into account as they are the receivers of the feedback. This can also be generalised to other areas, where the experts and the end users are not the same group of people. As the learned policy was not trained to optimise for the evaluation criteria, in future, we will explore reward functions that bear in mind both the expert knowledge and the student's preferences.

6 Conclusion

We have presented a statistical learning approach to summarisation from time-series data in the area of feedback reports. In our reports, we took into account the principles of good feedback provision as instructed by the Higher Education Academy. We also presented a method for data gathering from students and lecturers and show how we can use these data to generate feedback by presenting the problem as a Markov Decision Process and optimising it using Reinforcement Learning techniques. We also showed a way of constructing a data-driven reward function that can capture dependencies between the time-series data and the realisation phrases, in a similar way that the lecturers do when providing feedback. Finally, our evaluation showed that the learned report generation policy generates reports as well as lecturers.

7 Future Work

We aim to conduct further qualitative research in order to explore what factors and templates students find useful to be included in the feedback and inform our reward function with this information as well as what we have observed in the lecturer data collection. This way, we hope, not only to gain insights into what is important to students and lecturers but also to develop a data-driven approach that, unlike the rule-based system, does not require expensive and difficult-to-obtain expert input from Learning and Teaching experts. In addition, we want to compare RL techniques with supervised learning approaches and evolutionary algorithms. Finally, we want to unify content selection and surface realisation, therefore we will extend the action space in order to include actions for template selection.

8 Acknowledgements

The research leading to this work has received funding from the EC's FP7 programme: (FP7/2011-14) under grant agreement no. 248765 (Help4Mood).

References

Carole Ames. 1992. Classrooms: Goals, Structures, and Student Motivation. Journal of Educational Psychology, 84(3):p261-71.

Gabor Angeli, Percy Liang and Dan Klein. 2010. A simple domain-independent probabilistic approach to generation. EMNLP '10: Proceedings of the 2010 Conference on Empirical Methods in Natural Language Processing.

Regina Barzilay and Mirella Lapata. 2004. Collective content selection for concept-to-text generation. HLT '05: Proceedings of the conference on Human Language Technology and Empirical Methods in Natural Language Processing.

Regina Barzilay and Lillian Lee. 2004. Catching the drift: Probabilistic content models, with applications to generation and summarization. HLT-NAACL 2004: Proceedings of the Human Language Technology Conference of the North American Chapter of the Association for Computational Linguistics.

Anja Belz and Eric Kow. 2010. Extracting parallel fragments from comparable corpora for data-to-text generation. INLG '10: Proceedings of the 6th International Natural Language Generation Conference.

Rolf Black, Joe Reddington, Ehud Reiter, Nava Tintarev, and Annalu Waller. 2010. Using NLG and Sensors to Support Personal Narrative for Children with Complex Communication Needs. SLPAT '10: Proceedings of the NAACL HLT 2010 Workshop on Speech and Language Processing for Assistive Technologies.

Michelene T.H. Chi, Stephanie A. Siler, Heisawn Jeong, Takashi Yamauchi, Robert G. Hausmann. 2001. Learning from human tutoring. Journal of Cognitive Science, 25(4):471-533.

Scotty D. Craig, Arthur C. Graesser, Jeremiah Sullins, Barry Gholson. 2004. Affect and learning: an exploratory look into the role of affect in learning with AutoTutor. Journal of Educational Media, 29:241-250.

Nina Dethlefs and Heriberto Cuayahuitl. 2011. Combining hierarchical reinforcement learning and bayesian networks for natural language generation in situated dialogue. ENLG '11: Proceedings of the 13th European Workshop on Natural Language Generation.

Barbara Fox. 1993. The Human Tutorial Dialogue Project: Issues in the Design of Instructional Systems. Lawrence Erlbaum Associates, Hillsdale, New Jersey.

Albert Gatt, Francois Portet, Ehud Reiter, James Hunter, Saad Mahamood,Wendy Moncur, and Somayajulu Sripada. 2009. From Data to Text in the Neonatal Intensive Care Unit: Using NLG Technology for Decision Support and Information Management. Journal of AI Communications, 22:153-186.

Higher Education Academy. 2009. Providing individual written feedback on formative and summative assessments. `http://www.heacademy.ac.uk/assets/documents/resources/database/id353_senlef_guide.pdf`. Last modified September 16.

Jim Hunter, Yvonne Freer, Albert Gatt, Yaji Sripada, Cindy Sykes, and D Westwater. 2011. BT-Nurse: Computer Generation of Natural Language Shift Summaries from Complex Heterogeneous Medical Data. Journal of the American Medical Informatics Association,18:621-624.

Srinivasan Janarthenam, Helen Hastie, Oliver Lemon, Xingkun Liu. 2011. "The day after the day after tomorrow?" A machine learning approach to adaptive temporal expression generation: training and evaluation with real users. SIGDIAL '11: Proceedings of the SIGDIAL 2011 Conference.

Srinivasan Janarthanam and Oliver Lemon. 2010. Adaptive Referring Expression Generation in Spoken Dialogue Systems: Evaluation with Real Users. SIGDIAL '10: Proceedings of the 11th Annual Meeting of the Special Interest Group on Discourse and Dialogue.

Nicholas A. R. Johnson and David M. Lane. 2011. Narrative Monologue as a First Step Towards Advanced Mission Debrief for AUV Operator Situational Awareness. In the 15th International Conference on Advanced Robotics.

Ioannis Konstas and Mirella Lapata. 2012. Unsupervised concept-to-text generation with hypergraphs. NAACL HLT '12: Proceedings of the 2012 Conference of the North American Chapter of the Association for Computational Linguistics: Human Language Technologies.

Natalie K. Person, Roger J. Kreuz, Rolf A. Zwaan and Arthur C. Graesser. 1995. Pragmatics and Pedagogy: Conversational Rules and Politeness Strategies May Inhibit Effective Tutoring. Journal of Cognition and Instruction, 13(2):161-188.

Kaska Porayska-Pomsta and Chris Mellish. 2013. Modelling human tutors' feedback to inform natural language interfaces for learning. International Journal of Human-Computer Studies,71(6):703724.

Ehud Reiter and Robert Dale. 2000. Building Natural Language Generation systems. Cambridge University Press.

Verena Rieser, Oliver Lemon, and Xingkun Liu. 2010. Optimising Information Presentation for Spoken Dialogue Systems. ACL '10: Proceedings of the 48th Annual Meeting of the Association for Computational Linguistics.

Somayajulu Sripada, Ehud Reiter, I Davy, and K Nilssen. 2004. Lessons from Deploying NLG Technology for Marine Weather Forecast Text Generation. In Proceedings of PAIS session of ECAI-2004:760-764.

Somayajulu Sripada, Ehud Reiter, Jim Hunter, and Jin Yu. 2003. Generating English Summaries of Time Series Data using the Gricean Maxims. KDD '03: Proceedings of the ninth ACM SIGKDD international conference on Knowledge discovery and data mining.

Richart Sutton and Andrew Barto. 1998. Reinforcement Learning. MIT Press.

Deconstructing Human Literature Reviews – A Framework for Multi-Document Summarization

Kokil Jaidka, Christopher S.G. Khoo, Jin-Cheon Na
Division of Information Studies
Wee Kim Wee School of Communication and Information
Nanyang Technological University, Singapore
[kokil, chriskhoo]@pmail.ntu.edu.sg, tjcna@ntu.edu.sg

Abstract

This study is conducted in the area of multi-document summarization, and develops a literature review framework based on a deconstruction of human-written literature review sections in information science research papers. The first part of the study presents the results of a multi-level discourse analysis to investigate their discourse and content characteristics. These findings were incorporated into a framework for literature reviews, focusing on their macro-level document structure and the sentence-level templates, as well as the information summarization strategies. The second part of this study discusses insights from this analysis, and how the framework can be adapted to automatic summaries resembling human written literature reviews. Summaries generated from a partial implementation are evaluated against human written summaries and assessors' comments are discussed to formulate recommendations for future work.

1 Introduction

This project proposes a framework for literature reviews, which has applications in automatic summarization of scientific papers. A literature review is the traditional multi-document summary of research papers which is constructed by a researcher to survey previous findings and its structure follows certain linguistic rules. Several studies have identified that literature reviews are used to achieve distinct rhetorical purposes (Hart, 1998; Bourner, 1996; Boot & Beile, 2005; Jonsson, 2006; Massey, 2006; Torraco, 2005; Hinchliffe, 2003; Bruce, 1994), such as to:

- Compare and contrast previous research.
- Identify gaps in the literature
- Identify new research questions
- Define the proposed research contributions
- Build the justification for the current work
- Situate the work in the research literature
- Reinterpret and critique previous results

These rhetorical characteristics of literature reviews make it a challenging research problem in automatic multi-document summarization – not only should the summarizer identify salient information, but it should also synthesize the summary in a way that achieves certain argumentative purposes. The problem of summarization in context was first identified by Sparck Jones and Endres-Niggemeyer (1995) and subsequently in Sparck Jones' follow-up article (2007), wherein they questioned the usefulness of state-of-the-art summarization methods in addressing users' information needs. As articulated by Sparck Jones (2007) and echoed by Nenkova and McKeown (2011), summarization needs to be viewed as a part of the larger discourse (academic writing) it belongs to, tailored to the purpose (literature review) of summarization, the reader (in this case, a researcher) and the genre being summarized (research papers). Motivated by this research gap, we outline the aims of our analyses:

- To identify how to emulate the purpose of literature reviews, we conducted a discourse analysis to identify the macro-level structure and the sentence-level linguistic expressions embedded in literature review sections.
- To identify the relationship between research paper and literature review, we conducted an information analysis to identify rules for selecting and

transforming information from research papers.

The focus of the paper is to draw insights from the framework to propose strategies for automatic literature review generation. An automatic summary fashioned as a literature review can function as a tool to help literature review writers by pointing out ways in which information in the source papers can be compared and integrated. For information searchers, it can provide a customisable overview of a set of retrieval results that is more readable and more logical than a list of salient sentences.

2 Previous Work

This paper investigates the human summarization process through an extensive discourse analysis. Human summarization is a process comprising document exploration to investigate the document macrostructure, relevance assessment by constructing a mental representation and summary production by selecting and transforming text from the source(s) (Endres-Niggemeyer, Maier, and Sigel, 1995). The underlying principle is the theory of human synthesis of information, by Van Dijk and Kintsch (1983).

This study proposes a linguistically motivated framework for summarization. In previous work, a summarization framework developed by Marcu (2000) compressed information from general texts by identifying rhetorical relationships between clauses and sentences, and extracting sentence nuclei. Shiyan, Khoo & Goh (2008) summarized social science dissertation abstracts by referencing a social science taxonomy to identify important information and a specially constructed knowledge bank to identify important inter-relationships. In earlier work, a summarization framework designed by Teufel and Moens (2002) identified 7 categories of scientific arguments and extracted single-document summaries from chemistry and computational linguistics papers (Teufel, Siddharthan & Batchelor, 2009) based on user's queries. However, it required large corpora of manually annotated papers to be applied to any field, and it generated only single-document summaries.

Some other scientific summarization systems aim to model information relationships accurately without concerning themselves with summary structure. Centrifuser, a framework for summarizing medical literature (Elhadad, Kan, Klavans and McKeown, 2005) produced a multi-document, query-focused indicative summary highlighting the similarities and differences between source documents. The topic tree for the final summary was constructed offline by clustering a large number of documents, thus it was not suitable for real-time user queries. In a related recent approach, Hoang and Kan (2010) presented preliminary results from automatically generating related work sections for a target paper by taking a hierarchical topic tree as an input; however, the requirement of a pre-conceived topic tree limits the scalability of this system. To sum up, these scientific summarization systems are typically delimited by their scalability and generalizability for multiple documents and domains.

Newer approaches in scientific paper summarization rely on preselected information cited in other papers to judge whether information is influential or not, and generate a multi-document summary of a topic (Nanba, Kando & Okumura, 2011) or a single document summary for a paper using its relevant cited information (Qazvinian & Radev, 2008). A system for generating literature surveys through citations was proposed by Mohammad et al. (2009) which applied superficial analysis of research paper citation sentences to suggest model sentences; the present study describes parallel efforts to refine a summarization framework after extensive discourse analysis. We consider providing not just a synopsis of information, but also integrating the synopsis with the contextual and rhetorical features which make a human written literature review a coherent, cohesive and useful reference. Our study thus addresses a different, and more challenging, set of objectives than the citation-based summarizers of recent work.

3 Developing the Literature Review Framework

Following the first research aim, we carried out an analysis of the discourse structure of a sample of 30 literature review sections in research papers haphazardly selected from the Journal of the American Society for Information Science and Technology between the years 2000-2008, 2 or 3 from each year. On average, a literature review section was 1146 words in length and it cited 17 studies. The texts were analyzed at 3 levels of detail:

- Macro-level document structure: to identify the different sections of the literature, the types of information they contain and how they are organized hierarchically.
- Sentence-level rhetorical structure: to identify how sentences are framed according to the overall purpose of the literature review.
- Summarization strategies: to identify how information was selected and synthesized for the literature review.

Preliminary findings of these discourse analyses have been discussed in previous work by the authors, notably, in a discussion of the features of the macro-structure of information science literature reviews (Khoo, Na & Jaidka, 2011), rhetorical functions found in literature reviews (Jaidka, Khoo & Na, 2010) and associations between sections in source papers and their citing sentences in literature reviews (Jaidka, Khoo & Na, 2013). The current study applies the discourse characteristics thus identified to develop and test a literature review framework for multi-document summarization.

3.1 Designing Document Structure Templates

As noted in academic writing textbooks (Hart, 1998), literature reviews are structured as a hierarchy of topics and each "paragraph" fulfills certain functions. To identify these macro-structures and their functions, we conducted this discourse analysis, proceeding with the assumption that a literature is structured as a set of topic elements, with each topic having a set of embedded study elements (i.e. descriptions of research studies relevant to the topic). An exploratory study was conducted to identify the structures within these topics and their hierarchical relationships. Two Research Assistants holding graduate degrees annotated every sentence with one or more of the following tags:

- title tag: to provide a statement of the topic theme or study objective
- description tag: to encapsulate the details of the topic or study
- meta-summary tag: to provide the writers' comments as an overview summary of the research in the field
- meta-critique tag: to contain the writers' critique or interpretation of cited studies, critical comparison of research or justification for the current study
- current-study tag: to refers to and compare with the current work being described in the paper.
- method and result tags: to provide a description of the research methods and research results reported in the cited papers.

In this coding scheme, the meta-summary and meta-critique tags provide the writers' comments, citing one or more studies together. The rest of the elements comprise descriptive text about individual studies. The average inter-coder reliability score (Cohen's Kappa) obtained was high at 0.76. Disagreements between the coders were resolved through discussion until a mutually agreeable solution was reached. The analysis identified different types of literature reviews as well as different structures. In our literature review framework, these findings suggested rules for generating different types of literature reviews:

- Integrative literature reviews should comprise a large proportion of meta-summary and meta-critique elements. This is because they discuss and critique ideas from a number of studies in a high-level summary.
- Descriptive literature reviews should report the results of individual studies in detail, outlining their methodology and recommendations. This is because they were found to comprise significantly more study elements.
- Integrative literature reviews should be organized as a hierarchical structure with embedded topics. Comparatively, descriptive literature reviews should be organized as a flat structure, with many more topic elements per text but less embedded topics. This is because

integrative literature reviews were found to comprise an average of 2.5 embedded topics, and descriptive literature reviews had an average of 1.4 embedded sub-topics.

These rules have been applied in designing several integrative and descriptive literature review templates. Fig 1 illustrates one of the template integrative literature reviews we designed. It comprises a level 1 starting topic which acts as the overall topic of the literature review. The topic has other sub-topic elements within it, each of which begins with a meta-summary element which introduces it, followed by study elements to illustrate it. The topic elements determine the logical organization of the literature review; meta-summary are incorporated into the structure because they provide research overviews and highlight the similarities across related papers. The study elements highlight the unique features for individual papers. These templates will be instantiated in the automatic literature review generation process.

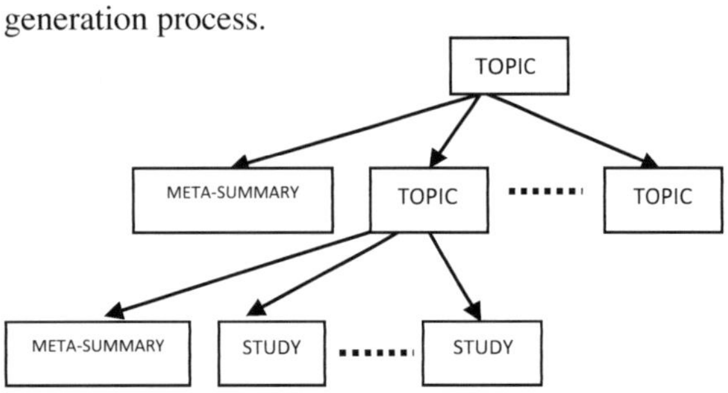

Figure 1. A template document structure in the literature review framework

3.2 Designing Sentence Templates

Previous studies of literature reviews (Bunton, 2002; Kwan, 2006) have highlighted the broad rhetorical "moves" which organize the text, but none have attempted to identify their linguistic structure or specific functions. In the clause-level analysis, we annotated linguistic expressions framing research descriptions, defined as discourse markers by Hyland (2004). Although discourse markers include generic logical connectives such as "so", "therefore" and "because", we followed Teufel's criteria (Teufel, 1999 pp. 76) to focus on only those discourse markers which are used in scientific discourse to perform one of the functions listed below:

- Describe a topic: Present a broad overview of research (e.g., "Previous research focused on") or its context (e.g., "Research in the area of")
- Describe a study: Cite an author (e.g., "In a study by") or describe research processes (e.g., "X identified…", "Y has conducted an experiment to…")
- Compare studies: Highlight similarities or differences in research (e.g., "Several studies have applied").
- Provide additional information: Frame examples or enumerate research studies (e.g., "For example", "A list includes").

It was found that a total of 110 expressions were used in 1298 variations to frame different types of information in different ways and achieve different rhetorical functions. We have applied these findings in the literature review framework to develop sentence templates for text generation, and to formulate rules for selecting templates which are significantly associated with the type of literature review and discourse element to be populated:

- In integrative literature reviews: apply regular expressions which describe research objectives in the description elements. In the meta-summary elements in integrative literature reviews, apply expressions which "state the common aims".
- In descriptive literature reviews: choose expressions which "state the research method" and "state the common approaches" in the description and meta-summary elements.

Regular expressions are applied for text-to-text generation, serving as a means to extract information from source papers as well as to map them into appropriate sentence templates. Those applied to extract and instantiate research objective sentences within topics, studies and comparisons are illustrated in Table 1.

3.3 Designing Information Selection and Summarization Strategies

In accordance with the second research aim, we conducted a content analysis to identify the relationship between the source papers and the final literature review. Similar work describing text editing strategies has been done by Jing and

McKeown (1999); however, in this analysis we extend their objectives to additionally identify:

- The source sections of the paper from where information was selected (i.e., Abstract Introduction, Methodology, Results or Conclusion).
- The types of transformations used to convert the source sentence to the referencing sentence (i.e., copy-paste, paraphrase, or higher-level summary).
- Identifying the types of information selected from the source papers (i.e., objective, methodology, results and critical summary).
- Analysis of the reasons for preference of one source sentence over another, despite providing similar information. This was inferred by comparing candidate source sentences against each other.

The corpus for analysis was constructed by analyzing the 20 literature reviews line-by-line and retaining all the sentences referencing previous work, either explicitly (e.g., "X and Y (1998) conducted experiments in transitive translation") or implicitly by adding onto the details of a cited study (e.g., "Studies have also focused on users' mental models of information seeking (X, 1989)".

A total of 349 references were collected from the twenty literature review sections. Sentence providing definitions, or citing sources other than research papers, were further discarded because they lay outside the scope of our analysis. The findings, revealed that more than a quarter of all selected information was from the Abstract of the source paper. The information selected by the reviewer is copy-pasted more often in descriptive as compared to integrative literature reviews. Some of these findings have been applied to suggest strategies for information selection and summarization in the literature review framework:

- For research objective information: choose sentences from the Abstract and Introduction of source papers; copy-paste it into descriptive literature reviews, but paraphrase it in integrative literature reviews.
- In descriptive literature reviews: provide detailed method information, copy-pasted from the Introduction or Method of source papers.
- In integrative literature reviews: provide detailed result information, summarized at a higher level from the Results and Conclusions.

When more than one sentence provides the same factual information, the sentence selection criteria listed in Table 2 should be followed to choose the more concise alternative.

Function	Type of Information Required	Regular Expression which map into Sentence Templates
Describe a topic	Introduce a topic through its research aspects	(Researchers I Research) (have Ihas) (in I are concerned with I have addressed Iproposed I observed I investigated I focused on)
	Introduce a topic through its literature review	The (literature review I prior work) (covered I dealt with I looked at I focused on)?
	Introduce area of research	research I studies I findings) in the (field I area I domain I context) of
Describe a study	State the study objective	(the study I we I who) (conducted Iexplored I proposed I pursued I described I attempted to I represented I analyzed I examined I investigated Ideals with I seeks to discover)
	State the study motivation	(The I Their) underlying research (question I objective) (was Iis)
	State the study hypothesis	(They) (argue I opine I hold Idebate I believe) that
Compare studies	State the common aim of studies	The (common)? (issue I motivation Iaim I principle) (for I behind) (many I mostI someI theseI such I existing) studies
		(ManyI Most IThese I Some I Such I Existing I Various)? (studies I work) have (explored I focused on)

Table 1. Regular expressions obtained from clause-level analysis

Type of Criteria	Order of Priority
Lexical	• "This article/paper..." • "The aim/goal/objective is..." • "We present/ describe..." • "Recent research into..." • Sentences with how/what/why questions
Syntactic	• Sentence having the main topic in its main clause • The sentence with fewer clauses • The sentence with no back-referencing
Surface	• Sentence from the first paragraphs of a section • The title of the source paper • The sentence which is the shortest

Table 2. Criteria for selecting sentences

4 Evaluation

To evaluate the framework, the objective was to compare its "human-ness" represented by its Comprehensibility, Readability and Usefulness against human-written literature reviews and machine-generated sentence extracts. For this purpose, the framework was partially adapted in a summarization method focusing on comparing research objective information extracted from Abstracts and Introduction sections, and presenting a topical overview resembling a three-level literature review. The output generated is similar to the summaries generated by Centrifuser (Elhadad et al., 2005) – sentences are extracted to provide a synopsis of similarities and unique features of studies are highlighted for individual papers; however our prototype does so without rely on external domain knowledge. The method was implemented in Java on the Eclipse IDE, and it comprised three stages:

- Text pre-processing: to extract sentences from the Abstract and Introduction of the input source papers. Here the text is segmented, tokenized, parsed, stop-words are filtered and n-grams of noun phrases are created to represent concepts in the source papers.
- Information selection and integration: to identify similarities and differences across the research objective sentences of source papers. It selects important concepts based on the document frequency of lexical concept chains (Barzilay and McKeown, 2005), and applies the research objective sentence selection rules developed in the framework to select important information for summarization.
- Text presentation: to produce text that has the characteristics of the literature review. It applies the document structure described in the framework, to organize the literature review, and sentence templates particular to research objective information in integrative literature reviews (the ones listed in Table 1).

The resultant summaries resemble a human written literature review because they are laid out as a topic tree and present a comparative overview of similarities and unique features. However, some grammatical errors can be spotted, which would need a post-processing module to remove.

30 sets of information science source papers were prepared by sampling topics from 30 literature reviews from 2000-2008 issues of JASIST, Journal of Documentation and Journal of Information Science and downloading the papers they cited. Only 3-10 source papers were downloaded for every sampled topic; this was so that the task could be manageable for the researchers constructing the human summaries. An excerpt system summary is provided in Table 3.

For each input set of related research papers, three types of summaries were generated, each with a different kind of method – framework-based structure (by our method), sentence-extraction structure (by the baseline, MEAD) and a human-written summary by a researcher:

- MEAD: The MEAD summarization system (Radev, Jing, Stys, & Tam, 2004) was the baseline; it followed a sentence-extraction approach to generate multi-document extracts of information (generally news articles).

- System: Our system based on the framework, and focusing on the similarities and differences between research objectives at the lexical and syntactic level.
- Human: Five researchers from the School of Humanities and Social Sciences of our university summarized the research objective sentences from set of source papers in the context of a given (main) topic.

This literature review presents research in relevance published by Barry (1994), Harter (1992), Tang and Solomon (1998), Vakkari and Hakala (2000) and Wang and Soergel (1998).
Studies by Barry (1994) and Tang et al. (1998) focus on retrieval mechanism.
Researchers in relevance have also considered users (Harter, 1992; Vakkari et al., 2000; Wang et al., 1998).
The study by Vakkari et al. (2000) demonstrates that it is productive to study relevance as a task and process-oriented user construct.
Studies by Wang et al. (1998) and Tang et al. (1998) focus on dynamic models.
The study by Tang et al. (1998) is a step in the empirical exploration of the evolutionary nature of relevance judgments.

Table 3: Excerpt from a system summary

In the human summaries, the coders selected an average of 3 sub-topics and 8 unique sub-topics in their summaries. Human summaries also had the highest compression rate of 18%, as compared to a compression rate of 25% by MEAD and our System. An inter-coder agreement was conducted over 10 summaries by taking the summaries done by one of the post-graduate researchers as reference and comparing each pair of summaries, considering each of the "similarities" or "differences" as a "common" or "unique" sub-topic. Comparisons revealed that the coders usually had the same idea of what constituted an important "similarity" or common sub-topic (percent agreement= 70%) though they often chose different "differences" or unique sub-topics in their summaries (percent agreement= 56%).

Content evaluation of the 30 sets of summaries by the ROUGE-1 metric (Lin & Hovy, 2003) revealed that system summaries had a higher but not significantly different effectiveness or f-measure of 0.38 as compared to the baseline (0.33). We developed our own version of ROUGE to measure information overlap by comparing the information concepts extracted from summaries. It was different from the standard ROUGE-1 in three ways: it filtered out "research stopwords" such as "method", "experiment" and "study", which didn't represent research information; it aggregated words which shared the same lemma; and it also conflated co-occurring adjacent words into the same information concepts. Consequently, we obtained real scores of effectiveness in terms of higher f-measure scores for both the system and the baseline. The system's f-measure (0.57) was a significant improvement over the baseline (0.50) at the 0.01 level. The results are provided in Table 4.

For the quality evaluation, 90 questionnaires were prepared from the 30 sets of summaries, using permutations of presentation orders to account for carry-over effects during assessment. To recruit assessors, a call for participation in the evaluation was broadcast over the internet, through postings in discussion boards, personal emails and library sciences mailing lists. The invitation was also personally extended to authors of other publications in JASIST, JDoc and JIS. The invitation for participation was restricted to only Library and Information Science and Computer Science researchers and PhD students who had passed their qualifying exam. It was anticipated that such assessors would be more familiar with the topics in the summary, and would be able to make meaningful comments about the summaries and their characteristics, such as lack of evident comparisons and generalizations, or incorrect comparisons and generalizations among unlike information. There were a total number of 35 assessors with a mean research experience of 6 years, who provided 67 responses, by filling out 1 or 2 each, over a period of two months. The assessors were from reputable international universities in different countries. The highest degrees held by the assessors varied from Bachelors (for PhD students who had passed their qualifying exam) to PhD. They scored the summaries on their Comprehensibility, Readability and Usefulness and also provided qualitative comments to the following questions:

- What did you like about this summary?
- What did you find confusing about this summary?
- How is this summary, a good/bad literature review?

The quantitative results in Table 5 show that the System summary was significantly more readable and more useful than the baseline at the 0.05 level. The qualitative results (provided in Table 6) are equally interesting and show that researchers with different number of years of research liked or disliked different things about the System summary. Researchers with 0-4 years of experience did not have any specific preference of one type of summary over another. Researchers with 5-8 years of experience were more conscious of grammatical errors and repetition mistakes in the system summary. Researchers with 9-12 years of experience ignored the grammatical errors in Human summaries and System and instead criticized their lack of detail. Researchers with 13 years or experience or more were sensitive to the overall "context" and "flow" of the summary. Most of the assessors were able to identify the main topic and its related sub-topics; however, they experienced the System as being more disjointed, lacking "focus" as compared to the Human summaries. On the whole, researchers were satisfied with the overview provided as well as the hierarchical organization. It would be interesting to see whether these findings and differences would be replicated in a larger study.

Measures	System	MEAD
Recall	0.70	0.63
Precision	0.49	0.44
F-measure	0.57	0.50

Table 4. Results from the content evaluation (N=30)

	MEAD	System	Human
Comprehensibility	5.6	5.6	6.2
Readability	4.9	5.3	5.6
Usefulness	5.7	6.4	6.3

Table 5. Results from the quality evaluation (N=67)

5 Conclusion and Future Work

This study has analyzed how authors select information, transform it and organize it in a definite discourse structure as a literature review. Our findings identified two styles of literature reviews – the integrative and descriptive literature reviews, with different profiles of discourse elements and rhetorical expressions. Integrative literature reviews present information from several studies in a condensed form as a critical summary, possibly complemented with a comparison, evaluation or comment on the research gap. The focus is on highlighting relationships amongst concepts or comparing studies against each other. Descriptive reviews present experimental detail about previous studies, such as the approach followed, their results and evaluation. The focus is on providing important details of previous studies in a concise form.

From these findings, we conjecture that authors begin a literature review with an overall strategy in mind. They select and edit the information content based on the style of literature review. They may choose to write an integrative style of literature review to guide the reader along a critical survey of previous research. To support their argument, they paraphrase information selected from the Abstract and Conclusion sections, and integrate information from the Results sections into a high-level overview of important findings. Accordingly, they choose the discourse structure and linguistic expressions to frame their argument.

Our framework has since been validated on a larger sample size of 90 articles selected from 3 top journals in information science. It is recommended for application in a complete automatic literature review generation system, wherein a user would be able to control the style of literature review, the level of detail and analysis required, as well as the structure of the layout and the number of topics. At the information selection stage, it would be able to apply different information selection and transformation strategies to generate different parts of a literature review. At the text generation stage, it would be able to introduce a topic and describe its context and core concepts, describe a study and its objectives, methods and findings, delineate a research gap and identify the common and different features among studies, and illustrate its argument with examples.

	Year 0-4	Year 5-8	Year 9-12	Year 13+
Comprehensibility	- It gives a good overview on the topic and points	- I liked the structure. - It summarizes the research and connects the authors to the topic by the use of "these authors." - It's not too short nor too long.	- Easy to read and understand. - It is better review than the others because it tries to tie the literature together in some fashion.	- There seemed to be no reason for the ordering of the sentences about the different research papers - Each individual statement in the summary seems relevant (of some objective value) by itself, but all together lacks uniformity in subject. - However it does seem to get the core issues.
Readability	- Continuity - Yet, the linking of sentence could be better. - Too many repetitions, but gives some information	- This summary is neither readable nor informative. - The same studies are cited several times - It kept repeating all the studies. - It felt very disjointed, maybe because of all the small paragraphs. - Badly written, hard to read.	- It flows well - Has some sentences seemingly unrelated to neighboring sentences	- Generally easy to read. - There are a few mistakes in grammar, which is distracting. - Very readable. - Like: seems to have a bit of flow.
Usefulness	- This summary seems quite good - I feel I got an overview over the research in the area. - The summary covered a good deal of literature - The overview is nice but still really flat.	- This is the best summary of the sample. - Comprehensively covers the text - The summary provides information about groups of studies researching certain topics - This summary provides an overview of research in web search with more informative details	- Comparison between studies is helpful. - More info required about study, including methods, findings. - It would be pretty useful for lit review. - While comparisons of different papers are well done, it would also be useful to have more description of each study.	- Should give an indication of these trends in order to help the reader contextualize the research field. - There is an attempt at relating studies to each other so that one gets an overview of the research area.

Table 6. Comments on System by assessors with different years of research experience

References

Barzilay, R., & McKeown, K. R. (2005). Sentence fusion for multidocument news summarization. Computational Linguistics, 31(3), 297-328.

Boote, D. N., & Beile, P. (2005). Scholars before researchers: On the centrality of the dissertation literature review in research preparation. Educational researcher, 34(6), 3-15.

Bourner, T. (1996). The research process: four steps to success. Research methods: guidance for postgraduates, Arnold, London, 7-11.

Bruce, C. S. (1994). Research students' early experiences of the dissertation literature review. Studies in Higher Education, 19(2), 217-229.

Bunton, D. (2002) Generic moves in Ph.D Introduction chapters. In J. Flowerdew (Ed.), Academic Discourse. London: Longman.

Cooper, H. M. (1988). The structure of knowledge synthesis. Knowledge in Society, 1, 104-126.

Hoang, C., & Kan, M.Y. 2010. Towards automated related work summarization. In Proceedings of the 23rd International Conference on Computational Linguistics (COLING'10): Posters (pp. 427–435).

DUC. (2002). The Document Understanding Conference. Retrieved Oct 2010, from http://duc.nist.gov.

Elhadad, N., Kan, M. Y., Klavans, J. L., & McKeown, K. R. (2005). Customization in a unified framework for summarizing medical literature.Artificial Intelligence in Medicine, 33(2), 179.

Endres-Niggemeyer, B., Maier, E., & Sigel, A. (1995). How to implement a naturalistic model of abstracting: four core working steps of an expert abstractor. Information Processing & Management, 31(5), 631-674.

Guo, Q., & Li, C. (2007, August). The Research on the Application of Text Clustering and Natural Language Understanding in Automatic Abstracting. In Fuzzy Systems and Knowledge Discovery, 2007. FSKD 2007. Fourth International Conference on (Vol. 4, pp. 92-96). IEEE.

Hart, C. (1998). Doing a literature review. London: Sage.

Hinchliffe, L. (2003). Having your say in a scholarly way. Research Strategies, 19, 163– 164.

Hyland, K. (2004). Disciplinary interactions: Metadiscourse in L2 postgraduate writing. Journal of Second Language Writing, 13(2), 133-151.

Jing, H., & McKeown, K. R. (1999). The decomposition of human-written summary sentences. In Proceedings of the 22nd annual international ACM SIGIR conference on Research and development in information retrieval (pp. 129-136). ACM.

Jaidka, K., Khoo, C., and Na, J.-C. (2010). Imitating Human Literature Review Writing: An Approach to Multi-Document Summarization. In Proceedings of the International Conference on Asian Digital Libraries (ICADL) (pp. 116-119). Australia: Springer-Verlag.

Jaidka, K., Khoo, C., & Na, J. C. (2013). Literature Review Writing: How Information is Selected and Transformed. Aslib Proceedings, 65(3), 303-325.

Khoo, C., Na, J. C., & Jaidka, K. (2011). Analysis of the macro-level discourse structure of literature reviews. Online Information Review, 35(2), 255-271.

Kwan, B. S. (2006). The schematic structure of literature reviews in doctoral theses of applied linguistics. English for Specific Purposes, 25(1), 30-55.

Lin, C. Y., & Hovy, E. (2003, May). Automatic evaluation of summaries using n-gram co-occurrence statistics. In Proceedings of the 2003 Conference of the North American Chapter of the Association for Computational Linguistics on Human Language Technology-Volume 1 (pp. 71-78). Association for Computational Linguistics.

Marcu, D. (1997, July). From discourse structures to text summaries. In Proceedings of the ACL (Vol. 97, pp. 82-88).

Nenkova, A., & McKeown, K. (2011). Automatic summarization. Now Publishers Inc.

Nanba, H., Kando, N., & Okumura, M. (2011). Classification of research papers using citation links and citation types: Towards automatic review article generation. Advances in Classification Research Online, 11(1), 117-134.

Ou, S., Khoo, C. S. G., & Goh, D. H. (2008). Design and development of a concept-based multi-document summarization system for research abstracts. Journal of information science, 34(3), 308-326.

Radev, D. R., Jing, H., Styś, M., & Tam, D. (2004). Centroid-based summarization of multiple documents. Information Processing & Management, 40(6), 919-938.

Saggion, H., & Lapalme, G. (2002). Generating indicative-informative summaries with sumum. Computational linguistics, 28(4), 497-526.

Mohammad, S., Dorr, B., Egan, M., Ahmed, H., Muthukrishan, P., Qazvinian, V., Radev, D., Zajic, D. (2009). Using citations to generate surveys of scientific paradigms. In Proceedings of Human Language Technologies: The 2009 Annual Conference of the North American Chapter of the Association for Computational Linguistics (pp. 584–592). Association for Computational Linguistics.

Sparck Jones, K., & Endres-Niggemeyer, B. (1995). Automatic summarizing. Information Processing & Management, 31(5), 625-630.

Sparck Jones, K. (2007). Automatic summarising: The state of the art. Information Processing & Management, 43(6), 1449-1481.

Teufel, S. (1999). Argumentative zoning: Information extraction from scientific text (Doctoral dissertation, University of Edinburgh).

Teufel, S., & Moens, M. (2002). Summarizing scientific articles: experiments with relevance and rhetorical status. Computational linguistics, 28(4), 409-445.

Teufel, S., Siddharthan, A., & Batchelor, C. (2009, August). Towards discipline-independent argumentative zoning: Evidence from chemistry and computational linguistics. In Proceedings of the 2009 Conference on Empirical Methods in Natural Language Processing: Volume 3 (pp. 1493-1502). Association for Computational Linguistics.

Torraco, R. J. (2005). Writing integrative literature reviews: Guidelines and examples. Human Resource Development Review, 4(3), 356-367.

Van Dijk, T. A., & Kintsch, W. (1983). Strategies of discourse comprehension. New York: Academic Press.

Abstractive Meeting Summarization with Entailment and Fusion

Yashar Mehdad* **Giuseppe Carenini*** **Frank W. Tompa**** **Raymond T. NG***
Department of Computer Science
*University of British Columbia **University of Waterloo
{mehdad, carenini, rng}@cs.ubc.ca fwtompa@cs.uwaterloo.ca

Abstract

We propose a novel end-to-end framework for abstractive meeting summarization. We cluster sentences in the input into communities and build an entailment graph over the sentence communities to identify and select the most relevant sentences. We then aggregate those selected sentences by means of a word graph model. We exploit a ranking strategy to select the best path in the word graph as an abstract sentence. Despite not relying on the syntactic structure, our approach significantly outperforms previous models for meeting summarization in terms of informativeness. Moreover, the longer sentences generated by our method are competitive with shorter sentences generated by the previous word graph model in terms of grammaticality.

1 Introduction

The huge amount of data generated every day in meetings calls for developing automated methods to efficiently process these data to meet users' needs. Automatic summarization is a popular task that can help users to browse a large amount of recorder speech in text format. This paper tackles the task of recorded meeting summarization, addressing the key limitations of existing approaches by proposing the following contributions:

1) Various approaches that were recently developed for meeting summarization (such as (Gillick et al., 2009; Garg et al., 2009)) focus on extracting important sentences (or dialogue acts) from speech transcripts, either manual transcripts or automatic speech recognition (ASR) output. However, it has been observed in the context of meeting summarization users generally prefer concise abstracts over extracts, and abstracts lead to higher objective task scores; likewise automatic abstractive summaries are preferred in comparison with human extracts (Murray et al., 2010). Moreover, most of the abstractive summarization approaches focus on one component of the system, such as generation (e.g., (Genest and Lapalme, 2010)) or content selection (e.g., (Murray et al., 2012)), instead of developing the full framework for abstractive summarization. To address these limitations, as the main contribution of this paper, we propose a full pipeline to generate an abstractive summary for each meeting transcript. Our system is similar to that of Murray et al. (2010) in terms of generating abstractive summaries for meeting transcripts. However, we take a lighter supervision for the content selection phase and a different approach towards the language generation phase, which does not rely on the conventional Natural Language Generation (NLG) architecture (Reiter and Dale, 2000).

2) We propose a word graph based approach to aggregate and generate the abstractive sentence summary. Our work extends the word graph method proposed by Filippova (2010) with the following novel contributions: *i)* We take advantage of lexical knowledge to merge similar nodes by finding their relations in WordNet; *ii)* We generate new sentences through generalization and aggregation of the original ones, which means that our generated sentences are not necessarily composed of the original words; and *iii)* We adopt a new ranking strategy to select the best path in the graph by taking the information content and the grammaticality (i.e. fluency) of the sentence into consideration.

3) In order to generate an abstract summary for a meeting, we have to be able to capture the overall content of the conversation. This can be done by identifying the essential content from the most informative sentences using the semantic relations among all sentences in a meeting transcript. However, most current methods disregard such relations in favor of statistical models of word distributions and frequencies. Moreover, the data from meeting transcripts often contains many highly redundant sentences. As one of the key contributions of this paper, we propose to build a multi-directional entailment graph over the sentences to identify and select relevant information from the most informative sentences.

4) The textual data from meeting conversation transcripts are typically in a casual style and do not exhibit a clear syntactic structure with proper grammar and spelling. Therefore, abstractive summarization approaches developed for formal texts, such as scientific or news articles, often are not satisfactory when dealing with informal texts. Our proposed method for abstractive meeting summarization requires minimal syntactic and structural information and is robust in dealing with text that suffers from transcription errors, ill-formed sentences and unknown lexical choices such as typically formed in meeting transcripts.

We evaluate our system over meeting transcripts. Our result compares favorably to the result of previous extractive and abstractive approaches in terms of information content. Moreover, we show that our method can generate longer sentences with competitive grammaticality scores, in comparison with previous abstractive approaches. Furthermore, we evaluate the impact of each component of our system through an ablation test. As an additional result of our experiments, we also show that using semantic relations (entailment graph) is important in efficiently performing the final step of our summarization pipeline (i.e., the sentence fusion).

2 Abstractive Summarization Framework

Similar to Murray et al. (2010), our goal is to generate a meeting summary, i.e. a set of sentences, that could capture the semantics of the meeting. While (Murray et al., 2010) requires extensive annotations to train several classifiers to detect important sentences, opinions and dialog acts, we only use a subset of that annotation, which includes a human abstract and links from each sentence in the abstract to the source meeting sentences. In addition, instead of generating an abstractive sentence via the conventional NLG pipeline (Reiter and Dale, 2000), we exploit a word graph approach.

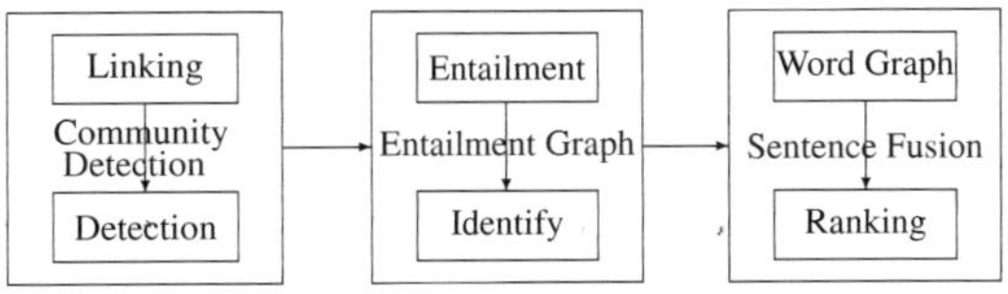

Figure 1: Meeting summarization framework.

As shown in Figure 1, our framework consists of three main components, which we describe in more detail in the following sections.

2.1 Community Detection

While some abstractive summary sentences are very similar to original sentences from the meeting transcript, others can be created by aggregating and merging multiple sentences into an abstract sentence. In order to generate such a sentence, we need to identify which sentences from the original meeting transcript should be combined in generated abstract sentences. This task can be considered as the first step of abstractive meeting summarization and is called "abstractive community detection (ACD)" (Murray et al., 2012). To perform ACD, we follow the same method proposed by Murray et al. (2012), in two steps:

First, we classify sentence pairs according to whether or not they should be realized by a common abstractive sentence. For each pair, we extract its structural and linguistic features, and we train a logistic regression classifier over all our training data (described in Section 3.1) exploiting such features. We run the trained classier over sentence pairs, predicting abstractive links between sentences in the document. The result can be represented as an undirected graph where nodes are the sentences, and edges represent whether two nodes are linked.

Second, we have to identify which nodes (i.e., sentences from the meeting transcript) can be clustered as a community to generate an abstract sentence. For this purpose, we apply the CONGA algorithm (Gregory, 2007) for community detection that uses betweenness to detect communities in a graph. The betweenness score for an edge is the number of shortest paths between pairs of nodes in the graph that run along that edge.

If a sentence is not connected to at least one other sentence in the first step, it's assigned to its own singleton community.

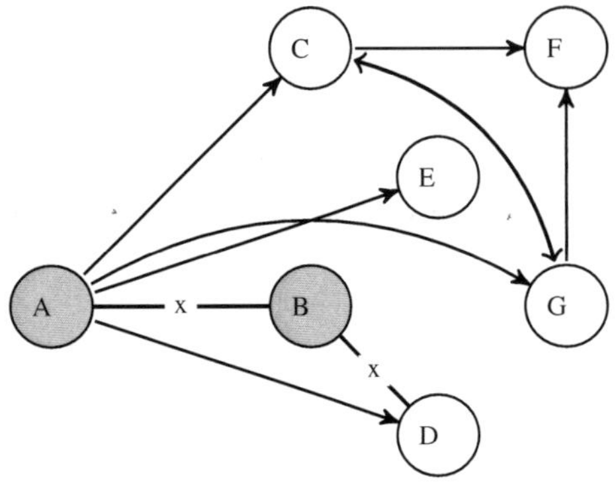

Figure 2: Building an entailment graph over sentences. Arrows and "x" represent the entailment direction and unknown cases respectively.

2.2 Entailment Graph

Sentences in a community often include redundant information which are semantically equivalent but vary in lexical choices. By identifying the semantic relations between the sentences in each community, we can discover the information in one sentence that is semantically equivalent, novel, or more/less informative with respect to the content of the other sentences.

Similar to earlier work (Lloret et al., 2008; Mehdad et al., 2010; Berant et al., 2011; Adler et al., 2012; Mehdad et al., 2013), we set this problem as a variant of the Textual Entailment (TE) recognition task (Dagan and Glickman, 2004). We build an entailment graph for each community of sentences, where nodes are the linked sentences and edges are the entailment relations between nodes. Given two sentences (s_1 and s_2), we aim at identifying the following cases:

i) s_1 and s_2 express the same meaning (*bidirectional* entailment). In such cases one of the sentences should be eliminated;

ii) s_1 is more informative than s_2 (*unidirectional* entailment). In such cases, the entailing sentence should replace or complement the entailed one;

iii) s_1 contains facts that are not present in s_2, and vice-versa (the "*unknown*" cases in TE parlance). In such cases, both sentences should remain.

Figure 2 shows how entailment relations can help in selecting the sentences by removing the redundant and less informative ones. As we show in the figure, the sentence "*A*" entails "*E*", "*F*" and "*G*", but not "*B*". So we can keep "*A*" and "*B*" and eliminate others. For example, the sentence "*we should discuss about the remote control and its color*" entails "*about the remote*", "*let's talk about the remote*" and "*um remote's color*", but not "*remote's size is also important*". So we can keep "*we should discuss about the remote control and its color*" and "*remote's size is also important*" and eliminate the others. In this way, TE-based sentence identification can be designed to distinguish meaning-preserving variations from true divergence, regardless of lexical choices and structures.

Similar to previous approaches in TE (*e.g.*, (Berant et al., 2011)), we use a supervised method. To train and build the entailment graph, we perform three steps described in the following subsections.

2.2.1 Training set collection

In the last few years, TE corpora have been created and distributed in the framework of several evaluation campaigns, including the Recognizing Textual Entailment (RTE) Challenge[1] and Cross-lingual textual entailment for content synchronization[2] (Negri et al., 2012). However, such datasets cannot directly support our application, since the RTE datasets are often composed of longer well-formed sentences and paragraphs (Bentivogli et al., 2009; Negri et al., 2011).

In order to collect a dataset that is more similar to the goal of our entailment framework, we select a subset of the sixth and seventh RTE challenge main task (*i.e.*, RTE within a Corpus). Our dataset choice is based on the following reasons: *i*) the length of sentence pairs in RTE6 and RTE7 is shorter than the others, and *ii*) RTE6 and RTE7 main task datasets are originally created for summarization purpose, which is closer to our work. We sort the RTE6 and RTE7 dataset pairs based on the sentence length and choose the first 2000 samples with an equal number of positive and negative examples. The average length of words in our training data is 7 words. There are certainly some differences between our training set and our sentences from the meeting corpus. However, the collected training samples was the closest available dataset to our needs.

2.2.2 Feature representation and training

Working with meeting transcripts imposes some constraints on feature selection. Meeting transcripts are not often well-formed in terms of sen-

[1] http://pascallin.ecs.soton.ac.uk/Challenges/RTE/

[2] http://www.cs.york.ac.uk/semeval-2013/task8/

tence structure and contain errors. This limits our features to the lexical level. Fortunately, lexical models are less computationally expensive and easier to implement and often deliver a strong performance for RTE (Sammons et al., 2011).

Our entailment decision criterion is based on similarity scores calculated with a sentence-to-sentence matching process. Each example pair of sentences (s_1 and s_2) is represented by a feature vector, where each feature is a specific similarity score estimating whether s_1 entails s_2.

We compute 18 similarity scores for each pair of sentences. Before aggregating the similarity scores to form an entailment score, we normalize the similarity scores by the length of s_2 (in terms of lexical items), when checking the entailment direction from s_1 to s_2. In this way, we can estimate the portion of information/facts in s_2 which is covered by s_1.

The first five scores are computed based on the exact lexical overlap between the phrases: word overlap, edit distance, ngram-overlap, longest common subsequence and Lesk (Lesk, 1986). The other scores were computed using lexical resources: WordNet (Fellbaum, 1998), VerbOcean (Chklovski and Pantel, 2004), paraphrases (Denkowski and Lavie, 2010) and phrase matching (Mehdad et al., 2011). We used WordNet to compute the word similarity as the least common subsumer between two words considering the synonymy-antonymy, hypernymy-hyponymy, and meronymy relations. Then, we calculated the sentence similarity as the sum of the similarity scores of the word pairs in Text and Hypothesis, normalized by the number of words in Hypothesis. We also use phrase matching features described in (Mehdad et al., 2011) which consists of phrasal matching at the level on ngrams (1 to 5 tokens). The rationale behind using different entailment features is that combining various scores will yield a better model (Berant et al., 2011).

To combine the entailment scores and optimize their relative weights, we train a Support Vector Machine binary classifier, SVMlight (Joachims, 1999), over an equal number of positive and negative examples. This results in an entailment model with 95% accuracy over 2-fold and 5-fold cross-validation, which further proves the effectiveness of our feature set for this lexical entailment model. The reason that we gained a very high accuracy is because our selected sentences are a subset of RTE6 and RTE7 with a shorter length (fewer words) which makes the entailment recognition task much easier than recognizing entailment between paragraphs or long sentences.

2.2.3 Entailment graph edge labeling

Since our training examples are labeled with binary judgments, we are not able to train a three-way classifier. Therefore, we set the edge labeling problem as a two-way classification task that casts multidirectional entailment as a unidirectional problem, where each pair is analyzed checking for entailment in both directions (Mehdad et al., 2012). In this condition, each original test example is correctly classified if both pairs originated from it are correctly judged ("*YES-YES*" for bidirectional,"*YES-NO*" and "*NO-YES*" for unidirectional entailment and "*NO-NO*" for unknown cases). Two-way classification represents an intuitive solution to capture multidimensional entailment relations.

2.2.4 Identification and selection

By assigning all entailment relations between the extracted sentence pairs, we identify relevant sentences to eliminate the redundant (in terms of meaning) and less informative ones. In order to perform this task we follow a set of rules based on the graph edge labels. Note that since entailment is a transitive relation, our entailment graph is transitive *i.e.*, if entail(s_1,s_2) and entail(s_2,s_3) then entail(s_1,s_3) (Berant et al., 2011).

Rule 1) Among the nodes that are connected with bidirectional entailment (semantically equivalent nodes) we keep only the one with more outgoing bidirectional and unidirectional entailment relations;

Rule 2) If there is a chain of entailing nodes, we keep the one that is the root of the chain and eliminate others.

2.3 Multi-sentence Fusion

Sentence fusion is a well-known challenge for summarization systems. In this phase, our goal is to generate an understandable informative sentence that maximally captures the content of the sentences in a sentence community.

There are several ways of generating an abstract sentence (e.g. (Barzilay and McKeown, 2005; Liu and Liu, 2009; Ganesan et al., 2010; Murray et al., 2010)); however, most of them rely heavily on the syntactic structure. We believe that such

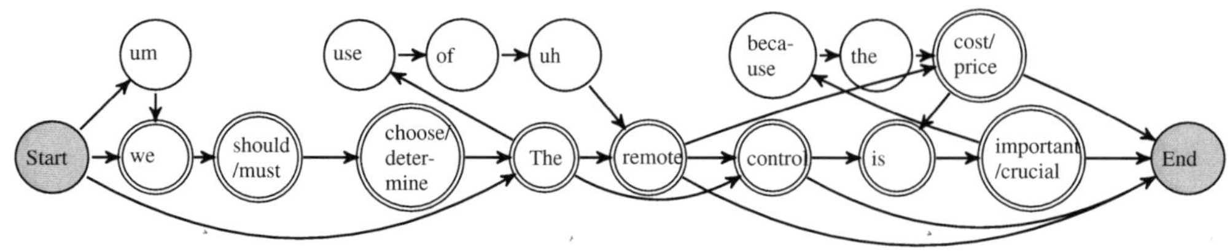

Figure 3: Word graph constructed from sentences (1-4) and possible fusion paths. Double line nodes represent merged words in the graph.

approaches are suboptimal, especially in dealing with written conversational data (e.g., email) or the data from speech transcripts, whether manual transcription or automatic speech recognition output. Instead, we apply an approach that does not rely on syntax, nor on a standard NLG architecture. More specifically, we build a word graph from all the words of the sentences in a community and aggregate them in order to generate a new abstractive sentence.

We perform the task of multi-sentence fusion in two steps. First, we construct a word graph over sentences in each community that were selected from the entailment graph. Second, we rank the valid paths in the word graph and select the top path as the abstract sentence summary.

2.3.1 Constructing a Word Graph

In order to construct a word graph, our model extends the word graph method proposed by Filippova (2010) with the following novel contributions:

1- The basic word graph method disregards semantic and lexical relations between the words in constructing the word graph, in favor of redundancy and word frequencies. To move beyond such limitation, we take advantage of lexical knowledge to map the similar nodes by finding their relations in WordNet. In this way, for example, two synonym words can be mapped into the same node.

2- Filippova's approach is essentially extractive in nature, which means the generated sentence is composed by the same words from the original sentences. We move beyond this by generating new sentences through generalization and aggregation of the original ones. This means that our generated sentences are not necessarily composed of the original words. In this way, we are one step closer to abstractive summarization.

3- Our proposed method aggregates and generates new readable sentences, regardless of their lengths, that can semantically imply several original sentences, by taking the information content and the readability (i.e. fluency) of the sentence into consideration.

Following Filippova's method, given a set of related sentences, we build a word graph by iteratively adding sentences to it. Figure 1 illustrates a small graph composed of 4 sentences, including the start and end nodes.

1- *we must determine the use of uh remote.*
2- *The remote control is important because the cost.*
3- *um we should choose the control.*
4- *The remote price is crucial.*

As one of the main steps of word graph construction, we merge the words that have the same POS tags under the following conditions:

1) The words are identical (e.g. *"remote"*).

2) The words are synonyms. The replacement choice is based on the word's commonality, i.e. *tfidf* (e.g. *"important"* and *"crucial"*).

3) The words form a hypernym/hyponym pair or share a common hypernym. Both words are replaced by the hypernym (e.g. *"price"* and *"cost"*).

4) The words are in an entailment relation. Both words are replaced by the entailed one (e.g. *"pay"* and *"buy"*).

Note that, similar to Filippova's approach, where merging is ambiguous we check the context (a word before and after in the sentence and the neighboring nodes in the graph) and select the candidate that has larger overlap in the context, or the one with a greater frequency. Similar to the original word graph model, we connect adjacent words with directed edges. For the new nodes or unconnected nodes, we draw an edge with a weight of 1. In contrast, weights between already connected nodes are increased by 1.

2.3.2 Path Selection and Ranking

The word graph, as described above, will generate many sequences connecting start and end. However, it is likely that most of the paths are not readable. Since we are aiming at generating a good abstractive sentence, some constraints need to be considered.

A good abstractive sentence should cover most of the concepts that exist in the original sentences. Moreover, it should be grammatically correct.

In order to satisfy these constraints we adopt a ranking strategy that combines the characteristics of a good summary sentence. To filter ungrammatical sentences, we prune the paths in which a verb does not exist. Our ranking formulation is summarized as below:

Fluency: Our word graph process generates many possible paths as abstractive summaries. We need now to decide which of these paths are more readable and fluent. As in other areas of NLP (e.g. machine translation and speech recognition), the answer can be estimated by a language model. We assign a probability $Pr(P)$ to each path P based on a n-gram language model.

$$Pr(P) = \prod_{i=1}^{m} Pr(p_i|p_1^{i-1}) \approx \prod_{i=1}^{m} Pr(p_i|p_{i-n+1}^{i-1})$$
$$\approx \sum_{i=1}^{m} -logPr(p_i|p_{i-n+1}^{i-1})$$

Coverage: To identify the summary with the highest coverage, we propose a second score that estimates the number of nouns that appear in the path. In order to reward the ranking score to cover more salient nouns, we also consider the *tfidf* score of nouns in the coverage formulation.

$$Coverage(P) = \frac{\sum_{p_i \in P} \mathit{tfidf}(p_i)}{\sum_{p_i \in G} \mathit{tfidf}(p_i)}$$

where the p_i are nouns and G is the graph.

Edge weight: As a third score, we adopt the Filippova's edge weighting formulation $w(p_i, p_j)$ and define the edge weight of the path $W(P)$ as below:

$$w(p_i, p_j) = \frac{\mathit{freq}(p_i) + \mathit{freq}(p_j)}{\sum_{\substack{P \in G\\ p_i, p_j \in P}} \mathit{diff}(P, p_i, p_j)^{-1}}$$
$$W(P) = \frac{\sum_{i=1}^{m-1} w(p_i, p_{i+1})}{m-1}$$

where the function $\mathit{diff}(P, p_i, p_j)$ refers to the distance between the offset positions $pos(P, p_i)$ of words p_i and p_j in path P and is defined as $|pos(P, p_j) - pos(P, p_i)|$ and m is the number of words in path P.

Ranking score: In order to generate a summary sentence that combines the scores above, we employ a ranking model. The purpose of such a model is three-fold: i) to generate a more readable and grammatical sentence; ii) to cover the content of original sentences optimally; and iii) to favor strong connections between the concepts. Therefore, the final ranking score of path P is calculated over the normalized scores as:

$$Score(P) = \frac{Pr(P) \times Coverage(P)}{W(P)}$$

We select all the paths that contain at least one verb and rerank them using our proposed ranking function to find the best path as the summary of the original sentences.

3 Experiments and Results

We now describe a preliminary, formative evaluation of our framework, whose main goal is to assess strengths and weaknesses of the various components and generate ideas for further developments.

3.1 Dataset

To verify the effectiveness of our approach, we experiment with the AMI meeting corpus (Carletta et al., 2005) that consists of 140 multi-party meetings with a wide range of annotations, including abstactive summaries for each meeting and links from each sentence in the summary to the set of sentences in the original transcripts that sentence is summarizing. We use this information as our gold standard since it provides many examples in which a set of sentences in the meeting (a community) is linked to a human written sentence summarizing that community.

In our experiments, we use human authored transcripts. Note that our approach is not specific to conversations, however it is designed to deal with ill-formed sentences and structural errors. Moreover, the first two components of our system are supervised, while the word-graph model is completely unsupervised and domain independent.

In order to train our logistic regression classifier for the first phase of our pipeline, we randomly select a training set that consists of 98 meetings. Note that there are about one million sentence pair instances in the training set since we consider every pairing of sentences within a meeting. The rest is selected as a test set for the evaluation phase.

3.2 Experimental Settings

For preprocessing our dataset we use OpenNLP[3] for tokenization and part-of-speech tagging. When the number of sentences in each community is more than 10 (which happens in around 10% of the cases), the community is first clustered using the MajorClust (Stein and Niggemann, 1999) algorithm when sentences are represented as normalized *tfidf* vectors and the similarity between the sentences is measured using cosine similarity. Then, each cluster is treated as a separate community. The clustering guarantees a higher overlap between the sentences as well as a word graph with fewer paths. Next, we construct a word graph over each cluster and rank the valid paths. We choose the first ranked path as the abstractive summary of the cluster. For our language model, we use a tri-gram smoothed language model trained using the newswire text provided in the English Gigaword corpus (Graff and Cieri,).

3.3 Evaluation Metrics

To evaluate performance, we use the ROUGE-1 and ROUGE-2 (unigram and bigram overlap) F1 score, which correlate well with human rankings of summary quality (Lin and Hovy, 2003). We also ignore stopwords to reduce the impact of high overlap when matching them.

Furthermore, to evaluate the grammaticality of our generated summaries in comparison with the original word graph method, following common practice (Barzilay and McKeown, 2005), we randomly selected 10 meeting summaries (total 150 sentences). Then, we asked annotators to give one of three possible ratings for each sentence in a summary based on grammaticality: perfect (2 pts), only one mistake (1 pt) and not acceptable (0 pts), ignoring the capitalization or punctuation. Each meeting was rated by two annotators (Computer Science graduate students).

[3]http://opennlp.apache.org/

Models	ROUGE-1	ROUGE-2
MMR-centroid	18	3
MMR-cosine	21	-
ILP	24	-
TextRank	25.0	4.4
ClusterRank	27.5	**5.1**
Orig. word graph	26.9	3.8
Our model (-ent)	**32.3**	**4.8**
Our model (GC)	**32.1**	4.0
Our model (full)	**28.7**	4.2

Table 1: Performance of different summarization algorithms on human transcripts for meeting conversations. [5]

3.4 Baselines

We compare our approach with various extractive baselines: 1) MMR-centroid system (Carbonell and Goldstein, 1998); 2) MMR-cosine system (Gillick et al., 2009); 3) ILP-based system (Gillick et al., 2009); 4) TextRank system (Mihalcea and Tarau, 2004); and 5) ClusterRank system (Garg et al., 2009) and with one abstractive baseline: 6) Original word graph model (Orig. word graph) (Filippova, 2010).

In order to measure the effectiveness of different components, we also evaluated our system using human-annotated sentence communities (GC) in comparison with our community detection model (full). Moreover, we measure the performance of our system (GC) ablating the entailment module (-ent).

3.5 Results

Table 1 shows the results for our proposed approach in comparison with these strong baselines for meeting summarization. The results show that our model outperforms the baselines significantly[4] for ROUGE-1 over human transcripts for meeting conversations, which proves the effectiveness of our approach in dealing with summarization of

[5]The MMR-cosine and ILP systems did not report the ROUGE-2 score.

[4]The statistical significance tests was calculated by approximate randomization described in (Yeh, 2000).

Models	Read.	R=2	R=1	R=0	Avg Len.
Orig. word graph	1.41	55%	32%	13%	8
Our model	1.34	47%	39%	14%	14

Table 2: Average rating and distribution over rating scores for abstractive word graph models.

meeting conversations. However, the ClusterRank and TextRank systems outperform our model for ROUGE-2 score. This can be due to word merging and word replacement choices in the word graph construction (see Section 2.3.1), which sometimes changes a word in a bigram and consequently decreases the bigram overlap score. A more detailed analysis of this problem is left as future work.

Note that there is a drop in ROUGE score when we use entailment in our system in comparison with ablating the entailment phase (-ent). This is mainly due to the fact that the entailment phase filters equivalent sentences. This affects the results negatively when such filtered sentences share many common words with our human-authored abstracts. We believe that this drop is partly associated with our evaluation metric rather than meaning. In other words, we expect no difference in performance when a human evaluation is applied. However, the entailment phase helps in improving the efficiency of our pipeline significantly. If each graph has e edges, n nodes, and p paths, then finding all the paths results in time complexity $O((np+1)(e+n))$, using depth-first search. Decreasing the number of sentences will reduce the number of nodes and edges, which leads to the smaller number of paths. This is even more significant when there are many sentences in a community in comparison with the gold standard. Note that it's impossible to finish the graph building phase after 12 hours on a 2.3 GHz quad-core machine without performing the entailment phase, when we use our community detection model. This would be especially problematic in a real-time setting.

Comparing the gold standard sentence communities (GC) and our fully automatic system, we can notice that inaccuracies in the community detection phase affects the overall performance. However, using our community detection model, we still outperform the previous models significantly.

Table 2 shows grammaticality scores, distributions over the three scores and average sentence lengths in tokens. The results demonstrate that 47% of the sentences generated by our method are grammatically correct and 39% of the generated sentences are almost correct. In comparison with the original word graph method, our model reports slightly lower results for the grammaticality score and the percentage of correct sentences. However, considering the correlation between sentence length and grammatical complexity, our model is capable of generating longer sentences with more information content (according to ROUGE) and competitive grammaticality scores.

4 Discussion

After analyzing the results and through manual verification of some cases, we observe that our approach produces some interestingly successful examples. Nevertheless, it appears that the performance is still far from satisfactory. This leaves an interesting challenge for the research community to tackle. We have identified five different sources of error:

Type 1: Abstractive human-authored summaries: the nature of our method is based on extracting the relevant sentences and generating an abstract sentence by aggregating such sentences. Also due to this, our generated abstracts are often informal and closer to the transcripts' style. However, in many cases, the human-written summaries are composed by understanding the original sentences and produce a formal style abstract sentence, often using a different vocabulary and structure. For example:

> Human-authored: *The industrial designer and user interface designer presented the prototype they created, which was designed to look like a banana.*
> System: *Working on the principle of a fruit it's basically designed around a banana.*

Type 2: Evaluation method: The current evaluation methods fail to capture the meaning and relies only on matching the words at uni- or bigram level. Therefore, we believe that a manual evaluation can reveal more potential of our system in generating abstractive summaries that are closer to human-written summaries.

> Human-authored: *the project manager recapped the decisions made in the previous meeting.*
> System: *I told you guys about the three new requirements ... so that was the last meeting.*

Type 3: Subjective abstractive summaries: often it is not easy for humans to agree on one summary for a meeting. It is well known that inter-annotator agreement is quite low for the summarization task (Mani, 2001). For example:

> Human-authored 1: *They do tool training with a whiteboard and each person introduces themselves and draws their favorite animal on the board.*
> Human-authored 2: *The group introduced themselves to each other and acquainted themselves with the meeting-room materials by drawing on the whiteboard.*
> System: *We are gonna know each other and then draw your little animal.*

Type 4: Speaker information: since the nature of our method is based on extracting the relevant sentences or speaker utterances, we do not take the speaker information into consideration. However, the human-written summaries for meetings take the speaker into account. We plan to extend our framework to include this feature. For example:

> Human-authored: *The project manager opened the meeting and stated the agenda to the team members.*
> System: *I hope you're ready for this functional design meeting know at the end projects requirement.*

Type 5: Transcription errors: as mentioned before, the meeting transcripts often contain structure, grammar, vocabulary choice and dictation errors. This always raises more challenges for algorithms dealing with such texts. For example:

> Transcript: *if it i if it isn't more expensive for us to k make because as far as I understand it.*

In light of this analysis, we conclude that a more comprehensive evaluation method (e.g., human evaluation), including speaker information in the pipeline and using text normalization techniques to reduce the effects of noisy transcripts can better reveal the potential of our system in dealing with meeting summarization.

5 Conclusion and Future Work

In this paper, we study the problem of abstractive meeting summarization, and propose a novel framework to generate summaries composed of grammatical sentences. Within this framework, this paper makes three main contributions. First, in contrast with most current methods based on fully extractive models, we propose to take advantage of a word graph model for sentence fusion to generate abstractive summary sentences. Second, beyond most of the current approaches which disregard semantic information, we integrate semantics by means of building textual entailment graphs over sentence communities. Third, our framework uses minimal syntactic information in comparison with previous methods and does not require a domain specific, engineered conventional NLP component.

We successfully applied our framework over a challenging meeting dataset, the AMI corpus. Some significant improvements over our dataset, in comparison with previous methods, demonstrates the potential of our approach in dealing with meeting summarization. Moreover, we prove that our model can generate longer sentences with only a minimal loss in grammaticality.

In light of the results of our preliminary formative evaluation, future work will address the improvement of the community detection and sentence fusion phases. On the one hand, we plan to improve our community detection graph by adding more relevant features into our current supervised model. On the other hand, we plan to incorporate a better source of lexical knowledge in the word graph construction (e.g., YAGO or DBpedia). We are also interested in improving our ranking model by assigning tuned weights to each component. In addition, we are exploring the replacement of pronouns by their referents (e.g., replacing *"I"* by the name or role of the speaker) to improve both the entailment and word graph models. Once we will have explored all these improvements, we plan to run more comprehensive human evaluations.

Acknowledgments

We would like to thank the anonymous reviewers for their valuable comments and suggestions to improve the paper, our annotators for their valuable work, and the NSERC Business Intelligence Network for financial support.

References

Meni Adler, Jonathan Berant, and Ido Dagan. 2012. Entailment-based text exploration with application to the health-care domain. In *Proceedings of the ACL 2012 System Demonstrations*, ACL '12, pages 79–84, Stroudsburg, PA, USA. Association for Computational Linguistics.

Regina Barzilay and Kathleen R. McKeown. 2005. Sentence Fusion for Multidocument News Summarization. *Comput. Linguist.*, 31(3):297–328, September.

Luisa Bentivogli, Ido Dagan, Hoa Trang Dang, Danilo Giampiccolo, and Bernardo Magnini. 2009. The Fifth PASCAL Recognizing Textual Entailment Challenge. In *Proc Text Analysis Conference (TAC09*.

Jonathan Berant, Ido Dagan, and Jacob Goldberger. 2011. Global Learning of Typed Entailment Rules. In *Proceedings of ACL*, Portland, OR.

Jaime Carbonell and Jade Goldstein. 1998. The use of MMR, diversity-based reranking for reordering documents and producing summaries. In *Proceedings of the 21st annual international ACM SIGIR conference on Research and development in information retrieval*, SIGIR '98, pages 335–336, New York, NY, USA. ACM.

Jean Carletta, Simone Ashby, Sebastien Bourban, Mike Flynn, Thomas Hain, Jaroslav Kadlec, Vasilis Karaiskos, Wessel Kraaij, Melissa Kronenthal, Guillaume Lathoud, Mike Lincoln, Agnes Lisowska, and Mccowan Wilfried Post Dennis Reidsma. 2005. The AMI meeting corpus: A pre-announcement. In *Proc. MLMI*, pages 28–39.

Timothy Chklovski and Patrick Pantel. 2004. VerbOcean: Mining the Web for Fine-Grained Semantic Verb Relations. In Dekang Lin and Dekai Wu, editors, *Proceedings of EMNLP 2004*, pages 33–40, Barcelona, Spain, July. Association for Computational Linguistics.

I. Dagan and O. Glickman. 2004. Probabilistic Textual Entailment: Generic applied modeling of language variability. In *PASCAL Workshop on Learning Methods for Text Understanding and Mining*.

Michael Denkowski and Alon Lavie. 2010. METEOR-NEXT and the METEOR paraphrase tables: improved evaluation support for five target language. In *Proceedings of the Joint Fifth Workshop on Statistical Machine Translation and MetricsMATR*, WMT '10, pages 339–342, Stroudsburg, PA, USA. Association for Computational Linguistics.

Christiane Fellbaum. 1998. *WordNet: An Electronic Lexical Database*. Bradford Books.

Katja Filippova. 2010. Multi-sentence compression: finding shortest paths in word graphs. In *Proceedings of the 23rd International Conference on Computational Linguistics*, COLING '10, pages 322–330, Stroudsburg, PA, USA. Association for Computational Linguistics.

Kavita Ganesan, ChengXiang Zhai, and Jiawei Han. 2010. Opinosis: a graph-based approach to abstractive summarization of highly redundant opinions. In *Proceedings of the 23rd International Conference on Computational Linguistics*, COLING '10, pages 340–348, Stroudsburg, PA, USA. Association for Computational Linguistics.

Nikhil Garg, Benoit Favre, Korbinian Reidhammer, and Dilek Hakkani Tür. 2009. ClusterRank: A Graph Based Method for Meeting Summarization. Idiap-RR Idiap-RR-09-2009, Idiap, P.O. Box 592, CH-1920 Martigny, Switzerland, 6.

Pierre-Etienne Genest and Guy Lapalme. 2010. Text Generation for Abstractive Summarization. In *Proceedings of the Third Text Analysis Conference*, Gaithersburg, Maryland, USA. National Institute of Standards and Technology, National Institute of Standards and Technology.

Dan Gillick, Korbinian Riedhammer, Benoit Favre, and Dilek Hakkani-tr. 2009. A global optimization framework for meeting summarization. In *Proc. IEEE ICASSP*, pages 4769–4772.

David Graff and Christopher Cieri. English Gigaword Corpus—, year = 2003, institution = Linguistic Data Consortium, address = Philadelphia,. Technical report.

Steve Gregory. 2007. An Algorithm to Find Overlapping Community Structure in Networks. In *Proceedings of the 11th European conference on Principles and Practice of Knowledge Discovery in Databases*, PKDD 2007, pages 91–102, Berlin, Heidelberg. Springer-Verlag.

T. Joachims. 1999. Making large-Scale SVM Learning Practical. LS8-Report 24, Universität Dortmund, LS VIII-Report.

Michael Lesk. 1986. Automatic sense disambiguation using machine readable dictionaries: how to tell a pine cone from an ice cream cone. In *Proceedings of the 5th annual international conference on Systems documentation*, SIGDOC '86, pages 24–26, New York, NY, USA. ACM.

Chin-Yew Lin and Eduard Hovy. 2003. Automatic evaluation of summaries using N-gram co-occurrence statistics. In *Proceedings of the 2003 Conference of the North American Chapter of the Association for Computational Linguistics on Human Language Technology - Volume 1*, NAACL '03, pages 71–78, Stroudsburg, PA, USA. Association for Computational Linguistics.

Fei Liu and Yang Liu. 2009. From extractive to abstractive meeting summaries: can it be done by sentence compression? In *Proceedings of the ACL-IJCNLP 2009 Conference Short Papers*, ACLShort '09, pages 261–264, Stroudsburg, PA, USA. Association for Computational Linguistics.

Elena Lloret, Óscar Ferrández, Rafael Muñoz, and Manuel Palomar. 2008. A Text Summarization Approach under the Influence of Textual Entailment. In *NLPCS*, pages 22–31.

I. Mani. 2001. *Automatic summarization*. Natural Language Processing, 3. J. Benjamins Publishing Company.

Yashar Mehdad, Matteo Negri, and Marcello Federico. 2010. Towards cross-lingual textual entailment. In *Human Language Technologies: The 2010 Annual Conference of the North American Chapter of the Association for Computational Linguistics*, HLT '10, pages 321–324, Stroudsburg, PA, USA. Association for Computational Linguistics.

Yashar Mehdad, Matteo Negri, and Marcello Federico. 2011. Using bilingual parallel corpora for cross-lingual textual entailment. In *Proceedings of the 49th Annual Meeting of the Association for Computational Linguistics: Human Language Technologies - Volume 1*, HLT '11, pages 1336–1345, Stroudsburg, PA, USA. Association for Computational Linguistics.

Yashar Mehdad, Matteo Negri, and Marcello Federico. 2012. Detecting semantic equivalence and information disparity in cross-lingual documents. In *Proceedings of the 50th Annual Meeting of the Association for Computational Linguistics: Short Papers - Volume 2*, ACL '12, pages 120–124, Stroudsburg, PA, USA. Association for Computational Linguistics.

Yashar Mehdad, Giuseppe Carenini, and Raymond NG T. 2013. Towards Topic Labeling with Phrase Entailment and Aggregation. In *Proceedings of NAACL 2013*, pages 179–189, Atlanta, USA, June. Association for Computational Linguistics.

R. Mihalcea and P. Tarau. 2004. TextRank: Bringing order into texts. In *Proceedings of the 2004 Conference on Empirical Methods in Natural Language Processing*, July.

Gabriel Murray, Giuseppe Carenini, and Raymond Ng. 2010. Generating and validating abstracts of meeting conversations: a user study. In *Proceedings of the 6th International Natural Language Generation Conference*, INLG '10, pages 105–113, Stroudsburg, PA, USA. Association for Computational Linguistics.

Gabriel Murray, Giuseppe Carenini, and Raymond Ng. 2012. Using the omega index for evaluating abstractive community detection. In *Proceedings of Workshop on Evaluation Metrics and System Comparison for Automatic Summarization*, pages 10–18, Stroudsburg, PA, USA. Association for Computational Linguistics.

Matteo Negri, Luisa Bentivogli, Yashar Mehdad, Danilo Giampiccolo, and Alessandro Marchetti. 2011. Divide and conquer: crowdsourcing the creation of cross-lingual textual entailment corpora. In *Proceedings of the Conference on Empirical Methods in Natural Language Processing*, EMNLP '11, pages 670–679, Stroudsburg, PA, USA. Association for Computational Linguistics.

Matteo Negri, Alessandro Marchetti, Yashar Mehdad, Luisa Bentivogli, and Danilo Giampiccolo. 2012. Semeval-2012 task 8: cross-lingual textual entailment for content synchronization. In *Proceedings of the First Joint Conference on Lexical and Computational Semantics - Volume 1: Proceedings of the main conference and the shared task, and Volume 2: Proceedings of the Sixth International Workshop on Semantic Evaluation*, SemEval '12, pages 399–407, Stroudsburg, PA, USA. Association for Computational Linguistics.

Ehud Reiter and Robert Dale. 2000. *Building natural language generation systems*. Cambridge University Press, New York, NY, USA.

Mark Sammons, V.G.Vinod Vydiswaran, and Dan Roth. 2011. Recognizing textual entailment. In *Multilingual Natural Language Applications: From Theory to Practice*. Prentice Hall, Jun.

Benno Stein and Oliver Niggemann. 1999. On the Nature of Structure and Its Identification. In *Proceedings of the 25th International Workshop on Graph-Theoretic Concepts in Computer Science*, WG '99, pages 122–134, London, UK, UK. Springer-Verlag.

Alexander Yeh. 2000. More accurate tests for the statistical significance of result differences. In *Proceedings of the 18th Conference on Computational Linguistics - Volume 2*, COLING '00, pages 947–953. Association for Computational Linguistics.

Automatic Voice Selection in Japanese based on Various Linguistic Information

Ryu Iida and **Takenobu Tokunaga**
Department of Computer Science, Tokyo Institute of Technology
W8-73, 2-12-1 Ookayama Meguro Tokyo, 152-8552 Japan
{ryu-i,take}@cl.cs.titech.ac.jp

Abstract

This paper focuses on a subtask of natural language generation (NLG), *voice selection*, which decides whether a clause is realised in the active or passive voice according to its contextual information. Automatic voice selection is essential for realising more sophisticated MT and summarisation systems, because it impacts the readability of generated texts. However, to the best of our knowledge, the NLG community has been less concerned with explicit voice selection. In this paper, we propose an automatic voice selection model based on various linguistic information, ranging from lexical to discourse information. Our empirical evaluation using a manually annotated corpus in Japanese demonstrates that the proposed model achieved 0.758 in F-score, outperforming the two baseline models.

1 Introduction

Generating a readable text is the primary goal in natural language generation (NLG). To realise such text, we need to arrange discourse entities (e.g. NPs) in appropriate positions in a sentence according to their discourse salience. Consider the two following Japanese texts, each of which consists of two sentences.

(1) *Tom$_i$-wa kouen$_j$-ni it-ta .*
Tom$_i$-TOP park$_j$-IOBJ go-PAST
(Tom$_i$ went to a park$_j$.)

Kare$_i$-wa soko$_j$-de ookina inu-ni oikake-rareta .
he$_i$-TOP there$_j$-LOC big dog-IOBJ chase-PASSIVE/PAST
(He$_i$ was chased by a big dog there$_j$.)

(2) *Tom$_i$-wa kouen$_j$-ni it-ta .*
Tom$_i$-TOP park$_j$-IOBJ go-PAST
(Tom$_i$ went to a park$_j$.)

Ookina inu-ga soko$_j$-de kare$_i$-o oikake-ta .
big dog-SUBJ there$_j$-LOC he$_i$-OBJ chase-PAST
(A big dog chased him$_i$ there$_j$.)

In (1), 'Tom$_i$' is topicalised in the first sentence, and then it appears at the subject position in the second sentence. In contrast, the same argument, i.e. 'he$_i$' is realised at the object position in the second sentence of text (2). Intuitively, text (1) is relatively more natural than text (2). Thus, given the two predicate argument relations, go(SUBJ:Tom$_i$, IOBJ:park$_j$) and chase(SUBJ:big dog, OBJ:Tom$_i$, IOBJ:park$_j$), a generation system should choose text (1).

The realisation from a semantic representation (e.g. predicate argument structures) to an actual text has been mainly developed in the area of natural language generation (Reiter and Dale, 2000), and has been applied to various NLP applications such as multi-document summarisation (Radev and McKeown, 1998) and tutoring systems (Di Eugenio et al., 2005). During the course of a text generation process, various kinds of decisions should be made, including decisions on textual content, clustering the content of each clause, discourse structure of the clauses, lexical choices, types of referring expressions and syntactic structures. Since these different kinds of decisions are interrelated to each other, it is not a trivial problem to find an optimal order among these decisions. This issue has been much discussed in terms of architecture of generation systems. Although a variety of architectures has been proposed in the past, e.g. an integrated architecture (Appelt, 1985) and a revision-based architecture (Inui et al., 1994; Robin, 1994), a pipeline architecture is considered as a consensus architecture in which decisions are made in a predetermined order (Reiter, 1994). Voice selection is a syntactic decision that tends to be made in a later stage of the pipeline architecture, even though it influences various decisions, such as discourse structure and lexical choice. Unlike referring expression generation, voice selection has received less attention and been less discussed in the past. Against this background, this research tackles the problem of voice selection considering a wide range of linguistic information that is assumed to be already decided in the preceding stages of a generation process.

The paper is organised as follows. We first overview the related work in Section 2, and then propose a voice selection model based on the four kinds of information that impact voice selection in Section 3. Section 4 then demonstrates the results of empirical evaluation using the NAIST Text Corpus (Iida et al., 2007) as training and evaluation data sets. Finally, Section 5 concludes and discusses our future directions.

2 Related work

The task of automatic voice selection has been mainly developed in the NLG community. However, it has attracted less attention compared with other major NLG problems, such as generating referring expressions. There is less work focusing singly on voice selection, but not entirely without exception, such as Abb et al. (1993). In their work, passivisation is performed by taking into account both linguistic and extra-linguistic information. The linguistic information explains passivisation in an incremental generation process; realising the most salient discourse entity in short term memory as a subject eventually leads to passivisation. In contrast, extra-linguistic information is used to move a less salient entity to a subject position when an explicit agent is missing in the text. Although these two kinds of information seem adequate for explaining passivisation, their applicability was not examined in empirical evaluations.

Sheikha and Inkpen (2011) focused attention on voice selection in the generation task distinguishing formal and informal sentences. In their work, passivisation is considered as a rhetorical technique for conveying formal intentions. However, they did not discuss passivisation in terms of discourse coherence.

3 Voice selection model

We recast the voice selection task into a binary classification problem, i.e. given a predicate with its arguments and its preceding context, we classify the predicate into either an active or passive class, taking into account predicate argument relations and the preceding context of the predicate.

As shown in examples (1) and (2) in Section 1, several factors have an impact on voice selection in a text. In this work, we take into account the following four information as features The details of the feature set are shown in Table 1.

Passivisation preference of each verb An important factor of voice selection is the preference for how frequently a verb is used in passive sentences. This means each verb has a potential tendency of being used in passive sentences in a domain. For example, the verb '*yosou-suru* (to expect)' tends to be realised in the passive in the newspaper domain because Japanese journalists tend to write their opinions objectively by omitting the agent role. To take into account this preference of verb passivisation, we define a preference score by the following formula:

$$score_{pas}(v_i) = \frac{freq_{pas}(v_i)}{freq_{all}(v_i)} \cdot \log freq_{all}(v_i) \quad (1)$$

where v_i is a verb in question[1], $freq_{all}(v_i)$ is the frequency of v_i appearing in corpora, and $freq_{pas}(v_i)$ is the frequency of v_i with the passive marker, *(ra)reru*. The logarithm of $freq_{all}(v_i)$ is multiplied due to avoiding the overestimation of the score for less frequent instances. In the evaluation, the preference score was calculated based on the frequency of each verb in the 12 years worth of newspaper articles, which had been morpho-syntactically analysed by a Japanese morphological analyser Mecab[3] and a dependency parser *CaboCha*[4].

Syntactic decisions As described in Section 1, various kinds of decisions are interrelated to voice selection. Particularly, syntactic decisions including voice selection directly impact sentence structure. Therefore, we introduce syntactic information except for voice selection which prescribes how an input predicate-argument structure will be realised in an actual text.

Semantic category of arguments Animacy of the arguments of a predicate has an impact on their syntactic positions. Unlike in English, inanimate subjects tend to be avoided in Japanese. In order to capture this tendency, we use the semantic category of the arguments of the verb in question (e.g.

[1]Note that the preference needs to be defined for each word sense. However, we here ignore the difference of senses because selecting a correct verb sense for a given context is still difficult.

[1]*Bunsetsu* is a basic unit in Japanese, consisting of at least one content word and more than zero functional words.

[2]http://nlp.cs.nyu.edu/irex/index-e.html

[3]https://code.google.com/p/mecab/

[4]https://code.google.com/p/cabocha/

type	feature	definition
PRED	score$_{pas}$	passivisation preference score defined in equation (1).
	lexical	lemma of P.
	func	lemma of functional words following P, excluding passive markers.
SYN	sent_end	1 if P appears in the last *bunsetsu*[1]-unit in a sentence; otherwise 0.
	adnom	1 if P appears in an adnominal clause; otherwise 0.
	first_sent (last_sent)	1 if P appears in the first (last) sentence of a text; otherwise 0.
	subj(obj,iobj)_embedded	1 if the head of the adnominal clause including P is semantic subject (object, indirect object) of P; otherwise 0.
ARG	subj(obj,iobj)_ne	named entity class (based on IREX[2]) of the subject (object, indirect object) of P.
	subj(obj,iobj)_sem	semantic class of the subject (object, indirect object) of P in terms of Japanese ontology, *nihongo goi taikei* (Ikehara et al., 1997).
COREF	subj(obj,iobj)_exo	1 if the subject (object, indirect object) of P is unrealised and it is annotated as exophoric; otherwise 0.
	subj(obj,iobj)_srl_order	order of the subject (object, indirect object) of P in the SRL.
	subj(obj,iobj)_srl_rank	rank of the subject (object, indirect object) of P in the SRL.
	subj(obj,iobj)_coref_num	number of discourse entities in the coreference chain including P's subject (object, indirect object) in the preceding context.

P stands for the predicate in question. The four feature types (PRED, SYN, ARG and COREF) correspond to each information described in Section 3.

Table 1: Feature set for voice selection

named entity labels provided by *CaboCha*, such as Person and Organisation, and the ontological information defined in a Japanese ontology, *nihongo goi taikei* (Ikehara et al., 1997)) as features.

Coreference and anaphora of arguments As discussed in discourse theories such as Centering Theory (Grosz et al., 1995), arguments which have been already most salient in the preceding context tend to be placed at the beginning of a sentence for reducing the cognitive cost of reading, as argued in Functional Grammar (Halliday and Matthiessen, 2004). In order to consider the characteristic, we employ an extension of Centering Theory (Grosz et al., 1995), proposed by Nariyama (2002) for implementing the COREF type features in Table 1. She proposed a generalised version of the forward looking-center list, called the *Salient Reference List* (SRL), which stores all salient discourse entities (e.g. NP) in the preceding contexts in the order of their saliency. A highly ranked argument's entity in the SRL tends to be placed in the subject position, resulting in a passive sentence if that salient entity has a THEME role in the predicate-argument structure. To capture this characteristic, the order and rank of discourse entities in the SRL are used as features[5].

In addition, as described in Abb et al. (1993), if the agent filler of a predicate is underspecified, the passive voice is preferred so as to unfocus the underspecified agent. Likewise, if the argument (in this case, the agent filler) of a predicate is exophoric, the passive voice is selected.

4 Experiments

We conducted an empirical evaluation using manually annotated newspaper articles in Japanese. To estimate the feature weights of each classifier, we used MEGAM[6], an implementation of the Maximum Entropy model, with default parameter settings. We also used SVM[7] with a polynomial kernel for explicitly handling the dependency of the proposed features.

4.1 Data and baseline models

For training and evaluation, we used the NAIST Text Corpus (Iida et al., 2007). Because the corpus contains manually annotated predicate argument relations and coreference relations, we used those for the inputs of voice selection. In our problem setting, we conducted an intrinsic evaluation; given manually annotated predicate argument relations and coreference relations of arguments, a model determines whether a predicate in question is actually realised in the *passive* or *active* voice in the original text. The performance is measured based on recall, precision and F-score of correctly detecting passive voice. For evaluation, we divided the texts in the corpus into two sets; one is used for training and the other for evaluation. The details of this division are shown in Table 2.

We employed two baseline models for compar-

[5]In Table 1 "*_srl_rank" stands for how highly the argument's referent ranked out of the discourse entities in the SRL, while "*_srl_order" stands for which slot (e.g. TOP slot or SUBJ slot, etc.) stores the argument's referent.

[6]http://www.cs.utah.edu/~hal/megam/

[7]http://svmlight.joachims.org/

	#articles	#predicates	#passive predicates
training	1,753	65,592	4,974 (7.6%)
test	696	24,884	1,891 (7.6%)

Table 2: Data set division for evaluation

	R	P	F
$\theta = 0.1$	0.768	0.269	0.399
$\theta = 0.2$	0.573	0.357	**0.440**
$\theta = 0.3$	0.403	0.450	0.425
$\theta = 0.4$	0.293	0.512	0.373
$\theta = 0.5$	0.161	0.591	0.253
$\theta = 0.6$	0.091	0.692	0.162
$\theta = 0.7$	0.060	0.717	0.111
$\theta = 0.8$	0.030	0.851	0.058
$\theta = 0.9$	0.014	1.000	0.027

Table 3: Effect of threshold θ for score_{pas}

model	R	P	F
baseline1: $\text{score}_{pas} \geq 0.2$	0.573	0.357	0.440
baseline2: exophora	0.493	0.329	0.395
ME: PRED	0.270	9.612	0.374
ME: SYN	0.000	N/A	N/A
ME: ARG	0.095	0.516	0.161
ME: COREF	0.092	0.574	0.159
ME: PRED+SYN	0.282	0.618	0.387
ME: PRED+ARG	0.380	0.647	0.479
ME: PRED+COREF	0.480	0.762	0.589
ME: SYN+ARG	0.133	0.558	0.215
ME: SYN+COREF	0.147	9.618	9.238
ME: ARG+COREF	0.267	0.661	0.380
ME: PRED+SYN+ARG	0.397	0.656	0.494
ME: PRED+SYN+COREF	0.485	0.760	0.592
ME: PRED+ARG+COREF	0.506	0.752	**0.605**
ME: SYN+ARG+COREF	0.281	0.673	0.397
ME: ALL	0.507	0.747	0.604
SVM(linear): ALL	0.456	0.792	0.579
SVM(poly-2d): ALL	0.679	0.858	**0.758**

Table 4: Results of automatic voice selection

ison. One is based on the passivisation preference of each verb. The model uses only $score_{pas}(v_i)$ defined in equation (1), that is, it selects the *passive* voice if the score is more than the threshold parameter θ; otherwise, it selects the *active* voice. The other baseline model is based on the information that the existence of an exophoric subject results in selecting the passive voice. To capture this characteristic, the model classifies a verb in question as *passive* if the annotated subject is exophoric; otherwise, it selects the *active* voice.

4.2 Results

We first evaluated performance of the first baseline model with various θ. The results are shown in Table 3, demonstrating that the baseline achieved its best F-score when θ is 0.2. Therefore, we set the θ to 0.2 in the following comparison.

Table 4 shows the results of the baselines and proposed models. To investigate the impact of each feature type, we conducted feature ablation when using the maximum entropy model (ME:* in Table 4). Table 4 shows that the model using the feature type PRED achieves the best performance among the four models when using a single feature type. In addition, by adding feature type(s), the F-score monotonically improves. Finally, the results of the model using the PRED, ARG and COREF features achieved the best F-score, 0.605, out of the two baselines and models based on the maximum entropy model. It indicates that each of the features except SYN feature contributes to improving performance in a complementary manner.

Furthermore, the results of the model using SVM with the second degree polynomial kernel show better performance than any model based on the maximum entropy model. This means that the combination of features is important in this task because of the dependency among the four kinds of information introduced in Section 3.

5 Conclusion

This paper focused on the task of automatic voice selection in text generation, taking into account four kinds of linguistic information: passivisation preference of verbs, syntactic decisions, semantic category of the arguments of a predicate, and coreference or anaphoric relations of the arguments. For empirical evaluation of voice selection in Japanese, we used the predicate argument relations and coreference relations annotated in the NAIST Text Corpus (Iida et al., 2007). Integrating the four kinds of linguistic information into a machine learning-based approach contributed to improving F-score by about 0.3, compared to the best baseline model, which utilises only the passivisation preference. Finally, we achieved 0.758 in F-score by combining features using SVM.

As future work, we are planning to incorporate the proposed voice selection model into natural language generation models for more sophisticated text generation. In particular, generating referring expressions and voice selection are closely related because both tasks utilise similar linguistic information (e.g. salience and semantic information of arguments) for generation. Therefore, our next challenge is to solve problems about generating referring expressions and voice selection simultaneously by using optimisation techniques.

References

B. Abb, M. Herweg, and K. Lebeth. 1993. The incremental generation of passive sentences. In *Proceedings of the 6th EACL*, pages 3–11.

Douglas E. Appelt. 1985. Planning English referring expressions. *Artificial Intelligence*, 26(1):1–33.

Barbara Di Eugenio, Davide Fossati, Dan Yu, Susan Haller, and Michael Glass. 2005. Natural language generation for intelligent tutoring systems: A case study. In *Proceedings of the 2005 conference on Artificial Intelligence in Education: Supporting Learning through Intelligent and Socially Informed Technology*, pages 217–224.

B. J. Grosz, A. K. Joshi, and S. Weinstein. 1995. Centering: A framework for modeling the local coherence of discourse. *Computational Linguistics*, 21(2):203–226.

M. A. K. Halliday and C. Matthiessen. 2004. *An Introduction to Functional Grammar*. Routledge.

R. Iida, M. Komachi, K. Inui, and Y. Matsumoto. 2007. Annotating a Japanese text corpus with predicate-argument and coreference relations. In *Proceeding of the ACL Workshop 'Linguistic Annotation Workshop'*, pages 132–139.

S. Ikehara, M. Miyazaki, S. Shirai A. Yokoo, H. Nakaiwa, K. Ogura, Y. Ooyama, and Y. Hayashi. 1997. *Nihongo Goi Taikei (in Japanese)*. Iwanami Shoten.

Kentaro Inui, Takenobu Tokunaga, and Hozumi Tanaka. 1994. Text revision: A model and its implementation. In *Aspects of Automated Natural Language Generation: Proceedings of the 6th International Natural Language Generation Workshop*, pages 215–230.

S. Nariyama. 2002. Grammar for ellipsis resolution in Japanese. In *Proceedings of the 9th International Conference on Theoretical and Methodological Issues in Machine Translation*, pages 135–145.

D. R. Radev and K. R. McKeown. 1998. Generating natural language summaries from multiple online sources. *Computational Linguistics*, 24(3):469–500.

E. Reiter and R. Dale. 2000. *Building Natural Language Generation Systems*. Cambridge University Press.

Ehud Reiter. 1994. Has a consensus NL generation architecture appeared, and is it psycholinguistically plausible? In *Proceedings of the Seventh International Workshop on Natural Language Generation*, pages 163–170.

Jacques Robin. 1994. *Revision-based Generation of Natural Language Summaries Providing Historical Background – Corpus-based Analysis, Design, Implementation and Evaluation*. Ph.D. thesis, Columbia University.

F. Abu Sheikha and D. Inkpen. 2011. Generation of formal and informal sentences. In *Proceedings of the 13th European Workshop on Natural Language Generation*, pages 187–193.

MIME - NLG in Pre-Hospital Care

Anne H. Schneider Alasdair Mort Chris Mellish Ehud Reiter Phil Wilson
University of Aberdeen
{a.schneider, a.mort, c.mellish, e.reiter, p.wilson}@abdn.ac.uk

Pierre-Luc Vaudry
Université de Montréal
vaudrypl@iro.umontreal.ca

Abstract

The cross-disciplinary MIME project aims to develop a mobile medical monitoring system that improves handover transactions in rural pre-hospital scenarios between the first person on scene and ambulance clinicians. NLG is used to produce a textual handover report at any time, summarising data from novel medical sensors, as well as observations and actions recorded by the carer. We describe the MIME project with a focus on the NLG algorithm and an initial evaluation of the generated reports.

1 Introduction

Applications of Natural Language Generation (NLG) in the medical domain have been manifold. A new area where NLG could contribute to the improvement of services and to patient safety is pre-hospital care: care delivered to a patient before arrival at hospital. There are many challenges in delivering pre-hospital care, making it different from care taking place in the controlled circumstances of emergency departments or hospital wards.

Some Ambulance Services have developed innovative models to care for patients whilst an ambulance is en-route. Community First Responder (CFR) schemes recruit volunteers from local communities and give them the necessary training and equipment to deal with a limited range of medical emergencies. The premise is that even those with basic first-aid skills can save a life. It is their task to attend the casualty while waiting for the ambulance and to record their observations and actions on a paper patient report form (PRF). They may also assess the patient's physiological measurements (e.g. heart rate). In practice, due to time constraints, a verbal handover is performed and the PRF is filled in later. Physiological measurements may be written in ink on the back of a protective glove, and are rarely passed on in any systematic way.

The MIME (Managing Information in Medical Emergencies)[1] project is developing technology to support CFRs in the UK when they respond to patients. The project aims to enable CFRs to capture a greater volume of physiological patient data, giving them a better awareness of a patient's medical status so they can deliver more effective care.

There are two parts to our work: the use of novel lightweight wireless medical sensors that are simple and quick to apply, and the use of novel software that takes these inherently complex sensor data, along with some other information inputted by the user (e.g. patient demographics or actions performed) on a tablet computer, and present it very simply. We are working with two sensors that provide measurements of the patient's respiratory rate, heart rate and blood oxygen saturation. Our software can use NLG to produce a textual handover report at any time. This can be passed to an arriving paramedic to give a quick summary of the situation and can accompany the patient to inform later stages of care. We anticipate that our system will also provide some basic decision support based upon the patients clinical condition.

2 Related Work

Many situations arise in the medical domain where vast amounts of data are produced and their correct interpretation is crucial to the lives of patients. Interpreting these data is usually a demanding and complex task. Medical data are therefore often presented graphically or preferably in textual summaries (Law et al., 2005) making NLG important for various applications in the medical domain.

A number of systems address the problem of presenting medical information to patients in a form that they will understand. Examples are

[1] www.dotrural.ac.uk/mime

STOP (Reiter et al., 2003), PILLS (Bouayad-Agha et al., 2002), MIGRANE (Buchanan et al., 1992), and Healthdoc (Hirst et al., 1997). Other systems, such as TOPAZ (Kahn et al., 1991) and Suregen (Hüske-Kraus, 2003), aim to summarise information in order to support medical decision-making.

In the case of MIME, the challenge is to summarise large amounts of sensor data, in the context of carer observations and actions, in a coherent way that supports quick decision making by the reader. The problem of describing the data relates to previous work on summarising time series data (e.g. (Yu et al., 2007)). In many ways, though, our problem is most similar to that of Babytalk BT-Nurse system (Hunter et al., 2012), which generates shift handover reports for nurses in a neonatal intensive care unit. The nature of the recipient is, however, different. Whereas BabyTalk addresses clinical staff in a controlled environment, MIME is aimed at people with little training who may have to deal with emergency situations very quickly. Further, while BT-Nurse works with an existing clinical record system, which does not always record all actions and observations which ideally would be included in a report, in MIME users enter exactly the information which MIME needs. This simplifies the NLG task, at the cost of adding a new task (interface construction).

3 The MIME project

In the first stage of MIME, we have developed a desktop application to prototype the generation of handover reports. We used simulated scenarios, where a panel of medical experts determined the sequence of events and predicted the stream of data from the simulated sensors.

The generated reports must provide a quick overview of the situation but at the same time be sufficiently comprehensive, while the format must enhance the readability. A general **structure for the handover reports** was determined in a user-centred development process together with ambulance clinicians. After the demographic description of the casualty and incident details (entered by the responder whenever they have an opportunity), two sections of generated text follow: the initial assessment section and the treatments and findings section. The initial assessment contains information on the patient gathered by the CFRs just after the sensors are applied and also any observations made during the first minute after the application of the sensors. The treatment and findings section is a report on the observations and actions of the CFRs while they waited for the ambulance to arrive. This includes a paragraph that sums up the condition of the patient at the time of handover.

Using sensors to capture physiological data continuously introduces the problem that irrelevant information needs to be suppressed in order not to overload the ambulance clinicians and hinder interpretation. The **NLG algorithm** that generates short as well as comprehensive handover reports accomplishes text planning in the two stages of document planning and micro-planning (Reiter and Dale, 2000). Document planning is responsible for the selection of the information that will be mentioned in the generated report. Events that will be mentioned in the text are selected and structured into a list of trees (similar to trees in Rhetorical Structure Theory (Scott and Sieckenius de Souza, 1990)). In the micro-planning step the structure of the document plan is linearised and sentences are compiled using coordination and aggregation.

Whereas some parts of the handover document (e.g. patient demographics) are relatively stylised, the main technically demanding part of the NLG involves the description of the "treatment and findings", which describes the events that happen whilst the patient is being cared for and relevant parts of the sensor data (see Figure 1). For this section of the report, the document planning algorithm is based on that of (Portet et al., 2007), which identifies a number of key events and creates a paragraph for each key event. Events that are explicitly linked to the key event or events that happen at the same time are added to the relevant paragraph. This is based on the earlier work of (Hallett et al., 2006).

4 Evaluation

In an initial evaluation we sought to assess how our reports would be received in comparison with the current situation – either short verbal reports or paper report forms (PRFs)– and also in comparison with what might be regarded as a "gold standard" report produced by an expert.

Materials: Two videos were produced independently of the NLG team, based on two scenarios of medical incidents typical of a CFRs caseload. These scenarios, a farm injury and chest pain, included a short description of the incident, similar

```
At 02:12, after RR remained fairly
constant around 30 bpm for 4 minutes,
high flow oxygen was applied, she took
her inhaler and RR decreased to 27
bpm. However, subsequently RR once
more remained fairly constant around
30 bpm for 8 minutes.

At 02:15 she was feeling faint.

At 02:15 the casualty was moved.

At 02:17 the casualty was once more
moved.
```

Figure 1: Part of the "Treatment and Findings" for an asthma scenario.

to the initial information a CFR would receive, a time line of events that happened before the ambulance arrived as well as simulated sensor data from the patient. The videos showed an actor in the role of CFR and another as patient, with the scenario time displayed in one corner. When the CFR performed readings of the physiological measures they were shown as subtitles.

The videos were presented to two CFRs and a paramedic, who were asked to imagine themselves in the situation of the CFR in the video, and to produce a handover report. Each video was only played once in order to produce more realistic results. We asked one CFR to construct a written "verbal" handover for the first scenario and to fill out a PRF for the other scenario, and the other CFR to do the "verbal" handover for the second scenario and to fill out the PRF for the first. To anonymise the PRF it was transcribed into a digital version. The paramedic received a blank sheet of paper and was requested to produce a handover report that he would like to receive from a CFR when arriving at the scene. Based on the scenarios we also generated two reports with the MIME system. This process resulted in four reports for each of the two scenarios, one transcribed verbal handover and a PRF from a CFR, a written handover report from a paramedic and the generated report.

Hypotheses: Our hypothesis was that the generated reports would improve on the current practice of verbal handovers and PRFs, and that paramedics would perceive them to be more suitable, hence rank them higher than the CFRs' verbal or PRF reports. The paramedic handover report might be regarded as a gold standard produced by an expert and we were interested in how the generated reports fared in comparison. Further, we hoped to gain information on how to improve our generated reports.

Participants: We approached paramedics in the Scottish Ambulance Service to participate in our study. Nine paramedics responded (eight male and one female; age range 32–56 years with 10–24 years' service).

Procedure: Participants received an invitation email with a link to a brief online survey and the eight reports as attachments. After an introduction and consent form they were forwarded to one of the two scenario descriptions and asked to rank the respective four reports. After that the participant was asked to rate the accuracy, understandability and usefulness of the generated report for this scenario on a 5-point Likert scale ranging from *very good* to *very bad* and to indicate what they liked or disliked about it in a free text box. This process was repeated for the second scenario.

4.1 Results

Ranking: An overview of the rankings can be found in Table 1. Apart from the rankings of participant 7 and 8, no large differences in how the reports were ranked could be observed between the two scenarios. We performed a Friedman test (Friedman, 1937) (farm injury scenario: chi-squared=4.3, df=3, p=0.23; chest pain scenario: chi-squared=12.44, df=3, p=0.006): some reports were ranked consistently higher or lower than others. The verbal CFR report was ranked worst in all but five cases. There is a high disparity in the rankings for the PRF, which was ranked first on eight occasions and in the other ten instances in third or fourth place. The generated report was ranked in first place only once, but eleven times in second place and in third place the other six times. In general the paramedic report, which was regarded as the "gold standard", was ranked better than the generated report, but in five cases the generated report was ranked better.

Rating: An overview of the ratings for the generated reports can be found in Table 2. The ratings for both scenarios were good on average, with a majority of ratings lying between very good to moderate. Only one rating (the accuracy of the generated report for the farm injury scenario) was bad; none was very bad. The ratings for the generated report of the chest pain scenario were on average better than those for the farm injury scenario. Accuracy had better ratings than usefulness and understandability in both scenarios.

Participant:	1	2	3	4	5	6	7	8	9	med	min	max
farm injury scenario												
Paramedic	2	2	3	1	1	3	3	2	1	2	1	3
Generated	3	3	2	2	2	2	2	3	2	2	2	3
CFR PRF	1	1	1	3	4	1	4	4	3	3	1	4
CFR verbal	4	4	4	4	3	4	1	1	4	4	1	4
chest pain scenario												
Paramedic	2	2	3	1	1	2	2	1	1	2	1	3
Generated	3	3	2	2	2	3	1	2	2	2	1	3
CFR PRF	1	1	1	3	4	1	4	3	3	3	1	4
CFR verbal	4	4	4	4	3	4	3	4	4	4	3	4

Table 1: Overview of the ranking results (*most preferred* (1) to *least preferred* (4)), median (med), maximum (max) and minimum (min) values for the patient report form (CFR PRF), paramedic report (Paramedic), generated report (generated) and verbal report (verbal CFR).

Participant:	1	2	3	4	5	6	7	8	9	med	min	max
farm injury scenario												
accuracy	1	2	1	4	2	2	1	1	1	1	1	4
useful.	3	3	2	2	1	2	2	1	1	2	1	3
unders.	2	3	2	2	1	3	3	1	1	2	1	3
chest pain scenario												
accuracy	2	2	1	1	1	3	1	2	1	1	1	3
useful.	2	3	2	1	1	2	1	1	1	1	2	3
unders.	2	3	2	1	1	3	2	1	1	2	1	3

Table 2: Overview of the rating results, median (med), maximum (max) and minimum (min) values for accuracy, usefulness (useful.) and understandability (unders.) of the generated reports, on a Likert scale (*very good* (1) to *very bad* (5)).

4.2 Discussion

We hypothesised that the generated reports would fare better than the verbal handovers and the PRFs. Results confirm a preference for the generated reports over the verbal handover. The paramedic reports, which were regarded as our "gold standard" were ranked higher than the generated reports. Interestingly, in almost half the cases there was a clear preference for the PRF and in the other cases the PRF ranked badly. This may have been affected by the familiarity of this medium and perhaps by the background assumption that this is how handover reports "should" be presented.

We regard this as a tentative confirmation that the generated texts compete favourably with the *status quo*. In a real world scenario the paramedics often get a verbal handover instead of the PRF and it should be noted that the PRF was printed and not handwritten. Furthermore, although the CFRs and paramedics only saw the scenario video once they were under no time pressure to submit the reports. Hence the quality of all the human reports in our experiment is likely to be better than normal.

Although each individual generally provided consistent responses across the two scenarios, there were variations between individuals. These different preferences may be merely stylistic choices or they may reflect in task performance. Preferences are not necessarily an indication of usefulness for a task (cf. (Law et al., 2005)).

In general the accuracy, understandability and usefulness of the generated reports received good ratings. Although participation was low, the qualitative data we gathered were valuable, every participant offered comments in the free text box on what they liked or disliked about the generated report. In general there seemed to be an impression that some sections were longer than necessary. One participant observed that reporting on observations a long time later is only useful if things have changed significantly. The structure and organisation of the report received some positive comments. For example one participant stated that he liked "the separate sections for information" and another commented that the report was "logically laid out", that it was "easy to obtain information" from the report and that it "clearly states intervention and outcome of intervention".

5 Conclusion and Future Work

Despite the fact that the experiment reported here involved a small number of participants, which implies that its results need to be interpreted with some caution, the generated reports produced by the MIME system appear to improve on the current practice of verbal handover. We aim to collect more responses and repeat the evaluation that has been presented. Our next step in evaluating the report generator will be to carry out a task based evaluation to see whether the preference ratings we have gathered can be reflected in performance measures.

We are now moving into the second stage of MIME and have started developing a new prototype, a mobile device that gets signals from two lightweight sensors. Here we will collect data from real emergency ambulance callouts by having a researcher join ambulance crews for their normal activity, which will be used to modify the NLG system (e.g. in order to allow for more reliable handling of noise).

6 Acknowledgments

This work is supported by the RCUK dot.rural Digital Economy Research Hub, University of Aberdeen (Grant reference: EP/G066051/1)

References

N. Bouayad-Agha, R. Power, D. Scott, and A. Belz. 2002. PILLS: Multilingual generation of medical information documents with overlapping content. In *Proceedings of LREC 2002*, pages 2111–2114.

B. Buchanan, J. Moore, D. Forsythe, G. Banks, and S. Ohlsson. 1992. Involving patients in health care: explanation in the clinical setting. In *Proceedings of the Annual Symposium on Computer Application in Medical Care*, pages 510–514, January.

M. Friedman. 1937. The Use of Ranks to Avoid the Assumption of Normality Implicit in the Analysis of Variance. *Journal of the American Statistical Association*, 32(200):675–701.

C. Hallett, R. Power, and D. Scott. 2006. Summarisation and visualisation of e-Health data repositories Conference Item Repositories. In *UK E-Science All-Hands Meeting*, pages 18–21.

G. Hirst, C. DiMarco, E. Hovy, and K. Parsons. 1997. Authoring and Generating Health-Education Documents That Are Tailored to the Needs of the Individual Patient. In Anthony Jameson, Cécile Paris, and Carlo Tasso, editors, *User Modeling: Proceedings of the Sixth International Conference, UM97*, pages 107–118. Springer Wien New York.

J. Hunter, Y. Freer, A. Gatt, E. Reiter, S. Sripada, and C Sykes. 2012. Automatic generation of natural language nursing shift summaries in neonatal intensive care: BT-Nurse. *Artificial Intelligence in Medicine*, 56:157–172.

D. Hüske-Kraus. 2003. Suregen-2: A Shell System for the Generation of Clinical Documents. In *Proceedings of the 10th Conference of the European Chapter of the Association for Computational Linguistics (EACL-2003)*, pages 215–218.

M. Kahn, L. Fagan, and L. Sheiner. 1991. Combining physiologic models and symbolic methods to interpret time-varying patient data. *Methods of information in medicine*, 30(3):167–78, August.

A. Law, Y. Freer, J. Hunter, R. Logie, N. McIntosh, and J. Quinn. 2005. A comparison of graphical and textual presentations of time series data to support medical decision making in the neonatal intensive care unit. *Journal of clinical monitoring and computing*, 19(3):183–94, June.

F. Portet, E. Reiter, J. Hunter, and S. Sripada. 2007. Automatic generation of textual summaries from neonatal intensive care data. In *In Proccedings of the 11th Conference on Artificial Intelligence in Medicine (AIME 07). LNCS*, pages 227–236.

E. Reiter and R. Dale. 2000. *Building Natural Language Generation Systems*. Studies in Natural Language Processing. Cambridge University Press.

E. Reiter, R. Robertson, and L. Osman. 2003. Lessons from a failure: Generating tailored smoking cessation letters. *Artificial Intelligence*, 144(1-2):41–58, March.

D. Scott and C. Sieckenius de Souza. 1990. Getting the message across in rst-based text generation. In R. Dale, C. Mellish, and M. Zock, editors, *Current Research in Natural Language Generation*. Academic Press.

J. Yu, E. Reiter, J. Hunter, and C. Mellish. 2007. Choosing the content of textual summaries of large time-series data sets. *Natural Language Engineering*, 13(1):25–49.

Generation of Quantified Referring Expressions: Evidence from Experimental Data

Dale Barr
Dept. of Psychology
University of Glasgow
dale.barr@glasgow.ac.uk

Kees van Deemter
Computing Science Dept.
University of Aberdeen
k.vdeemter@abdn.ac.uk

Raquel Fernández
ILLC
University of Amsterdam
raquel.fernandez@uva.nl

Abstract

We present the results from an elicitation experiment in which human speakers were asked to produced quantified referring expressions (QREs), as in *'The crate with 10 apples'*, *'The crate with many apples'*, etc. These results suggest that some subtle contextual factors govern the choice between different types of QREs, and that numerals are highly preferred for subitizable quantities despite the availability of coarser-grained expressions.

1 Introduction

Speakers can express quantities in different ways. For instance, a speaker may specify a meeting time with the expression *'in the morning'* or with the more precise, numeric expression *'at 10:30am"*; she may choose to specify a temperature as *'5 degrees Celsius'* or instead use the less precise but more qualifying expression *'cold'*. One area of NLG where these choices are important is the generation of referring expressions. In particular, a referent may be identified by means of some quantitative value or other (e.g., *'the tall man*; *'the man who is 198cm tall'*), or by means of the number of other entities to which it is related. Henceforth, let's call these *quantified* referring expressions (QREs). An example of a QRE arises, for instance, when a person is identified by means of the number of his children (*'the man with 5 daughters'*), when a directory is identified by means of the number of files in it (*'the directory with 520/many PDF files in it'*), or when a crate is identified by means of the number of apples in it (*'the crate with 7 /a few apples'*).

Green and van Deemter (2011) asked under what circumstances it might be beneficial, for a reader or hearer, for referring expressions of this kind to contain vague expressions (e.g., like *many*). The present paper addresses the same phenomena focussing, more broadly, on all the different ways in which reference may be achieved; unlike these previous authors, we shall address this question from the point of view of the speaker, asking how human speakers refer in such cases, rather than how useful a given referring expression is to a hearer (e.g., as measured by their response times in a manipulation task).

We start by making our research questions more precise in the next section. We then describe the production experiment we run online in Section 3 and present an analysis of the data in Section 4. We end with some pointers on how our results could inform an NLG module for QREs.

2 Research Questions

Suppose you want to point out one crate amongst several crates with different numbers of apples. You may use a numeral (*'the crate with seven apples'*) or, if the crate in question is the one with the largest or smallest amount of apples, you may use superlatives (*'the crate with the most apples'*), comparatives (*'with more apples'*) or vague quantifiers (*'with many apples'*); if your crate is the only one with any apples in it at all, you might simply say *'the crate with apples'*). In many situations, several of these options are applicable. It is not obvious, however, which of these is preferred. The Gricean Maxim of Quantity (Grice, 1975) urges speakers to make their contribution as informative as, but not more informative than, it is required for the current purposes of the exchange. This might be taken to predict that speakers will tend to use the most coarsely grained expression that identifies the referent (unless they want some nontrivial implicatures to be inferred). This would predict, for example that it is odd to say *'the box with 27 apples'* when *'the box with apples'* suffices, because the latter contains a boolean property (contains apples), whereas the former relies

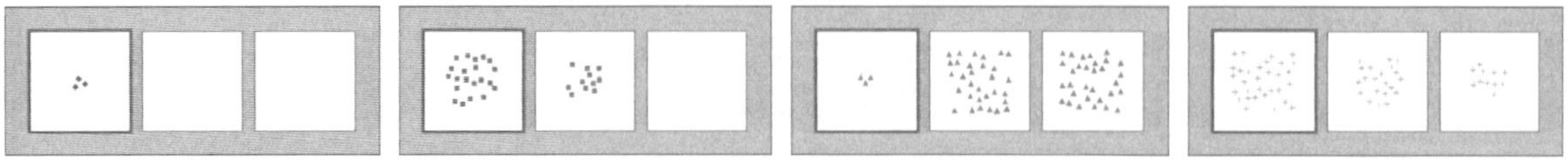

Figure 1: Sample stimuli in contexts X__, XY_, XYY with big gap, and XYZ with small gap.

on a special case on what is essentially much more finely grained property (contains x apples).

Our hunch, however, was that this is not the whole story. For example, the literature on human number processing suggests that numbers below 5 or 6 are handled almost effortlessly; these numbers are called *subitizable* (Kaufman et al., 1949) Furthermore, we hypothesized that it matters to what extent the number of apples in the target crate "stands out". We had the following expectations:

1. Speakers do not always use the coarsest-grained level that is sufficient.
2. Whether a quantity is subitizable or not interferes with the speakers' choice.
3. The frequency of vague forms (such as *'many'*) will be higher in contexts where the gap between the target quantity and the quantities in the distractors is large than when it is small.[1]

We wanted to put these ideas to the test and, more generally, find out how human speakers use QREs in different contexts. Our interest was also in creating a corpus of human-produced QREs that can serve future research.

3 Experimental Setup

The elicitation experiment was run online. Subjects first encountered a screen with instructions. They were told that they would be presented with situations consisting of three squares, with each of them having none, one or more shapes in it. In each of these situations, one of the three squares would be highlighted and subjects were asked to describe this target square in a way that would enable a reader of their expression to identify it. Subjects were told that the recipient of their description may see the three squares arranged differently on the screen with their contents possibly being scrambled around. That is, they were indirectly asked to concentrate on the *quantity* of shapes in the squares (rather than on their relative position or on the spatial configuration of the shapes in them). Figure 1 shows some sample stimuli.

The experiment included a total of 20 items, generated according to the following parameters:

- *Subitizability*: the amount of shapes in the target is within the subitizable range (SR) (1-4 shapes) or within a non-subitizable range (NR); we included three non-subitizable ranges, with around 10, 20, and 30 shapes, respectively.
- *Context*: we considered four types of scenarios:
  1. X__: only the target square is filled.
  2. XY_: two squares are filled.
  3. XYY: all squares filled; with two ranges.
  4. XYZ: all squares filled; with three ranges.

  The symbol X in the first position stands for the referent square, while the symbols in the other two positions indicate for each of the other two squares whether it contains a number of shapes within the same range as the referent square (X), within a different range (Y/Z), or whether it does not contain any shapes at all (_).
- *Relative Size*: the target contains either the smallest or the largest amount of shapes.
- *Gap Size*: there is either a big or a small quantity difference between the target and other squares. A big gap size is only possible with target squares that contain the largest amount of shapes within a non-subitizable range and those that contain the smallest amount of shapes within a subitizable range.

Participants were recruited by publishing a call in the Linguist List. A total of 82 subjects participated in the experiment, including participants who only responded to some items. We eliminated 6 sessions where the participant had responded to less than 10 items. The final dataset includes 76 participants and a total of 1508 descriptions.

4 Results

Each description produced by the participants was annotated with one of the categories in Table 1.

[1] Later on we refer to vague forms as "base", a common term used to describe the vague, unmodified form of relative scalar adjectives (e.g., *tall*) as opposed to their comparative (*taller*) and superlative (*tallest*) forms.

Category	Examples
ABS [absolute]	*the one with pacmans / the square that's not blank*
BASE [base]	*the square with lots of dark dashes / it has a few crosses in it*
COMP [comparative]	*the one with fewer dashes / the square with more crosses in it*
NUM [numeric]	*the square with 11 black dots / 3 grey ovals*
SUP [superlative]	*it has the largest number of purple squares / the square with the least minuses*
OTH [other]	*about a dozen blue diamonds / big droup of circles in the centre*

Table 1: Categories used to code the expressions produced by the participants.

The classification was first done automatically by pattern matching and then revised manually.

To analyse the data, we used mixed-effects logistic regression with crossed random effects for subjects and items (Baayen et al., 2008). All models had by-subject and by-item random intercepts, and by-subject random slopes for the within-subject factors of context and range (subitizability). The models were fit using maximum likelihood estimation with p-values derived from likelihood ratio tests. Model estimation was performed using the lme4 package (Bates et al., 2013) of R statistical software (R Core Team, 2013).

Table 2 shows the overall distribution of expression types used by the participants. As can be seen, numerical expressions were the most common type of expression used overall (65%). We found, however, that there was a strong subitizability effect in the use of these expressions: for non-subitizable targets, subjects used numerical expressions only 39% of the time, while for subitizable targets they did so 90% of the time. This main effect of subitizability was significant ($\chi^2(1) = 47.92$, $p < .001$). There was high variability across subjects in the effect ($\chi^2(1) = 25.00$, $p < .001$), with a higher rate of numerical expressions associated with a smaller effect of subitizability ($r = -.61$). Note that 17 of the 82 subjects ($\sim$ 20%) *always* used numerical expressions, even when the target was not subitizable. Of the remaining 65 subjects, 64 show a very significant preference for using numeric expressions to describe targets within the subitizable range.

Figure 2 shows the proportion of expression types for each type of context and subitizability condition.[2] Sensitivity to context differed for subitizable and non-subitizable targets, supported by a reliable interaction between these factors ($\chi^2(1) = 17.31$, $p < .001$). Despite the strong overall preference for numerical expressions with subitizable targets, the effect of context was still reliable ($\chi^2(1) = 22.63$, $p < .001$). For subitizable targets (Figure 2, bottom row), numeric expressions were almost always used (96%) except in contexts where the target was the only filled square (X__). In this context, participants occasionally used absolute expressions instead (e.g. *the one with shapes*) 33% of the time. In sum, subitizable targets overwhelmingly triggered the use of numerals, predominating even when a Gricean account would prefer coarser-grained expressions.

For non-subitizable targets (first row of plots in Figure 2), in contexts without distractors (X__) absolute expressions were preferred over numerical ones; this differed from the behaviour of subitizable targets in this context, where numerical expressions predominated ($\chi^2(1) = 4.25$, $p = .039$). In contexts with non-empty distractors (XY_, XYY, and XYZ), expressions other than numeric are used significantly more often than they were for subitizable targets ($\chi^2(1) = 52.93$, $p < .001$). Superlative expressions (e.g. *the square with the least dots*) were preferred in contexts where the three squares were filled ($\chi^2(1) = 7.74$, $p = .005$). In contexts with one distractor (XY_), superlatives were also rather common, and comparative expressions (e.g. *the one with fewer dashes*) occurred at higher rates than in other types of context ($\chi^2(1) = 42.34$, $p < .001$).

The comparison between the contexts with two distractors (XYY and XYZ) suggests that they differed largely in the use of vague expressions (BASE; e.g. *the one with many diamonds*), which had a higher rate in context XYY where there were only two quantity ranges ($\chi^2(1) = 5.01$,

	ABS	BASE	COMP	NUM	SUP	OTH	Total
NR	73	33	26	294	308	17	751
SR	51	1	0	684	21	0	757
Total	124	34	26	978	329	17	1508

Table 2: Row counts of expression types for non-subitizable (NR) and subitizable (SR) targets.

[2]Category OTH (other) is not shown in Figure 2 to avoid clutter. Table 2 shows the row counts for all categories.

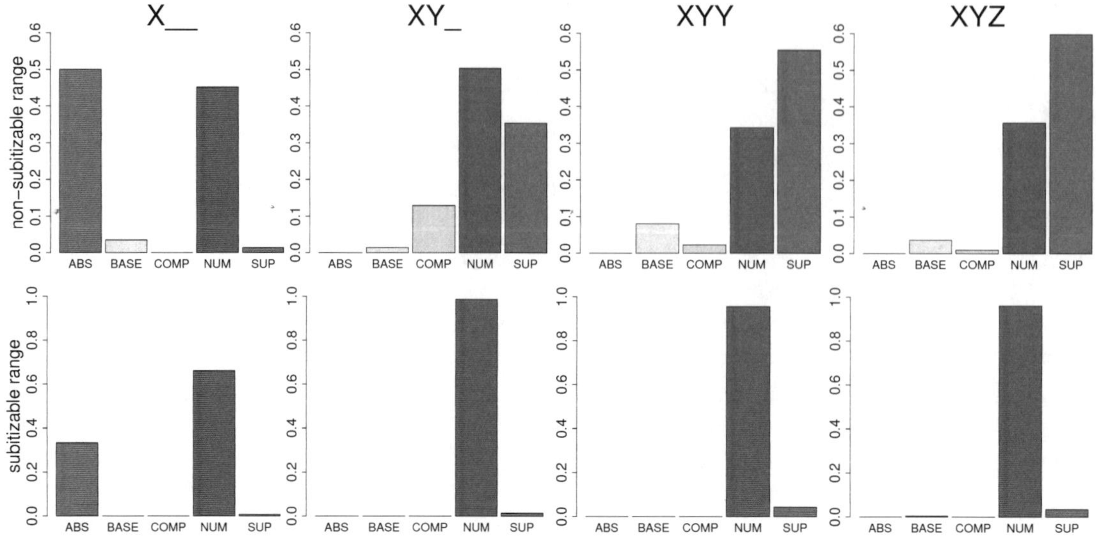

Figure 2: Proportion of expression types in each context for subitizable and non-subitizable targets.

$p = .025$). For this context we also found an effect of gap size (see Figure 3): the relative odds of choosing a vague expression over a numeric or superlative one is significantly higher when there is a big difference between the target quantity and the distractor quantities ($\chi^2(1) = 5.68, p = .017$); that is, when the chance of there being borderline cases is reduced. A small gap between the quantities makes the preference for superlative (and thus non-vague) expressions stronger.

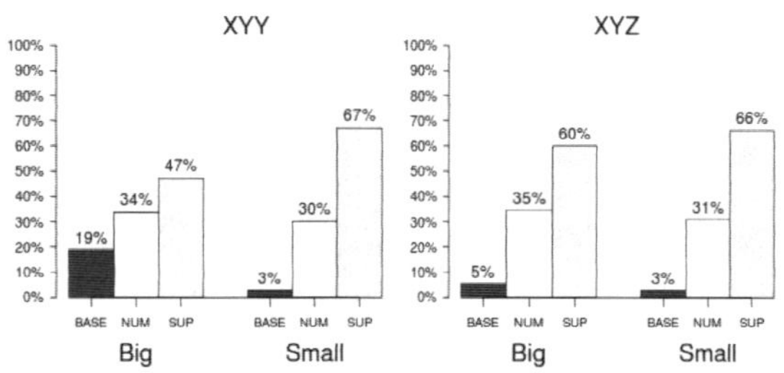

Figure 3: The effect of gap size.

5 Conclusions

In line with our expectations (see Section 2), our data are not easy to reconcile with the type of Gricean account that predicts a preference for the most coarsely grained QRE that identifies the target. The most obvious deviation from this Gricean account arises from the subitizable items in our study, where numerical expressions turned out to be much preferred over other QREs. The natural explanation seems to be that such expressions *come naturally* to speakers (and to hearers too as shown by Green and van Deemter (2011)). In other words, our study suggests an intriguing variant on Grice, in which the most relevant factor is not one of *informativeness* – as Grice's writings suggest – but one of effort. It suggests that speakers tend to produce expressions that identify the referent *with least effort*.

Our expectation 3 was also confirmed: vague forms (BASE) are more frequent with big gap sizes, although they are not produced with high frequency. (The same pattern of results was found by van Deemter (2004)). Thus, in the scenarios we considered vague QREs are never the most favoured option. The high frequency of superlatives over comparatives is also noteworthy. Comparatives are used very seldom overall but are more frequent in contexts with only one distractor (XY_). This indicates that some speakers opt for a less strong expression than a superlative (an expression that means *more than x* rather than *more than any other x*) in contexts where this does not lead to ambiguity. However, numerals and superlatives are still largely preferred in those contexts.

These observations suggest that a given type of situation (i.e., a given context + subitizability condition) should not always map to the same type of QRE. If human QRE behaviour is to be mimicked, the best approach seems to be to use a stochastic NLG program that seeks to replicate the frequencies that are found in human usage.

The collected data is freely available at `http://www.illc.uva.nl/~raquel/xprag/`.

References

R. Baayen, D. Davidson, and D. Bates. 2008. Mixed-effects modeling with crossed random effects for subjects and items. *Journal of memory and language*, 59(4):390–412.

D. Bates, M. Maechler, and B. Bolker, 2013. *lme4: Linear mixed-effects models using S4 classes*. R v. 0.999999-2.

M. Green and K. van Deemter. 2011. Vagueness as cost reduction: An empirical test. In *Proc. of Production of Referring Expressions workshop at CogSci 2011*.

H. P. Grice. 1975. Logic and conversation. In *The Logic of Grammar*, pages 64–75. Dickenson.

E. Kaufman, M. Lord, T. Reese, and J. Volkmann. 1949. The discrimination of visual number. *American Journal of Psychology*, 62(4):498–525.

R Core Team, 2013. *R: A Language and Environment for Statistical Computing*. R Foundation. v. 3.0.0.

K. van Deemter. 2004. Finetuning NLG through experiments with human subjects: the case of vague descriptions. In *Proc. of the 3rd INLG Conference*.

POS-tag based poetry generation with WordNet

Manex Agirrezabal, Bertol Arrieta, Aitzol Astigarraga
University of the Basque Country (UPV/EHU)
IXA NLP Group
Dept. of Computer Science
20018 Donostia
sgpagzam@ehu.es
bertol@ehu.es
aitzol.astigarraga@ehu.es

Mans Hulden
University of Helsinki
Department of Modern Languages
Helsinki, Finland
mhulden@email.arizona.edu

Abstract

In this paper we present the preliminary work of a Basque poetry generation system. Basically, we have extracted the POS-tag sequences from some verse corpora and calculated the probability of each sequence. For the generation process we have defined 3 different experiments: Based on a strophe from the corpora, we (a) replace each word with other according to its POS-tag and suffixes, (b) replace each noun and adjective with another equally inflected word and (c) replace only nouns with semantically related ones (inflected). Finally we evaluate those strategies using a Turing Test-like evaluation.

1 Introduction

Poetry generation is one of the dream tasks of Natural Language Processing (NLP). In this text we point out an approach to generate Basque strophes automatically using some corpora, morphological information and a lexical database. The presented method is not tied to a specific language, but it is especially suitable for inflected languages, as the POS information used in some tasks with success in non inflected languages is not enough for inflected ones. We have used the POS-tags with their inflectional information to learn usual structures in Basque poetry.

This work is part of a more general and complete project, called *BertsoBOT* (Astigarraga et al., 2013). BertsoBOT is a robot capable of creating and singing Basque verses automatically. The robot joins together in a single system techniques from robotics, NLP and speech synthesis and recognition. The work presented in this paper comes to improve the generation module of the mentioned system.

Although our intention is to create whole verses, in this paper we present the first steps towards it: the creation of strophes. Additionally, Basque verses have to rhyme, but in these first experiments we have not considered it.

Basque language

Basque language is spoken along the Basque Country[1] by approximately 700.000 people. Although there is a standardized form of the language, it is common the use of non-standard dialects in certain regions, mainly in spoken language.

Basque is a morphologically rich language, which is an obvious feature if we analyze the multiple declension cases[2] that can be used with only one word. For example, the phrase "with the friends" can be expressed with only one word, "*lagunekin*".

lagunekin = *lagun* (friend) + *ak* (plural determiner) + *kin* (with)

Art of *bertsolaritza*

The art of *impromptu* verse-making, *bertsolaritza*, is very ingrained in the Basque Country. The performances of verse-makers are quite usual and a big championship is held every four years which congregates 15.000 people, approximately. One tipical work to do for the verse-makers is to sing verses extempore, given a topic. The particularity of these verses is that they have to follow strict constraints of meter and rhyme. In the case of a metric structure of verses known as "*zortziko txikia*"

[1] http://en.wikipedia.org/wiki/Basque_Country_(greater_region)
[2] en.wikipedia.org/wiki/Basque_grammar#Declension

(small of eight), the poem must have eight lines. The union of each odd line with the next even line, form a strophe. Each strophe, has a small structure[3] and must rhyme with the others. Below, you can see an example of a verse, with *lauko txikia*[4] stanza:

Neurriz eta errimaz	With meter and rhyme
kantatzea hitza,	to sing the word
horra hor ze kirol mota	bertsolaritza is
den bertsolaritza.	that kind of sport

2 State of the art

A good review of computer guided poetry can be found in (Gervás, 2010). Most relevant ones include:

WASP

The WASP system (Gervás, 2000) can be considered one of first serious attempts to build an automatic poetry generator system. It is based on the generate-and-test paradigm of problem solving. Simple solutions are generated and then coupled with an evaluation function for metric constraints, producing acceptable results.

ASPERA

ASPERA (Gervás, 2001) is a case-based reasoning (CBR) system for poetry generation. It generates poetry based on the information provided by the user: a prose description of the intended message, a specific stanza for the final poem, a set of verse examples on that stanza, and a group of words that the final poem must contain.

The system was implemented using CLIPS rule-based system, and follows the four typical CBR steps: Retrieval, Reuse, Revise and Retain.

POEVOLVE

Levy (Levy, 2001) went on to develop an evolutionary model of poetry generation. POEVOLVE creates limericks taking as a reference the human way of poetry writing. The POEVOLVE system works as follows: an initial population is created from a group of words that include phonetic and stress information. Rhymes that meet the requirements are selected and then more words are selected to fill the rest of the verse-line based on their stress information. A genetic algorithm is employed to modify the words that compose the limerick. Evaluation is performed by a neural network trained on human judgements. It must be said that this system does not take syntax and semantics into account.

McGonnagall

Manurung presented also an evolutionary approach to generate poetry (Manurung, 2003). The poem generation process is formulated as a state space search problem using stochastic hill-climbing. The overall process is divided in two steps: evaluation and evolution. During the evaluation phase, a group of individuals is formed based on initial information, target semantics and target phonetics. This group of initial individuals is then evaluated taking into account different aspects such as phonetics, semantics and surface form. Each individual receives a score, and in the evolution step, the subset with higher scores is selected for reproduction. The resulting mutated individuals derive, hopefully, in better versions of the poem.

3 Creating strophes

Our goal is to create Basque strophes automatically. But strophes written by combining words randomly usually do not have any sense. For words have any meaning when combined together, they must be organized following particular patterns. Towards this end we have applied and tested different methodologies. We use a morphological analyzer to extract POS and inflection patterns in strophes, and to create new ones following those schemes. The idea is to find the most commonly used patterns so that we can use them in new strophes. We also improve the results taking semantics into account. In the next lines we are going to describe some resources we have used.

3.1 Corpora

For the learning process of the usual POS-tag patterns we have employed some Basque verse corpora yielded by the Association of the Friends of Bertsolaritza[5] (*AFB*). Those are impromptu verses sung by Basque verse-makers and the transcriptions of this collection have been done by members of the information center[6] of the *AFB*.

For this work, we are going to exploit three corpora,

[3] 13 syllables with a *caesura* after the 7th syllable

[4] Lauko txikia: The same as *zortziko txikia* but with four lines, instead of eight.

[5] http://www.bertsozale.com/en

[6] http://bdb.bertsozale.com/en/orriak/get/7-xenpelar-dokumentazio-zentroa

each one following a classic stanza in Basque verses: (a) small stanza, (b) big stanza and (c) habanera.

a) Small stanza

This corpus has approximately 10.000 lines. Each line of this corpus is composed by a strophe containing 13 syllables with a *caesura* between the 7th and the 8th syllable. This stanza is used to sing sprightly verses composed by compact ideas.

b) Big stanza

In this case, this corpus has about 8.000 lines and each line has 18 syllables with a caesura after the 10th syllable. Depending on the chosen melody, this stanza can also have a complementary pause in the 5th syllable. The topics of this type of verses tend to be more epic or dramatic.

c) Habanera

This corpus has just about 1000 lines and they are composed by 16-syllable lines with a caesura after the 8th syllable. It is commonly used when the verse-maker has to compose a verse alone about a topic.

3.2 POS sequence extraction

To extract the POS-tags, we use a Basque analyzer developed by members of IXA NLP group (Aduriz et al., 2004), which involve phrasal morphologic analysis and disambiguation, among other matters.

Once calculated the POS-tags, we estimated the most probable POS sequences using POS-tag ngrams. We did this in order to know which POS-tag sequence would better fit for each stanza. For example, an acceptable POS-tag sequence in the small stanza corpus would be "NN-NN-JJ-VB". This pattern could be extracted from this strophe, which is correct.

Mirenekin+NN *zakurra*+NN *zoriontsua*+JJ *da*+VB.
(With Miren)+NN (the dog)+NN is+VB happy+JJ.

But to have the POS-tag pattern is not enough for a good generation.

Special issues in the categorization of words in Basque

The gist is that Basque is an agglutinative language, so there is plenty information included in the suffixes of the words. Because of that, if we don't retain any information about suffixes, we would lose some important data. In Basque, we can apply declension to nouns, pronouns, adjectives and determiners. Therefore, we need to save the declension case information to do a correct generation. When a set of words compound a noun phrase, only one of the words will be inflected.

Some verbs, when they are part of a subourdinate clause, can also be inflected. In these cases, we have to extract the suffixes of the verb of that clause, because it expresses the type of clause.

All this information is essential if we do not want to lose the meaning of the clause. Below, you can see an example of generation of strophes in Basque using only POS-tags:

Mirenekin+NN *lagunekin*+NN *zoriontsua*+JJ *da*+VB.
(With Miren)+NN (with the friends)+NN is+VB happy+JJ.

As you can see, the phrase "with Miren with the friends is happy" is not grammatically correct. Storing the declension information, that creation would not be allowed and one of the clauses created by the system could be:

Mirenekin+NN_COM *mahaia*+NN_ABS *zoriontsua*+JJ_ABS *da*+VB.
(With Miren)+NN_COM (the desk)+NN_ABS is+VB happy+JJ_ABS.

The addition of the declension information will avoid some grammatical errors in the generation process. But when the changed element is a verb, the system can insert one that does not follow the same subcategorization[7], which will lead us to a grammatical error too. So, changing the verb without more information can be uncertain.

3.3 Semantic information

On the other hand, if we take a look at the last example, it is not correct to say that the desk is happy. To avoid these cases, we posed the use of the Basque WordNet (Fellbaum, 2010) (Pociello et al., 2011). We used it to change words with related ones.

3.4 Morphological generation

Finally, it is important the fact that Basque is an inflected language. So, we need to have a morphological generator (Alegria et al., 2010) to create the corresponding inflected forms of the words. This generator is based on the Basque morphology description (Alegria et al., 1996).

4 Experiments

In this work, we have performed a set of experiments to analyze different strategies for the generation of stro-

[7]The subcategorization indicates the syntactic arguments required or allowed in some lexical items (usually verbs).

phes in Basque. In the following lines, we explain the ameliorations we get in each experiment.

The first experiment creates strophes by inserting words that are consistent with each POS-tag and its inflection information. We first get some of the most common POS-tag sequences and for each POS-tag sequence the application returns two strophes. The first strophe uses words from the same verse corpus to make substitutions. The second one uses words from the EPEC corpus (Aduriz et al., 2006).

The second experiment creates clauses, but changing only the nouns and adjectives from original strophes from the corpus. We mantain the inflection information. In this experiment we also get two strophes for each pattern sequence, as in the previous attempt (verse corpus and EPEC corpus). With this constraint we avoid the creation of incorrect strophes because of the problem of subcategorization (explained in section 3.2).

The third experiment makes small changes in the original strophes (from the corpus), as it only replaces each noun for a semantically related noun. The related noun can be: (a) Antonym of the original word or (b) hyponym of the hypernyms of the original word. In order of preference, first we try to change each name with one of its antonyms. If there is no antonym, then we try to get the hypernyms of the word to return their hyponims. Once the new word has been found, we add the needed suffixes (the same ones that had the words from the corpus) in order to fit correctly in the strophe, using the morphological generator. The change of words with related ones gives us the chance to express semantically similar sentences using different words.

5 Evaluation

Once the experiments were finished, we made an evaluation in order to analyze the quality of the automatically generated strophes. The evaluation of computer generated poetry is nowadays fuzzy, so we defined a Turing Test-like evaluation. We contacted two linguists that had not done any work on this project, so that the evaluation be as objective as possible. We prepared 135 strophes interleaving some created by the machine with others from the corpus. We asked the evaluators to guess if the strophe was done by the machine or by a human. We only draw conclusions using machine-generated strophes, as we want to know how many of them percolate as human-generated ones. In the next table you can see the rate of sentences created by the machine and suposed to be done by humans:

	EXPERIMENT		
Evaluator 1	1	2	3
Percolated as human	0.033	0.259	0.75
Evaluator 2			
Percolated as human	0.333	0.481	0.75

As you can see, according to *Evaluator 1*, the first experiment was not very worthy, as the only 3.3% of the machine generated strophes percolated as human generated ones. The second experiment got better results, and the 26% of the strophes were thought to be human generated ones. As expected, the strophes of the third experiment are the most trustworthy ones. The results given by the second evaluator are higher, but the important fact is the increase of the progression over the experiments.

6 Discussion & Future Work

In this paper we have presented a set of experiments for the automatic generation of poetry using POS and inflectional tag patterns and some semantics. In the last section we show the Turing Test-like evaluation to measure the reliability of each experiment. This will be part of a whole poetry analysis and generation system.

In the future, we intend to change verbs from strophes controlling the subcategorization of them in order to enable the creation of well-formed strophes about a constrained topic. Also, we plan to use a frame semantics resource, such as FrameNet, and after creating a strophe, make some modifications to get an acceptable semantic meaning.

References

Aduriz, I., Aranzabe, M., Arriola, J., de Ilarraza, A., Gojenola, K., Oronoz, M., and Uria, L. (2004). A cascaded syntactic analyser for Basque. *Computational Linguistics and Intelligent Text Processing*, pages 124–134.

Aduriz, I., Aranzabe, M. J., Arriola, J. M., Atutxa, A., de Ilarraza, D. A., Ezeiza, N., Gojenola, K., Oronoz, M., Soroa, A., and Urizar, R. (2006). Methodology and steps towards the construction of EPEC, a corpus of written Basque tagged at morphological and syntactic levels for automatic processing. *Language and Computers*, 56(1):1–15.

Alegria, I., Artola, X., Sarasola, K., and Urkia, M. (1996). Automatic morphological analysis of Basque. *Literary and Linguistic Computing*, 11(4):193–203.

Alegria, I., Etxeberria, I., Hulden, M., and Maritxalar, M. (2010). Porting Basque morphological grammars to foma, an open-source tool. *Finite-State Methods and Natural Language Processing*, pages 105–113.

Astigarraga, A., Agirrezabal, M., Lazkano, E., Jauregi, E., and Sierra, B. (2013). Bertsobot: the first minstrel robot. *6th International Conference on Human System Interaction, Gdansk.*

Fellbaum, C. (2010). *WordNet*. Springer.

Gervás, P. (2000). Wasp: Evaluation of different strategies for the automatic generation of Spanish verse. In *Proceedings of the AISB-00 Symposium on Creative & Cultural Aspects of AI*, pages 93–100.

Gervás, P. (2001). An expert system for the composition of formal spanish poetry. *Knowledge-Based Systems*, 14(3):181–188.

Gervás, P. (2010). Engineering linguistic creativity: Bird flight and jet planes. In *Proceedings of the NAACL HLT 2010 Second Workshop on Computational Approaches to Linguistic Creativity*, pages 23–30. Association for Computational Linguistics.

Levy, R. P. (2001). A computational model of poetic creativity with neural network as measure of adaptive fitness. In *Proccedings of the ICCBR-01 Workshop on Creative Systems*. Citeseer.

Manurung, R. (2003). *An evolutionary algorithm approach to poetry generation*. PhD thesis, School of informatics, University of Edinburgh.

Pociello, E., Agirre, E., and Aldezabal, I. (2011). Methodology and construction of the Basque Wordnet. *Language resources and evaluation*, 45(2):121–142.

Greetings Generation in Video Role Playing Games

Björn Schlünder
Ruhr-Universität Bochum
Department of Linguistics
Germany
bjoern.schluender@rub.de

Ralf Klabunde
Ruhr-Universität Bochum
Department of Linguistics
Germany
ralf.klabunde@rub.de

Abstract

We present first results of our project on the generation of contextually adequate greeting exchanges in video role playing games. To make greeting exchanges computable, an analysis of the factors influencing greeting behavior as well as the factors influencing greeting exchanges is given. Based on the politeness model proposed by Brown & Levinson (1987) we develop a simple algorithm for the generation of greeting exchanges. An evaluation, comparing dialog from the video role playing game *Skyrim* to dialog determined by our algorithm, shows that our algorithm is able to generate greeting exchanges that are contextually more adequate than those featured by *Skyrim*.

1 Introduction

Though there has been a steep rise in interest in video games during the past decade, both culturally as well as commercial, little has been done in getting language technology involved in game development. There is a huge contrast between the steep development of almost every other aspect of game development and the usage of language technology. To our knowledge there is not one game of one of the major game companies that uses sophisticated NLG-methods for the generation of contextually adequate utterances. Modern games feature rich voice acting, but often lack realistic conversational situations. Voice acting, which became standard in commercial productions around the year 2000, hampered usage of language technology for quite some time, since e.g. speech synthesis did not reach sufficient quality and therefore would hurt immersion. Since then not only quality of synthesis systems has increased, but synthesis-like voice acting has also been used in successful productions (e.g. Portal 1 & 2).

There is some work in the NLG community on NLG in games (e.g., Koller et al. 2004; Khosmood and Walker 2010), but an intimate cooperation between game design and NLG does not exist on a commercial level. Research in the fields of NLG & game design is e.g. conducted at Expressive Intelligence Studio at UC Santa Cruz, with current projects (e.g. SpyFeet) focussing on combining NLG methods and computational dialog management in simple role playing games (Reed et al. 2011).

By nature of their modern design, video games, especially of the role playing genre, provide detailed information on the spatial and social environment, the agent types, their behavior and motivation, the progress on and steps in certain goals etc., so that context-related language generation should be a feasible task.

In our paper, we show by means of an apparently simple generation task, viz. the generation of greetings in greeting exchange situations, how more appropriate linguistic expressions can be generated if context features are taken into account. Our examples will be taken from the video role playing game *The Elder Scrolls V: Skyrim*, which shall henceforth simply be referenced as *Skyrim*.

2 Video Role Playing Games (VRPGs)

Video games involve two kinds of players or agents, respectively: player characters are agents acting in the virtual game environment on behalf of and controlled by the player, and non-player characters (NPCs) are agents controlled by the game software. Both agents interact with each other by non-verbal and verbal means, the latter typically realized by the selection of canned text from an agent-dependent discourse tree.

The ultimate goal of a video game is immersion: the player should get emotionally involved with the environment, the NPCs and his character. Text presented in video games is vital to the immersion process. Form and content of the texts presented depend on the player types and the story telling method.

The essential features of VRPGs are the high number of appearing NPCs, their multifaceted models (skills, attributes, "karma", etc.), a branching story line and the possibility to take different approaches to solve problems, many of the former being conversational. As a result, in VRPGs conversations mostly take place directly within the games virtual environment (as opposed to cutscenes in many action games, i.e. episodes the player is not able to control), which leads to the high immersion factor of the genre.

2.1 Text in Video Games

Game texts are the major component in telling and driving a game's story. In most recent games they are fully voice acted. Game texts can either be categorized as storytelling text, written documents appearing in the game, or dialog, which can be further categorized as either scripted or interactive dialog. The latter is mostly featured in games of the branching storytelling type like VRPGs. These games make rich use of interactive dialogue and use it to fuel their story. Players have multiple choices in dialogs and are able to use different verbal approaches to solve conversational problems. Nevertheless all possible dialog lines are still prewritten during development – there is just a lot more of them. According to web sources *Skyrim* comprises more than 60,000 dialog lines.

This demonstrates that game developers must use an enormous amount of text that will be presented in the different episodes of a story. However, there is little variation within these texts to keep development costs down. As a result, conversations may get an inappropriate character by means of an iterated use of one and the same text unit in subsequent scenes, or the constant, inappropriate avoidance of ingame variables that would bloat the number of dialog lines (e.g. gender of agents).

In *Skyrim* this leads to constant skipping of real conversation openers and real passing greetings. As our evaluation below shows, even a minimalistic greeting exchange will be perceived as more appropriate and therefore improve immersion.

3 Greeting Exchanges

Greeting exchanges are social practices that agents in VRPGs should be able to master. According to Firth (1972) the aim of a greeting exchange is to establish or reestablish social relations in case of conversation openers, or in case of passing greetings – if the agents are strangers – guaranteeing a safe passage. Both may also serve acknowledgement of a different allocation of status.

Politeness is a central aspect of every type of greeting exchange. Greeting exchanges as adjacency pairs comprise a linguistic, a sociolinguistic, and an anthropological aspect (Williams 2001). Some of the variables influencing form and content of a greeting exchange are:

- Attention of player and agents (e.g. are the agents facing each other?)
- Time since last encounter between the two parties (e.g. Skyrim's NPCs do not make a difference between the character leaving for five minutes and leaving for days)
- Gender as social variable (e.g. in the society in question, is a woman supposed to greet first?)
- Physical variables: time of the day, physical distance, noisiness of surroundings, crowdedness of the immediate environment. E.g., the last three variables influence wether a verbal or a gestural greeting should be performed.

In *Skyrim*, instantiations of these variables are available during runtime because they are tracked for various other functions of the game engine, but only gender (*"Hello master / mistress"*) and distance (passing greetings will only occur in the immidiate vicinity of the player character) are actually utilized for greeting purposes. Also the necessary variables underlying the politeness effect of a greeting are implicitly given in a game; e.g. in Skyrim the player will encounter kings as well as peasants, and the sum of her deeds for certain factions are also tracked.

4 Computing Greeting Exchanges

Brown & Levinson's (1987) well-known politeness model uses the concepts of negative and positive face to explain polite behavior. The negative face comprises the want of every agent that his actions be unimpeded by others. The positive

Trait	Par.	Value	Motivation
shy	α	1.2	misinterprets social distance
	β	1.3	afraid of authority
	γ	1.8	fears social impositions more than anything else
uncouth	α	0.2	unaware of social distance
	β	1.6	does recognize and respect power
	γ	0.2	does not mind the impositions of the FTA

Table 1: Values of α-, β- and γ-parameters for shy and uncouth stereotypes

face is the want of every agent that his wants be desirable to at least some others. Face threating acts (FTAs) threaten the positive and/or the negative face of the addressee and/or the speaker. Politeness is just a verbal or non-verbal means to attenuate the FTA. According to Brown & Levinson (1987) the weight W_x of a FTA x is calculated as follows:

$$W_x = D(S, H) + P(H, S) + R_x$$

where D is the social distance between speaker S and hearer H, P is the relative power the hearer has over the speaker, and R_x is the ranking of the impositions of a particular FTA x.

In *Skyrim* the background information for the generation of appropriate greetings is available in the course of the game, but the software makes very limited use of the variables at its disposal. Time since the last encounter is not taken into account as well as attention: Characters might have been gone for days of ingame time and will hear the same phrases as if they just left the room. The character is also addressed by NPCs while they are passing behind his back or sometimes while talking to other NPCs. This is clearly impolite greeting behavior that is not licensed by urgency and rudeness as an agent's trait, since this affects all NPCs.

More information available could be used to calculate the social distance D and power P. The social distance could be calculated by taking into account the interacting agent's ethnicities, their profession, social skills etc., while relative power could be calculated through factors like rank in or standing with an organisation.

Finally and most importantly personal influences are implemented by the use of parameters which simply adjust the impact of the social variables:

$$W_x = \alpha \times D(S, H) + \beta \times P(H, S) + \gamma \times R_x$$

This allows for easy contrasting between character types. If we assume that a "normal" greeting behavior is based on a value of 1 for each of α, β and γ, we assume exemplary values for the parameters for stereotypical *shy* and *uncouth* as seen in Table 1.

As a result, our method not only generates different greetings w.r.t. different instantiations of the physical and social variables, but also different greetings for different agent types. Our algorithm outlined in Table 2 generates a simple passing greeting exchange or a simple conversation opener.

We assume that for every pair of agents (character and NPC) there is a Question Under Discussion (QUD) stack of information that has not yet been resolved (see, e.g., Djalali et al. 2011). A QUD-model for short-term discourse history can also be utilized to lock the NPC in a certain conversational state (urgent quests), therefore giving access to the notion of urgency which mitigates the impact of impolite behavior, e.g. skipping greeting exchanges, and also helps to keep discourse coherent.

Besides the QUD stack we assume a database which keeps record of the discourse history beyond the QUD-stack. Elements resolved (popped from the stack) are stored in the database. This database also helps to keep track of relations between the two agents and directly affects the social distance component. Relative power is untouched. The database also keeps track of agent-specific information like faction, rank, and others as well as agent-pair specific data, like time since last encounter.

Since we do not have access to *Skyrim*'s source code, our algorithm has not been implemented yet. However, given greetings from *Skyrim*, the outlined algorithm can be used to determine modified greetings whose quality has been evaluated by players. For example, when entering an alchemist's store the following example dialog might occur in *Skyrim* (**A** being the alchemist, **P** being the player character):

A: You look rather pale. Could be Ataxia. It's quite a problem back home in Cyrodiil.
P: [not realized]
P: [initiates conversation; not realized]
A: Pardon me, but do I detect a case of the Rattles? I've got something for that.

check for possibility of a greeting exchange:
- checking agent type (normal, shy, uncouth)
- line of sight between agents?
- agents paying attention to e.o.?
- distance between agents appropriate?
- one of agents trying to hide?

gather possible and situationally fitting greeting phrases / schemes for either.:.
- A passing greeting or
- A conversation opener

look for physical modifiers that influence mode of greeting (e.g. noisiness of surrounding)

look for situational modifiers that override politeness calculation

calculate politeness with regards to agent types

if greeting character is a player character:
- generate passing greeting or conversational opener.
- present player with options to choose from.
- add greeting phrase to discourse history.
- check for circumstances that might reduce impact of FTA (e.g. urgency)
- apply politeness impact on standing and/or karma.

else if greeting character is a NPC:
- choose greeting according to NPCs role and model
- generate chosen phrase.
- add chosen phrase to discourse history

output to player

Table 2: Proposed algorithm for greeting exchange generation.

P: [not realized]
P: [chooses from variety of conversation topics]

Utilizing our algorithm, the following dialog might unfold.

A: Good morning and welcome to my store.
P: Good morning.
A: How may I serve you?
P: [chooses from variety of conversation topics]

One can see that while the pre-written dialog lines give a lot of background information about the game world, their usage in the initial dialog stages seems a bit odd.

5 Evaluation

To evaluate the suggested method of computing greeting exchanges, we designed a questionnaire containing descriptions (in a pen & paper RPG style) of five different situations from Skyrim. These situations have been chosen because of their unfitting pragmatic realisation. For each situation, we presented a set of follow-up dialog situations which contained the original dialog from Skyrim, dialog determined by our algorithm (minus urgency, as it would allow to skip greeting exchanges) as well as by a simple approach that only took into account attention and minimalistic greetings.

We used transcripts from the original dialog to eliminate potential bias from different methods of presentation as well as to ensure that subjects would not recognize the original dialog from Skyrim. The subjects were then asked to evaluate the dialog situations according to appropriateness, politeness, social distance, relative power as well as feeling a sense of urgency. In addition we asked the subjects for a short self-evaluation of their experience with video and role playing games as well as their experience with Skyrim. Out of seven participants two did not have any experience with video or role playing games. Two participants had played Skyrim. They evaluated the overall linguistic realisation with a score of 7 out of 9 and were able to recognize the situations as well as the dialog options from Skyrim. Table 3 shows the overall evaluation results.

	very	medium	not
Skyrim	1.4	1.4	4.2
simple	2	4	1
our alg.	4.2	1.4	1.2
Skyrim	0.2	1.8	5
simple	1.6	4	1.4
our alg.	4.6	1.6	0.8

Table 3: Average no. of choices for appropriateness (above) and politeness (below)

In this setting, Skyrim's passing greetings and conversation openers generally were perceived as much less appropriate than the alternatives presented, while greetings determined by our algorithm were perceived as the most appropriate in all scenarios by the majority of all participants. Skyrim's greeting exchanges were also mostly associated with only little social distance and were perceived as relatively impolite. The opposite was true for greetings determined by our algorithm: in every scenario the majority of participants chose them as the most polite one.

References

Penelope Brown and Stephen C. Levinson. 1987. *Politeness: Some universals in language usage*. Cambridge University Press, Cambridge

Alex Djalali, David Clausen, Sven Lauer, Karl Schultz and Christopher Potts. 2011. Modeling Expert Effects and Common Ground Using Questions Under Discussion. *Proceedings of the AAAI Workshop on Building Representations of Common Ground with Intelligent Agents.*

Raymond Firth. 1972. Verbal and Bodily Rituals of Greeting and Parting. *The Interpretation of Ritual*: 1–38.

J.S. La Fontaine (Ed.). 1972. *The Interpretation of Ritual*. Tavistock Publications, London.

Alexander Koller, Ralph Debusmann, Malte Gabsdil and Kristina Striegnitz. 2004. Put my galakmid coin into the dispenser and kick it: Computational Linguistics and Theorem Proving in a Computer Game. *Journal of Logic, Language and Information, 13 (2)*: 187–206.

Foaad Khosmood and Marilyn Walker. 2010. Grapevine: a gossip generation system. *Proceedings of the 5th International Conference on the Foundations of Digital Games, New York, NY, USA*: 92–99.

Aaron A. Reed, Ben Samuel, Anne Sullivan, Ricky Grant, April Grow, Justin Lazaro, Jennifer Mahal, Sri Kurniawan, Marilyn Walker and Noah Wardrip-Fruin. 2011. SpyFeet: An Exercise RPG. *Proceedings of the 6th International Conference on the Foundations of Digital Games.*

Jesse Schell. 2008. *The Art of Game Design: A book of lenses*. Elsevier/Morgan Kaufmann, Amsterdam and Boston.

Kenneth E. Williams. 2001. An Evaluation of Greeting Exchanges in Textbooks and Real Life Settings. *Sophia Junior College Faculty Journal*, 21:49–64.

On the Feasibility of Automatically Describing n-dimensional Objects

Pablo Ariel Duboue
Les Laboratoires Foulab
999 du College
Montreal, Quebéc
pablo.duboue@gmail.com

Abstract

This paper introduces the problem of generating descriptions of n-dimensional spatial data by decomposing it via model-based clustering. I apply the approach to the error function of supervised classification algorithms, a practical problem that uses Natural Language Generation for understanding the behaviour of a trained classifier. I demonstrate my system on a dataset taken from CoNLL shared tasks.

1 Introduction

My focus is the generation of textual descriptions for n-dimensional data. At this early stage in this research, I introduce the problem, describe a potential application and source of interesting n-dimensional objects and show preliminary work on a traditional NLG system built on off-the-shelf text planning and surface realization technology plus a customized sentence planner.

This work was inspired by a talk by Kathleen McCoy in which she described a system that produces Natural Language explanations of magazine infographics for the blind by combining Computer Vision techniques with NLG (Carberry et al., 2013). She mentioned an anecdote in which she asked a blind user of the system what would the user would want added to the text description and the user replied *"I don't know, I have never seen an infographic."* I found the comment very inspiring and it led to the realization that n-dimensional objects (for $n > 3$) were also something which we, as humans, have never seen before and which we will profit from having a computer system to describe to us.

A type of n-dimensional objects that are of particular practical interest are the error function for a machine learning algorithm for particular training data. That is the case because, for NLP practitioners using supervised classification, the task of debugging and improving their classifiers at times involves repeated steps of training with different parameters. Usually, at each stage the trained model is kept as an opaque construct of which only aggregate statistics (precision, recall, etc) are investigated. My technology improves this scenario by generating Natural Language descriptions for the error function of trained machine learning models.

My system, Thoughtland,[1] (Fig. 1) is a pipeline with four stages, accessed through a Web-based interface (Duboue, 2013), further discussed in the next section.

This early prototype is already able to tackle descriptions of existing, non-trivial data. These results are very encouraging and the problem merits attention from other NLG researchers. To further broad interest in this problem, I am distributing my prototype under a Free Software license,[2] which should encourage extensions and classroom use. I have already found the current descriptions useful for telling apart the output of two different algorithms when run on the same data.

I will now describe the algorithm and then dive into the NLG details. I conclude with related and future work discussions.

2 Algorithm

Thoughtland's architecture is shown in Fig. 1. While the first stage lies clearly outside the interest of NLG practitioners, the next two stages (Clustering and Analysis) are related to the *message generation* aspect of content planning (Reiter and Dale, 2000),[3] as they seek to transform the data into units that can be communicated verbally (the last stage is the more traditional NLG system itself).

[1] http://thoughtland.duboue.net
[2] https://github.com/DrDub/Thoughtland
[3] pages 61-63.

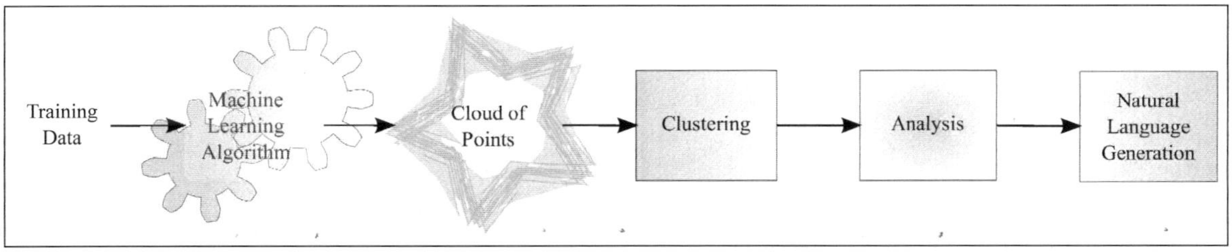

Figure 1: Thoughtland's architecture.

2.1 Cross-Validation

The error function is computed as the error for each point in the input data. For a numeric target class, that would mean that for every training instance $(\vec{x}, y)$, $e = \left\| f(\vec{x}) - y \right\|$, where the error is computed using f trained on the folds that do not contain $(\vec{x}, y)$.[4] This stage produces a cloud of points in n-dimensions, for $n = F + 1$, where F is the number of features in the training data (the extra dimension is the error value).

2.2 Clustering

The cloud of error points obtained in the previous step is then clustered using a mixture of Dirichlet models (McCullagh and Yang, 2008) as implemented by Apache Mahout (Owen et al., 2011).[5] I choose this clustering approach because each of the obtained clusters has a geometrical representation in the form of n-balls, which are n-dimensional spheres. These representations are important later on for the natural language generation approach.

Some input features present a natural geometric groupings which will interfere with a clustering set to elucidate the error function. To make the error coordinate the most prominent coordinate for clustering, I re-scale the error coordinate using the radius of an n-ball that encompasses all the input features.

2.3 Analysis

In Fig. 1, the Analysis Stage involves determining the overall size, density, distances to the other n-balls and extension in each dimension for each n-ball. These numbers are put into perspective with respect to the n-ball encompassing the whole cloud of points. The distance between two n-balls, for example, is said to be *big* if in any dimension it is above half the radius of the large n-ball in that particular dimension. Each n-ball is also compared to each other in terms of distance.

I have so far determined these thresholds by working on the mileage data discussed elsewhere (Duboue, 2013). Objective-function optimization-based techniques (discussed in the next section) might prove useful here.

This stage is at its infancy, in future work I want to analyze the pairs of n-balls in terms of rotations as they are particularly important to determine how many dimensions are actually being used by the sets of n-balls.

3 Natural Language Generation

As I go exploring the different aspects of the problem, I opt for a very traditional generation system and architecture. Approaches based on learning (Mairesse et al., 2010; Varges and Mellish, 2010; Oh and Rudnicky, 2000) are not particularly easy to apply to this problem as I am producing a text for which there are no available examples. I do hope to explore objective-function optimization-based techniques such as Lemon (2011) or Dethlefs and Cuayáhuitl (2011) in the near future.

The NLG system is thus implemented on top of McKeown's (1985) Document Structuring Schemata (using the recent implementation OpenSchema[6]) and SimpleNLG (Gatt and Reiter, 2009). I use two schemata, in one the n-balls are presented in order while in the other the attributes are presented in order. One of the schemata I am using is shown in Fig. 2. Document structuring schemata are transition networks of rhetorical predicates that can contain free and bound variables, with restrictions on each variable. The system presents the user the shorter description.

Either strategy should emphasize similarities, simplifying aggregation (Reape and Mellish, 1999). I employ some basic aggregation rules, that

[4] The error is different if the target class is not numeric (nominal target classes). In that case the error is 1.0 if the class is different from the target or 0 if it the same.

[5] See Section 9.4.2, "Dirichlet clustering."

[6] `http://openschema.sf.net`

is, for each aggregation segment I assemble all n-balls with the same property together to make complex sentences. That works well for size and density. To verbalize distances, I group the different pairs by distance value and then look for cliques using the Bron-Kerbosch clique-finding algorithm (Bron and Kerbosch, 1973), as implemented in JGraphT.[7] I also determine the most common distance and verbalize it as a defeasible rule (Knott et al., 1997), which significantly shortens the text.

This pipeline presents a non-trivial NLG application that is easy to improve upon and can be used directly in a classroom setting.

3.1 Case Study

I will now illustrate Thoughtland by virtue of an example with training data from the CoNLL Shared Task for the year 2000 (Sang and Buchholz, 2000). The task involved splitting a sentence into syntactically related segments of words:

> (NP He) (VP reckons) (NP the current account deficit) (VP will narrow) (PP to) (NP only # 1.8 billion) (PP in) (NP September) .

The training contains for each word its POS and its Beginning/Inside/Outside chunk information:

He	PRP	B-NP
reckons	VBZ	B-VP
the	DT	B-NP
current	JJ	I-NP
account	NN	I-NP
deficit	NN	I-NP
will	MD	B-VP
narrow	VB	I-VP

I transformed the data into a classification problem based on the current and previous POS, rendering it a two dimensional problem. The provided data consists of 259,104 training instances. Over this data Naïve Bayes produces an accuracy of 88.9% and C4.5, 89.8%. These numbers are very close, but do the two algorithms produce similar error function? Looking at Thoughtland's descriptions (Fig. 3) we can see that is not the case.

In later runs I add the current and previous words, to make for a three and fourth dimensional problem. These are extra dimensions with a nominal class with 20,000 distinct values (one for each word). Interestingly, when the classifiers become good enough, there is no discriminating information left to verbalize. A similar situation happens when the classifiers have poor accuracy.

[7] http://jgrapht.sourceforge.net/

```
schema by-attribute(whole: c-full-cloud)
  ; first sentence, overall numbers
  pred-intro(cloud|whole)
  aggregation-boundary
  star
    pred-size()
  aggregation-boundary
  star
    pred-density()
  aggregation-boundary
  star
    pred-distance()

predicate pred-density
  variables
    req def component : c-n-ball
    req attribute : c-density
  properties
    component == attribute.component
  output
    pred has-attribute
    pred0 component
    pred1 attribute
    pred2 magnitude
```

Figure 2: One of the two schemata employed by Thoughtland. This schema produces descriptions focusing on the similar attributes of each of the n-balls. I include one of the predicates for reference.

4 Related Work

The problem of describing n-dimensional objects is a fascinating topic which Thoughtland just starts to address. It follows naturally the long term interest in NLG for describing 3D scenes (Blocher et al., 1992), spatial/GIS data (De Carolis and Lisi, 2002) or just numerical data (Reiter et al., 2008).

In the more general topic of explaining machine learning decisions, ExOpaque (Guo and Selman, 2007) takes a trained system and uses it to produce training data for an Inductive Logic Programming (Muggleton and Raedt., 1994) system, presenting the resulting Horn-clauses directly to the user. Focusing on explaining the impact of specific attributes in the prediction outcome of a particular instance, Robnik-Sikonja and Kononenko (2008) analyze changes to the classification outcome under different input variations, weighted by their priors, an idea explored early on in agent-based systems (Johnson, 1994). In general, systems based on Bayesian networks seem to have a stronger probabilistic framework that facilitates explanations (Lacave and Diez, 2000).

By far, most of the attention in understanding the error function for machine learning algorithms has come from the graphical visualization commu-

Naive Bayes	C4.5
THREE DIMENSIONS	
Accuracy 88.9%	Accuracy 89.8%
There are five components and three dimensions. Component One is big and components Two, Three and Four are small. Component Four is dense and components Two and Three are very dense. Components Three and Five are at a good distance from each other. The rest are all far from each other.	There are six components and three dimensions. Component One is big, components Two, Three and Four are small and component Five is giant. Component Five is sparse and components Two, Three and Four are very dense. Components One and Two are at a good distance from each other. The rest are all far from each other.
FOUR DIMENSIONS	
Accuracy 90.4%	Accuracy 91.4%
There are six components and four dimensions. Components One, Two and Three are big and components Four and Five are small. Component Three is dense, component One is sparse and components Four and Five are very dense. Components Two and Three are at a good distance from each other. The rest are all far from each other.	There are six components and four dimensions. Components One, Two and Three are big and components Four and Five are small. Component One is dense, component Three is sparse and components Four and Five are very dense. Components Three and Four are at a good distance from each other. Components Six and Four are also at a good distance from each other. The rest are all far from each other.
FIVE DIMENSIONS	
Accuracy 91.6%	Accuracy 91.6%
There is one component and five dimensions.	There is one component and five dimensions.

Figure 3: Example generated descriptions.

nities. However, as stated by Janert (2010):[8]

> *As soon as we are dealing with more than two variables simultaneously, things become much more complicated – in particular, graphical methods quickly become impractical.*

The focus is then in dimensionality reduction[9] and projection (Kaski and Peltonen, 2011), usually as part of an integrated development environment (Kapoor et al., 2012; Patel et al., 2010). The usual discussion regarding the complementary role of text and graphics, as studied for a long time in NLG (McKeown et al., 1997), applies also here: there are things like generalizations and exceptions that are easier to express in text. We look forward for NLG-based approaches to be included in future versions of ML IDEs such as Gestalt.

Finally, Thoughtland uses the error function for an ML algorithm as applied to training data. A similarly worded term which should not be confused is *error surface* (Reed and Marks, 1999),[10] which refers to the space of possible ML *models*. Error surfaces are particularly important for training algorithms that explore the said surface, for example by gradient descent.

[8]Chapter 5, page 99.

[9]A reviewer suggested combining dimensionality reduction and NLG, an idea most definitely worth exploring.

[10]Chapter 8.

5 Final Remarks

I have presented Thoughtland, a working prototype addressing the problem of describing clouds of points in n-dimensional space. In this paper I have identified the problem and shown it to be approachable with a solution based on model-based clustering.

For future work, I want to enrich the analysis with positional information: I want to find planes on which a majority of the n-balls lie so as to describe their location relative to them. I am also considering hierarchical decomposition in up to five to seven n-balls (to make it cognitively acceptable (Miller, 1956)) as it will translate well to textual descriptions.

My preliminary experiments suggest there is value in generating *comparisons* for two error functions. I can therefore employ the existing body of work in NLG for generating comparisons (Milosavljevic, 1999).

While the pilot might speak of the feasibility of the task, Thoughtland still needs to be evaluated. For this, I want to start with simple cases such as overfitting or feature leaks and see if the descriptions help humans detect such cases faster.

Acknowledgements

The author would like to thank Annie Ying, Or Biran, Samira Ebrahimi Kahou and David Racca.

References

A. Blocher, E. Stopp, and T. Weis. 1992. ANTLIMA-1: Ein System zur Generierung von Bildvorstellungen ausgehend von Propositionen. Technical Report 50, University of Saarbrücken, Sonderforschungsbereich 314, Informatik.

Coenraad Bron and Joep Kerbosch. 1973. Finding all cliques of an undirected graph (algorithm 457). *Commun. ACM*, 16(9):575–576.

Sandra Carberry, Stephanie Elzer Schwartz, Kathleen Mccoy, Seniz Demir, Peng Wu, Charles Greenbacker, Daniel Chester, Edward Schwartz, David Oliver, and Priscilla Moraes. 2013. Access to multimodal articles for individuals with sight impairments. *ACM Trans. Interact. Intell. Syst.*, 2(4):21:1–21:49, January.

Berardina De Carolis and Francesca A Lisi. 2002. A NLG-based presentation method for supporting KDD end-users. In *Foundations of Intelligent Systems*, pages 535–543. Springer.

Nina Dethlefs and Heriberto Cuayáhuitl. 2011. Hierarchical reinforcement learning and hidden markov models for task-oriented natural language generation. In *Proceedings of the 49th Annual Meeting of the Association for Computational Linguistics: Human Language Technologies: short papers-Volume 2*, pages 654–659. Association for Computational Linguistics.

P.A. Duboue. 2013. Thoughtland: Natural Language Descriptions for Machine Learning n-dimensional Error Functions. In *Proceedings of ENLG'13*.

Albert Gatt and Ehud Reiter. 2009. SimpleNLG: a realisation engine for practical applications. In *Proceedings of the 12th European Workshop on Natural Language Generation*, ENLG '09, pages 90–93, Stroudsburg, PA, USA. Association for Computational Linguistics.

Yunsong Guo and Bart Selman. 2007. ExOpaque: A framework to explain opaque machine learning models using Inductive Logic Programming. In *ICTAI (2)*, pages 226–229. IEEE Computer Society.

Philipp K. Janert. 2010. *Data Analysis with Open Source Tools*. O'Reilly.

W Lewis Johnson. 1994. Agents that learn to explain themselves. In *Proceedings of the twelfth national conference on Artificial intelligence*, volume 2, pages 1257–1263.

Ashish Kapoor, Bongshin Lee, Desney Tan, and Eric Horvitz. 2012. Performance and preferences: Interactive refinement of machine learning procedures. In *Twenty-Sixth AAAI Conference on Artificial Intelligence*.

Samuel Kaski and Jaakko Peltonen. 2011. Dimensionality reduction for data visualization [applications corner]. *Signal Processing Magazine, IEEE*, 28(2):100–104.

Alistair Knott, Mick O'Donnell, Jon Oberlander, and Chris Mellish. 1997. Defeasible rules in content selection and text structuring. In *Proceedings of the Sixth European Workshop on Natural Language Generation*, pages 50–60, Duisburg, Germany, March.

Carmen Lacave and Francisco J. Diez. 2000. A review of explanation methods for bayesian networks. *Knowledge Engineering Review*, 17:2002.

Oliver Lemon. 2011. Learning what to say and how to say it: Joint optimisation of spoken dialogue management and natural language generation. *Computer Speech & Language*, 25(2):210–221.

François Mairesse, Milica Gašić, Filip Jurčíček, Simon Keizer, Blaise Thomson, Kai Yu, and Steve Young. 2010. Phrase-based statistical language generation using graphical models and active learning. In *Proceedings of the 48th Annual Meeting of the Association for Computational Linguistics*, pages 1552–1561. Association for Computational Linguistics.

Peter McCullagh and Jie Yang. 2008. How many clusters? *Bayesian Analysis*, 3(1):101–120.

Kathleen McKeown, Shimei Pan, James Shaw, Jordan Desmond, and Barry Allen. 1997. Language generation for multimedia healthcare briefings. In *Proceedings of the Fifth Conference on Applied Natural Language Processing (ANLP-97)*, Washington (DC), USA, April.

Kathleen Rose McKeown. 1985. *Text Generation: Using Discourse Strategies and Focus Constraints to Generate Natural Language Text*. Cambridge University Press, Cambridge, England.

George Miller. 1956. The magical number seven, plus or minus two: Some limits on our capacity for processing information. *The psychological review*, 63:81–97.

Maria Milosavljevic. 1999. *Maximising the Coherence of Descriptions via Comparison*. Ph.D. thesis, Macquarie University, Sydney, Australia.

S. Muggleton and L. D. Raedt. 1994. Inductive logic programming: Theory and methods. *Journal of Logic Programming*, (19/20):629–679.

Alice Oh and A. Rudnicky. 2000. Stochastic language generation for spoken dialogue systems. In *Proceedings of the ANLP/NAACL 2000 Workshop on Conversational Systems*, pages 27–32, Seattle, WA, May.

Sean Owen, Robin Anil, Ted Dunning, and Ellen Friedman. 2011. *Mahout in Action*. Manning Publications Co., Manning Publications Co. 20 Baldwin

Road PO Box 261 Shelter Island, NY 11964, first edition.

Kayur Patel, Naomi Bancroft, Steven M Drucker, James Fogarty, Andrew J Ko, and James Landay. 2010. Gestalt: integrated support for implementation and analysis in machine learning. In *Proceedings of the 23nd annual ACM symposium on User interface software and technology*, pages 37–46. ACM.

Mike Reape and Chris Mellish. 1999. Just what *is* aggregation anyway? In *Proceedings of the European Workshop on Natural Language Generation (EWNLG'99)*, pages 20 – 29, Toulouse, France, May.

Russell D. Reed and Robert J. Marks. 1999. *Neural Smithing: Supervised Learning in Feedforward Artificial Neural Networks*. MIT Press.

Ehud Reiter and Robert Dale. 2000. *Building Natural Language Generation Systems*. Cambridge University Press.

Ehud Reiter, Albert Gatt, François Portet and Marian van der Meulen 2008. The importance of narrative and other lessons from an evaluation of an NLG system that summarises clinical data. In *INLG '08*.

Marko Robnik-Sikonja and Igor Kononenko. 2008. Explaining classifications for individual instances. *IEEE Trans. Knowl. Data Eng.*, 20(5):589–600.

Tjong Kim Sang and Sabine Buchholz. 2000. Introduction to the CoNLL-2000 shared task: Chunking. In *Proceedings of the 2nd workshop on Learning language in logic and the 4th conference on Computational natural language learning, September*, pages 13–14.

Sebastian Varges and Chris Mellish. 2010. Instance-based natural language generation. *Natural Language Engineering*, 16(3):309.

GenNext: A Consolidated Domain Adaptable NLG System

Frank Schilder, Blake Howald and Ravi Kondadadi*
Thomson Reuters, Research & Development
610 Opperman Drive, Eagan, MN 55123
firstname.lastname@thomsonreuters.com

Abstract

We introduce GenNext, an NLG system designed specifically to adapt quickly and easily to different domains. Given a domain corpus of historical texts, GenNext allows the user to generate a template bank organized by semantic concept via derived discourse representation structures in conjunction with general and domain-specific entity tags. Based on various features collected from the training corpus, the system statistically learns template representations and document structure and produces well–formed texts (as evaluated by crowdsourced and expert evaluations). In addition to domain adaptation, GenNext's hybrid approach significantly reduces complexity as compared to traditional NLG systems by relying on templates (consolidating micro-planning and surface realization) and minimizing the need for domain experts. In this description, we provide details of GenNext's theoretical perspective, architecture and evaluations of output.

1 Introduction

NLG systems are typically tailored to very specific domains and tasks such as text summaries from neonatal intensive care units (SUMTIME-NEONATE (Portet et al., 2007)) or offshore oil rig weather reports (SUMTIME-METEO (Reiter et al., 2005)) and require significant investments in development resources (e.g. people, time, etc.). For example, for SUMTIME-METEO, 12 person months were required for two of the system components alone (Belz, 2007). Given the subject matter of such systems, the investment is perfectly reasonable. However, if the domains to be generated are comparatively more general, such as financial reports or biographies, then the scaling of development costs becomes a concern in NLG.

NLG in the editorial process for companies and institutions where content can vary must be domain adaptable. Spending a year or more of development time to produce high quality market summaries, for example, is not a viable solution if it is necessary to start from scratch to produce other reports. GenNext, a hybrid system that statistically learns document and sentence template representations from existing historical data, is developed to be consolidated and domain adaptable. In particular, GenNext reduces complexity by avoiding the necessity of having a separate document planner, surface realizer, etc., and extensive expert involvement at the outset of system development.

Section 2 describes the theoretical background, architecture and implementation of GenNext. Section 3 discusses the results of a non–expert and expert crowdsourced sentence preference evaluation task. Section 4 concludes with several future experiments for system improvement.

2 Architecture of GenNext

In general, NLG systems follow a prototypical architecture where some input data from a given domain is sent to a "document planner" which decides content and structuring to create a document plan. That document plan serves as an input to a "micro planner" where the content is converted into a syntactic expression (with associated considerations of *aggregation* and *referring expression generation*) and a text specification is created. The text specification then goes through the final stage of "surface realization" where everything is put together into an output text (McKeown, 1985; Reiter and Dale, 2000; Bateman and Zock, 2003).

In contrast, the architecture of GenNext (summarized in Figure 1) is driven by a domain-specific

*Ravi Kondadadi is now affiliated with Nuance Communications, Inc.

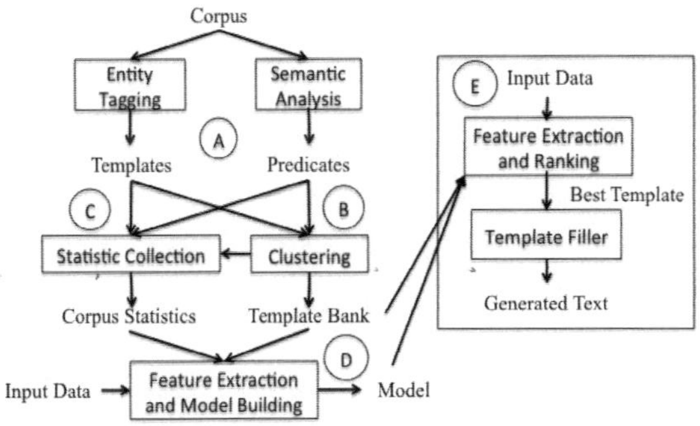

Figure 1: GenNext System Architecture.

corpus text. There is often a structured database underlying the domains of corpus text, the fields of which are used for domain specific entity tagging (in addition to domain general entity tagging [e.g. DATE, LOCATION, etc.]). An overview of the different stages, which are a combination of statistical (e.g., Langkilde and Knight (1998)) and template–based (e.g., van Deemter, et al. (2005)) approaches, follows in (A-E).[1]

A: Semantic Representation - We take a domain specific training corpus and reduce each sentence to a Discourse Representation Structure (DRS) - formal semantic representations of sentences (and texts) from Discourse Representation Theory (Kamp and Reyle, 1993; Basile and Bos, 2011). Each DRS is a combination of domain general named entities, predicates (content words) and relational elements (function words). In parallel, domain specific named entity tags are identified and are used to create templates that syntactically represent some conceptual meaning; for example, the short *biography* in (1):

(1) *Sentence*
a. Mr. Mitsutaka Kambe has been serving as Managing Director of the 77 Bank, Ltd. since June 27, 2008.
b. He holds a Bachelor's in finance from USC and a MBA from UCLA.

Conceptual Meaning
c. SERVING | MANAGING | DIRECTOR | PERSON | ...
d. HOLDS | BACHELOR | FINANCE | MBA | HOLD | ...

Once the semantic representations are created, they are organized and identified by semantic concept ("CuId") (described in (B)). Our assumption is that each cluster equates with a CuId represented by each individual sentence in the cluster and is contrastive with other CuIds (for similar approaches, see Barzilay and Lapata (2005), Angeli, et al. (2010) and Lu and Ng (2011)).

[1]For more detail see Howald, et al. (2013) - semantic clustering and micro-planning and Kondadadi, et al. (2013) - document planning.

B: Creating Conceptual Units - To create the CuIds (a semi-automatic process), we cluster the sentences using k-means clustering with k set arbitrarily high to over-generate (Witten and Frank, 2005). This facilitates manual verification of the generated clusters to merge (rather than split) them if necessary. We assign a unique CuId to each cluster and associate each template in the corpus to a corresponding CuId. For example, in (2), using the sentences in (1a-b), the identified named entities are assigned to a clustered CuId (2a-b) and then each sentence in the training corpus is reduced to a template (2c-d).

(2) *Content Mapping*
a. $\{CuId : 000\}$ – *Information*: **person**: Mr. Mitsutaka Kambe; **title**: Managing Director; **company**: 77 Bank, Ltd.; **date**: June 27, 2008
b. $\{CuId : 001\}$ – *Information*: **person**: he; **degree**: Bachelor's, MBA; **subject**: finance; **institution**: USC; UCLA

Templates
c. $\{CuId : 000\}$: **[person]** has been serving as **[title]** of the **[company]** since **[date]**.
d. $\{CuId : 001\}$: **[person]** holds a **[degree]** in **[subject]** from **[institution]** and a **[degree]** from **[institution]**.

At this stage, we will have a set of CuIds with corresponding template collections which represent the entire "micro-planning" aspect of our system.

C: Collecting Statistics - For the "document planning" stage, we collect a number of statistics for each domain, for example:

- Frequency distribution of CuIds by position
- Frequency distribution of templates by position
- Frequency distribution of entity sequence
- Average number of entities by CuId and position

These statistics, in addition to entity tags and templates, are used in building different features used by the ranking model (D).

D: Building a Ranking Model - The core component of our system is a statistical model that ranks a set of templates for a given position (e.g. sentence 1, sentence 2, ..., sentence n) based on the input data (*see also* Konstas and Lapata (2012). The learning task is to find the rank for all the templates from all CuIds at each position. To generate the training data, we first exclude the templates that have named entities not specified in the input data (ensuring completeness). We then rank templates according to the edit distance (Levenshtein,

1966) from the template corresponding to the current sentence in the training document. For each template, we build a ranking model with features, for example:

- Prior template and CuId
- Difference in number of words given position
- Most likely CuId given position and previous CuId
- Template 1-3grams given position and CuId

We use a linear kernel for a ranking SVM (Joachims, 2002) to learn the weights associated with each feature. Each domain has its own model that is used when generating texts (E).

E: Generation: At generation time, our system has a set of input data, a semantically organized template bank and a model from training on a given domain of texts. For each sentence, we first exclude those templates that contain a named entity not present in the input data. Then we calculate the feature values times the model weight for each of the remaining templates. The template with the highest score is selected, filled with matching entities from the input data and appended to the generated text. Example generations for each domain are included in (3).

(3) *Financial*
a. First quarter profit per share for Brown-Forman Corporation expected to be $0.91 per share by analysts.
b. Brown-Forman Corporation July first quarter profits will be below that previously estimated by Wall Street with a range between $0.89 and $0.93 per share and a projected mean per share of $0.91 per share.
c. The consensus recommendation is Hold.

Biography
d. Mr. Satomi Mitsuzaki has been serving as Managing Director of Mizuho Bank since June 27, 2008.
e. He was previously Director of Regional Compliance of Kyoto Branch.
f. He is a former Managing Executive Officer and Chief Executive Officer of new Industrial Finance Business Group in Mitsubishi Corporation.

Weather
g. Complex low from southern Norway will drift slowly NNE to the Lofoten Islands by early tomorrow.
h. A ridge will persist to the west of British Isles for Saturday with a series of weak fronts moving east across the North Sea.
i. A front will move ENE across the northern North Sea Saturday.

3 Evaluation and Discussion

We have tested GenNext on three domains: Corporate Officer and Director Biographies (1150 texts ranging from 3-10 period ended sentences), Financial Texts (Mutual Fund Performances [162 texts, 2-4 sentences] and Broker Recommendations [905 texts, 8-20 sentences]), and Offshore Oil Rig Weather Reports (1054 texts, 2-6 sentences) from SUMTIME-METEO (Reiter et al., 2005). The total number of templates for the *financial* domain is 1379 distributed across 38 different semantic concepts; 2836 templates across 19 concepts for *biography*; and 2749 templates across 9 concepts for *weather* texts.

We have conducted several evaluation experiments comparing two versions of GenNext, one applying the ranking model (*rank*) and one with random selection of templates (*non-rank*) (both systems use the same template bank, CuId assignment and filtering) and the original texts from which the data was extracted (*original*).

We used a combination of automatic (e.g. BLEU–4 (Papineni et al., 2002), METEOR (Denkowski and Lavie, 2011)) and human metrics (using crowdsourcing) to evaluate the output (*see generally*, Belz and Reiter (2006). However, in the interest of space, we will restrict the discussion to a human judgment task on output *preferences*. We found this evaluation task to be most informative for system improvement. The task asks an evaluator to provide a binary preference determination (100 sentence pairs/domain): "Do you prefer Sentence A (from *original*) or the corresponding Sentence B (from *rank* or *non-rank*)". This task was performed for each domain.[2] We also engaged 3 experts from the financial and 4 from the biography domains to perform the same preference task (average agreement was 76.22) as well as provide targeted feedback.

For the preference results, summarized in Figure 2, we would like to see no statistically significant difference between GenNext-*rank* and *original*, but statistically significant differences between GenNext-*rank* and GenNext-*non-rank*, and *original* and GenNext-*non-rank*. If this is the case, then GenNext-*rank* is producing texts similar to the *original* texts, and is providing an observable improvement over not including the model at all (GenNext-*non-rank*). This is exactly what we see for all domains.[3] However, in general, there

[2]Over 100 native English speakers contributed, each one restricted to providing no more than 50 responses and only after they successfully answered 4 initial gold data questions correctly and continued to answer periodic gold data questions. The pair orderings were randomized to prevent click bias. 8 judgments per sentence pair was collected (2400 judgments) and average agreement was 75.87.

[3]*Original* vs. GenNext-*rank* : *financial* - χ^2=.29, $p\leq$.59; *biography* - χ^2=3.01, $p\leq$.047; *weather* - χ^2=.95, $p\leq$.32. *Original* vs. GenNext-*non-rank* : *financial* - χ^2=16.71, $p\leq$.0001; *biography* - χ^2=45.43, $p\leq$.0001; *weather* -

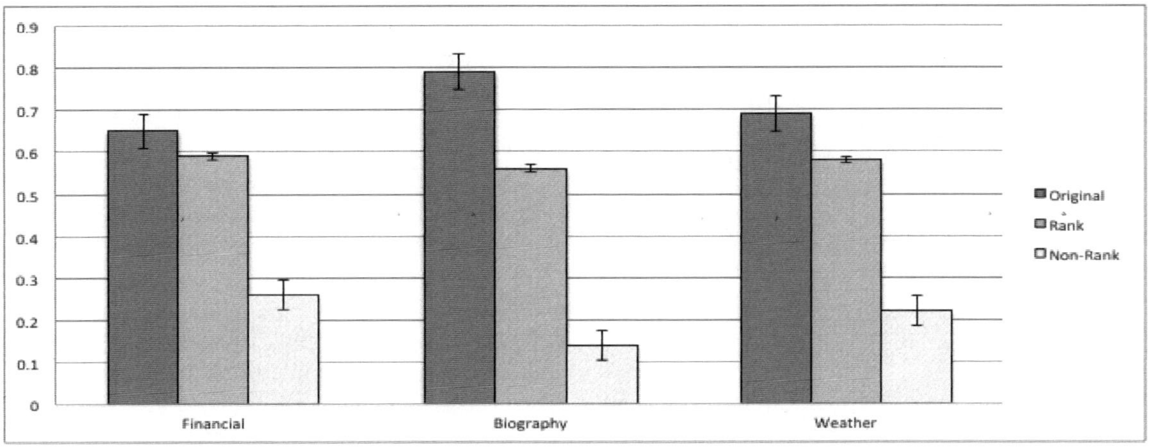

Figure 2: Cross-Domain Non-Expert Preference Evaluations.

is a greater difference between the *original* and GenNext-*rank biographies* compared to the *financial* and *weather* texts. We take it as a goal to approach, as close as possible, the preferences for the *original* texts.

The original *financial* documents were machine generated from a different existing system. As such, it is not surprising to see similarity in performance compared to GenNext-*rank* and potentially explains why preferences for the originals is somewhat low (assuming a higher preference rating for well-formed human texts). Further, the original *weather* documents are highly technical and not easily understood by the lay person, so, again, it is not surprising to see similar performance. *Biographies* were human generated and easy to understand for the average reader. Here, both GenNext-*rank* and GenNext-*non-rank* have some ground to make up. Insights from domain experts are potentially helpful in this regard.

Expert evaluations provided similar results and agreements compared to the non–expert crowd. Most beneficial about the expert evaluations was the discussion of integrating certain editorial standards into the system. For example, shorter texts were preferred to longer texts in the *financial* domain, but not the *biographies*. Consequently, we could adjust weights to favor shorter templates. Also, in *biographies*, sentences with subordinated elaborations were not preferred because these contained subjective comments (e.g. *a leader in industry*, *a well respected individual*, etc.). Here, we could manually curate or could automatically detect templates with subordinated clauses and remove them. These types of comments are useful to adjust the system accordingly to end user expectations.

χ^2=24.27, $p \leq .0001$. GenNext-*rank* vs. GenNext-*non-rank* : *financial* - χ^2=12.81, $p \leq .0003$; *biography* - χ^2=25.19, $p \leq .0001$; *weather* - χ^2=16.19, $p \leq .0001$.

4 Conclusion and Future Work

We have presented our system GenNext which is domain adaptable, given adequate historical data, and has a significantly reduced complexity compared to other NLG systems (*see generally*, Robin and McKeown (1996)). To the latter point, development time for semantically processing the corpus, applying domain general and specific tags, and building a model is accomplished in days and weeks as opposed to months and years.

Future experimentation will focus on being able to automatically extract templates for different domains to create preset banks of templates in the absence of adequate historical data. We are also looking into different ways to increase the variability of output texts from selecting templates within a range of top scores (rather than just the highest score) to providing additional generated information from input data analytics.

Acknowledgments

This research is made possible by Thomson Reuters Global Resources (TRGR) with particular thanks to Peter Pircher, Jaclyn Sprtel and Ben Hachey for significant support. Thank you also to Khalid Al-Kofahi for encouragement, Leszek Michalak and Andrew Lipstein for expert evaluations and three anonymous reviewers for constructive feedback.

References

Gabor Angeli, Percy Liang, and Dan Klein. 2012. A simple domain-independent probabilistic approach to generation. In *Proceedings of the 2010 Conference on Empirical Methods for Natural Language Processing (EMNLP 2010)*, pages 502–512.

Regina Barzilay and Mirella Lapata. 2005. Collective content selection for concept-to-text generation. In *Proceedings of the 2005 Conference on Empirical Methods for Natural Language Processing (EMNLP 2005)*, pages 331–338.

Valerio Basile and Johan Bos. 2011. Towards generating text from discourse representation structures. In *Proceedings of the 13th European Workshop on Natural Language Generation (ENLG)*, pages 145–150.

John Bateman and Michael Zock. 2003. Natural language generation. In R. Mitkov, editor, *Oxford Handbook of Computational Linguistics*, Research in Computational Semantics, pages 284–304. Oxford University Press, Oxford.

Anja Belz and Ehud Reiter. 2006. Comparing automatic and human evaluation of NLG systems. In *Proceedings of the European Association for Computational Linguistics (EACL'06)*, pages 313–320.

Anja Belz. 2007. Probabilistic generation of weather forecast texts. In *Proceedings of Human Language Technologies 2007: The Annual Conference of the North American Chapter of the Association for Computational Linguistics (NAACL-HLT'07)*, pages 164–171.

Michael Denkowski and Alon Lavie. 2011. Meteor 1.3: Automatic metric for reliable optimization and evaluation of machine translation systems. In *Proceedings of the EMNLP 2011 Workshop on Statistical Machine Translation*, pages 85–91.

Blake Howald, Ravi Kondadadi, and Frank Schilder. 2013. Domain adaptable semantic clustering in statistical NLG. In *Proceedings of the 10th International Conference on Computational Semantics (IWCS 2013)*, pages 143–154. Association for Computational Linguistics, March.

Thorsten Joachims. 2002. *Learning to Classify Text Using Support Vector Machines*. Kluwer.

Hans Kamp and Uwe Reyle. 1993. *From Discourse to Logic; An Introduction to Modeltheoretic Semantics of Natural Language, Formal Logic and DRT.* Kluwer, Dordrecht.

Ravi Kondadadi, Blake Howald, and Frank Schilder. 2013. A statistical NLG framework for aggregated planning and realization. In *Proceedings of the Annual Conference for the Association of Computational Linguistics (ACL 2013)*. Association for Computational Linguistics.

Ioannis Konstas and Mirella Lapata. 2012. Concept-to-text generation via discriminative reranking. In *Proceedings of the 50th Annual Meeting of the Association for Computational Linguistics*, pages 369–378.

Irene Langkilde and Kevin Knight. 1998. Generation that exploits corpus-based statistical knowledge. In *Proceedings of the 36th Annual Meeting of the Association for Computational Linguistics (ACL'98)*, pages 704–710.

Vladimir Levenshtein. 1966. Binary codes capable of correcting deletions, insertions, and reversals. *Soviet Physics Doklady*, 10:707–710.

Wei Lu and Hwee Tou Ng. 2011. A probabilistic forest-to-string model for language generation from typed lambda calculus expressions. In *Proceedings of the 2011 Conference on Empirical Methods for Natural Language Processing (EMNLP 2011)*, pages 1611–1622.

Kathleen R. McKeown. 1985. *Text Generation: Using Discourse Strategies and Focus Constraints to Generate Natural Language Text.* Cambridge University Press.

Kishore Papineni, Slim Roukos, Todd Ward, and Wei-Jing Zhu. 2002. BLEU: A method for automatic evaluation of machine translation. In *Proceedings of the 40th Annual Meeting of the Association for Computational Linguistics (ACL'02)*, pages 311–318.

Franois Portet, Ehud Reiter, Jim Hunter, and Somayajulu Sripada. 2007. Automatic generation of textual summaries from neonatal intensive care data. In *In Proccedings of the 11th Conference on Artificial Intelligence in Medicine (AIME 07). LNCS*, pages 227–236.

Ehud Reiter and Robert Dale. 2000. *Building Natural Language Generation Systems.* Cambridge University Press.

Ehud Reiter, Somayajulu Sripada, Jim Hunter, and Jin Yu. 2005. Choosing words in computer-generated weather forecasts. *Artificial Intelligence*, 167:137–169.

Jacques Robin and Kathy McKeown. 1996. Empirically designing and evaluating a new revision-based model for summary generation. *Artificial Intelligence*, 85(1-2).

Kees van Deemter, Mariët Theune, and Emiel Krahmer. 2005. Real *vs.* template-based natural language generation: a false opposition? *Computational Linguistics*, 31(1):15–24.

Ian Witten and Eibe Frank. 2005. *Data Mining: Practical Machine Learning Techniques with Java Implementation (2nd Ed.).* Morgan Kaufmann, San Francisco, CA.

Adapting SimpleNLG for bilingual English-French realisation

Pierre-Luc Vaudry and Guy Lapalme
RALI-DIRO – Université de Montréal
C.P. 6128, Succ. Centre-Ville
Montréal, Québec, Canada, H3C 3J8
{vaudrypl,lapalme}@iro.umontreal.ca

Abstract

This paper describes SimpleNLG-EnFr, an adaption of the English realisation engine SimpleNLG (Gatt and Reiter, 2009) for bilingual English-French realisation. Grammatical similarities between English and French that could be exploited and specifics of French that needed adaptation are discussed.

1 Introduction

Surface realisation is the last step in natural language generation. It takes as input an abstract representation where lexical units and syntactic structures have been determined. Its output is formatted natural language text. SimpleNLG, as described in Gatt and Reiter (2009), is a realisation engine for English in the form of a Java library. It handles inflection, derivation, word order, auxiliaries, agreement, pronominalisation, punctuation, spacing, etc. This paper describes SimpleNLG-EnFr 1.1[1], a bilingual realisation engine for English and French derived from SimpleNLG 4.2, and explains the design choices and the challenges encountered. Grammatical similarities and differences between English and French that influenced the design are discussed. The current version of SimpleNLG is 4.4, but all mentions of SimpleNLG in this paper refer to version 4.2.

2 Subset of French covered

The English grammatical coverage of SimpleNLG-EnFr is the same as that of SimpleNLG 4.2. Its French grammatical coverage is equivalent to its English one.

Le français fondamental (1er Degré) (Ministère de l'Éducation nationale, 1959) was used as a reference for French grammatical coverage. That document results from empirical studies and aims at describing the essential notions for teaching French as a foreign language. Almost all of the grammar points enumerated in this document are covered by SimpleNLG-EnFr. The detailed French grammar rules used in the implementation come mainly from Grevisse (1993) and Mansouri (1996).

SimpleNLG-EnFr has a 3871 entry default French lexicon covering *L'échelle Dubois-Buyse d'orthographe usuelle française* (Ters et al., 1964). It contains the most important and commonly used French vocabulary (including function words), so as not to interfere with a particular application domain vocabulary. A domain specific lexicon can easily be added as SimpleNLG supports using multiple lexicons. Most of the inflected forms in the default French lexicon were taken from Morphalou 2.0 (CNRTL).

3 SimpleNLG parts pooled for English and French

Most of the basic framework, which defined the class hierarchy covering lexical units, phrases and document elements such as paragraphs, could be kept in common for both English and French. Some shared grammar rules and principles were put in abstract classes from which language-specific modules could be derived. The other grammar rules were rewritten for French, with the corresponding English ones serving as references. Many static methods in the English modules in SimpleNLG were changed to regular instance methods in order to be able to override them in the new subclasses.

[1] Available online, along with the source code, at `http://www-etud.iro.umontreal.ca/~vaudrypl/snlgbil/snlgEnFr_english.html`

3.1 General characteristics

Features: SimpleNLG uses a system of features for various functions: encoding morphological and syntactic properties of lexical units; letting the user set the parameters of a particular phrase (plural, verb tenses, etc.); and internally keeping track of the content of a phrase and various information needed during realisation. This system is generic enough to be used for other languages. Most features are reusable and others can be added as needed. In SimpleNLG-EnFr, most of the already present features were reused for French.

Lexicon: In SimpleNLG, the lexicon is already relatively well separated from the grammar. The basic lexicon class provides an interface to a simple XML file containing the necessary information about the lexical units. The list of available fields in this file can easily be extended by adding lexical features to the ones used for English. In SimpleNLG-EnFr, many lexical features were added mainly to account for the higher complexity of French morphology.

3.2 Syntax

Verb phrase and clause: First, English and French have the same basic clause constituent order: Subject-Verb-Object (SVO). Even more importantly for SimpleNLG-EnFr, this constituent order is relatively stable (compared with other languages like German or Russian), at least for the purpose of practical NLG applications. This frees us in most cases from having to choose between different syntactically correct word orders. We thus did not have to make such big changes to the syntactic representation as were needed in adapting SimpleNLG to German (Bollmann, 2011). Indeed, in German the subject has the same syntactic status in the clause than the object(s) and they can all occupy the same varying positions relative to the verb. However, Bollmann (2011) had more leeway because he had decided not to keep the English grammar alongside the German one in his implementation. In contrast, in SimpleNLG-EnFr we wanted to be able to change freely between English and French grammars during the generation of a single text.

English and French also have a very similar passive construction. In French, it is used less frequently because other options exist to avoid mentioning the subject of a sentence (for example, using the indefinite personal pronoun *on*), but choosing between those constructions is not the role of the realisation engine.

Noun phrase: English and French can both have a determiner at the beginning of a noun phrase.

Prepositional phrase: Both languages use prepositions (not postpositions) for introducing various complements.

Coordinated phrase: Both have a coordination conjunction in penultimate position and both use commas as separators between coordinates.

3.3 Morphology

In both languages, nouns and verbs are marked morphologically for singular/plural. In addition, personal pronoun forms differ based not only on number and person, but also on grammatical function and gender. This last similarity facilitated adapting pronominalisation.

4 Adaptations for French

The rules for each processing level are encoded in separate modules for each language. The following adaptations were made for French by adding syntactic and lexical features and encoding the corresponding rules in the French versions of the grammar rules modules.

4.1 Syntax

Verb phrase and clause: French negation has some similarities but also big differences with its English counterpart. It is usually expressed with not one but two adverbs (*ne* and *pas*), which come respectively before and after the first word of the verb group, as in example (1). Moreover, *pas* can be replaced by other negation auxiliaries to specify a different kind of negation, as in (2). Finally, no negation auxiliary is used (only *ne*) when the sentence already carries another negative element, for example a negative indefinite pronoun as in (3).

(1) *il ne parle pas*
"he does not speak"

(2) *il ne parle plus*
he not speaks more
"he does not speak anymore"

(3) *personne ne parle*
nobody not speaks
"nobody speaks"

In French, some complement pronouns, instead of being placed after the verb as in the regular SVO word order, are placed just before it. Furthermore, some of them sometimes take in that case a different form. The rules governing the acceptable combinations and sequencings of those complements that can be cliticised in this way are very precise. Examples (4) and (5) illustrate this phenomenon.

(4) *il la leur réfère*
he her them refers
"he refers her to them"

(5) *il nous réfère à eux*
he us refers to them
"he refers us to them"

The complexity of French past participle agreement is well known, particularly because it manifests itself mostly in written French. French verbs can have *être* (to be) or *avoir* (to have) as auxiliaries in compound tenses. This influences whether the past participle agrees with the subject (*être*) or the direct object if it is placed before the past participle (*avoir*). Combined with clitic complement pronouns and relative clauses, among others, it can get very complex. In addition, French past participles are inflected in gender and number, like adjectives.

Noun phrase: In SimpleNLG, a noun phrase can have pre-modifiers and post-modifiers. Adjectives are by default considered pre-modifiers and everything else post-modifiers. In contrast, in French, most adjectives are placed after the noun, but some (the most common) are most frequently placed before the noun. In SimpleNLG-EnFr this is achieved by referring to an extra lexical feature.

In addition, in French the determiner and adjectives agree with the noun in number and gender. Instead of adding a new mechanism to propagate relevant features of the noun phrase to where they are needed, as with subject-verb agreement in SimpleNLG, the solution implemented was to let the determiner and adjectives get themselves the information they needed from their parent constituent. This more flexible way of managing agreement is more amenable to multilingual realisation.

Interrogative clause: A simple way of building an interrogative sentence in French is to prepend the expression *est-ce que* (is it that), like in (6). This is what we chose.

(6) *est-ce que tu as mangé?*
is it that you have eaten?
"did you eat?"

This kind of interrogative clause can be built in part by using the relative clause rules (see below).

Relative clause: A mechanism for building relative clauses has been added to the French part of SimpleNLG-EnFr that has no direct equivalent in the English implementation. The phrase that must be replaced by a relative pronoun is specified by setting a feature on the clause. This phrase will not appear in the realised clause. Even if this phrase was not present in the clause, it will still be used to choose a relative pronoun, which can be useful. The grammatical function of that phrase can in that case be set manually.

The resulting relative pronoun takes the place that is normally reserved for the complementiser. Its form is chosen according to two sources: the grammatical function and preposition, if any, of the phrase it replaces; and the person and gender of its antecedent (the noun or pronoun that the relative clause modifies). Examples (7), (8) and (9) illustrate this.

(7) *la tarte que tu as mangée*
the pie that.obj you have eaten.fem
"the pie that you ate"

(8) *la tarte qui a été mangée*
the pie that.subj has been eaten.fem
"the pie that was eaten"

(9) *l'homme dont j'ai mangé la tarte*
the man whose I have eaten the pie
"the man whose pie I ate"

4.2 Morphology

Number and gender: French determiners and adjectives must be inflected in number and gender. Additionally, number and gender interact with each other in the inflection process.

Verb tenses: Verb inflected forms are more varied in French than in English. In addition, French verbs are classified in three conjugation groups. The first group is comprised of the regular verbs. The third group is a catchall category for miscellaneous irregular verbs. Several morphological rules govern the combination of the verb inflection morphemes.

Detached form of personal pronouns: In French, personal pronouns are often cliticised (see subsection 5.1), but where they are not, they take a different form, which is called *forme disjointe* (detached form). See *leur* versus *eux* in examples (4) and (5).

4.3 Morphophonology

The morphophonological level is a new processing level introduced in SimpleNLG-EnFr to account for a range of phenomena very common in French and other languages. They are best described using rules that use both morphological and phonological conditions. The only obvious example of this kind of rule in written English, which was included in the morphology module in SimpleNLG, is illustrated by examples (10) and (11).

(10) a + book → a book

(11) a + apple → **an** apple

Here the morphological condition is the presence of the indefinite singular determiner *a* and the phonological one is the presence of a vowel at the beginning of the next word.

The morphology rules operate on one word at a time. The morphophonology rules may need to have access to adjacent words and to be applied after all inflection and derivation rules have been applied. This justifies a separate processing level. In SimpleNLG-EnFr, the morphophonological level is used mainly for external sandhi, i.e. phenomena occurring at word boundaries.

Elision: In French some words have their last vowel elided when in front of a word beginning by a vowel or a so-called *h aspiré* (aspired h). Indeed, an extra lexical feature is needed for French words beginning with the letter *h* to know if that kind of rule applies. Note that the letter *h* itself is never pronounced in French. Examples (12) and (13) illustrate elision, while it does not occur in (14).

(12) *la* + *amitié* → *l'amitié*
the friendship

(13) *le* + *homme* → *l'homme*
the man

(14) *la* + *honte* → *la honte*
the shame

Liaison: *Liaison* is a phenomenon akin to elision, except that it involves adding and/or replacing phonemes. Its "goal" is to avoid contact between the vowel at the end of some words and the beginning vowel of the next word. It is mostly apparent in speech, although it sometimes has an effect in written French, as in (15).

(15) *le* + *beau* + *homme* → *le bel homme*
the handsome man

Prepositions: Some prepositions interact with definite determiners in French, as in (16).

(16) *à* + *le* → *au*
at the

5 Bilingual generation

Building a bilingual realisation engine rather than just adapting SimpleNLG for unilingual French realisation was a design choice dictated mainly by practical considerations. Being able to use the same realisation engine (and thus the same API) for several or all target languages when developing a multilingual NLG application is convenient. In the case of English and French, this could be most useful when targeting Canadian or European populations, for example.

In SimpleNLG-EnFr, bilingual generation is implemented by being able to determine dynamically the language of each processing unit: phrases for the syntax module, lexical units for the morphology module, etc. The factories used by the library's user to create syntactic structure specifications and access or create lexical units each use a language-specific lexicon. Each processing module then chooses at realisation time which set of rules to apply to a given processing unit based on the language of its lexicon. Thus, sentences, phrases and words of different languages can be mixed freely.

6 Conclusion

A bilingual realisation engine for English and French was built. It took five months to complete, including the writing of a detailed French manual. Despite many internal changes, it retains almost the same API as the original.

Future improvements could include enlarging the default lexicon and adding specialised lexicons for French, implementing a complete textual representation for numbers, and adapting the changes in SimpleNLG since version 4.2, like the XML realiser.

More languages could be added to SimpleNLG-EnFr. However, it would perhaps be easier to include many languages if the grammar of each language could be specified in a common grammar formalism, instead of programmatically in the processing modules themselves. This would necessitate changing the architecture.

In the process of developing SimpleNLG-EnFr, a great deal was learned about what kind of challenges multilingual realisation poses. A common grammatical ground must be found and exploited for the group of languages considered, which should not be too far apart in that respect. For the rest, care must be taken not to make too many assumptions about the inner workings of the grammar of each language. Indeed, every language has its own grammatical peculiarities.

Acknowledgments

We would like to thank the SimpleNLG team for having made available its source code. This work was supported by two Undergraduate Student Research Awards (USRA) from the Natural Sciences and Engineering Research Council of Canada (NSERC).

References

Marcel Bollmann. 2011. Adapting SimpleNLG to German. In *Proceedings of the 13th European Workshop on Natural Language Generation (ENLG 2011)*, pages 133-138.

CNRTL. *CNRTL : Centre National de Ressources Textuelles et Lexicales – Morphalou,* button *Télécharger Morphalou 2.0*, [http://www.cnrtl.fr/lexiques/morphalou/] (consulted on 14 July 2011).

Albert Gatt and Ehud Reiter. 2009. SimpleNLG: A realisation engine for practical applications. In *Proceedings of the 12th European Workshop on Natural Language Generation (ENLG 2009)*, pages 90-93.

Maurice Grevisse, (1993). *Le bon usage, grammaire française,* 12e édition refondue par André Goosse, 8e tirage, Éditions Duculot, Louvain-la-Neuve, Belgique.

Mohammed Issaoui Mansouri, (1996). *Le Mansouris, tous les verbes usuels entièrement conjugués et orthographiés*. CAPT, Éditeurs, Montréal, Canada.

Ministère de l'Éducation nationale, Direction de la Coopération avec la Communauté et l'Étranger (France) (1959). *Le français fondamental (1er Degré)*, Publication de l'Institut Pédagogique National, Paris, France.

François Ters, Daniel Reichenbach and Georges Mayer. (1964). *L'échelle Dubois-Buyse d'orthographe usuelle française*. Messeiller.

A Case Study Towards Turkish Paraphrase Alignment

Seniz Demir **İlknur Durgar El-Kahlout** **Erdem Unal**
TUBITAK-BILGEM
Gebze, Kocaeli, TURKEY
{seniz.demir,ilknur.durgar,erdem.unal}@tubitak.gov.tr

Abstract

Paraphrasing is expressing the same semantic content using different linguistic means. Although previous work has addressed linguistic variations at different levels of language, paraphrasing in Turkish has not been yet thoroughly studied. This paper presents the first study towards Turkish paraphrase alignment. We perform an analysis of different types of paraphrases on a modest Turkish paraphrase corpus and present preliminary results on that analysis from different standpoints. We also explore the impact of human interpretation of paraphrasing on the alignment of paraphrase sentence pairs.

1 Introduction

Paraphrases are alternative linguistic expressions that convey the same content. Natural languages allow linguistic variations at different levels (e.g., lexical and phrasal) and a change at a level of language may trigger other changes at different levels. Paraphrasing has attracted a growing interest from the research community in a broad range of tasks such as language generation (Power and Scott, 2005), machine translation (Callison-Burch et al., 2006), and question answering (France et al., 2003). Moreover, research on acquisition (Max et al., 2012), generation (Zhao et al., 2010), and recognition (Qiu et al., 2006) of paraphrases has been on the rise for the last decade. Paraphrasing is also an increasingly studied problem by the generation community. One particular text-to-text generation problem being addressed is the generation of sentence-level paraphrases by converting a sentence into a new one with approximately the same meaning (Wubben et al., 2010).

One aspect of paraphrasing is the specification of paraphrase types via a typology. Building paraphrase typologies from different perspectives (e.g., linguistics analysis and discourse analysis) has been an active research area for a number of years now (Vila et al., 2011). In particular, linguistic grounds govern the typologies built by language processing systems (Kozlowski et al., 2003) which are often very generic or system specific.

Research on paraphrase alignment focuses on identifying links between semantically related word strings. Such monolingual alignments can be later used as training data for several natural language processing approaches (e.g., textual entailment and multidocument summarization) (Thadani et al., 2012). Although a wealth amount of research has studied various problems related to Turkish, we here focus on a problem which has not been studied earlier. We present our initial explorations on Turkish paraphrase alignment by considering how alignment is affected by human interpretation of paraphrasing. We conducted a study on a modest corpus from four different sources to investigate answers to the following questions: i) What are the types of paraphrases that can be observed at different levels of Turkish? ii) Do humans agree on the existence of paraphrasing between Turkish paraphrase sentences? iii) How does human interpretation of paraphrasing affect the alignment of paraphrase sentences?

Our study is unique in that it presents a generic typology of paraphrase types found in our Turkish paraphrase corpus and discusses the agreement of human annotators on the identification and classification of observed correspondences between paraphrases. This study also presents our aggregated observations on the relation between interpretation and alignment of paraphrase casts.

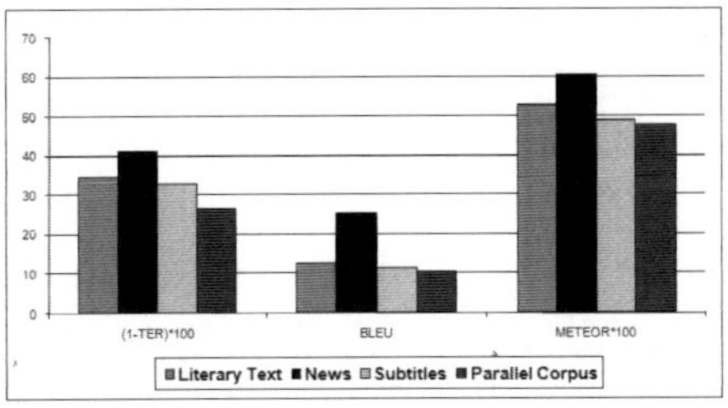

Figure 1: Sentence similarity scores of the corpus.

	Literary Text	News Articles	Subtitles	Parallel Corpus
# Tokens	1879	3379	1632	1581
# Unique Tokens	811	1473	824	609
# Shared Tokens	519	1125	402	354
Lexical Overlap	72.5	82.9	63.2	62.7
Lexical Overlap (lem. cont. words)	68.4	67.2	48.6	45

Table 1: Characteristics of the selected 400 pairs.

2 Paraphrase Corpora

The Turkish paraphrase corpus (Demir et al., 2012) comprises 1270 paraphrase pairs from four different sources: i) translations of a literary text, ii) multiple reference translations of English tourism-related sentences, iii) news articles, and iv) subtitles of a movie. We measured sentence similarities of all paraphrase pairs from each domain via three measures typically used in statistical machine translation evaluations: TER (Matthew Snover, 2006), BLEU (Papineni et al., 2002), and METEOR (Lavie and Agarwal, 2007). As shown in Figure 1, the ordering of domains with respect to all metrics are the same where the pairs from the news domain and those from the parallel corpus are the most and the least similar pairs respectively. Since there are divergences across different domains, we randomly drew from each domain an equal number of sentences (i.e., 100 paraphrase pairs[1]). Some characteristic features of the paraphrase pairs selected for this study are shown in Table 1.

3 Paraphrase Typology

To our best knowledge, a Turkish paraphrase typology that we can apply to this study does not yet exist in the literature. On the other hand, building a comprehensive typology is not one of our objectives. There are a number of available typologies built for English (Dras, 1999; Vila et al., 2011). Since our focus in this work is on characterizing paraphrasing at different levels of language, we greatly drew from the linguistically-motivated typology by Vila et al. (2011) while building our generic typology. We examined the selected 400 paraphrase pairs and constructed a typology that covers all paraphrases occurring within these pairs. Our typology covers three levels of language and consists of four classes.

The **lexical class** covers all changes that arise from exchanging words within a phrase with other words and includes four subclasses (i.e., substitution, substitution with opposite polarity, deletion, and pronominalization)[2]:

(1) "Su bize takip edebileceğimiz hiçbir$_1$ iz$_1$ bırakmıyor$_1$." (Water leaves$_1$ no$_1$ trace$_1$ that we can follow.)

(2) "Su olayın takip edilebilecek bütün$_1$ izlerini$_1$ yok$_1$ ediyor$_1$." (The water destroys$_1$ all$_1$ traces$_1$ of the event that can be followed.)

The **morphological class** covers inflectional and derivational changes within words and includes two subclasses (i.e., inflectional changes and derivational changes):

(1) "Böyle bir ilaç almaktansa hasta$_1$ kalmak$_1$ iyidir." (Staying$_1$ sick$_1$ is better than taking such a drug.)

(2) "Hasta$_1$ kalırım$_1$ da yine de bu ilacı içmem."(I$_1$ stay$_1$ sick$_1$ still I don't take this drug.)

The **phrasal class** includes changes that arise from exchanging fragments with same meaning:

1) "Bunları biliyorum fakat emri ben$_1$ vermedim$_1$." (I know all that, but I$_1$ did$_1$ not$_1$ give$_1$ the order.)

(2) "Bunları biliyorum ama, emri veren$_1$ ben$_1$ değilim$_1$." (I know all that, but I'm$_1$ not$_1$ the$_1$ one$_1$ who$_1$ gave$_1$ the order.)

The **other class** is for all other changes that imply different lexicalizations for the same contextual meaning:

(1) "Savaş çıkınca pek çok çingene eskilerdeki gibi kötü$_1$ kişiler$_1$ oldular$_1$." (When war broke out, many gypsies became$_1$ just$_1$ as bad$_1$ people$_1$ as those of the past.)

(2) "Savaşta birçok çingene eskiden olduğu gibi yine çok$_1$ kötülük$_1$ yaptılar$_1$." (Many gypsies did$_1$ much$_1$ evil$_1$ in the war again as in the past.)

[1]The number of paraphrase pairs in the subtitle domain limits the study to 100 pairs from each domain.

[2]Each word in a paraphrase cast receives the same subscript.

Although these classes are language independent, they include several Turkish specific aspects such as morphophonemic processes. For instance, Turkish word changes due to vowel harmony, vowel drops, and consonant drops/changes are all covered by the morphological class.

4 Paraphrase Alignment

While manually aligning the paraphrase sentence pairs, our goal was to jointly identify the paraphrase casts (i.e., the substitutable word strings) and specify the types correspondences between them. We asked three native speakers to align the selected paraphrase sentences by aligning word strings[3] as much as possible and marking the strength of observed correspondences as either "certain" (the correspondences that hold in any context) or "possible" (the correspondences that are context-specific). The annotators were also told to assign each identified correspondence between paraphrase casts to one of the classes in our typology. In cases where the same word strings were aligned, the correspondence was not classified with a class from the typology. Before aligning the corpus, the annotators were trained on a different set of paraphrases using an annotation guideline. Table 2 reports some statistics of the alignment process. The column labelled as "Common" represents the alignments common to all annotators. The rows labelled as "C", "P", and "U" represent the number of certain and possible alignments, and the number of unaligned words respectively[4]. It is noteworthy that the percentage of common certain alignments is significantly higher than the percentage of common possible alignments in all domains.

5 Corpus Study Findings

In this study, we aim to explore whether humans agree on the existence (i.e., identifying two word strings as paraphrases) and type of paraphrasing between Turkish paraphrase sentences. We are also interested in how the alignment of paraphrase casts is affected from human interpretation of paraphrasing between Turkish paraphrase sentences. Please note that the alignment of paraphrase casts consequently affects the sentence alignment of paraphrase sentence pairs.

Domain		Ant.1	Ant. 2	Ant. 3	Common
Literary Text	C	647	639	578	376 (58%)
	P	88	121	178	10 (5.62%)
	U	165	140	144	101 (61.2%)
News Articles	C	1384	1330	1259	988 (71.4%)
	P	53	186	214	3 (1.4%)
	U	203	124	167	102 (50.2%)
Subtitles	C	578	546	530	306 (52.9%)
	P	101	112	119	13 (10.9%)
	U	104	122	131	71 (54.2%)
Parallel Corpus	C	565	531	542	313 (55.4%)
	P	109	126	70	6 (4.8%)
	U	112	129	174	80 (45.9%)

Table 2: Alignment statistics of paraphrase pairs.

Our analysis started with examining how often our annotators agreed on identifying paraphrasing between two word strings. The agreement scores in Table 3 show that the annotators (pairwise) had a reasonable level of agreement in all domains. In majority of these cases, the annotators also agreed on the strength of the correspondence (i.e., both annotators either classified the correspondence as "Certain-Certain" or "Possible-Possible").

Domain	Ant.1&2	Ant. 1&3	Ant. 2&3
Literary Text	0.78%	0.73%	0.77%
News Articles	0.81%	0.86%	0.81%
Subtitles	0.68%	0.72%	0.86%
Parallel Corpus	0.59%	0.61%	0.78%

Table 3: Agreement on paraphrase identification.

The agreement scores in Table 3 show the agreement of annotators on the fact that two word strings are paraphrases and thus should be aligned. But it does not mean that the reason behind similar identifications is the same. We thus explored whether the annotators similarly classified the word strings that they identified as paraphrases. In all domains, the agreement scores between the annotators (given in Table 4) are dramatically lower than the scores in Table 3. It is particularly noteworthy that the smallest drop is observed in the parallel corpus domain (the domain that contains the least similar sentences). In cases where the annotators (pairwise) classified the same word strings with the same paraphrase class, they had a high agreement (between 78% and 91%) on the strength of the correspondence in all domains. We also computed the inter-annotator agreement via Kappa (Cohen, 1960). Kappa scores (shown bold in Table 4) represent fair to good agreement be-

[3]A word string consists of one or more words which may not be contiguous. Two word strings are aligned when one or more words in one string are paired with one or more words in the other string.

[4]Please note that these scores represent all alignments including the alignments of the same word strings.

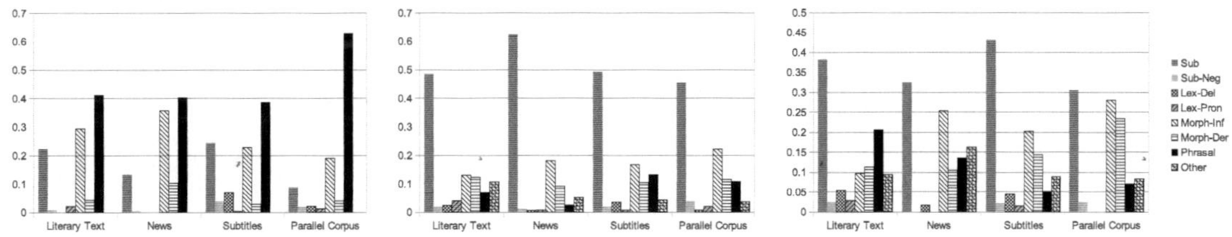

(a) Annotator 1 (b) Annotator 2 (c) Annotator 3

Figure 2: Distribution of paraphrase classes across domains.

tween the annotators.

Domain	Ant.1&2	Ant. 1&3	Ant. 2&3
Literary Text	0.37% **(0.34)**	0.34% **(0.33)**	0.56% **(0.63)**
News Articles	0.40% **(0.38)**	0.51% **(0.48)**	0.54% **(0.53)**
Subtitles	0.37% **(0.41)**	0.37% **(0.38)**	0.70% **(0.72)**
Parallel Corpus	0.33% **(0.46)**	0.35% **(0.46)**	0.64% **(0.75)**

Table 4: Agreement on paraphrase classes.

Figure 2 presents the distribution of paraphrase classes identified by each annotator across different domains. Notably, the identified paraphrase classes between word strings appear to diverge in several respects. We are currently exploring the reason behind this poor annotator agreement on paraphrase classes. One possible reason might be different understanding of the typology.

As a second step, we explored the impact of different interpretations of paraphrasing between sentence pairs on the alignment of these sentences. We analyzed the alignment differences of sentences and classified them into four classes:

- **Different Classification:** Although both annotators identify the same correspondence between two word strings, they classify that correspondence differently.
- **Missing Alignment:** One annotator identifies an alignment between two word strings but the other annotator does not identify a correspondence between these word strings.
- **Missing Word:** The annotators identify a correspondence of the same paraphrase class between two word strings which differ only in one word.
- **Different Grouping:** Two word strings are identified as having a single correspondence by one annotator whereas a number of disjoint correspondences between these word strings are identified by the other annotator.

All these differences except those classified as "different classification" result in different alignments between word strings. Such different alignments of paraphrase casts then change the alignment of paraphrase sentences.

6 Conclusion and Future Work

In this paper, we present our initial explorations on Turkish paraphrase alignment by exploiting a modest corpus. We built a generic and linguistically grounded Turkish paraphrase typology that covers the types of paraphrases observed in the corpus. In the study, the paraphrases identified by human annotators were aligned and annotated with paraphrase classes from the typology. The agreement of the annotators with respect to the existence and alignment of paraphrases as well as the associated paraphrase classes were reported. The study showed that the way how humans interpret paraphrasing between Turkish paraphrase sentences has an impact on how they align these sentences.

We have two main directions for future research: i) conducting a larger corpus study for drawing generalizations about Turkish paraphrasing and enhancing the typology if necessary, and ii) building Turkish paraphrase applications (e.g., automatic paraphrase acquisition) in correlation with the collected insights. We believe that the current findings for Turkish paraphrase alignment and our corpus enriched with paraphrase types enable future research on paraphrase phenomena in different fields such as language generation, textual entailment, summarization, and machine translation to be empirically assessed.

References

Chris Callison-Burch, Philipp Koehn, and Miles Osborne. 2006. Improved statistical machine translation using paraphrases. In *Proceedings of the main conference on Human Language Technology Conference of the North American Chapter of the Association of Computational Linguistics*, HLT-NAACL '06, pages 17–24.

Jacob Cohen. 1960. A coefficient of agreement for nominal scales. *Educational and Psychological Measurement*, 20(1):37–46.

Seniz Demir, Ilknur Durgar El-Kahlout, Erdem Unal, and Hamza Kaya. 2012. Turkish paraphrase corpus. In *Language Resources and Evaluation Conference - LREC*.

Mark Dras. 1999. *Tree Adjoining Grammar and the Reluctant Paraphrasing of Text*. Ph.D. thesis, Macquarie University.

Florence Duclaye France, Franois Yvon, and Olivier Collin. 2003. Learning paraphrases to improve a question-answering system. In *EACL Workshop NLP for Question-Answering*.

Raymond Kozlowski, Kathleen F. McCoy, and K. Vijay-Shanker. 2003. Generation of single-sentence paraphrases from predicate/argument structure using lexico-grammatical resources. In *Proceedings of the second international workshop on Paraphrasing - Volume 16*, PARAPHRASE '03, pages 1–8.

Alon Lavie and Abhaya Agarwal. 2007. Meteor: an automatic metric for mt evaluation with high levels of correlation with human judgments. In *Proceedings of the Second Workshop on Statistical Machine Translation*, StatMT '07, pages 228–231.

Richard Schwartz. Matthew Snover, Bonnie J. Dorr. 2006. A study of translation edit rate with targeted human annotation. In *Proceedings of AMTA*.

Aurélien Max, Houda Bouamor, and Anne Vilnat. 2012. Generalizing sub-sentential paraphrase acquisition across original signal type of text pairs. In *EMNLP-CoNLL*, pages 721–731.

Kishore Papineni, Salim Roukos, Todd Ward, and Wei-Jing Zhu. 2002. Bleu: a method for automatic evaluation of machine translation. In *Proceedings of the 40th Annual Meeting on Association for Computational Linguistics*, ACL '02, pages 311–318.

Richard Power and Donia Scott. 2005. Automatic generation of large-scale paraphrases. In *IWP*.

Long Qiu, Min-Yen Kan, and Tat-Seng Chua. 2006. Paraphrase recognition via dissimilarity significance classification. In *Proceedings of the 2006 Conference on Empirical Methods in Natural Language Processing*, EMNLP '06, pages 18–26.

Kapil Thadani, Scott Martin, and Michael White. 2012. A joint phrasal and dependency model for paraphrase alignment. In *COLING*, pages 1229–1238.

Marta Vila, M. Antonia Marti, and Horacio Rodriguez. 2011. Paraphrase concept and typology: A linguistically based and computationally oriented approach. *Procesamiento del Lenguaje Natural*, 46:83–90.

Sander Wubben, Antal van den Bosch, and Emiel Krahmer. 2010. Paraphrase generation as monolingual translation: data and evaluation. In *Proceedings of the 6th International Natural Language Generation Conference*, INLG '10, pages 203–207.

Shiqi Zhao, Haifeng Wang, Xiang Lan, and Ting Liu. 2010. Leveraging multiple mt engines for paraphrase generation. In *Proceedings of the 23rd International Conference on Computational Linguistics*, COLING '10, pages 1326–1334.

Towards NLG for Physiological Data Monitoring with Body Area Networks

Hadi Banaee, Mobyen Uddin Ahmed and Amy Loutfi
Center for Applied Autonomous Sensor Systems
Örebro University, Sweden
{hadi.banaee,mobyen.ahmed,amy.loutfi}@oru.se

Abstract

This position paper presents an on-going work on a natural language generation framework that is particularly tailored for summary text generation from body area networks. We present an overview of the main challenges when considering this type of sensor devices used for at home monitoring of health parameters. This paper describes the first steps towards the implementation of a system which collects information from heart rate and respiration rate using a wearable sensor. The paper further outlines the direction for future work and in particular the challenges for NLG in this application domain.

1 Introduction

Monitoring of physiological data using body area networks (BAN) is becoming increasingly popular as advances in sensor and wireless technology enable lightweight and low costs devices to be easily deployed. This gives rise to applications in home health monitoring and may be useful to promote greater awareness of health and prevention for particular end user groups such as the elderly (Ahmed et al., 2013). A challenge however, is the large volumes of data which is produced as a result of wearable sensors. Furthermore, the data has a number of characteristics which currently make automatic methods of data analysis particularly difficult. Such characteristics include the multivariate nature of the data where several dependent variables are captured as well as the frequency of measurements for which we still lack a general understanding of how particular physiological parameters vary when measured continuously.

Recently many systems of health monitoring sensors have been introduced which are designed to perform massive and profound analysis in the area of smart health monitoring systems (Baig and Gholamhosseini, 2013). Also several research have been done to show the applications and efficiency of data mining approaches in healthcare fields (Yoo et al., 2012). Such progress in the field would be suitable to combine with state of the art in the NLG community. Examples of suitable NLG systems include the system proposed by Reiter and Dale (2000) which suggested an architecture to detect and summarise happenings in the input data, recognise the significance of information and its compatibility to the user, and generate a text which shows this knowledge in an understandable way. A specific instantiation of this system on clinical data is BabyTalk project, which is generated summaries of the patient records in various time scales for different end users (Portet et al., 2009; Hunter et al., 2012). While these works have made significant progress in the field, this paper will outline some remaining challenges that have yet to be addressed for physiological data monitoring which are discussed in this work. The paper will also present a first version of an NLG system that has been used to produce summaries of data collected with a body area network.

2 Challenges in Physiological Data Monitoring with BAN

2.1 From Data Analysis to NLG

One of the main challenges in healthcare area is how to analyse physiological data such that valuable information can help the end user. To have a meaningful analysis of input signals, preprocessing the data is clearly an important step. This is especially true for wearable sensors where the signals can be noisy and contain artifacts in the recorded data. Another key challenge in physiological data monitoring is mapping from the many data analysis approaches to NLG. For example finding hidden layers of information with unsupervised mining methods will be enable the system to make a representation of data which is not producible by human analysis alone. However, domain rules and expert knowledge are important in order to consider a priori information in the data analysis. Further external variables (such as medication, food, stress) may also be considered in a supervised analysis of the data. Therefore, there is a challenge to balance between data driven techniques that are able to find intrinsic patterns in the data and knowledge driven techniques which take into account contextual information.

2.2 End User / Content

A basic issue in any design of a NLG system is understanding the audience of the generated text. For health monitoring used e.g. at home this issue is highly relevant as a variety of people with diverse backgrounds may use a system. For example, a physician should have an interpretation using special terms, in contrast for a lay user where information should be presented in a simple way. For instance, for a decreasing trend in heart rate lower than defined values, the constructed message for the doctor could be: *"There is a Bradycardia at ..."*. But for the patient itself it could be just: *"Your heart rate was low at ..."*. It is also important to note that the generated text for the same user in various situations should also differ. For instance a high heart rate at night presents a different situation than having a high heart rate during the high levels of activity. Consequently, all the modules in NLG systems (data analysis, document planning, etc.) need to consider these aspects related to the end user.

2.3 Personalisation / Subject Profiling

Personalisation differs from context awareness and is effective to generate messages adapted to the personalised profile of each subject. One profile for each subject is a collection of information that would be categorised to: metadata of the person (such as age, weight, sex, etc.), the history of his/her signals treatments and the extracted features such as statistical information, trends, patterns etc. This profiling enables the system to personalise the generated messages. Without profiling, the represented information will be shallow. For instance, two healthy subjects may have different baseline values. Deviations from the baseline may be more important to detect than threshold detection. So, one normal pattern for one in-

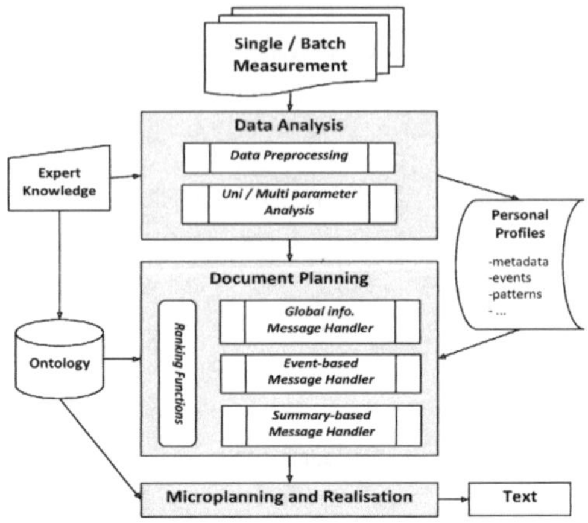

Figure 1: System architecture of text generation from physiological data.

dividual could be an outlier for another individual considering his/her profile.

3 System Architecture

In this section we outline a proposed system architecture, which is presented in Figure 1. So far the handling of the single and batch measurements and the data analysis have been implemented as well as first version of the document planning. For microplanning and realisation modules, we employed the same ideas in NLG system proposed by Reiter and Dale (2000).

3.1 Data Collection

By using wearable sensor, the system is able to record continuous values of health parameters simultaneously. To test the architecture, more than 300 hours data for two successive weeks have been collected using a wearable sensor called Zephyr (2013), which records several vital signs such as heart rate, respiration, temperature, posture, activity, and ECG data. In this work we have primarily considered two parameters, heart rate (HR) and respiration rate (RR) in the generated examples.

3.2 Input Measurements

To cover both short-term and long-term healthcare monitoring, this system is designed to support two different channels of input data. The first channel is called single measurement channel which is a continuous recorded data record. Figure 2 shows an example of a single measurement. In the figure, the data has been recorded for nine continuous hours of heart rate and respiration data which capture health parameters during the sequential activi-

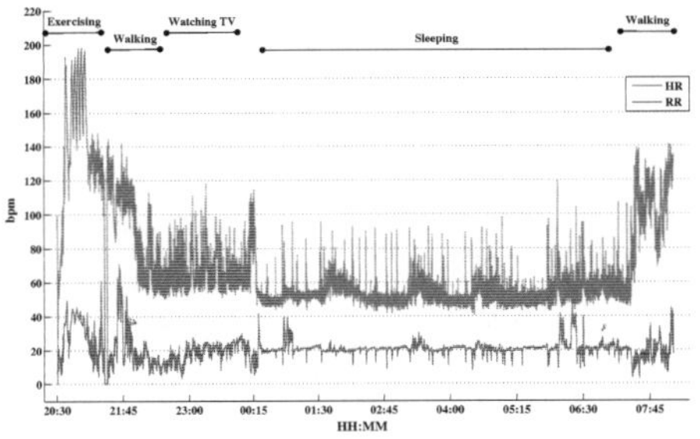

Figure 2: An example of single measurement, 13 hours of heart rate (HR) and respiration rate (RR).

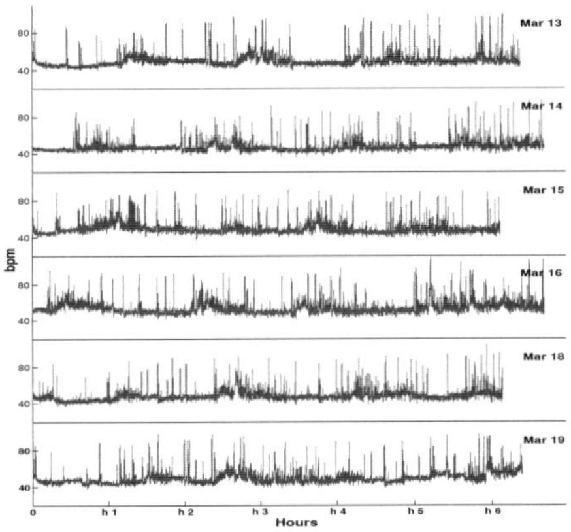

Figure 3: An example of batch measurement included heart rate for 6 nights.

ties such as exercising, walking, watching TV, and sleeping. To have a long view of health parameters, the system is also designed to analyse a batch of measurements. Batch measurements are sets of single measurements. Figure 3 presents an example of a batch of measurements that contain all the readings during the night for a one week period. This kind of input data allows the system to make a relation between longitudinal parameters and can represent a summary of whole the dataset.

3.3 Data Analysis

To generate a robust text from the health parameters, the data analysis module extracts the informative knowledge from the numeric raw data. The aim of data analysis module is to detect and represent happenings of the input signals. The primary step to analyse the measurements is denoising and removing artifacts from the raw data. In this work, by using expert knowledge for each health parameter, the artifact values are removed. Meanwhile, to reduce the noise in the recorded data, a series of smoothing functions (wavelet transforms and linear regression (Loader, 2012)) have been applied.

In this framework an event based trend detection algorithm based on piecewise linear segmentation methods (Keogh et al., 2003) for the time series has been used. In addition, general statistics are extracted from the data such as mean, mode, frequency of occurrence etc. that are fed into the summary based message handler. As an ongoing work, the system will be able to recognise meaningful patterns, motifs, discords, and also determine fluctuation portions among the data. Also for multi-parameter records, the input signals would be analysed simultaneously to detect patterns and events in the data. Therefore the particular novelty of the approach beyond other physiological data analysis is the use of trend detection.

3.4 Document Planning

Document planning is responsible to determine which messages should appear, how they should be combined and finally, how they should be arranged as paragraphs in the text. The messages in this system are not necessarily limited to describing events. Rather, the extracted information from the data analysis can be categorised into one of three types of messages: global information, event based, and summary based messages. For each type of message category there is a separate ranking function for assessing the significance of messages for communicating in the text. The order of messages in the final text is a function based on (1) how much each message is important (value of the ranking function for each message) (2) the extracted relations and dependencies between the detected events. The output of document planning module is a set of messages which are organised for microplanning and realisation. Document planning contains both event based and summary based messages as described below.

Event based Message Handler: Most of the information from the data analysis module are categorised as events. Event in this system is an extracted information which happens in a specific time period and can be described by its attributes. Detected trends, patterns, and outliers and also identified relations in all kinds of data analysis (single/batch measurement or uni/multi parameter) are able to be represented as events in the text. The main tasks of the event based message handler are to determine the content of events, construct and combine corresponding messages and their relations, and order them based on a risk function.

The risk function is subordinate to the features of the event and also expert knowledge to determine how much this event is important.

Summary based Message Handler: Linguistic summarisation of the extracted knowledge data is a significant purpose of summary based message handler. With inspiration from the works done by Zadeh (2002) and Kacprzyk et. al (2008), we represent the summary based information considering the possible combination of conditions for the summary of data. The proposed system uses fuzzy membership function to map the numeric data into the symbolic vocabularies. For instance to summarise the treatments of heart rate during all nights of one week in linguistic form, we define a fuzzy function to identify the proper range of low/medium/high heart rate level or specify a proper prototype for representing the changes such as steadily/sharply or fluctuated/constant. Here, the expert knowledge helps to determine this task.

The validity of these messages is measured by a defined formula in linguistic fuzzy systems called truth function which shows the probability of precision for each message. The system uses this indicator as a ranking function to choose most important messages for text. The main tasks of summary based message handler are: determining the content of the summaries, constructing corresponding messages, and ordering them based on the truth function to be appeared in the final text. The summary based message handler is not considered in previous work in this domain.

3.5 Sample Output

The implemented interface is shown in Figure 4 which is able to adapt the generated text with features such as health parameters, end user, message handler etc.. Currently our NLG system provides the following output for recorded signals which covers global information and trend detection messages. Some instances of generated text are shown, below. The first portion of messages in each text is global information which includes basic statistical features related to the input signals. An example of these messages for an input data is:

"This measurement is 19 hours and 28 minutes which started at 23:12:18 on February 13th and finished at 18:41:08 on the next day."

"The average of heart rate was 61 bpm. However most of the time it was between 44 and 59 bpm. The average of respiration rate was 19 bpm, and it was between 15 and 25 bpm."

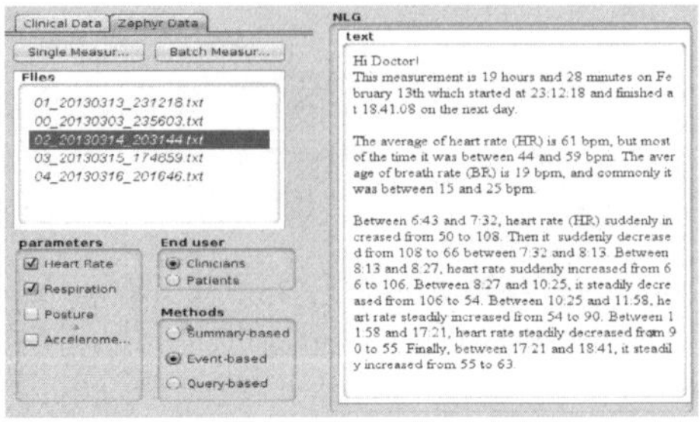

Figure 4: A screenshot of the implemented interface.

Regarding to the event based messages, an example of the output text extracted from the trend detection algorithm is:

"Between 6:43 and 7:32, the heart rate suddenly increased from 50 to 108 and it steadily decreased from 90 to 55 between 11:58 and 17:21."

4 Future Work

So far we have described the challenges and the basic system architecture that has been implemented. In this section we outline a number of sample outputs intended for future work which captures e.g. multivariate data and batch of measurement. We foresee that there is a non-trivial interaction between the event message handler and the summary message handler. This will be further investigated in future work.

Samples for single measurement:

"Since 9:00 for half an hour, when respiration rate became very fluctuated, heart rate steadily increased to 98."

"Among all high levels of heart rate, much more than half are very fluctuated."

Samples for batch of measurements:

"During most of the exercises in the last weeks, respiration rate had a medium level."

"During most of the nights, when your heart rate was low, your respiration rate was a little bit fluctuated."

Other messages could consider the comparison between the history of the subject and his/her current measurement to report personalised unusual events e.g.:

"Last night, during the first few hours of sleep, your heart rate was normal, but it fluctuated much more compared to the similar times in previous nights."

In this work we have briefly presented a proposed NLG system that is suitable for summarising data from physiological sensors using natural language representation rate. The first steps towards an integrated system have been made and an outline of the proposed system has been given.

References

Mobyen U. Ahmed, Hadi Banaee, and Amy Loutfi. 2013. Health monitoring for elderly: an application using case-based reasoning and cluster analysis. *Journal of ISRN Artificial Intelligence*, vol. 2013, 11 pages.

Mirza M. Baig and Hamid Gholamhosseini. 2013. Smart health monitoring systems: an overview of design and modeling. *Journal of Medical Systems*, 37(2):1–14.

James Hunter, Yvonne Freer, Albert Gatt, Ehud Reiter, Somayajulu Sripada, and Cindy Sykes. 2012. Automatic generation of natural language nursing shift summaries in neonatal intensive care: BT-Nurse. *Journal of Artificial Intelligence in Medicine*, 56(3):157–172.

Janusz Kacprzyk, Anna Wilbik, and Slawomir Zadrożny. 2008. Linguistic summarization of time series using a fuzzy quantifier driven aggregation. *Fuzzy Sets and Systems*, 159(12):1485–1499.

Eamonn J. Keogh, Selina Chu, David Hart, and Michael Pazzani. 2003. Segmenting time series: a survey and novel approach. *Data Mining In Time Series Databases*, 57:1–22.

Catherine Loader. 2012. Smoothing: local regression techniques. *Springer Handbooks of Computational Statistics*, 571-596.

Franois Portet, Ehud Reiter, Albert Gatt, Jim Hunter, Somayajulu Sripada, Yvonne Freer, and Cindy Sykes. 2009. Automatic generation of textual summaries from neonatal intensive care data. *Journal of Artificial Intelligence*, 173:789–816.

Ehud Reiter and Robert Dale. 2000. Building natural language generation systems. *Cambridge University Press, Cambridge, UK.*

Illhoi Yoo, Patricia Alafaireet, Miroslav Marinov, Keila Pena-Hernandez, Rajitha Gopidi, Jia-Fu Chang, and Lei Hua. 2012. Data mining in healthcare and biomedicine: a survey of the literature. *Journal of Medical Systems*, 36(4):2431–2448.

Lotfi A. Zadeh. 2002. A prototype centered approach to adding deduction capabilities to search engines. *Annual Meeting of the North American Fuzzy Information Processing Society, (NAFIPS 2002)* 523–525.

Zephyr. http://www.zephyr-technology.com, Accessed April 10, 2013.

MIME- NLG Support for Complex and Unstable Pre-hospital Emergencies

Anne H. Schneider Alasdair Mort Chris Mellish Ehud Reiter Phil Wilson
University of Aberdeen
{a.schneider, a.mort, c.mellish, e.reiter, p.wilson}@abdn.ac.uk

Pierre-Luc Vaudry
Université de Montréal
vaudrypl@iro.umontreal.ca

Abstract

We present the first prototype of a handover report generator developed for the MIME (Managing Information in Medical Emergencies) project. NLG applications in the medical domain have been varied but most are deployed in clinical situations. We develop a mobile device for pre-hospital care which receives streamed sensor data and user input, and converts these into a handover report for paramedics.

1 Introduction

Natural Language Generation underlies many applications in the medical domain but most are employed under relatively predictable clinical situations. The MIME project employs a mobile device with novel lightweight sensors to improve pre-hospital care service delivery. The term pre-hospital care denotes the treatment delivered to a patient before they arrive at hospital. Usually this entails paramedics and ambulance teams, but it can also include a wide range of voluntary and professional care groups. Care for rural pre-hospital patients can sometimes be carried out by volunteers from local communities: Community First Responders (CFR). Their task is to assess patients, perform potentially life-saving first aid procedures and record medical observations whilst the ambulance clinicians are en-route. These data are then handed over to the receiving ambulance team upon arrival. Because of their time-critical nature, handover reports are often verbal and hence maybe incomplete or misunderstood.

MIME was inspired by the Babytalk BT-Nurse system (Hunter et al., 2012), which generates shift handover reports for nurses in a neonatal intensive care unit. While BT-Nurse works with an existing clinical record system, which does not always record all actions and observations which ideally would be included in a report, in MIME the electronic record and user interface for acquiring exactly the desired information are effectively designed. This simplifies the NLG task, at the cost of adding a new task (interface construction).

```
At 02:12, after RR remained fairly
constant around 30 bpm for 4 minutes,
high flow oxygen was applied, she took
her inhaler and RR decreased to 27
bpm. However, subsequently RR once
more remained fairly constant around
30 bpm for 8 minutes.

At 02:15 she was feeling faint.

At 02:15 the casualty was moved.

At 02:17 the casualty was once more
moved.
```

Figure 1: Part of the "Treatment and Findings" for an asthma scenario.

2 The MIME project

Pre-hospital care is especially challenging because the environment in which it is delivered is inherently unpredictable. The clinical condition of a patient may have improved or deteriorated since the original call for help. The unpredictability of the environment at the scene of the call and the minimal level of clinical training of the CFRs contributes to the challenges presented to developers of a mobile device for this situation. In particular, the continuous capture of physiological data introduces the problem that irrelevant material needs to be suppressed in order not to overload the ambulance clinicians and hinder interpretation. The generated reports must provide a quick overview of the situation but at the same time be comprehensive. It is also vital that the format must enhance the readability, and the user-interface be simple and intuitive in order to avoid what has

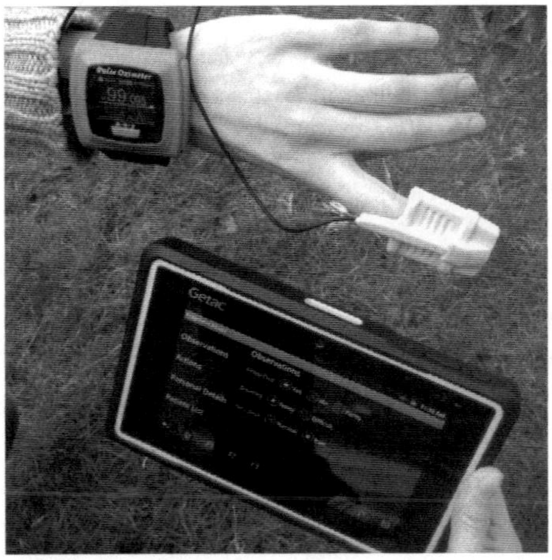

Figure 2: First hardware prototype of the MIME project (GETAC Z710 tablet and Pulse Oxymeter sensor).

been termed 'creeping featurism' (His and Potts, 2000), whereby option saturation hinders task performance.

In a user centred development process we established a structure for the handover reports. After the demographic description of the casualty (i.e. age and gender) and incident details that were relayed to the CFR by the ambulance control centre two elements of generated text follow, the initial assessment section and the treatment and findings section. The initial assessment contains information on the casualty that is gathered by the CFRs before the sensors are applied including baseline observation during the first minute after the application of the sensors. The treatment and findings section (Figure 1) is a report of the observations and actions of the CFRs while they attended the casualty and waited for the ambulance to arrive. This includes a paragraph that sums up the condition of the patient at the time of handover. There are three types of events included in the report: discrete events (action and observation) and continuous events (trends in sensor readings). Actions (e.g. applying oxygen) and observations (e.g. the patient feels faint) have to be entered by the CFR through an interface. Continuous events are derived from the medical sensors: currently respiratory rate, blood oxygen saturation, and heart rate are recorded. Since some events, especially those that deviate from the norm are more important than others (Hallett et al., 2006), in the document planning stage we employ an algorithm that decides which events are mentioned in the report and in which order. This process is loosely based on similar decision processes reported in (Hallett et al., 2006) and (Portet et al., 2007).

3 Summary and Conclusion

We have developed a first prototype of the system which uses simulated data to produce handover reports. This runs on standard desktop PCs. For our second prototype, which is currently being developed, we port the NLG algorithm onto a GETAC Z710 tablet[1] which has been chosen for it's robustness, capacitative touch screen, and long battery life (Figure 2). Our research also includes the establishment of a connection between the tablet and sensors, the recording of the incoming data stream and the development of an interface for the tablet, which can be used by the CFR to enter observations and actions taken or any other useful information.

At the ENLG workshop we will present our first hardware prototype alongside the desktop computer version, highlighting the challenges that the project faces in developing a handover report generator for pre-hospital care.

4 Acknowledgments

This work is supported by the RCUK dot.rural Digital Economy Research Hub, University of Aberdeen (Grant reference: EP/G066051/1)

References

C. Hallett, R. Power, and D. Scott. 2006. Summarisation and visualisation of e-Health data repositories. In *UK E-Science All-Hands Meeting*, pages 18–21, Nottingham, UK.

I. His and C. Potts. 2000. Studying the Evolution and Enhancement of Software Features. In *Proceedings of the International Conference on Software Maintenance*, ICSM '00, pages 143–151, Washington, DC, USA.

J. Hunter, Y. Freer, A. Gatt, E. Reiter, S. Sripada, and C Sykes. 2012. Automatic generation of natural language nursing shift summaries in neonatal intensive care: BT-Nurse. *Artificial Intelligence in Medicine*, 56:157–172.

F. Portet, E. Reiter, J. Hunter, and S. Sripada. 2007. Automatic generation of textual summaries from neonatal intensive care data. In *Proccedings of the 11th Conference on Artificial Intelligence in Medicine (AIME 07). LNCS*, pages 227–236.

[1] http://en.getac.com/products/Z710/Z710_overview.html

Thoughtland: Natural Language Descriptions for Machine Learning n-dimensional Error Functions

Pablo Ariel Duboue
Les Laboratoires Fouláb
999 du College
Montreal, Quebéc
pablo.duboue@gmail.com

Abstract

This demo showcases Thoughtland, an end-to-end system that takes training data and a selected machine learning model, produces a cloud of points via cross-validation to approximate its error function, then uses model-based clustering to identify interesting components of the error function and natural language generation to produce an English text summarizing the error function.

1 Introduction

For Machine Learning practitioners of supervised classification, the task of debugging and improving their classifiers involves repeated iterations of training with different parameters. Usually, at each stage the trained model is kept as an opaque construct of which only aggregate statistics (precision, recall, etc.) are investigated. Thoughtland (Duboue, 2013) improves this scenario by generating Natural Language descriptions for the error function of trained machine learning models. It is a pipeline with four components:

(1) A cross-validation step that uses a machine algorithm from a given learning library run over a given dataset with a given set of parameters. This component produces a cloud of points in n-dimensions, where $n = F + 1$, where F is the number of features in the training data (the extra dimension is the error value). (2) A clustering step that identifies components within the cloud of points. (3) An analysis step that compares each of the components among themselves and to the whole cloud of points. (4) A verbalization step that describes the error function by means of the different relations identified in the analysis step.

2 Structure of the Demo

This demo encompasses a number of training datasets obtained from the UCI Machine Learning repository (attendees can select different training parameters and see together the changes in the text description). It might be possible to work with some datasets provided by the attendee at demo time, if they do not take too long to train and they have it available in the regular Weka ARFF format.

A Web demo where people can submit ARFF files (of up to a certain size) and get the different text descriptions is will also be available at **http://thoughtland.duboue.net** (Fig. 1). Moreover, the project is Free Software[1] and people can install it and share their experiences on the Website and at the demo booth.

3 An Example

I took a small data set from the UCI Machine Learning repository, the Auto-Mpg Data[2] and train on it using Weka (Witten and Frank, 2000). Applying a multi-layer perceptron with two hidden layers with three and two units, respectively, we achieve an accuracy of 65% and the following description:

> There are four components and eight dimensions. Components One, Two and Three are small. Components One, Two and Three are very dense. *Components Four, Three and One are all far from each other.* The rest are all at a good distance from each other.

When using a single hidden layer with eight units we obtain an accuracy 65.7%:

[1] https://github.com/DrDub/Thoughtland.

[2] http://archive.ics.uci.edu/ml/machine-learning-databases/auto-mpg/

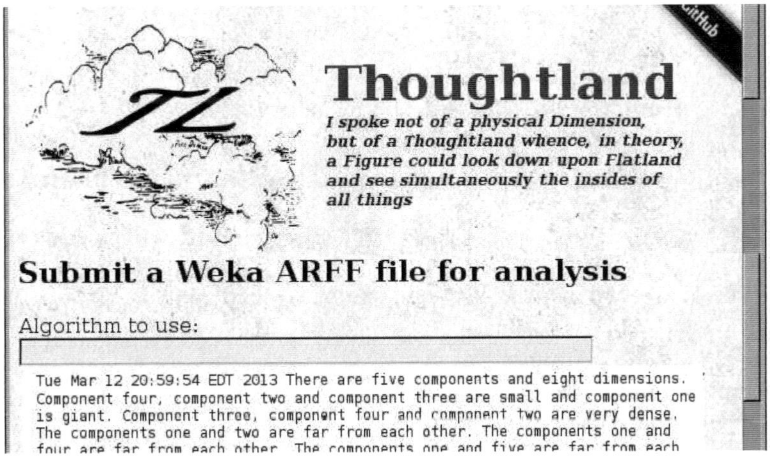

Figure 1: Web Interface to Thoughtland (composite).

> There are four components and eight dimensions. Components One, Two and Three are small. Components One, Two and Three are very dense. *Components Four and Three are far from each other.* The rest are all at a good distance from each other.

As both descriptions are very similar (we have emphasized the difference, which in the first case is also an example of our clique-based aggregation system), we can conclude that the two systems are performing quite similarly. However, if we use a single layer with only two units, the accuracy lowers to 58% and the description becomes:

> There are five components and eight dimensions. Components One, Two and Three are small and Component Four is giant. Components One, Two and Three are very dense. Components One and Four are at a good distance from each other. Components Two and Three are also at a good distance from each other. Components Two and Five are also at a good distance from each other. The rest are all far from each other.

4 Final Remarks

Thoughtland follows the example of Mathematics, where understanding high dimensional objects is an everyday activity, thanks to a mixture of formulae and highly technical language. It's long term goal is to mimic these types of descriptions automatically for the error function of trained machine learning models.

The problem of describing n-dimensional objects is a fascinating topic which Throughtland just starts to address. It follows naturally the long term interest in NLG for describing 3D scenes (Blocher et al., 1992).

Thoughtland is Free Software, distributed under the terms of the GPLv3+ and it is written in Scala, which allow for easy extension in both Java and Scala and direct access to the many machine learning libraries programmed in Java. It contains a straightforward, easy to understand and modify classic NLG pipeline based on well understood technology like McKeown's (1985) schemata and Gatt and Reiter's (2009) SimpleNLG project. This pipeline presents a non-trivial NLG application that is easy to improve upon and can be used directly in classroom presentations.

References

A. Blocher, E. Stopp, and T. Weis. 1992. ANTLIMA-1: Ein System zur Generierung von Bildvorstellungen ausgehend von Propositionen. Technical Report 50, University of Saarbrücken, Informatik.

P.A. Duboue. 2013. On the feasibility of automatically describing n-dimensional objects. In *ENLG'13*.

A. Gatt and E. Reiter. 2009. SimpleNLG: A realisation engine for practical applications. In *Proc. ENLG'09*.

K.R. McKeown. 1985. *Text Generation: Using Discourse Strategies and Focus Constraints to Generate Natural Language Text.* Cambridge University Press.

Ian H. Witten and Eibe Frank. 2000. *Data Mining: Practical Machine Learning Tools and Techniques with Java Implementations.* Morgan Kaufmann Publishers.

An Automatic Method for Building a Data-to-Text Generator

Sina Zarrieß **Kyle Richardson**
Institut für Maschinelle Sprachverarbeitung
University of Stuttgart, Germany
sina.zarriess,kyle@ims.uni-stuttgart.de

1 Introduction

We describe our contribution to the Generating from Knowledge Bases (KBgen) challenge. Our system is learned in a bottom-up fashion, by inducing a probabilistic grammar that represents alignments between strings and parts of a knowledge graph. From these alignments, we extract information about the linearization and lexical choices associated with the target knowledge base, and build a simple generate-and-rank system in the style of (Langkilde and Knight, 1998).[1]

2 Semantic Parsing and Alignments

A first step in building our generator involves finding alignments between phrases and their groundings in the target knowledge base. Figure 1 shows an example sentence from training paired with the corresponding triple relations. A partial lexicon is provided, indicating the relation between a subset of words and their concepts.

Using the triples, we automatically construct a probabilistic context-free grammar (PCFG) by converting these triples to rewrite rules, using ideas from (Börschinger et al., 2011). The right hand side of the rules represent the constituents of the triples in all orders (initially with a uniform probability) since the linear realization of a triple relation in the language might vary. This is rewritten back to each of its constituents to allow for interaction with other concepts that satisfy further domain relations. Individual concepts, represented in the grammar as preterminals, are assigned to the associated words in the lexicon, while unknown words are mapped to all concepts with equal probability.

Following (Börschinger et al., 2011), sentences in the training are restricted to analyses corresponding to their gold triple relations, and the inside-outside algorithm, a variant of EM, is applied to learn the corresponding PCFG parameters. In intuitive terms, the learning algorithm iteratively maximizes the probability of rules that derive the correct triple relations in training, looking over several examples. For example, the unknown word *are* in Figure 1 is learned to indicate the relation *object* since it often occurs in training contexts where this relation occurs between entities surrounding it. The syntax of how triples are composed and ordered in the language is also learned in an analogous way.

We annotate the development data with the most probable trees predicted by the PCFG. Figure 1 shows the viterbi parse for the given sentence after training. Bascially, it defines a spanning tree for the knowledge graph given in the input. Each ternary subtree indicates a triple relation detected in the sentence, and the root node of this subtree specifies the head (or first argument) of the triple relation. Note that some triple relations are not found (e.g. the *base* relation), since they are implicit in the language.

3 Grammar and Lexicon Extraction

The viterbi trees learned in the previous step for the development set are used for constructing a generation grammar that specifies the mapping between triples and surface realizations. The tree in Figure 1 indicates, for example, that the second argument of an *object* relation can be realized to the left of the relation and its first argument. We also learn that the *site* relation can be lexicalized as the phrase *in the*.

Grammar A non-lexical production in a tree corresponds to a surface realization of an input triple. We iterate over all productions of the trees in the development data and aggregate counts of concept orderings over all instances of a relation. We distinguish preterminal concepts ($preterm$) that map to a lexical entry and nonterminal concepts ($nonterm$) that embed another subtree. Example (1) and (2) illustrate rules that apply to the tree in Figure 1 for ordering the *site* and *object* relation. The rule for *object* introduces ambiguity. Note that (2-a) deletes the *object* phrase.

(1) *Input*: ($A_{nonterm}$,r-site,$B_{nonterm}$)

[1]This work was supported by the Deutsche Forschungsgemeinschaft (German Research Foundation) in SFB 732 *Incremental Specification in Context*, project D2 (PI: Jonas Kuhn). We thank Thomas Müller for help with the language models.

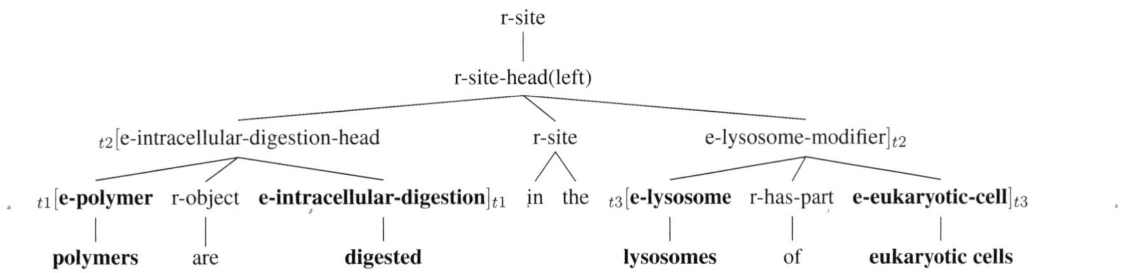


```
:TRIPLES ( (|Intracellular-Digestion36204| |object| |Polymer36220|)
           (|Intracellular-Digestion36204| |base| |Eukaryotic-Cell36203|)
           (|Intracellular-Digestion36204| |site| |Lysosome36202|)
           (|Eukaryotic-Cell36203| |has-part| |Lysosome36202|))
```

Figure 1: A semantic parse (top) learned from the the triples (bottom) provided during training. Words/concepts in bold are known from the lexicon, while the rest is learned along with the syntax of triple combination. Triple instances in the tree are marked with square brackets.

a. *rhs*: $A_{nonterm}$ r-site $B_{nonterm}$; 1.0

(2) *Input*: ($A_{preterm}$,r-object,$B_{preterm}$)

a. *rhs*: $A_{preterm}$ $B_{preterm}$; 0.33

b. *rhs*: $B_{preterm}$ r-object $A_{preterm}$; 0.3

c. ...

Lexicon For each preterminal in the trees, we extract its lexical span in the surface sentence. For instance, we extract 15 phrases as possible realizations for the *base* relation (e.g. "for the", "in the", "of a", "from a"). This is merged with the provided lexicon, to create an expanded lexicon.

4 Generation Pipeline

The main idea of the generator is to produce a (possibly large) set of output candidates licensed by the grammar and the lexicon. In a final step, these candidates are ranked with the help of a language model, a common approach in statistical generation (Langkilde and Knight, 1998). We train our language model on the GENIA corpus (Ohta et al., 2002). Below is our overall pipeline.

1. compute all spanning trees licensed by the input triples
2. for each spanning tree from step 1, compute all surface linearizations licensed by the generation grammar
3. for each linearized tree from step 2, compute all surface sentences licensed by the expanded lexicon
4. rank surface candidates with a language model

The set of spanning trees produced in step 1 is typically small. We prune the set of possible linearizations based on the counts in the generation grammar, and consider only the two most likely orderings for each input triple. We also prune the set of possible lexicalizations and refine it with some linguistic constraints described below.

Linguistic Constraints The viterbi trees learned in the alignment step do not capture any linguistic properties of the sentences in terms of morpho-syntactic categories. As a consequence, most of the output candidates coming from step 3 are ungrammatical. Ungrammatical sentences do not necessarily get low scores from the language model as it captures local relations between neighbouring words. We introduce some simple candidate filters to ensure some basic linguistic constraints. With the help of the lexicon and some heuristics, we tag all lexical entries containing a finite verb. In step 3, we filter all candidates that a) have no finite verb, b) have a finite verb as the first or last word, c) realize two finite verbs next to each other.

Conclusion We explore the use of Semantic Parsing techniques, coupled with corpus-based generation. We expect that our prototype would benefit from further development of the linguistic components, given that it is built with minimal resources.

References

Börschinger, Benjamin, Jones, Bevan K, Johnson, Mark. 2011. Reducing Grounded Learning to Grammatical Inference In *Proc. of EMNLP'11*, pages 1416-1425.

Irene Langkilde and Kevin Knight. 1998. Generation that exploits corpus-based statistical knowledge. In *Proc. of ACL 1998*, pages 704–710.

Tomoko Ohta, Yuka Tateisi, and Jin-Dong Kim. 2002. The genia corpus: an annotated research abstract corpus in molecular biology domain. In *Proc. of HLT '02*, pages 82–86.

LOR-KBGEN, A Hybrid Approach To Generating from the KBGen Knowledge-Base

Bikash Gyawali
Université de Lorraine, LORIA, UMR 7503
Vandoeuvre-lès-Nancy, F-54500, France
bikash.gyawali@loria.fr

Claire Gardent
CNRS, LORIA, UMR 7503
Vandoeuvre-lès-Nancy, F-54500, France
claire.gardent@loria.fr

Abstract

This abstract describes a contribution to the 2013 KBGen Challenge from CNRS/LORIA and the University of Lorraine. Our contribution focuses on an attempt to automate the extraction of a Feature Based Tree Adjoining Grammar equipped with a unification based compositional semantics which can be used to generate from KBGen data.

Introduction Semantic grammars, i.e., grammars which link syntax and semantics, have been shown to be useful for generation and for semantic parsing. This abstract outlines an attempt to automatically extract from the KBGen data, a Feature Based Tree Adjoining Grammar which can be used for generation from the KBGen data.

Data The KBGen data consists of sets of triples extracted from the AURA knowledge base which encodes knowledge contained in a college-level biology textbook. Each set of triple was selected to be verbalisable as a simple, possibly complex sentence. For instance, the input shown in Figure 1 can be verbalised as[1]:

(1) The function of a gated channel is to release particles from the endoplasmic reticulum

Sketch of the Overall Grammar Extraction and Generation Procedure To generate from the KBGen data, we parsed each input sentence using the Stanford parser; we aligned the semantic input with a substring in the input sentence; we extracted a grammar from the parsed sentences provided with the input triples; and we generated using an existing surface realiser. In addition some of the input were preprocessed to produce a semantics more compatible with the assumption underlying the syntax/semantic interace of SemTAG;

```
:TRIPLES (
(|Release-Of-Calcium646|
 |object| |Particle-In-Motion64582|)
(|Release-Of-Calcium646|
 |base| |Endoplasmic-Reticulum64603|)
(|Gated-Channel64605|
 |has-function||Release-Of-Calcium646|)
(|Release-Of-Calcium646|
 |agent| |Gated-Channel64605|))
:INSTANCE-TYPES
(|Particle-In-Motion64582|
 |instance-of| |Particle-In-Motion|)
(|Endoplasmic-Reticulum64603|
 |instance-of| |Endoplasmic-Reticulum|)
(|Gated-Channel64605|
 |instance-of| |Gated-Channel|)
(|Release-Of-Calcium646|
 |instance-of| |Release-Of-Calcium|))
```

and a procedure was used to guess missing lexical entries.

Alignment and Index Projection Given a Sentence/Input pair (S, I) provided by the KBGen Challenge, we match each entity and event variable in I to a substring in S. Matching uses the variable name, the name of the unary predicate true of that variable and the word form assigned to that predicte in the KBGen lexicon. Digits occurring in the input are removed and the string in the input sentence which is closest to either of the used units is decorated with that variable. Index variables are then projected up the syntactic trees to reflect headedness. For instance, the variable indexed with a noun is projected to the NP level; and the index projected to the NP of a prepositional phrase is project to the PP level.

Grammar Extraction Grammar extraction proceeds in two steps as follows. First, the subtrees whose root node are indexed with an entity variable are extracted. This results in a set of NP and PP trees anchored with entity names and associated with the predication true of the indexing variable.

Second, the subtrees capturing relations between variables are extracted. To perform this ex-

[1] For space reasons, we slightly simplified the KBGen input and removed type information.

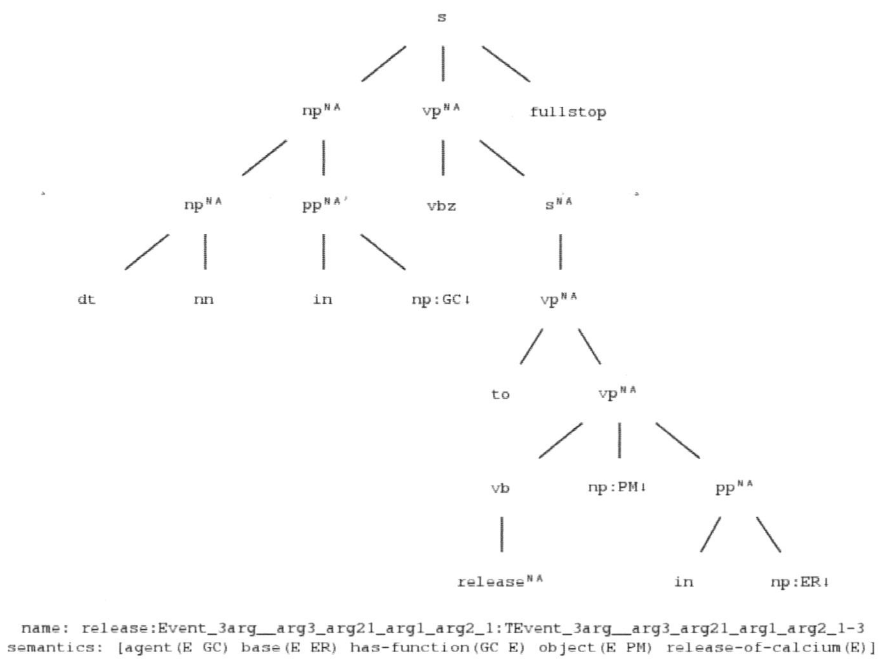

traction, each input variable X is associated with a set of dependent variables i.e., the set of variables Y such that X is related to Y ($R(X,Y)$). The minimal tree containing all and only the dependent variables $D(X)$ of a variable X is then extracted and associated with the set of literals Φ such that $\Phi = \{R(Y,Z) \mid (Y = X \wedge Z \in D(X)) \vee (Y, Z \in D(X))\}$. This procedure extracts the subtrees relating the argument variables of a semantics functors such as an event or a role.

The extracted grammar is a Feature-Based Tree Adjoining Grammar with a Unification-based compositional semantics as described in (Gardent, 2008). Each entry in the grammar associates a natural language expression with a syntactic tree and a semantic representation thereby allowing both for semantic parsing and for generation. Figure 1 shows the tree extracted for the *release* predicate in Example 1.

Pre-Processing The parse trees produced by the Stanford parser are pre-processed to better match TAG recursive modeling of modification. In particular, the flat structure assigned to relative clauses is modified into a recursive structure.

The input semantics provided by the KBGen task is also preprocessed to allow for aggregation and to better match the assumptions underlying the syntax/semantics interface of SemTAG.

For aggregation, we use a rewrite rule of the form shown below to support the production of e.g., *A cellulose-synthase which contains a polypeptide and* ***two glucose*** *synthesizes cellulose.*.

$$R(X,Y_1),\ldots,R(X,Y_n),P(Y1),\ldots,P(Y_n) \\ \Rightarrow R(X,Y),P(Y),quantity(Y,n)$$

For relative clauses, we rewrite input of the form *plays(X Y),in-event(Y E), P(E), R(E X)* to *plays(X Y),in-event(Y E), P(E), R(E Y)*. This captures the fact that in sentences such as *A biomembrane is a barrier which blocks the hydrogen ion of a chemical.*, the entity variable bound by the relative clause is that associated with *barrier*, not that of the main clause subject *biomembrane*.

Guessing Missing Lexical Entries To handle unseen input, we start by partitioning the input semantics into sub-semantics corresponding to events, entities and role. We then search the lexicon for an entry with a matching or similar semantics. An entry with a similar semantics is an entry with the same number and same type of literals (literals with same arity and with identical relations). Similar entries are then adapted to create lexical entries for unseen data.

References

Claire Gardent. 2008. Integrating a unification-based semantics in a large scale lexicalised tree adjoining grammar for french. In *COLING'08*, Manchester, UK.

Team UDEL KBGen 2013 Challenge

Keith Butler, Priscilla Moraes, Ian Tabolt, Kathleen F. McCoy
Computer and Information Science Department
University of Delaware
Newark, DE 19716
keithb@udel.edu, pmoraes@udel.edu, itabolt@udel.edu, mccoy@cis.udel.edu

Abstract

This document describes the University of Delaware's entry into KBGen 2013 Challenge which provided teams with input data representation from the AURA knowledge base (KB), developed in the context of the HALO Project at SRI International, along with a lexicon mapping for concepts present on those input files. Training sentences were also provided. The task was to accurately generate an English sentence depicting the information from a set of triples from the knowledge base.

1 Approach

Our approach to the problem was to develop a set of rules for translating KB structures into English structures and to use an existing generator, such as SimpleNLG (Gatt & Reiter, 2009) or FUF-SURGE (Elhadad, 1993) to generate the sentences.

Our analysis of pre-release data provided by the KBGen organization (triple-files, training sentences, tree graphs, lexicon) was facilitated by writing a mashup program (KBGenMashup) that enabled viewing/searching the data. The program initially loads all the training sentences into a clickable list box. When a sentence is clicked, all data relating to that sentence is displayed: corresponding triples, tree-graph, and Stanford parse of the sentence. The displayed triples are given "hot spots" so clicking on them will present a list of other sentences containing (or NOT containing) that same relation or instance type. Finally, KBGenMashup enables a search for other sentences that contain a given word or phrase. Using this tool allowed us to discover common realization patterns for certain KB triples.

2 Major sentence types

Our initial generator implementation utilized SimpleNLG in a java wrapper. Our tack was to focus on the realization of major sentence types, generally identified by the presence of a particular function in the KB triples, e.g. has-function, subevent, plays. These functions provided the main verb and sentence structures, and other KB relations were fit into this structure (in subject/object position or as adjuncts) in a rule-based way.

For instance, Figure 1 shows a triples file from the testing data that was identified under the cluster *has-function*, along with the sentence generated by our system and the rule used to realize the cluster for this relation type.

```
(KBGEN-INPUT
    :ID "ex03a.266-1-eval"
    :TRIPLES (
            (|Hold-Together6620| |object| |Hydrogen6637|)
            (|Hold-Together6620| |object| |Nitrogen6584|)
            (|Hold-Together6620| |instrument| |Single-Bond6596|)
            (|Hold-Together6620| |agent| |Peptide-Bond6571|)
            (|Peptide-Bond6571| |has-function| |Hold-Together6620|))
    :INSTANCE-TYPES (
            (|Hydrogen6637| |instance-of| |Hydrogen|)
            (|Nitrogen6584| |instance-of| |Nitrogen|)
            (|Single-Bond6596| |instance-of| |Single-Bond|)
            (|Peptide-Bond6571| |instance-of| |Peptide-Bond|)
            (|Hold-Together6620| |instance-of| |Hold-Together|))
    :ROOT-TYPES (
            (|Hold-Together6620| |instance-of| |Event|)
            (|Hydrogen6637| |instance-of| |Entity|)
            (|Nitrogen6584| |instance-of| |Entity|)
            (|Single-Bond6596| |instance-of| |Entity|)
            (|Peptide-Bond6571| |instance-of| |Entity|)))
```

Figure 1: A triples file from the testing data.

Sentence generated: *The function of the peptide bond is to hold together hydrogen and nitrogen using a single bond.*

The identified rule for this input is the *has-function* rule. The main entity is the entity that is related to the event of the instance by the *has-function* relation type. The rule states that the subject of the sentence is the "*the function of [main entity]*". For this template the verb *to be* is identified as the main verb and the object of the sentence is a verb phrase (VP) composed of the events present in the triples file in the infinitive form, and the existing secondary entities. Each secondary entity is related to an event by a semantic relation type. The nature of this relation defines which role the secondary entity plays in the sentence (e.g. the "object" relation, when present, usually links the event to the head(s) of the noun phrase (NP) within the VP). Although the majority of the input files have secondary entities that are related to the main event by the object relation, some other cases do not present them. The head of the noun phrases can be represented, in those cases, by secondary relations connected to the main event by one of *agent, base, result, raw-material*, relation types. Heuristics are applied in order to define the head of the noun phrase since the relation that will define which entity is the head of the NP is based on the combination of the existing relations. The relations in the set of triples that are not already realized as one of the previous roles in the sentence are then realized recursively for each event, complementing the VP. Those relations are represented by prepositional phrases (PP) and the preposition chosen for each PP represents the semantic role of the relation type (e.g. *instrument* relations often use the prepositions **with** or **using**, while *donor* and *origin* relations often use **from**).

3 No-Events and other sentence types

The simple strategy described above worked well for some sentence types, but others required more sophisticated triple traversal. In particular, realizing triple sets not containing an event was problematic. With time running short, we implemented a second realizer to handle these types. It used its own heuristics, plus stored the sets of triples in a database that allowed for flexible traversing. Consider its heuristics to handle no-event triple sets (events generally provide the verb and sentence structure). No-event sentences would use a form of "be" as the main verb, but we still needed to identify the sentence's main subject. To do this, the software looks for the Entity that is on the left side of the most triples. Why? There is more information about this Entity than about any other. Consider ex29b.4 (Figure 2). The tree graph shows that "Restriction-Site" is on the left side of five triples. It should be the subject of the sentence, which could be realized as "A restriction site is a short DNA sequence which consists of 2 deoxyribose and a deoxyribonucleoside monophosphate." Note the order of the Entities in the sentence. The subject is mentioned first, then its adjective ("short"), then class ("DNA sequence"), then remaining entities. In realizing the remaining Entities, a common routine is used to check for cardinality and perform any rewording as appropriate.

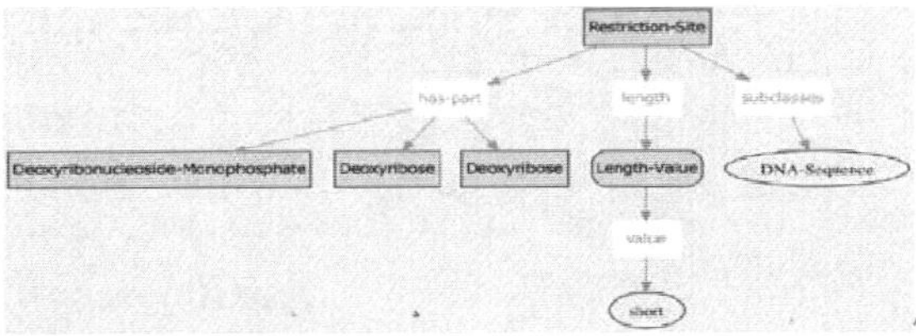

Figure 2: ex29b.4

In many cases, there was a tie among the times Entities were on the left. In one type of "tie" (ex05a2.265, Figure 3), there is a cycle in the graph (see "Fibronectin, "Carbohydrate-Side-Chain", "Surface".) In these cases, the heuristic chooses the "middle" Entity in the cycle (Carbohydrate in this case) as the subject. Then in choosing mention-order, the software (usually) starts the sentence by putting the adjective before the subject (i.e. "branched" & "carbohydrate side chain"), then visits each Entity around the cycle, then traverses up to the "Top" Entity. This sentence is realized as "There are branched carbohydrate side chains at the surface of the fibronectin of an animal plasma membrane."

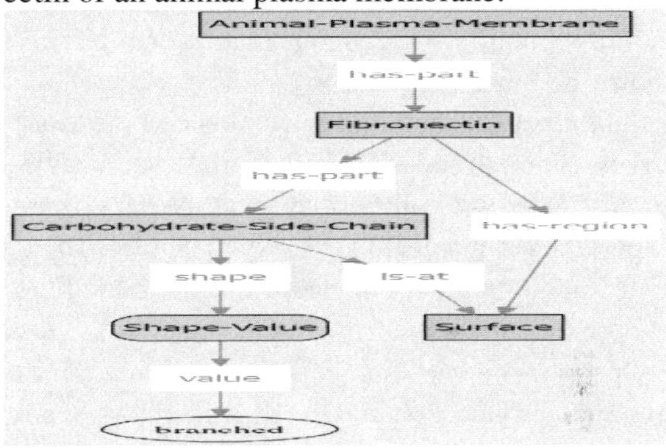

Figure 3: ex05a2.265

4 Conclusions

We have described a template-based generation entry based on two different paradigms. In one, sentences are formed on the basis of a major relation that generally selects the main verb and fits the realization of the other pieces according to the structures specific for that sentence type. The second piece that we needed is based on flexibly traversing the knowledge base and realizing based on patterns found in the triples.

References

Albert Gatt and Ehud Reiter. 2009. *SimpleNLG: A realization engine for practical applications*, Proceedings of the 12th European Workshop on Natural Language Generation, pages 90–93, Athens, Greece, 30 – 31 March 2009.

Michael Elhadad. 1993. FUF: the Universal Unifier User Manual Version 5.2.

Content Selection Challenge - University of Aberdeen Entry

Roman Kutlak
Chris Mellish
Kees van Deemter
Department of Computing Science
University of Aberdeen
Aberdeen AB24 3UE, UK
r.kutlak, c.mellish, k.vdeemter @abdn.ac.uk

1 Introduction

Bouayad-Agha et al. (2012) issued a content determination challenge in which researchers were asked to create systems that can automatically select content suitable for a first paragraph in a Wikipedia article from an RDF knowledge base of information about people. This article is a description of the system built at the University of Aberdeen.

Our working assumption is that the target text should contain information that is commonly known about the target person. The Wikipedia's manual of style mentions that "The lead [section] serves as an introduction to the article and a summary of its most important aspects[1]." What is most important about a person is likely to be often mentioned in biographies and hence it is more likely to be commonly known.

Our system was motivated by the notion of common ground, especially the way it was accounted for by (Clark and Marshall, 1981). Clark and Marshall (1981) introduce two categories of common ground: *personal common ground* shared by a small group of individuals and *communal common ground* shared by a community of people. We are most interested in the concept of communal common ground, which arises from the exposure to the same information within a community. For example, if there is a statue in front of your work place, you expect your colleagues to also know about this statue and so the information that there is a statue in front of you workplace becomes a part of the community knowledge (where the community are people who work at the same place).

Our hypothesis is that if we take a corpus of documents produced by some large community (e.g., English speakers), we should be able to approximate the community's knowledge of certain facts by counting how frequently they are mentioned in the corpus. For example, if a corpus contains 1000 articles about Sir Isaac Newton and 999 of the examined documents mention the property of him being a physicist and only 50 documents mention that he held the position as the warden of the Royal Mint in 1696 we should expect more people to know that he was a physicist.

We implemented the heuristic for approximating communal common ground and tested it in an experiment with human participants to measure whether there is a correlation between the heuristic's predictions and actual knowledge of people (Kutlak et al., 2012). In our implementation, we used the Internet as a corpus of documents and we used the Google search engine for counting the number of documents containing the properties. Although the number of hits is only an estimate of the actual number of documents containing a particular term, the heuristic achieved a Spearman correlation of 0.639 with $p < 0.001$ between the knowledge of people and the numbers of hits returned by Google.

Although there are some issues with the use of a proprietary search engine such as Google (for example, the search engine can perform stemming; see Kilgarriff (2007) for a discussion) search engines have been successfully used previously (Turney, 2001; Goudbeek and Krahmer, 2012).

2 Algorithm

The submitted system employs the heuristic outlined in in the previous section. The input is a collection of files containing information about people and a collection of human readable strings for each of the files. The data were taken from Freebase - a community created repository of information about people, places and other things. Each file is a small knowledge base containing a set of RDF triples describing the entity.

[1] http://en.wikipedia.org/wiki/Wikipedia:Manual_of_Style/Lead_section

The data is encoded in machine-readable form (e.g., the fact that Newton was an astronomer is encoded as `ns:m.03s9v ns:type.object.type ns:astronomy.astronomer` .) so in order to find collocations in a human written text, each RDF triple has to be "lexicalised." This is done by mapping the RDF values to human produced strings provided by Freebase. After substituting the lexicalisations and removing some unnecessary information the algorithm adds the name of the target, which results in text such as *Isaac Newton type Astronomer*.

The algorithm reads one file at a time and creates a human readable string for each of the properties in the file. In the second step, the system removes disambiguations (text in brackets) and filters out properties that have the same string representation (duplicates). Additionally, properties with certain attributes are filtered out to reduce the number of queries[2].

In the third step, the system uses Google custom search API (a programming interface to the search engine) to estimate the score of each property. Properties that contain the name of the entity are penalised. This is done to reduce the importance of properties such as the target's parents or relatives. For example, if the algorithm was ranking properties of Sir Isaac Newton and a property contained the string *Newton*, the score assigned to that property was multiplied by 0.75. The properties were then ordered by the number of corresponding hits in descending order.

In the last step the algorithm selects the top ranked properties. The number of properties to select was calculated by the following equation $5 * log(|properties|)$. This equation was chosen by intuition so that a larger proportion of properties was selected for entities with a small number of properties than for entities with a large number of properties. The set of properties in the above equation is the set obtained after the filtering.

To prevent the system from selecting too many properties with the same attribute and to introduce variation, the system selected only five properties with the same attribute (e.g., five films, five books).

[2]For example, the knowledge base describing Antonín Dvořák contains 5670 properties of which 5154 have the attribute `music.artist.track`.

3 Concluding Remarks

The implemented system uses a simple document-based collocation heuristic to decide what properties to select. This makes it prone to favouring properties that contain common words or the name of the described entity. The advantage is that the system is relatively simple and versatile. The "common ground" heuristic could be combined with another heuristic that assigns negative score to properties that contain common words or a heuristic that estimates how interesting the property is.

Finally, we do not expect the system to perform better than machine learning based approaches such as that of Duboue and McKeown (2003) but it will certainly be interesting to see how far one can get with a simple heuristic.

References

Nadjet Bouayad-Agha, Gerard Casamayor, Leo Wanner, and Chris Mellish. 2012. Content selection from semantic web data. In *Proceedings of INLG 2012*, pages 146–149, Stroudsburg, PA, USA. Association for Computational Linguistics.

Herbert H. Clark and Catherine Marshall. 1981. Definite reference and mutual knowledge. In A. K. Joshi, B. L. Webber, and I. A. Sag, editors, *Elements of discourse understanding*, pages 10–63. Cambridge University Press, New York.

Pablo A. Duboue and Kathleen R. McKeown. 2003. Statistical acquisition of content selection rules for natural language generation. In *Proceedings of the 2003 EMNLP*, pages 121–128, Morristown, NJ, USA. Association for Computational Linguistics.

Martijn Goudbeek and Emiel Krahmer. 2012. Alignment in interactive reference production: Content planning, modifier ordering, and referential overspecification. *Topics in Cognitive Science*, 4(2):269–289.

Adam Kilgarriff. 2007. Googleology is bad science. *Comput. Linguist.*, 33:147–151, March.

Roman Kutlak, Kees van Deemter, and Chris Mellish. 2012. Corpus-based metrics for assessing communal common ground. *Proceedings of the 34th Annual Meeting of the Cognitive Science Society*.

P. Turney. 2001. Mining the web for synonyms: PMI-IR versus LSA on TOEFL. In *Proceedings of the twelfth european conference on machine learning (ecml-2001)*.

UIC-CSC: The Content Selection Challenge entry from the University of Illinois at Chicago

Hareen Venigalla
Computer Science
University of Illinois at Chicago
Chicago, IL, USA
hareen058@gmail.com

Barbara Di Eugenio
Computer Science
University of Illinois at Chicago
Chicago, IL, USA
bdieugen@uic.edu

Abstract

This paper described UIC-CSC, the entry we submitted for the Content Selection Challenge 2013. Our model consists of heuristic rules based on co-occurrences of predicates in the training data.

1 Introduction

The core of the Content Selection Challenge task is formulated as *Build a system which, given a set of RDF triples containing facts about a celebrity and a target text (for instance, a Wikipedia - style article about that person), selects those triples that are reflected in the target text.* The organizers provided training data consisting of 62618 pairs of texts and triple sets. The text is the introductory text $tf_{\mathcal{C}}$ of the Wikipedia article corresponding to celebrity $\mathcal{C}$; the set of triples $tr_{\mathcal{C}}$ concerning $\mathcal{C}$ was grepped from the Freebase official weekly RDF dump. It is important to note that we do not know which specific triples from $tr_{\mathcal{C}}$ are rendered in $tf_{\mathcal{C}}$.

A sample triple in the file is as follows:

```
ns:m.04wqr
ns:award.award_winner.awards_won
ns:m.07ynmx5
```

In the above triple, `ns:m.04wqr` is the subject id, of Marilyn Monroe in this case (`ns` denotes `namespace`); `ns:award.award_winner.awards_won` is the predicate and `ns:m.07ynmx5` is the object id of the award. Since this format is not readable, the organizers provided a script to transform the turtle file into a human readable form, where the object id is replaced by its actual value:

```
/award/award_winner/awards_won ''Golden
Globe Awards for Actress - Musical or
Comedy Film - 17th Golden Globe Awards
- Some Like It Hot - 1960 - earliye -
Award Honor'' /m/07ynmx5
```

In the following, we will refer to the first element of these expressions as the *predicate*. Our approach relies on heuristics derived from clustering predicates directly, or clustering them based on the co-occurrence of the argument of predicate p_i in a text tf and in turtle files tr that contain both p_i and another predicate p_j.

2 Deriving heuristic rules

We observed that in total there are 613 distinct predicates. Out of these 613 predicate, only 11 are present in over 40 percent of the files and only 19 predicates are present in over 10 percent of the files. This means that a large number of predicates are present only in a few files. This makes it harder to decide whether we have to include these predicates or not. Conversely, nearly 40 percent of text files only contain one or two sentences, which compounds the sparsity problem.

Predicate Clustering. In the first method, we generate predicate clusters by simply removing the leaf from each predicate expression. For example, `/people/person/place_of_birth`, and `/people/person/education` belong to the same cluster, labelled `/people/person` as they have the same parent `/people/person`. We found 35 such clusters. We then analyzed the frequency of each predicate p_i on its own, and conditional on other predicates in the same cluster: for example, how frequent `/people/person/education` is, and how often it occurs in those triple files, where `/people/person/place_of_birth` is also present.

Intersection on Arguments. For each predicate p_i, we compute the set of its intersection sets $IS_{i,j}$. Each set $is_{i,j}$ comprises all the turtle files $tr_{i,j}$ where p_i co-occurs with a second predicate p_j. For each $tr_{i,j}$, we retrieve the corresponding text file tf (recall that each turtle file is associated with one text file) and check whether the argument of

p_i occurs in tf – this is indirect evidence that the text does include the information provided by p_i (of course this inference may be wrong, if this argument occurs in a context different from what p_i conveys). If the argument of p_i does occur in tf, we keep $tr_{i,j}$, otherwise we discard it. As above, we then proceed to compute the frequencies of the occurrences of p_i on its own, and of p_i when p_j is also present, over all the turtle files $tr_{i,j} \in is_{i,j}$ that have not been filtered out as just discussed.

Given these two methods, we derive rules such as the following:

```
IF /baseball/baseball_player/position ∈ tr_k
  AND
  /baseball/baseball_player/batting_stats
  ∈ tr_k
THEN
  select
  /baseball/baseball_player/position
```

The set of rules is then filtered as follows. On a small development set, we manually annotated which triples are included in the corresponding text files. We keep a rule if the F-measure concerning predicate p_i (i.e., concerning the triples whose predicate is p_i) improves when using the rule, as opposed to including p_i if it belongs to a set of frequent predicates.

We also need to deal with multiple occurrences of p_i in one single turtle file. Predicates such as `/music/artist/track` can have multiple instances, up to 30, in a certain tr_k, with different arguments; however, those predicates may occur far fewer times in the corresponding text files – because say tr_{MM} on Marilyn Monroe includes one triple for each of her movies, but the corresponding tf_{MM} only mentions a few of those movies. Hence, we impose an upper limit of 5 on the number of occurrences in the same turtle file, for a certain predicate to be included, for example:

```
IF      /music/artist/track
        AND its count ≤ 5
THEN    select /music/artist/track
```

3 Evaluation

Apart from our participation in the Challenge, we evaluated our system on a small test set composed of 96 pairs of text and turtle files, randomly selected from the data released by the organizers. This resulted in a total of 153 unique predicates (hence, about $\frac{1}{4}$ of the total number of distinct predicates). We manually annotated the predicates in the turtle files as present/absent in the corresponding text file.

We consider four domains:

1. *Basic facts*: general, very frequent information, such as `people/person/profession`, `people/person/nationality`.
2. *Books*: predicates whose root is `book`, like `book/author/works_written`, `book/book_subject/works`.
3. *Sports*: predicates whose root is a sport, like `baseball/baseball_player/position_s`, `ice_hockey/hockey_player/former_team`.
4. *Film and Music*: predicates whose root is `film` or `music`, like `/film/director/film`, `/music/artist/track`.
5. Television: predicates whose root is `tv`, like `/tv/tv_director/episodes_directed`.

As apparent from Table 1, the performance of our system varies considerably according to the domain of the predicates. Specifically, we believe that the exceedingly low precision for predicates of type `book, film & music, tv` is due to the sparseness of the data. As we noted above, 40% of the text files only include one or two sentences. Hence, our system selects many more predicates than are actually present in the corresponding text file.

Table 1: Performance on in-house test set

Domain	**P**	**R**	**F-score**
Basic Facts	79.83	51.25	62.40
Sports	79.84	49.22	60.90
Books	12.80	66.30	21.47
Film & Music	5.77	55.19	10.45
TV	5.46	43.36	9.70

4 Future Enhancements

UIC-CSC could be improved by more closely analyzing the features of the text files, especially the shortest ones: when they include only few sentences, which kinds of predicates (and arguments) do they include? For example, if only two movies are mentioned as far as Monroe is concerned, what else can we infer from the Monroe turtle file tr_{MM} about those two movies?

Author Index